MODERN SPORT AND THE AFRICAN AMERICAN EXPERIENCE

Second Edition
Edited by Gary Sailes
Indiana University, Bloomington

cognella®
academic publishing

Bassim Hamadeh, CEO and Publisher
Michael Simpson, Vice President of Acquisitions and Sales
Jamie Giganti, Senior Managing Editor
Miguel Macias, Graphic Designer
Angela Schultz, Senior Field Acquisitions Editor
Natalie Lakosil, Licensing Manager
Kat Ragudos, Interior Designer

First published in the United States of America in 2016 by Cognella, Inc.

Cover image copyright © Depositphotos/ArenaCreative.

Printed in the United States of America

ISBN: 978-1-63189-386-5 (pbk) / 978-1-63189-387-2 (br)

www.cognella.com   800-200-3908

Preface

01 The Paradigm of Race and Sport in American Culture

02 African American Culture & Sport

03 Myths, Stereotypes, & Images of the African American Athlete

04 Performance Differences

Contents

Modern Sport and the African American Experience, Second Edition, is a collection of essays from some of higher education's most brilliant and forward thinking Sport Sociology and Critical Race Theory scholars in the United States today.

This book was constructed to address my inability to find a comprehensive text that addressed the topics and critical issues I examine in my research and which I teach in my classes at Indiana University. The focus of this text highlights more of the experiences of African Americans in modern sport that any other text I could find. The essays contained within this work allow me to provide interesting and provocative topics on the African American experience in modern sport, which I hope will lead to vibrant discussions inside and outside the classroom. It was my intent to stimulate and maintain the interest and attention of readers and to initiate dialogue about topics that are sometimes classified as either taboo or politically incorrect. I think I have accomplished that with this compilation of a few previous and some new and updated essays.

The experiences of African Americans in modern sport are unique. My thirty years of research in this area has taught me that those unique experiences are important, worth writing about, and surely would stimulate interesting conversations among scholars, students, and sports fans alike. It was my intent to stimulate the senses, to evoke emotional responses, and most importantly, to educate. Many of the essays in this book reignited images of my own experiences as an African American athlete, coach, and administrator. My head was filled with familiarity, frustration, and anger, all of which eventually served as the foundation for my work as a sport sociologist and critical race scholar.

This collection of essays represents the central themes in the discussion on African American participation in modern sport. Certainly, there are other provocative issues that are absent from this work and are a part of daily critical race discussions. It would take two to three volumes to cover all the diverse topics that emerge in the discussion on African American participation in American sport. However, the central theme and essays contained in this work are the ones my colleagues and students indicate are the more prominent and provocative issues today. My favorite aspect of this text is that it gets my students talking and encourages their participation in class. I am happy to disclose that we have overcome personal bias and barriers emanating from political correctness. As a class, we are

By Gary Sailes

able to reach the plateau of understanding and enlightenment in the oftentimes difficult discussion about gender and race.

The articles in this text represent the most popular issues in the discussion on African American sport participation. In the second edition, I have kept the timeless essays that examined issues critical to the book's theme, but also included new essays that are more current. Chapter 1 includes essays from two of my contemporaries, Jay Coakley and Harry Edwards. Coakley's text *Sports in Society* is the most prominent sport sociology textbook in the United States. His essay confirms the thought that the social world of the African American community is organized such that it fosters a sense of sports destiny within its own culture, a great lead-off essay to introduce the reader to the intricacies of race and sport in American culture, and the intersections between race and sport. The second essay is from my mentor and colleague, Harry Edwards, considered by many to be the individual who got America thinking and talking about race in sport with his seminal work, "The Revolt of the Black Athlete." I have the highest regard for Edwards's essay, because he got us thinking about Critical Race Theory in sport long before the term was coined. It was Edwards's work that drew me into this discipline and his early writings made me aware that race truly was an issue in sport as it was in society. As always, Edwards delivered a compelling and thought-provoking essay on what he perceived would be the immediate future of the African American athlete.

There IS something very special occurring in America's black communities relative to preparing male youth for adulthood. Specific social aspects of that experience (rites of passage) intersect on many levels on the basketball courts, tracks, and football fields within black communities throughout the United States. Richard Lapchick, founder of the Center for the Study of Sport in Society, claimed that a black family is seven times more likely to push a male child into sport than a white family. Chapter 2 is dedicated to this assertion and further investigates why this phenomenon exists. Othello Harris's essay, while somewhat dated, is actually still current in its conceptual framework. Sport takes on a particularly significant role in the black community among its youth. Keith Harrison, Reggie Saunders, Scott J. Buckstein, Cliff Parks, and Dave Heikkinen further explore this point by detailing the intersection between basketball, black male youth, and branding oneself as a player. The concluding essay focuses on the adjustments being made in the black community as the NBA and other basketball institutions change the dynamics for participation of the Basketball

Conveyor Belt, which is the process through which elite African American basketball players attempt to reach professional status within the NBA.

I have studied the myths, stereotypes and media images of the African American athlete for over three decades. I find it both fascinating and frustrating that, with extensive current exposure and representation of the black athlete in the media on so many different fronts, many of the cultural stereotypes about the black athlete from several decades ago still exist today. Chapter 3 focuses on the historical and contemporary bias, myths, stereotypes, and media images of the black athlete that I am sure will stimulate discussion and debate on many fronts. There exists the belief that African American athletes are natural athletes and are better athletic performers than their white counterparts, but lack the intelligence and leadership skills that white athletes possess. This chapter examines not only the stereotypes about the differences between black and white athletes but also asks the questions: where did this all begin, where are we now, and where are we headed? Stephen A. Smith, we need your input on this one!

Chapter 4 focuses on the performance differences between black and white athletes and is a continuation of Chapter 3. If one were to watch basketball on television, a sport where black participation is highest, there would be noticeable differences in the performance patterns among the black and white athletes. Not wanting to give in to stereotyping but definitely serving as a witness to this phenomenon, it is liberating for my class to finally talk about the performance differences among black and white ballers. However, once the cultural manifestations are identified and the reasons behind performance differences are identified as social and not so much genetic, discussions take off. An interesting paradigm is when we are able to identify white athletes who perform like African American athletes and who adopt an African American lifestyle. It truly is revealing when we are able to witness that cultural phenomenon.

Five years ago, one of my African American female students led me to recognize the fact that my research and my class focused almost exclusively on male athletes. She felt the absence of research on female athletes in the literature and in my own publication and teaching initiatives slighted the presence and contributions of African American women athletes. Following that discussion, I was compelled to become more accountable and I have included readings about the sports participation and contributions of

African American women in sport in my publications and in my class. Additionally, I have presented a number of papers at scholarly conferences and dedicated a chapter in this text to African American women athletes. Chapter 5 is titled African American Women and Sport. The essays in this chapter focus on the factors that influence the participation of African American women, the sexism and racism these women face in sport, and the images that portray them in the media. While this chapter is not nearly comprehensive in covering all the issues, it is time that this topic made its way to the forefront in the discussions on American sport and it is my intent to contribute to that initiative.

Chapter 6 is a discussion on college sports, the most popular topic among my students at Indiana University. Every semester I conduct a class survey to determine what percentage of students factored in IU sports in any capacity in their decision to attend Indiana University. Approximately ninety percent of my students, at least in part, decided to enroll at IU because of the culture and tradition of our sports teams. This chapter focuses on two points: the perceptions of college students about African American student athletes and the perceptions and experiences of African American student athletes on the campuses of Predominantly White Institutions (PWI) like Indiana University. I was hoping to receive a manuscript focusing on the experiences of white student athletes at Historically Black Colleges and Universities (HBCU), but did not receive any submissions. I can say this, based on interviews of my graduate students who played sports at HBCUs, the experience of the white student athlete at an HBCU is different from that of a black athlete at a PWI. Generally, white student athletes are more accepted at HBCUs than black students are at PWIs. More on that at another time. This chapter focuses on the marginalization of the black athlete competing at PWIs.

The final section, Chapter 7, is titled Power, Conflict, and Cultural Identity. College-educated, wealthy white males control commercial sports in the United States as owners, managers, and head coaches. The vast majority of the athletes in the chief revenue-producing sports are African American. In fact, less than five percent of all the athletes participating in college sports—those African American student athletes participating in basketball and football—are responsible for generating the lion's share of the revenue in college athletics. That revenue is used to subsidize athletic scholarships for all of the remaining sports in college athletics, coaching and administrative staff salaries, and athletic department operating expenses. However, when it comes to control, there is an obvious lack of African American and female representation in the power and control leadership roles in commercial and college sports. The divergent cultures of those in power and those seeking control and power create a conflict that is worthy of inclusion and discussion in this chapter.

This work would not have been possible without the essays from the contributing scholars. To them, I would like to say "thank you!" I would also like to thank University Readers for the opportunity to place my work in a vessel that would make it available to my students, and the sport sociology academy for providing me a platform to share my research findings. Lastly, I would like to thank my sons Grant and William for their unconditional love and patience, which provided me with the time, space, and motivation to complete this work.

Chapter 1

The Paradigm of Race and Sport in American Culture

Race and Ethnicity in the Sociology of Sport in the United States

Jay Coakley

The problem of the twentieth century is the problem of the color line, the question as to how far differences of race will hereafter be made the basis of denying to over half the world the right of sharing the opportunities and privileges of modern civilization.

—W.E.B. Dubois

THESE WORDS, WRITTEN IN 1900 AS DUBOIS PREPARED FOR THE FIRST
Pan African Congress in London, predated a similarly prophetic statement in the forward of his classic book, The Souls of Black Folk (1903). For six decades Dubois used sociological theory and methods to study race and racial relations in the United States, producing numerous books and hundreds of insightful essays. However, it wasn't until 1944 when Swedish sociologist Gunnar Myrdal wrote An American Dilemma: The Negro Problem and Modern Democracy that the topic of race attracted concerted attention from sociologists and other scholars in the United States.

When the sociology of sport emerged as a sub-discipline in the fields of sociology and physical education during the 1960s, race and racial relations attracted immediate attention from scholars and social activists. Two scholarly publications in the early 1960s focused on the sociological dynamics underlying the desegregation of professional baseball (Broom and Selznick, 1963; Blalock, 1962), but the most provocative discussions of race and sport were published in the late 1960s and early 1970s by sociologist-activist Harry Edwards, an organizer of the boycott by black U.S. athletes of the 1968 Summer Olympic Games in Mexico City. Edwards' book, The Revolt of the

Black Athlete, published in 1969, clearly described the exclusion and exploitation of blacks in sports and challenged popular assumptions that sports were free of racism and provided African Americans with opportunities for upward social mobility and social acceptance in society at large.

Edwards' work was complimented by the writing of other scholar-activists (Scott, 1969; Hoch, 1972) and developed further in his Sociology of Sport (1973), the first textbook in the field. Edwards (1971) also was the most visible sociologist to critique a widely-read article in Sports Illustrated, a major weekly sport magazine, in which a sportswriter (Kane, 1971) argued that blacks were physiologically superior to whites and that the success of blacks in certain sports was due their natural abilities as athletes.

Early Research on Race and Sports

At the same time that Edwards and other scholar-activists were writing in popular sources and publicly debating issues related to race and sports, scholars in various disciplines initiated research that statistically documented patterns of racial segregation and discrimination in sports and provided general explanations for why those patterns existed.

Dozens of empirical studies beginning in the 1970s provided evidence showing that the structure of race relations and the prevailing racial ideology in the United States shaped and constrained patterns of desegregation in sports. This research focused on a combination of topics, including entry barriers faced by black athletes, patterns of racial stacking in which black athletes were over- or under-represented in particular positions on sport teams, and the exclusion of blacks and other ethnic minorities from positions of off-the-field leadership, such as coaching and management, in sport organizations.

These patterns, when observed by many whites who viewed the world in racialized terms, generally reinforced the racist ideology that created them. In this sense, the initial desegregation of sports reaffirmed racist notions about the physical superiority and intellectual inferiority of blacks relative to whites. Among whites in the United States during the 1960s and 1970s it was widely believed that blacks excelled in sports and team positions that demanded power and speed at the same time that inferior intellectual abilities prevented them from assuming leadership positions on the field and in coaching and management positions off the field. The success of white athletes, on the other hand, was explained in terms of character, hard work, intelligence, well planned strategies, and superior organizational skills.

Entry Barriers

Research done between the late 1960s and early 1980s indicated that blacks were recruited only into certain sports. For example, when Jackie Robinson broke the color line in major league baseball by signing a contract with the Brooklyn Dodgers in 1947, baseball was the most financially profitable team sport in the United States. Branch Rickey, the man who signed Robinson to a contract, convinced his fellow owners, all of whom were white, that Robinson would increase gate receipts and help the Dodgers win more games. Although owners of other teams initially objected to desegregation, they changed their minds as it became clear that Robinson attracted both white and black spectators to games and increased profits for all teams.

As the white owners in baseball and other major revenue producing sports in the United States slowly desegregated, they recruited only black athletes with exceptional physical skills. The existence of a selection bias in professional sport was first noted by Rosenblatt (1967) in his study of major league baseball. Using performance data from 1953 through 1965 he found that black players outperformed white players during every season. His findings were supported by others who studied baseball (Pascal and Rapping, 1972; Eitzen and Yetman, 1977; Lapchick, 1984), football at the college and professional levels (Scully, 1973; Tolbert, 1975), and basketball on both the intercollegiate and professional levels (Yetman and Eitzen, 1972; Lapchick, 1984).

In sports where there were no economic incentives for whites to permit or promote desegregation, it did not occur, or it occurred very slowly in limited situations. In sports where athletes learned skills and played in social settings, such as the club sports of golf and tennis, there was strong resistance to desegregation. This was due to whites who wanted to maintain social distance from blacks and feared social and possible sexual contact between black men and white women.[1]

Anecdotal information published in the print media during these years also suggested that there were informal racial quotas that restricted the number of blacks on any given team. White team owners, managers, and coaches, it was hypothesized, feared that attendance might decline if the proportion of black players on a team surpassed what white spectators defined as appropriate. This was consistent with Blalock's (1970) theory of race relations in which he noted that such quotes would be set at the point where blacks can no longer make it profitable for team owners and administrators to treat them in nondiscriminatory terms.

Racial "Stacking"

Through the 1980s the most popular research topic in the sociology of sport was racial stacking. The first and most influential study on this topic was done by John Loy and Joseph McElvogue (1971). Using team photos and public information about players, Loy and McElvogue identified the race of all players on the starting rosters of major league baseball and professional football teams for the 1967 and 1968 seasons, respectively. They analyzed their data in light of Oscar Grusky's (1963) theory of formal organizations. Grusky theorized that individuals who occupied centrally located positions in an organizational structure were more likely than those who occupied non-central positions to (1) engage in frequent interaction with others in the organization, and (2) be involved in interdependent tasks requiring interpersonal cooperation and coordination. Therefore, Loy and McElvogue hypothesized that racial segregation on a sport team would be positively related to the centrality of positions in the organizational structure of the team. The patterns in baseball

---

1   See Coakley, 1986 for a complete documentation of this research.

and football strongly supported their hypothesis: blacks rarely played central positions and they were heavily overrepresented in the non-central positions; at the same time, whites rarely played non-central positions and were heavily overrepresented in central positions. Loy and McElvogue suggested that these patterns could be explained by a combination of two factors: (1) a desire on the part of white players and team management to maintain a form of organizational segregation that preserved social distance between whites and blacks on teams, and (2) beliefs on the part of management that blacks were less able than whites to successfully play positions that required interpersonal coordination and decision-making.

This form of position segregation within teams was relatively easy to study because it involved counting and classifying athletes by race and position. Consequently, there were numerous studies of stacking in a wide range of men's and a few women's team sports (see Coakley, 1998 and Smith and Leonard, 1997 for a full list of references to this research). Although the pattern of racial stacking in certain U.S. sports was undeniable (and continues to exist in some cases) there were debates over how it should be explained. Scholars from different disciplines offered a range of biological, psychological, economic, and sociological explanations of stacking (Coakley, 1998). Although research in sociology and psychology suggested that the patterns were due to the use of racial stereotypes by coaches and other administrators who make player personnel decisions, the data never led to any widely accepted theory.

Exclusion from Positions of Leadership

A third topic studied in early sociological research on race and sport focused on the exclusion of blacks from positions of leadership, such as coaching and management, in sport organizations. During the 1970s it became clear that desegregation on the playing field did not mean that blacks would have access to positions in the power structures of sport organizations. The popular press occasionally published stories about this issue and presented data documenting the absence of black coaches, general managers, and top administrators.

It was not until the mid-1980s that systematic data on this phenomenon was published in a source that was widely accessible to scholars in the sociology of sport. In 1984, scholar-activist Richard Lapchick founded the Center for the Study of Sport in Society (CSSS) at Northeastern University in Boston. The center began to present data on the racial makeup of sport management, and in 1989 published its first annual Racial Report Card, a comprehensive statistical description of race in the hiring practices of the National Basketball Association, the National Football League, and Major League Baseball. Lapchick's national reputation and personal connections with former and current African American players in professional sports, led this document to receive nationwide media coverage; it also served to publicize continuing patterns of racial exclusion in sports and to put sport organizations on notice for their racialized personnel practices.

None of these data were used to generate and test theories of race relations, but they inspired speculation among many people, including those of us in the sociology of sport, about various explanations of this form of racial exclusion. These speculations have continued as data have been published annually since 1990.

Current Research on Race, Ethnicity, and Sports

The early research on entry barriers, racial stacking, and racial exclusion established that there were clear patterns of racial differentiation and stratification in U.S. sports and sport organizations. However, by the late 1980s it was apparent that this research added little to a critical theoretical understanding of race as a cultural construction, as a structure of power relations, as identity, and as a category of experience influenced by the material conditions of everyday life in a capitalist society. This was clearly pointed out in an influential essay written by Susan Birrell and published in the Sociology of Sport Journal in 1989. Birrell noted the following as she addressed colleagues in the field:

"We continue to produce studies on centrality and stacking, not because of their theoretical significance hut because the data are there. Twenty years ago such studies provided major insight into stratification by race, and it is startling to know that such patterns persist today, but there is no theoretical news in this tradition. We need to move to more powerful questions . ... A more profound approach is to conceive of race as a culturally produced marker of a particular relationship of power, to see racial identity as contested, and to ask how racial relations are produced and reproduced through sport (1989: 214)."

Birrell's critique was part of an overall "cultural turn" in sociology and an emphasis on exploring the dynamics of cultural formation and the connections between culture and structure. Additionally, one of her observations was that research in the sociology of sport focused almost exclusively on the impact of racial discrimination on the participation of black males in sports; absent was research on (a) the experiences of women from ethnic minority backgrounds; (b) the intersections of race, gender, and class; and (c) ethnic dynamics apart from issues of race. Future research on race and sport, she said, would benefit from "a blending of critical theories: cultural studies, socialist feminism, feminist cultural studies, materialist and cultural racial relations theories" (1989, p. 223).

Since Birrell's critique, some scholars in the sociology of sport have continued to statistically document differential treatment and stratification related to race and ethnicity, but others have focused research attention on race and ethnicity as they are related to processes of cultural formation, power relations, identity politics, and the meanings given to sport-related phenomena and experiences. The methods used in the latter studies primarily include in-depth interviews, critical ethnography, historical analyses, and textual/semiotic analyses.

The research that has been done since 1990 is diverse, but it generally falls into three main categories. First, there are studies focusing on racial and ethnic differences and the existence of differential treatment and discrimination. These are mostly atheoretical but they document continuing manifestations of racism in U.S. sports. Second, there are studies focusing on the experiences of athletes from various ethnic minority backgrounds. Some of this research is purely descriptive, but much of it links experiences to identity, the dynamics of racial and ethnic relations in organizational and community contexts, the material conditions underlying identity formation and ethnic relations, and more general processes of cultural production and reproduction. Third, there are studies that focus on images and narratives, usually represented in the media, through which race and ethnicity is constructed, contested, and re-imagined over time and across social contexts. Most of these studies deal with the social construction of race and racial classification systems, the dynamics of racial ideology, and the appropriation of Native American names and images by sport teams. The following three sections present selected examples of research in each of these categories.

Difference and Discrimination

As noted above, there is a strong tradition of research on difference and discrimination in the sociology of sport and related fields in the sport sciences. For example, recently published historical research documents the existence of racial politics and the changing contours of the color line through the twentieth century (Miller and Wiggins, 2004; Wiggins and Miller, 2003).

In 1997 John Hoberman published a "racial history of modern sport that explored the connections between sports, racial ideology, and biological racism during the 20th century. Provocatively titled Darwin's Athletes, the book was intended to document race as a dangerous, socially constructed myth and to show how sports have consistently served as sites for preserving dominant racial ideology, especially in the United States. In the absence of systematic data on the ways that African Americans have given meaning to and integrated sports and sport participation into their lives, Hoberman argued that "the cult of the black athlete [has] exacerbated the disastrous spread of anti-intellectual attitudes among African American youth" (p. xiii). Furthermore, he claimed that black intellectuals, especially black male scholars in the late-twentieth century, have failed to critique black athleticism thereby allowing the myth of race as well as popular ideas about black male physicality to be preserved in contemporary U.S. culture (pp. 76-95). Not surprisingly, Hoberman's inference that blacks have perpetuated their own victimization was not well received by African American scholars. Despite his insightful critique of racialist science and the role sports have played in the reproduction of racist ideas through the twentieth century, Hoberman's book has been cited with caution in the sociology of sport literature. However, it remains an important source of historical information about sports, the social construction of race, and the dynamics of dominant racial ideology in the United States.

Most research on difference and discrimination continues to focus on differential participation opportunities, often related to a combination of racism and constraints associated with social class and poverty, and on the dynamics of differential treatment and exclusion in particular sports and sport organizations. For example, Sailes (1998) and Brooks and Althouse (2000) have edited collections of research articles and commentaries that describe continuing racial myths and stereotypes, critique biological theories of race and athletic performance, and document the relative lack of ethnic minorities in coaching and administrative jobs in university athletic departments and the racism and sexism faced by African American women in college sports.

A primary source of data on patterns of racial and ethnic exclusion in the management positions of major sport organizations continues to be the annual Racial and Gender Report Card (gender was first included in the 1998 report; see http://www.sportinsociety.org/rgrc.html). Since 2002 this report has been published by the Institute for Diversity and Ethics in Sports at the University of South Florida. The current report (www.bus.ucf.edu/sport/public/downloads/media/ides/release_05.pdf) includes data on women and all people of color in the major men's team sports (football, baseball, basketball, and hockey), the Women's National Basketball Association, and the National Collegiate Athletic Association. Future reports will include data from the motor sports industry and Olympic sport organizations in the United States.

Although the 2003 Racial and Gender Report Card included data on African Americans, Latinos, Native Americans, and Asian Americans, there are few current sociological studies of difference and discrimination related to populations other than African Americans. This is not because people in these populations do not experience discrimination in sports. More likely, it is because ethnic stereotypes about each of these populations vary in content and how they are applied in sports. This makes it difficult to study issues of difference and discrimination except on a local level through qualitative research. Finally, it is important to note that the research on difference and discrimination has not been used as a basis for developing or testing theories of racial and ethnic relations.

Experiences Among People in Racial and Ethnic Populations

The extent of racial and ethnic diversity in the United States creates many research possibilities related to the sport experiences of people in different ethnic populations. Although most of this research has focused on African American men, there are studies describing the experiences of African American women and Latinos and Latinas. Only a few studies focus on Native Americans and the diverse Asian American populations in the United States.

Research on sport-related experiences ranges from descriptive to highly analytical, with the latter guided by a combination of theoretical frameworks. For example, Messner (1992) used critical feminist theory to guide his research on masculinity among men who were former elite athletes. His in-depth interviews indicated that because AfricanAmerican men from low income backgrounds had fewer educational and occupational opportunities than white athletes from middle- and upper class families, they were more likely to see sports as contexts in which they could establish their masculinity and achieve success in a culturally valued activity. Additional studies have confirmed that black men in the U.S. often face a race logic that encourages them to give priority to sport-related identities. The extent to which this interferes with the development of other identities among African American men and unrealistically constrains developmental choices is difficult to study and there are no systematic data on this issue.

Researchers exploring the intersections of race and gender have found that the dynamics associated with racial ideology are different for black women than for black men (Corbett and Johnson, 2000; Daniels, 2000; Smith, 1992, 2000). In ideological terms, the bodies of black men have been socially constructed and viewed differently than the bodies of black women.

Other research on identity dynamics indicates that there is a diversity of traditions and norms associated with gender and sport participation for girls and women from Latino cultures (Acosta, 1999; Jamieson, 2003). Latinas whose families have recently immigrated to the U.S. receive less parental support to play sports, especially if participation is perceived as separating them from their traditional culture. Latinas from families that have been in the US for more than one generation are often encouraged by parents and other relatives to play whatever they wish, although they sometimes face the challenge of negotiating normative differences between the dominant and Latino cultures.

One of the most notable studies that links sport-related experiences to material conditions was done by French sociologist Loic Wacquant who spent over three years studying the social world of boxers in a ghetto gym in Chicago (1992; 1995a, b, c; 2004). His observations and interviews as well as his personal experiences as an apprentice boxer gave him unique access to the social logic and meanings associated with boxing as it is learned by men living in a black ghetto. Guided by Bourdieu's notion that "we learn by the body" and that "the social order inscribes itself in bodies," Wacquant immersed himself into the social world of a boxing gym. He explained that the gym he studied was organized in connection with destructive social forces present in the ghetto at the same time that it sheltered black men from the full negative impact of those forces. As the men trained at the gym they engaged in an intense regime of body regulation demanding physical, visual, and mental discipline. As boxing became central in their lives, they developed a "socialized lived body" that was at the very core of their identities and actions. For these men, boxing constituted a powerful socializing experience that cannot be understood apart from the cultural and structural contexts in which their training occurred.

Additional ethnographic studies have linked the sport-related experiences of ethnic minorities to larger community processes. For example, Foley (1990a, b) gave special attention to Mexicano-Anglo relations in his study of high school football in a south Texas town. He identified the working-class vatos (young Mexicano males) who rejected sport participation but used football games and other sport events to publicly display their "cultural style" and establish their social reputations in the community. Foley described cases in which Mexicanos in the local population used high school football as a site to resist the dominant culture of the town, but he concludes that Mexicano resistance was largely symbolic and did not alter the prevailing culture and structure of power in the town.

Similar community dynamics were noted by Grey (1992) in his study of high school sports and relations between immigrants from Southeast Asia and the established residents of Garden City, Kansas. When students from immigrant families failed to participate in football, basketball, baseball, and softball, they were perceived by established residents as unwilling to become "true

Americans." This increased the marginalization of Asian students in the school and exacerbated ethnic tensions in the town. In contrast to Grey's research there is anecdotal information indicating that third and fourth generation Asian American families are generally well integrated in many U.S. communities, play the same sports that others play, and even use sports participation as an expression of cultural assimilation and as a reaffirmation of social relationships with peers–but systematic research on such processes has not been done.

Images and Narratives

The most provocative and theoretically rich research on race and sports has involved various forms of textual and semiotic analyses focusing on popular discourses representing athletes of color and on sports as sites for the construction of whiteness as a form of privilege. For example, scholars have used combinations of critical and postmodernist theories to study the complex connections between racial ideology, commodification, and "cultural stories" representing black athletes, especially Michael Jordan (Andrews, 1996a, b, 2001; Baker and Boyd, 1997). Critical studies scholar Todd Boyd explains that because sports and "the discourses that surround them, have become one of the master narratives of twentieth-century culture" they can be used as a barometer for assessing the American character (1997, p. ix). Cultural studies scholar David Andrews has built on this notion as he and his colleagues have deconstructed Michael Jordan and used representations of Jordan as a basis "for developing progressive understandings of the broader social, economic, political, and technological concerns that frame contemporary culture" (2001, p. xv). Andrews analyzes commercial advertising and other media coverage to explain how Jordan as a mediated icon represents "the convergence of corporate and media interests" and how Jordan has become "a cultural site around which particular neoconservative racial ideologies have been embodied and authorized" in late modem America (2001, p. xvii). African American Studies scholar Michael Eric Dyson, reading Jordan from a black cultural perspective concludes that even though Jordan was appropriated by corporate capitalism "his big, black body–graceful and powerful, elegant and dark–symbolizes the possibilities of other black bodies to remain safe long enough to survive within the limited but significant sphere of sport" 1993, p. 74). Jordan's body, says Dyson, is "a fluid metaphor" that has been used to represent multiple conflicting desires.

Focusing more directly on the struggles over the significance of race and cultural meanings, some scholars in the sociology of sport have studied the dynamics and implications associated with the uniquely American practice of using Native American names and images as a basis for team names, logos, and mascots in interscholastic and professional sports (Davis, 1993; King, 2004; King and Springwood, 2001a, b). This practice is a legacy of centuries of Native-Euro-American relations through which whiteness has become normalized and Native Americans and all people of color have been cast as "others." The concrete and highly visible logos and mascots used by sport teams have provoked activism as well as academic analysis (King, 2004). Analyses, grounded primarily in a framework of critical cultural studies, have focused on the cultural and structural dynamics involved as sport teams have resisted the objections of Native Americans and others who identify the names, logos, and mascots as offensive and racist. This research has made a significant contribution to the sociology of sport in that it has demonstrated "how racial difference animates much of the popular aesthetics of sport" (King and Springwood, 2001b, p. 12).

Conclusion

Research on sport, race, and ethnicity is important because the proportion of ethnic populations in the U.S. continues to increase relative to whites with European ancestry, and because professional and college teams often recruit athletes from Africa and Latin America. As of mid-2003, there were nearly 40 million Latinos in the U.S. population (14 percent); blacks numbered over 37 million (13 percent); people with Asian ancestry numbered 12 million (4 percent), and Native Americans numbered 2.8 million (1 percent). Demographic trends indicate that whites with European ancestry will constitute only 50% of the population in 2050, and they will be in a numerical minority in many U.S. states. If the color line was a dominant feature of the social and cultural landscape in the United States during the twentieth century, ethnic relations will be a dominant feature of the twenty-first century. The task in the sociology of sport will be to use sports as sites for theorizing and inspiring progressive forms of ethnic relations.

References

Acosta, Vivien. 1999. Hispanic women in sport. *Journal of Physical Education, Recreation & Dance* 70(4), 44–46.

Andrews, David L. 1996a. The fact(s) of Michael Jordan's blackness: Excavating a floating racial signifier. *Sociology of Sport Journal* 13, 2: 125–58.

Andrews, David L., ed. 1996b. Deconstructing Michael Jordan: Reconstructing postindustrial America. *Sociology of Sport Journal* 13, 4. Special issue.

——— 2001. Michael Jordan, Inc.: *Corporate sport, media culture, and late modern America.* Albany, NY: State University of New York Press.

Baker, Aaron, and Todd Boyd, eds. 1997. *Out of bounds: Sports, media, and the politics of identity.* Bloomington, IN: Indiana University Press.

Birrell, Susan. 1989. Race relations theories and sport: Suggestions for a more critical analysis. *Sociology of Sport Journal* 6, 3: 212–27.

Blalock, H. M. 1962. Occupational discrimination: Some theoretical propositions. *Social Problems* 9: 240-247.

——— 1970. *Toward a theory of minority-group relations.* New York: Capricorn Books.

Boyd, Todd, 1997. The day the Niggaz took over: Basketball, commodity culture, and Black masculinity. Pp. 123-144 in Baker, Aaron, and Todd Boyd, eds. *Out of Bounds: Sports, media, and the politics of identity*. Bloomington, IN: Indiana University Press.

Brooks, D. D., and R. C. Althouse, eds. 2000. *Racism in College Athletics: The African-American athlete's experience*. Morgantown, WV: Fitness Information Technology, Inc.

Broom, Leonard, and Phillip Selznick. 1963. *Sociology: A test with adapted readings* (3rd ed.). Evanston, IL: Row, Peterson.

Coakley, Jay. 1986. *Sport in Society: Issues and controversies* (3rd ed.). St. Louis, MO: The C. V. Mosby Company.

——— 1998. *Sport in Society: Issues and controversies* (6th ed.). New York: McGraw-Hill.

Corbett, Doris, and W. Johnson. 2000. The African American female in collegiate sport: Sexism and racism. Pp. 199–226 in D. Brooks & R. Althouse, eds. *Racism in College Athletics: The African American athlete's experience*. Morgantown, WV: Fitness Information Technology, Inc.

Davis, L. 1993. Protest against the use of Native American mascots: A challenge to traditional American identity. *Journal of Sport & Social Issues* 17, 1: 9–22.

Dubois, W.E.B. 1903/1989. *The Souls of Black Folk*. New York: Bantam Books.

Dyson, Michael Eric. 1993. *Reflecting Black: African-American cultural criticism*. Minneapolis, MN: University of Minnesota Press.

Edwards, Harry. 1969. *The Revolt of the Black Athlete*. New York: The Free Press.

——— 1971. The sources of the Black athlete's superiority. *The Black Scholar* (November): 32–41.

Edwards, H. 1973. *Sociology of Sport*. Homewood, IL: Dorsey Press.

Edwards, Harry. 1969. *The Revolt of the black athlete*. New York: The Free Press.

Eitzen, D. S., and N. Yetman, 1977. Immune from racism? *Civil Rights Digest* 9, 2: 3–13.

Foley, Douglas. 1990a. *Learning Capitalist Culture*. Philadelphia: University of Pennsylvania Press.

Foley, Douglas. 1990b. The great American football ritual: Reproducing race, class, and gender inequality. *Sociology of Sport Journal* 7, 2: 111–35.

Grusky, Oscar. 1963. The effects of formal structure on managerial recruitment: A study of baseball organization. *Sociometry* 26: 345–353.

Hoberman, John. 1997. *Darwin's Athletes: How sport has damaged Black America and preserved the myth of race*. Boston: Houghton Mifflin Company.

Hoch, P. 1972. *Rip Off the Big Game*. Garden City, NY: Anchor Books.

Jamieson, Katherine M. 2003. Occupying a middle space: Toward a Mestiza sport studies. *Sociology of Sport Journal,* 20,1:1–16.

Kane, M. 1971. An assessment of "Black is Best." *Sports Illustrated* 34, 3 (January 18): 72–83.

King, C. Richard, ed., 2004. Re/claiming Indianness: Critical perspectives on Native American mascots. *Journal of Sport and Social Issues* (special issue), 28, 1.

King, C. Richard, and Charles Fruehling Springwood, eds. 2001a. *Team Spirits: The Native American mascots controversy*. Lincoln, NB: Bison Books and University of Nebraska Press.

King, C. Richard, and Charles Fruehling Springwood. 2001b. *Beyond the Cheers: Race as spectacle in college sport.* Albany, NY: State University of New York Press.

Lapchick, R. 1984. *Broken Promises: Racism in American sports.* New York: St. Martin's/Marek.

Loy, John W., and Joseph F. McElvogue. 1971. Racial segregation in American sport. *International Review of Sport Sociology* 5: 5–24.

Messner, M. A. 1992. *Power at Play: Sports and the problem of masculinity.* Boston, MA: Beacon Press.

Miller, Patrick B., and David K. Wiggins, eds. 2004. *Sport and the Color Line: Black athletes and race relations in twentieth-century America.* New York/London: Routledge.

Myrdal, G. 1944. *An American Dilemma: The Negro problem and modern democracy.* New York: Harper and Brothers.

Pascal, A. H., and L. A. Rapping. 1972. The economics of racial discrimination in organized baseball. In A. H. Pascal and L. A. Rapping, eds. *Racial Discrimination in Economic Life.* Lexington, MA: D.C. Heath and Company.

Rosenblatt, A. 1967. Negroes in baseball: The failure of success. *Trans-action* 4, 9: 51–53.

Sailes, Gary A., ed. 1998. *African Americans in Sport.* New Brunswick, NJ/London: Transaction Publishers.

Scott, J. 1969. *The Athletic Revolution.* New York: The Free Press.

Scully, G. W. 1973. Economic discrimination in professional sports. *Law and Contemporary Problems* 38, 1: 67–84.

Smith, Earl, and Wib Leonard. 1997. Twenty-five years of stacking research in Major League Baseball: A theoretical assessment. *Sociological Focus* 30: 321–331.

Smith, Y. 1992. Women of color in society and sport. *Quest* 44, 2: 228–50.

——— 2000. Sociohistorical influences on African American elite sportswomen. Pp. 173–198 in D. Brooks & R. Althouse, eds., *Racism in college athletics: The African American athlete's experience.* Morgantown, WV: Fitness Information Technology, Inc.

Tolbert, C. M. II. 1975. *The black athlete in the Southwest Conference: A study of institutional racism.* Unpubished doctorial dissertation, Baylor University, Waco, Texas.

Wacquant. L. J. D. 1992. The social logic of boxing in Black Chicago: Toward a sociology of pugilism. *Sociology of Sport Journal* 9(3), 221–254.

Wacquant, L. J. D. 1995a. The pugilistic point of view: How boxers think and feel about their trade. *Theory and Society* 24: 489–535.

Wacquant, L. J. D. 1995b. Why men desire muscles. *Body & Society* 1,1: 163–79.

Wacquant, L. J. D. 1995c. Pugs at work: Bodily capital and bodily labour among professional boxers. *Body & Society* 1,1: 65–93.

Wacquant, Loic. 2004. *Body and Soul.* New York: Oxford University Press.

Wiggins, David K., and Patrick B. Miller, eds. 2003. *The Unlevel Playing field: A documentary history of the African American experience in sport.* Urbana, IL: University of Illinois Press.

Yetman, N. R., and D. S. Eitzen. 1972. Black Americans in sports: Unequal opportunity for equal ability. *Civil Rights Digest* 5, 2: 20–34.

Crisis of Black Athletes on the Eve of the 21st Century

Harry Edwards

FOR MORE THAN TWO DECADES I HAVE BEEN ADAMANT IN MY CONTEN-
tion that the dynamics of black sports involvement, and the blind faith of black youths and their
families in sport as a prime vehicle of self-realization and social-economic advancement, have
combined to generate a complex of critical problems for black society. At the root of these problems is the fact that black families have been inclined to push their children toward sports career
aspirations, often to the neglect and detriment of other critically important areas of personal and
cultural development.

Those circumstances have developed largely because of: (1) a long-standing, widely held, racist, and ill-informed presumption of innate, race-linked black athletic superiority and intellectual
deficiency; (2) media propaganda portraying sports as a broadly accessible route to black social
and economic mobility; and (3) a lack of comparably visible, high-prestige black role models
beyond the sports arena. The result is a single-minded pursuit of sports fame and fortune that
has spawned an institutionalized triple tragedy in black society: the tragedy of thousands upon
thousands of black youths in obsessive pursuit of sports goals that the overwhelming majority
of them will never attain; the tragedy of the personal and cultural under-development that af-
flicts so many successful and unsuccessful black sports aspirants; and the tragedy of cultural and
institutional underdevelopment throughout black society at least in some part as a consequence
of the drain in talent potential toward sports and away from other vital areas of occupational and
career emphasis, such as medicine, law, economics, politics, education, and technical fields.

Today there has developed a serious decline not only in the fact, but in the perception and even the hope of mainstream life choices and life chances for an increasing number of black youths. One-way integration and the resulting exit of the black middle-class from the traditional black community has contributed to a spiraling deterioration in institutional viability in many black communities—a deterioration encompassing the functionality of the family, education, the economy, the political infrastructure, and even the black church. This unfortunate situation has combined with the ongoing legacies of anti-black racism and discrimination in America, the erosion or elimination of civil rights gains such as affirmative action, and structural economic shifts in the broader society to generate the epidemics of crime, drugs, violence, gangs and gang warfare, and a pervasive despair, malaise, and hopelessness that now afflict broad sectors of black society.

In that environment, literally thousands of young black people have institutionally, culturally, and inter-personally disconnected: they attend school only infrequently, if at all; they have given up any hope of ever holding a legitimate job or of being otherwise productively involved in the mainstream economy; they respect only their closest peers and seek only their peers' respect; and, in many instances, they see no future for themselves or their generation and have little expectation of living beyond their teens or twenties. Some go so far as to pick out the coffin and the clothes in which they expect to be buried.

Predictably sports participation opportunities for those youths have also deteriorated. Playgrounds, sandlots, parks, and even backyard recreational sites in many instances have been taken over by drug dealers, or they have become battlegrounds in gang disputes, or they have simply become too dangerously exposed to eruptions of violence to be safely used. Cutbacks in educational budgets and shifts in funds from school athletic, physical education, and recreation programs to concerns deemed more vital in these fiscally strapped, troubled communities (including campus and classroom security) have further narrowed sports participation opportunities. Even where interscholastic sports participation opportunities have survived, security problems and fears of violence and other disruptions in an increasing number of cases have restricted both the scheduling of events and spectator attendance.

In the face of such discouraging circumstances, many black youths have opted to go with the flow, exchanging team colors for gang colors or simply dropping out of everything and chillin'. They move utterly beyond the reach and scope of established institutional involvements and contacts—save the criminal justice system, hospital emergency services, and the mortuary services industry.

The social circumstances facing young black males are particularly germane here. Nationally at least a quarter of all black males aged 16 to 29 are under the control of the courts; in some states (such as California) this figure is approaching one-third of the black males in this age range. One-third of all the deaths in this group nationally are homicides (usually perpetrated by other black males), and suicide ranks only behind homicides and accidents as a cause of death. Moreover, since the age range 16 to 29 represents the prime years of self-development and career establishment, it should be no surprise that black males are declining as a proportion of the population in virtually every institutional setting (e.g. higher education, the workforce, the church) save the prison system.

Predictably, black sports involvement is threatened as well. As alluded to earlier, developments at the intersection of race, sports, and education have over the years generated a situation wherein increasing numbers of black youths have focused their efforts on athletic achievement only to find themselves underdeveloped academically and unable to compete in the classroom.

Nonetheless, their talents were so critical to the success of revenue producing sports programs—most notably basketball and football—at major colleges and universities competing at the Division I level that those athletes were typically recruited out of high school or junior college notwithstanding their educational deficiencies, with the predictable result of widespread black athlete academic underachievement and outright failure. It was this tragedy and the attention it generated from sports activists and the media from the late 1960s into the 1980s that ultimately prompted the most far-reaching reform efforts in modern collegiate sports history.

But because black athletes' academic problems are in large part rooted in and intertwined with black youths' societal circumstances more generally there can be no effective resolution of the educational circumstances of black athletes at any academic level except in coordination with commensurate efforts in society. In fact, to the extent that remedial efforts neglect such a coordinated dual approach, they are virtually guaranteed to exacerbate rather than better the situation of the black athletes that they impact.

Indeed, that has been the impact of much recent activity aimed at academic reform in athletics. At the high school level, the institution of more demanding academic requirements for athletic participation prompted many black athletes who subsequently have been declared academically ineligible to drop out of high school altogether.

At the collegiate level the establishment of Proposition 48, officially National Collegiate Athletic Association (N.C.A.A.) Bylaw 14.3, has had even more negative consequences. Proposition 48 required that before he could participate in Division I college varsity sports, a student had to have a minimum grade point average (GPA)of 2.0 in at least 11 courses in core subjects in high school and a minimum SAT score of 700 (ACT score of 17). The rule was instituted to counteract academically lenient recruitment practices, and though the specific requirements mandated under the regulation have been adjusted to accommodate various sliding scales of eligibility over the last decade, the essential thrust and intent of regulatory efforts remains the same today—as does their disparate impact on black athletes.

In the first two years of Proposition 48 enforcement (1984–1986), 92 percent of all academically ineligible basketball players and 84 percent of academically ineligible football players were black athletes. As late as 1996, the overwhelming majority of Proposition 48 casualties were still black student-athlete prospects. Despite attempts to the contrary such horrifically disproportionate numbers cannot be justified on grounds that ineligible athletes would not have graduated anyway. Richard Lapchick, director of the Center for the Study of Sports in Society, reports that if Proposition 48 had been in use in 1981, 69 percent of black male scholarship athletes would have been ineligible to participate in sports as freshmen, but 54 percent of those athletes eventually graduated.

Complicating the effects of Proposition 48 is Proposition 42, which was passed by the N.C.A.A. in 1989 and was designed to strengthen Proposition 48 by denying athletes who failed to meet Proposition 48 eligibility requirements all financial aid during the freshman year. Proposition 42 effectively prevented prospective scholarship athletes who did not qualify under Proposition 48 and who could not pay their own college expenses from attending college at all. Of course, this regulation disproportionately affected black athletes, since they numbered disproportionately among Proposition 48 casualties.

In 1990, following widespread objections to the draconian nature of Proposition 42 (most notably the protest efforts of Georgetown basketball coach John Thompson), Proposition 42 was modified to allow student-athletes who were "partially qualified" (i.e., who met either minimum grade point average or test score requirements) to receive non-athletic, need-based financial aid during the freshman year. Those who did not qualify under either test score or grade point average requirements still could not receive any type of financial aid. Still, black athlete prospects, always among the poorest and neediest of athlete recruits, continued to bear the brunt of the measure's negative impact.

It is now clear that the greatest consequence of Proposition 42, and similar regulations has been to limit the opportunities—both educational and athletic—that would otherwise be available to black youths. Those measures were neither conceived nor instituted with due consideration of black youths' circumstances beyond the academy and the sports arena. In consequence, while there has been some minor improvement in such concerns as black athlete college graduation rates (an increase estimated to be about 8 percent and possibly due as much to improved academic support services for black student-athletes after they arrive on college campuses as to any pre-recruitment screening function of propositions 48 or 42), those results must be weighed against the profoundly negative cost of lost opportunities and more subtle consequences such as the stigmatizing of black youths as Proposition 48 cases or casualties.

The diminution of opportunities for black youths to succeed at the high school and collegiate levels must inevitably register and be manifest in all sports and at all levels traditionally accessible to black athletes in numbers. Already many high schools are unable to field teams or schedule dependable competition. Beyond the high school ranks, in recent years there has been disturbing evidence of a downward trend in the statistics of virtually every skill category in Division I collegiate basketball: team and individual points per game averages; individual and team field goals percentages; individual and team free throw percentages; and assists.

Both college coaches and officials, and the media, tend to assume that such declining performance figures are due mostly to early entry into the professional ranks by star collegiate players. Many star players leave college after only one or two years of collegiate competition, and, in some instances, talented high school players skip college altogether and go directly into the National

Basketball Association (NBA). But the NBA itself appears to be slumping statistically and, in any event, the league shows no evidence of having benefited from any would-be talent windfall.

In 1997, the average NBA team scored only 96.7 points, the lowest regular season league average since the 24-second shot clock was instituted. Moreover, in the 1996–1997 season the average age of players in the NBA was the highest in league history—older players are apparently able to hold on to their jobs and stay around longer because younger players are not able to displace them. Thus, regardless of how many collegiate basketball players are leaving or skipping college for the professional ranks, they are having no discernible impact as basketball talents at the professional level.

Other trends that individually would seem of little significance appear more troubling when considered within the context of emerging trends in black sports involvement. For example, black attendance at sporting events other than basketball and football games is virtually nonexistent. As ticket prices continue to increase and more leagues and teams choose "pay per view" and cable television broadcast options, ever fewer numbers of blacks will be watching even basketball and football either in person or on television. Those trends are likely to affect most severely people abiding in the lower and working-class strata of black society that have traditionally produced the greater proportion of black athlete talent. With school and community sports and recreation programs and opportunities on the decline, declining personal access and exposure to elite athletic performances virtually guarantees that both the interest and the involvement of that population in sport are likely to wane.

In this regard, the character of black involvement in baseball may be a harbinger of the future of black involvement in sports overall. Though major league baseball teams claim not to keep track of the race of their players and other personnel, it is estimated that approximately 18 percent of major league players are black. (In 1996, in a team by team count, I arrived at figures of 14 to 17 percent, depending on how some players of Caribbean or black Latino heritage counted themselves.) Eighteen percent is approximately the same black player representation in the major leagues as ten years ago.

Relatively speaking, this stagnation in the proportion of black players in the major leagues may be the good news. It has been fairly well established that, for the most part, in urban areas (where over 80 percent of the black population lives) black adolescents and teenagers no longer either follow baseball or play it. Few black adults take their children to baseball games; in fact only about one percent of all major league baseball tickets sold are bought by blacks. Indeed, on opening day of the 1997 baseball season—a day which marked the fiftieth anniversary of Jackie Robinson breaking the color barrier against black participation in the major leagues—Jackie Robinson's former team had the same number of black players on its roster as it did the day that he fast stepped on the field in a Dodger uniform—ONE!

All considered, unless steps are taken to reverse present trends in both sport and society, we could be witnessing the end of what in retrospect might well come to be regarded as the golden age of black sports participation. We are, quite simply disqualifying, jailing, and burying an increasing number of our potential black football players, basketball players baseball players, and other prospective athletes—right along with our potential black lawyers, doctors, and teachers.

In the past I have resoundingly rejected the priority of play books over textbooks because of the triple tragedy scenario outlined above. So long as the traditional black community and the larger society—particularly in the wake of hard-won civil rights advances and opportunities—effectively created and sustained some realistic broad spectrum access to legitimate means of personal and career development for the black youths in question (that is, access beyond the dream of sports stardom), criticisms and admonitions warning of a black overemphasis on sports participation and achievement not only were justified but necessary and even obligatory correctives to misguided attitudes and dispositions toward sports in black society. But today there is no option but to recognize that for increasing legions of black youths, the issue is neither textbooks nor playbooks—the issue is survival, finding a source of hope, encouragement, and support in developing lives and building legitimate careers and futures.

Without question, the ultimate resolution to this situation must be the overall institutional development of black communities and the creation of greater opportunity for black youths in the broader society. In the meantime, however, if community and school sports programs can provide a means of reconnecting with at least some of those black youths who we have already lost and strengthening our ties with those who. by whatever miracle of faith and tenacity, have managed to hold on to hope and to stay the course, then those programs and the youths involved deserve our strongest support and endorsement.

Therefore, I now say that we must reconstitute and broaden access to school sports programs. We must create secure and supervised playgrounds park recreation areas, and community sports facilities; open school sports facilities for supervised weekend community use and midnight basketball, volleyball, tennis, bowling, badminton, swimming, and other sports opportunities; recruit counselors, teachers, people trained in the trades, health care professionals, and religious leaders to advise, mentor, and tutor young people at those sports sites; network with corporate and government agencies to establish apprenticeship and job opportunities; and bring in students of sport and society who understand and can articulate the applicability of the great lessons and dynamics of black youths' sports success and achievement to their life circumstances and goals more generally.

Far from de-emphasizing or abandoning sport, or simply allowing our involvement to wane, black people must now more than ever intelligently, constructively, and proactively pursue sports involvement. We cannot afford to wait passively for better times or allow ourselves to be swept and herded along in the flow of events and developments at the interface of race, sports, and society. We must understand the forces threatening black sports participation while also recognizing that black sports participation need not become an obsession or preoccupation.

Today it is desirable, even necessary that black youths and black society as a whole continue to harbor dreams of achieving excellence in sports—there is much to be learned and gained from both the challenges of sports competition and the experiences of meeting those challenges. But all involved must learn to dream with their eyes open, always remaining fully cognizant of participation's pitfalls no less than its positive possibilities, of its potential as a dead end trap no less than its promise as a vehicle for outreach and advancement. As in the past, the responsibility for perpetually mapping the sports terrain and for the ongoing acculturation and education of black youths as they seek to productively navigate the possibilities of athletic achievement fall most heavily upon black people themselves.

In the final analysis, exploiting black youths' overemphasis on sports participation and achievement may be our only remaining avenue for guiding increasing numbers of them out of circumstances that today lead to even more devastating destructiveness and a greater waste of human potential than that which I, and others, have long decried in connection with unrealistic black sports aspirations. Not at all coincidentally it could also salvage the golden age of black sports participation.

Chapter 2

African American Culture and Sport

The Role of Sport in the Black Community

Othello Harris

Athletics is to the Black community what technology is to the Japanese and what oil is to the Arabs. We're allowing that commodity to be exploited. ... We really need to turn it around ... if those schools cannot do for us what we need done, i.e., provide an education for the next generation, then we should be looking to steer clear of those institutions.

—Charles Farrell, Director, Rainbow

Coalition for Fairness in Athletics

FARRELL'S QUOTE, ABOVE, REVEALS WHAT MANY BELIEVE ABOUT SPORT and the black community: that the athletic prowess of young black males is a precious commodity to the black community. No longer ignored by collegiate athletic programs, sports franchises, fans and the media, African Americans have come to define certain sports and/or sports positions. For example, the image one typically gets when listening to a sportscaster describe a game battle between a wide receiver and a cornerback is of black contenders engaged in a contest of skill. Black is the cornerback, receiver, basketball all-star, boxer and all-around athlete. The black athlete has arrived, conquered many challenges and displaced many whites on the playing field.

Therefore, sport, we are told by some, has opened its doors to African Americans, offering untold direct and indirect opportunities for social mobility. Farrell, cited above, while acknowledging the exploitation that occurs in many college programs, appears to believe that college sport can and should provide a gateway to a better life for African Americans. He is like many observers, coaches and former players, at least in his belief about what sport could provide. Yet, others like Edwards (1973, 1979), Coakley (1994), Eitzen and Sage (1993), Curry and Jiobu (1984) and Leonard (1997) dismiss the idea that sport is an easy route to social mobility for African Americans. What is the role of sport in the black community?

To understand the meaning of sport to the black community this paper examines some of the crucial athletic events in American sport and their impact on the black community. It begins with Jack Johnson at the turn of the century.

A Black Champion

In 1908 Jack Johnson defeated Canadian Tommy Burns to become the first black heavyweight champion of the world. But Burns was a lightly regarded champion: He had won the title from the dull Marvin Hart, who occupied the title after Jim Jeffries retired and named Hart one of the contenders for his crown (Roberts, 1983). Johnson, perhaps realizing that there was little interest in boxing at the time, seized the opportunity to position himself for a match with the newly crowned champion. He followed Burns to England and Australia, seeking what he believed to be his rightful place in the sport of boxing—as holder of the most prestigious title in the sportsworld—the heavyweight champion.

Johnson was not the first African American to fight for the heavyweight title; that honor goes to Tom Molineaux, a former slave from Virginia who won his freedom as a result of defeating another slave in a match that earned his slave owner $100,000.00 (Harris, in press). Molineaux bolted from America to England where he would, eventually, meet the white heavyweight champion, Tom Cribb, in "the battle of the century" nearly 100 years before Johnson fought a white champion for the title. In a controversial match, Molineaux lost to Cribb.

Despite Molineaux's unsuccessful bid for the belt, the fact that he and a few other slaves received special privileges and were, in rare cases, manumitted undoubtedly led some to proclaim sport's ability to elevate the status of African Americans. However, Frederick Douglass, himself a former slave, proclaimed, boxing and wrestling, drinking and other merriments during holiday periods were the most effective means slaveholders had for keeping down insurrection" (quoted in Sammons, 1988, pp. 31–32). For him, sport was a means of social control used by planters, not a way to a better life for America's black population. Thus, even before Johnson and the black boxing champions who preceded him (e.g., Dixon, Walcott and Gans) took the stage, the discussion about the role of sport in the black community had begun.2 Johnson's accomplishments would accelerate the debate. According to Sammons:

Since prizefighting has been characterized by some as a true test of skill, courage, intelligence, and manhood, boxing champions have traditionally stood as symbols of national and racial superiority. Consequently, black challengers to white American champions have been perceived as threats to white and national superiority. (1988, p. 31)

Johnson as champion was, therefore, a threat to social order and whites' beliefs about their black brethren. His defeat of Burns so outraged some whites that they began to search for a "Great White Hope." When Great White Hope Tournaments yielded no suitable prospects for returning the crown to white America (Roberts, 1983), Jim Jeffries, the former champ who had retired undefeated, was coaxed out of retirement to "wipe the Golden smile" from Johnson's face (London, 1992). In a fight fraught with implications for social Darwinism and racial superiority, Johnson easily defeated the white hope, setting off nationwide celebrations in black America. The fight also resulted in riots across America, principally whites attacking African Americans (Gilmore, 1973, 1975).

More important to this paper are perceptions, then, about sport and the elevation of people physically similar to the new heavyweight champion. For he had knocked down an important wall of segregation; he had defeated notions of black athletic inferiority (at least as far as boxing was concerned); he had challenged the widely held belief that, amazing as it seems now, African Americans lacked the physical wherewithal to compete with whites.

This caused whites to anguish about Johnson's impact on the black community as well as what his accomplishment would mean to businesses that employed African Americans. At least one cotton-buying firm was concerned that there would be a shortage of field laborers after Jack Johnson won the heavyweight title because African Americans would, in large numbers, enter the field of boxing (Roberts, 1983). Of course, boxing could no more offer opportunities to the masses of African American males than other sports can now offer positions to the black populace. Nevertheless, there was concern about a shift in the employment and aspirations of black workers.

On the other hand, Booker T. Washington, while castigating Johnson for public behaviors that Washington found to be injurious to African Americans,3 seemed also to be circumspect about sport's ability to uplift his people when he stated that "all men should be educated along mental and spiritual lines in connection with their physical education. A man with muscle minus brains is a useless creature" (quoted in Gilmore, 1973, p. 25). Washington did not view sport as the vehicle that would take African Americans from subordinate to equal status with whites. And some whites, threatened by the prospect of blacks challenging whites on their terms in physical feats, thought it wise to counsel blacks against both seeking equality (upward mobility) through sport and behaving like Johnson. For example, Mrs. James Crawford, vice-president of the California Women's Club, who declared herself a friend of the black race, offered that: the Negroes ... are to some extent a childlike race, needing guidance, schooling and encouragement. We deny them this by encouraging them to believe that they have gained anything by having one of their race as a champion fighter. Race riots are inevitable, when we, a superior people, allow these people to be deluded and degraded by such false ideals (Roberts, p. 112).

There were, during Johnson's reign, disparate beliefs about the role of sport in the black community. Interestingly, much of the opposition to any new found hope for prestige through sport for African Americans came from whites. This would change when new black superstars, more to their liking, took center stage.

Black Athletic Heroes to Americans

Unlike Jack Johnson, who was despised by whites, especially for his behavior towards them (i.e., he behaved as if he were whites' equal), Joe Louis and Jesse Owens were, to some extent, loved by many white Americans. And they should have been. They were both careful to follow whites' prescription for black behavior; that is, they were compliant and obsequious and showed the proper amount of deference in the presence of whites. But they also represented American might and superiority. Whereas Johnson was seen as a hero to some segments of black America, Louis and Owens became the first black athletic heroes to white America.

Owens was in the spotlight for a relatively short period of time. His claim to fame was his outstanding 4-gold-medal-performance at the 1936 Olympics, which was supposed to "check" Hitler's arrogance about his "master race." Louis's tenure was much longer, as he held the heavyweight title for 12 years. He, too, was catapulted to prominence and accepted by much of white America largely as a result of his encounter with Nazism. Even now, he is perhaps more renowned for his defeat of the German, Max Schmeling, than for winning the heavyweight title from James Braddock.

The effect of Louis's and Owens's accomplishments was to heighten the discussion about what sport had done, or could do, for African Americans. Sport, it was argued, might be the first rung on the social ladder for blacks. Louis and Owens were credited with opening doors for others in and apart from sport. If those who followed behaved like them, African Americans were told, sport and other institutions would be more accepting of black presence. For example, the Governor of Michigan took it upon himself to write Louis and proclaim:

"Destiny seems to have pointed you for a high rank in pugilism. Your ability to overpower others by skill and physical force is something of which you may be Proud. ... You'll have world prominence and money. They will mean little, Joe, if you do not use them as God intended that gifts of Nature should be used. ... Your race, at times in the past, has been misrepresented by others who thought they had reached the heights. ... The qualities which may soon make you a world champion should call to the attention of people the world over, that the good in you can also be found in others of your race. ... So Joe, you may soon have on your strong hands the job of representative-at-large of your people." (quoted in Mead 1985, pp. 55–56)

Others, especially whites, from all sorts of occupations found it necessary to counsel Louis and Owens about the impact of their public behavior. They were groomed to favorably represent African Americans. Today, countless prominent African Americans such as John Thompson, Andrew Young, Vernon Jordan and Jesse Jackson often cite Louis's and/or Owens's accomplishments for catalyzing their own achievement. Many felt their situations would improve or decline as a result of Owens's, or especially Louis's, performance. Maya Angelou wrote:

"If Joe lost we were back in slavery and beyond help. It would all be true, the accusations that we were lower types of human beings. Only a little higher than apes. True that we were stupid and ugly and lazy and dirty and, unlucky and worst of all, that God Himself hated us and ordained us to be be hewers of wood and drawers of water, forever and ever, world without end." (1970)

It is ironic that Louis and Owens are both credited with opening the doors to sport and other institutions for African Americans, improving race relations (even black newspapers said Owens was "good for the race"), and demonstrating the path from rags to riches for blacks (through sport), yet neither retired with substantial wealth or income and both had trouble with the IRS. Both were success stories without the usual spoils of success. Still, they attained everlasting, if not universal, fame, heretofore unknown to African Americans. The message from their era seemed to be "look at what Joe and Jesse have done for race relations in America, and look at what sport has done for them" (and by extension, "Negroes"). Whites and African Americans, it seemed, felt that American society and, in particular, the sportsworld were more open to African Americans. Louis and Owens had paved the way for black athletes in other sports. Jackie Robinson would pick up where they left off.

Jackie Robinson: Breaking the Color Barrier in Team Sports

Joe Louis and Jesse Owens changed whites' perceptions about black presence in individual sports, but professional (and most college) team sports remained segregated. Numerous reasons were given for this phenomenon, including that African Americans lacked the interest, talent and training to compete alongside whites. But the absence of black ballplayers in team sports had more to do with whiles' reluctance to socially interact with African Americans—or to rub elbows with blacks—than to any of the above reasons. It was feared that many whites—players, fans, managers, owners, etc.—would take offense at blacks acting as whites' peers in so public an institution as sport. Also, if blacks were included in sport, what would happen to whites' protected status in other areas?

Branch Rickey, the Brooklyn Dodger general manager who presided over baseball's desegregation, worried about whites' reaction to his plan to recruit black ballplayers. Rickey wanted to be very sure to recruit not necessarily the best black ballplayer but one who would be tough and courageous and able to allay white fears about the threatening nature of novel interracial interactions. During their first meeting Rickey said to Robinson:

> "We can't fight our way through this, Robinson. We've got no army. There's virtually nobody on our side. No owners, no umpires, very few newspapermen. And I'm afraid that many fans will be hostile. We'll be in a tough position. We can win only if we can convince the world that I'm doing this because you're a great ballplayer and a fine gentleman." [Robinson asked] "Mr. Rickey, are you looking for a Negro who is afraid to fight back?" Rickey replied, "I'm looking for a ballplayer with guts enough not to fight back." (quoted in Levine, 1989, pp. 131–132)

While Robinson was not the first African American to play on a professional sport team with and against whites, his accomplishment is, nonetheless, a significant one. He was the first African American to play in "professional baseball" (i.e., white major league baseball) in the twentieth century. Finally, African Americans had reintegrated the most sacred of American athletic institutions—baseball. Soon the belief in white athletic superiority would be crushed and replaced with a belief in African Americans' "natural athletic advantages." With this belief came a shift in the meaning of sport for the black community. More and more Americans believed that sports could be a way to improve African Americans' social status.

Sociologist Hubert Blalock offers an example. In an article which purports to describe how and why professional baseball is an occupation which is remarkably free of racial discrimination," Blalock asserted that:

"Historically, most American minorities have entered the labor force at or very near the bottom of the occupational ladder ... each immigrant group was followed by more recent arrivals to take its place at the base of the pyramid ... [but] the Negro has been exposed to a different situation in several important respects." (1962, p. 242)

After pointing out the problems faced by skin color and condescendingly commenting on the tendency for the Northern born Negro to be confused with the criminally-prone recent black immigrants from the south," Blalock argues his main point, which is that, unlike other white-collar occupations that African Americans find all but closed to them, "Professional baseball has provided Negroes with one of the relatively few avenues for escape from traditional blue-collar occupations" (1962, p. 242). Following Jackie Robinson's desegregation of baseball and the subsequent desegregation of professional football and basketball, many African Americans and whites, undoubtedly, believed the same.

The 1968 Olympic Protest Movement

For years the dominant theme concerning sport and the black community during the period preceding the proposed Olympic boycott was that sport had taken black men, and a few black women, out of the "ghettoes" and provided them with opportunities for social mobility. For example, George McCarty, athletic director at the University of Texas at El Paso (UTEP), proclaimed, "In general, the nigger athlete is a little hungrier, and we have been blessed with having some real outstanding ones. We think they've done a lot for us, and we think we've done a lot for them" (Olsen, 1968, p. 15). The evidence seemed clear to many: Joe Louis and Jesse Owens, Hank Aaron and Willie Mays, Althea Gibson and Wilma Rudolph and many others could be used to demonstrate sports' capacity to increase African Americans' social status.

However, some present and former black athletes repudiated this claim. Harry Edwards, who later organized the Olympic Project for Human Rights, argued that sport exploited African Americans. For example, African American collegiate athletes were denied the same housing, hotel and restaurant accommodations as their white teammates; they were often demeaned by fans, coaches and teachers; and they were "stacked" into positions, leaving many spots on the roster open for white competition only. Edwards advised black collegiate athletes to become activists and to boycott the 1968 Olympics as a way to bargain for better treatment by the sports establishment. He stated that:

> "... once their athletic abilities are impaired by age or injury, only the ghetto
> beckons and they are doomed once again to that faceless, hopeless, ignominious
> existence they had supposedly forever left behind. At the end of their athletic
> career, black athletes do not become congressmen, as did Bob Mathias, the white
> former Olympic decathlon champion, or Wilmer Mizell, ex-Pittsburgh Pirate
> pitcher. Neither does the black athlete cash in on the thousands of dollars to be
> had from endorsements, either during his professional career or after he retires."
> (Edwards, 1969, p. xxvii)

Edwards led a movement during the late 1960s that demanded a change in the treatment of African Americans students, sometimes by disrupting collegiate football and basketball contests at campuses all across America. Some colleges were forced to cancel football games because of expected disturbances. This movement also signaled a change in black athletes' (and perhaps the black community's) relationship to white leadership in sports. While many whites and some African Americans still touted sports' role as an escalator to social mobility for "ghetto blacks, many African Americans—athletes and others—began to condemn the sport establishment for blatant exploitation and racial discrimination. No longer would a belief in sport as the route to increased status go unchallenged. If whites had renewed their faith in sports' ability to elevate the status of the black community, they were not joined in this belief by many of those principally involved—black athletes.

Proposition 48 and Other Legislation by the NCAA.

> For at least the last two decades we've told Black kids who bounce balls, run around tracks and catch touchdown passes that these things are ends unto themselves. We've raped them. We can't afford to do it to another generation. (cited in Edwards, 1984, p. 14)

According to Harry Edwards (1984), the above statement, which was made from the floor of the 1983 NCAA convention floor, was, in part, responsible for the adoption of Proposition 48. This required freshmen collegiate athletes, beginning in 1986, to attain a minimum 700 SAT or 15 ACT score and a 2.0 average in 11 core high school courses to receive an athletic scholarship. The minimum SAT and ACT scores have since been raised. It was evident that the debate over new standards for providing athletic grants-in-aid was directly related to African American athletes' success, or lack of success, in academic programs at colleges and universities.

Edwards has been a leader in castigating colleges for their failure to graduate minority student athletes. Colleges, he has often said, bring black athletes to campus to do one thing: play sport. They are not serious about the academic concerns of black athletes, often providing them with "Mickey Mouse" courses and giving them grades for courses never completed or mastered. So, for him there was irony in the fact that opposition to higher academic standards for student athletes came from black college presidents and civil rights leaders who criticized the NCAA for attempting to limit the participation of black student-athletes by imposing rules based on scores earned by taking racially or culturally biased examinations.

Both sides recognized that sport is unlikely to provide professional sport opportunities for most African American student-athletes, but those in opposition to Proposition 48 (and later Proposition 42) often point to the role sport has played in the black community for the student who would otherwise be least-disposed to go to college. Sport, they argue, may provide the means necessary (i.e., a scholarship) for the student-athlete to improve his or her station in life. But this is only possible through educational attainment (i.e., graduation from college). From this view sport facilitates upward mobility.

Others believe the athlete and student roles to be incompatible for most student-athletes in revenue-generating sports (Harris, 1991, 1994). A few experience upward mobility—directly or indirectly—through sport involvement, but for far too many, sport participation results in the abuse of student athletes.

As this essay indicates, perceptions about sport and its role in the black community are ever shifting. At times there has been optimism about its capacity to enhance the status of an entire group of people. At other times it has been cautiously embraced as an escalator to a better life. During the 1960s, sport was interrogated as a path to the American Dream. Today there is a brighter outlook than during the sixties among those who believe sport can provide opportunities for advancement outside of the sport world. (The phrase often used now is "don't let sport use you, use it.")

While the role of sport in the black community appears to be unclear, the media seem to be less cloudy about their view of race and sport. They bombard us with endless articles and vignettes about how black athletes had little going for them—they would come from broken or father-absent homes in dreadful neighborhoods where residents succumbed to dashed hopes—until they found, or were found by, sport. This is typically followed by the athlete's "admission" that if it had not been for sport, he (and sometimes she) would be out on the street or working a menial job. (Mississippi State University basketball player Dante Jones and the Seattle Supersonic's Ervin Johnson are but two of the many players who were reportedly rescued from low-paying, unfulfilling jobs by basketball.) And, in the end, the athlete, showing a bit of humility, informs the audience that they, too, can be lifted out of undesirable circumstances, if they would work hard at sport. The sports media would have us hold on to the belief that sport is the way to a better life. Many are not at ease with this assessment of sport in the black community.

Notes

1. Direct mobility refers to one's attainment of a player position, while indirect mobility refers, typically, to educational attainment or occupational sponsorship resulting from sport participation.
2. In 1888, George "Little Chocolate" Dixon became the first African American champion in any sport; he was bantamweight and featherweight champion. Joe Walcott followed in 1901 as welterweight champion, Joe Gans won the lightweight bile in 1902 (Rust, 1985).
3. Johnson had a penchant for dating and marrying white women and for being indiscreet about his affairs. Washington and many whites abhorred this and Johnson's ostentatious public manner.

References

Angelou, Maya. 1970. *I Know Why the Caged Bird Sings*. New York: Random House.
Blalock Jr., Hubert M. 1962. "Occupational Discrimination: Some Theoretical Propositions," *Social Problems* 9:240–247.
Coakley, Jay J. 1994. *Sport in Society: Issues and controversies*. 5th ed. St. Louis: Mosby.

Curry, Timothy J. and Robert Jiobu. 1984. *Sports: A social perspective.* Englewood Cliffs, NJ: Prentice-Hall.

Edwards, Harry, 1973. "Black Athletes: 20th Century Gladiators for White America." *Psychology Today* 7:43 52.

——— 1979. "Sport within the Veil: The Triumphs, Tragedies and Challenges of Afro-American Involvement." *Annals of the American Academy of Political and Social Science* 445:116–127. 1984.

"The Collegiate Athletic Arms Race: Origins and Implications of the 'Rule 48' Controversy." *Journal of Sport and Social Issues* 8:4–22.

Eitzen, D. Stanley and George H. Sage. 1993. *Sociology of North American Sport.* 6th ed. Madison, Wl: Brown & Benchmark Publishers.

Gilmore, Al-Tony. 1973. "Jack Johnson and white women: The national impact." *Journal of Negro History* (Jan.): 18–38.

——— 1975. *Bad Nigger!: The National Impact of Jack Johnson.* Port Washington, NY: Kennikat Press.

Harris, Othello. 1991. "Athletics and academics: Contrary or complementary activities?" Pp. 58–73 in *Sport, Racism and Ethnicity*, edited by Grant Jarvie, London: Falmer Press.

——— 1994. "Balancing athletics and academics: Some reflections from African American male student-athletes." Paper presented at the annual Association of Black Psychologists Meetings (August, Toronto).

——— (in press). "African Americans in sport from shadow to summit." In *Sport and International Politics in the 20th Century*, edited by Jim Riordan. E & FN Spon (Chapman and Hall),

Leonard II, Gilbert M. 1997. *A Sociological Perspective of Sport.* 6th ed. Boston: Allyn and Bacon.

Levine, Peter. 1989. *American Sport: A documentary history.* Englewood Cliffs, NJ: Prentice Hall.

London, Jack. 1992. "Tommy Burns versus Jack Johnson." Pp. 142–150 in *Jack London*, edited by James Bankes. Dubuque, IA; Wm C. Brown Publishers.

Olsen, J. 1968. "The Black athlete: A shameful story. The cruel deception, Part I." *Sports Illustrated* 29(1) (1 July); 15–17.

Roberts, Randy. 1983. *Papa Jack: Jack Johnson and the era of white hopes.* New York: Free Press.

Rust Jr., Art and Edna Rust. 1985. *Art Rust's Illustrated History of the Black Athlete.* Garden City, NJ: Doubleday.

Sammona, Jeremy, 1988. *Beyond the Ring: The role of boxing in American society.* Urbana, IL: University of Illinois Press.

"My Sick J's"

Impacting the Cultural Identity of Future Generations via the Scholar-Baller® and Jordan Brand Collaborative Partnership

C. Keith Harrison
Reggie Saunders
Scott J. Bukstein
Cliff Parks
S. Malia Lawrence

On a mission trying to shift the culture.

—Drake, *Tuscan Leather*, 2013

DURING THE VIDEO BASED ON THE SONG "BROTHERS IN PARIS" (2012), mogul Jay-Z is seen walking through Paris, France, with a stroll like a ballplayer. Larger than life is the depiction—a cool, confident, casual but fresh look. He gestures like a basketball player shooting a sweet jumper, which, in urban and other pop culture means "ballin" (performing at the highest level). He sings the song and spits a verse—**MY SICK J'S.**

Jay-Z is not the only cultural icon or rapper to express the impact of the Jordan Brand. Drake articulates, "I get so much Jordan people think I play for North Carolina." The point is that Jordan Brand and the apparel connected to it reaches far beyond Michael Jordan and the sport of basketball on the court. This essay asks the following question: can we maximize this powerful (Jordan) brand in a way that positions education and the academic performance of African Americans and other ethnic groups so that their identity is shaped in a way that is synergistic with school, learning, and performing in the classroom? What follows is an analysis of this question.

Identity Construct One: It's Gotta Be the Shoes

Brian Wilson and Robert Sparks conducted a study, "'It's Gotta Be the Shoes': Youth, Race and Sneaker Commercials," that is informative as we think about how youth and young adults embrace the very popular Jordan Brand sneaker known as J's. Their (1996) article is concerned with the processes demonstrated in this case, and with the impacts of athletic apparel commercial messages on youth and youth cultures. The paper focuses on youth interpretations of athletic footwear commercials and athletic apparel in Black and non-Black youth cultures. The use of celebrity Black athletes like Michael Jordan is well-established in North American athletic apparel marketing. Critics like Harry Edwards (1969, 1973) have argued for years that the media successes of Black athletes give Black youth an inflated sense of the very high-profile Black athletes in advertising, television shows, and film would appear to only extend this problem. As well, advertisements featuring high-profile athletes take advantage of youth. (p. 399)

This quote sets the stage for the current essay, as we all feel (the authors of this essay) that these platforms of fashion and popular culture can be utilized to be a solution—not a problem. This will be addressed in the next section.

Identity Construct Two: Check Out My Swag

The outward appearance of humans in general is a powerful expression of self-confidence and personal esteem. With this in mind, we have observed that linking academic performance to the Jordan Brand enables an innovative and new discourse about education and sport to evolve. Currently, individuals and groups across the globe wear any and everything Jordan Brand to show their affinity and affiliation with the brand. Jordan Brand and Scholar-Baller have already been co-branded on a smaller level with some university athletic departments. For example, Arizona State University since 2004 has worn the Scholar-Baller patch on their game-day jerseys in football, softball, and baseball.

Further, there is a tradition (since 2004) during football camp each August for the Arizona State University football team. Jordan Brand/Scholar-Baller shorts are given out to all football student athletes with a 3.0 grade point average or higher. This ceremony is a tradition that the late Dr. Myles Brand (former NCAA president) said "shows pride" for academics. There are cheers, chanting, and sincere enthusiasm by each teammate cheering for the recipients of this "swag," highlighting peer group validation by the Division I football players, coaches, athletic administrators, and faculty present. While Jordan Brand and Scholar-Baller officially partnered in 2013 in terms of educational content in concert with other apparel items (e.g., bags, hats, shorts, shirts), the real innovation will be released in 2016—the Scholar-Baller Jordan's and Jordan Brand Scholar-Ballers. This will be elaborated on in the next section.

Identity Construct Three: Changing the Cultural Identity Formation of Future Generations Through an Icon Sneaker and Concept Based on Two Decades of Research

As we have discussed previously, extending the Scholar-Baller concept through the power of Jordan Brand is culturally relevant and influential to many diverse populations of student athletes and youth in general. Considering the fact that Jordan Brand sneakers literally have a cult following, are a spectacle with new releases occurring periodically, and have even resulted in theft and violence by those obsessed with the brand, it appears the time for this innovative partnership is ripe. Education and academic performance will be the differentiator, but it must be acknowledged that the "baller" identity has some unhealthy aspect to its construct. In the next section we analyze the lyrics and themes from one of the most popular songs during the mid-1990s, "I Wish" by Skee-Lo.

Case Study: A Content Analysis of a Cultural Song from 1995/1996

Music is an important cultural form that both impacts and shapes identity. A closer look at each of the fourteen themes coded from a very popular song in the mid-1990s reveals some key insights related to the overall tone of this essay. One, African American and other youth dream of being "ballers"—an identity that women and girls broadly find attractive and appealing. Second, Skee-Lo in this particular song "I Wish" does not think that he even exists in the urban or American mind because he is not tall and does not play ball (see the lyrics and themes that follow below). This song is an important snapshot for understanding what the Jordan Brand and Scholar-Baller partnership seeks to address—narrow identities focused only on "ballin," without education being a part of the conceptualization process of positive identity development. The question is, what if Skee-Lo remixed this song in 2016 and rapped about "I wish I had Scholar-Baller Jordan's," and his lyrical content focused on what it would take with this *mind* to attain this status, apparel, and so on? Once again, there is another opportunity through a popular culture platform to shift the culture and identity constructs in a positive way. The next few sections capture the lyrics, critical analysis based on the themes from the song, and a complete list of the themes from the song based on a content analysis with coding.

"I Wish" (1995/1996) by Skee-Lo (Note: Shortened version of the song's lyrics. Themes and the analysis are based on the entire song's lyrics).[1]

I wish I was a little bit taller
I wish I was a baller

---

1   Skee-Lo, "I Wish." Copyright © 1996 by Peer Music.

I wish I had a girl who looked good, I would call her

I wish I had a rabbit in a hat with a bat

And a six four Impala

I wish I was like six-foot-nine

So I can get with Leoshi

Cause she don't know me but yo she's really fine

Major Themes

1. Envious of jocks
2. Feelings of rejection and mockery
3. Low self-esteem
4. Desire to be fresh and cool

The deeper meaning and themes coded from the song reveals his urban identity construct. The list below covers the remaining minor or subthemes:

1. Dreaming and wishing (wacky wishes—this practice seems wacky to him)
2. Infatuation with a girl
3. Envious of jocks
4. Feels ignored and unnoticed
5. Wannabe baller
6. Feels bypassed and ignored
7. Feels made fun of
8. Low self-esteem
9. Makes fun of himself
10. Feels left out
11. Trying to be cool and noticed
12. Tough life, trying to keep up with others
13. Compares himself to others
14. Desire to be fresh and cool

Critical Analysis of Themes

What do the major four themes mean in the broader social context of identity, education, and sport? First, Skee-Lo understands that he lives in an urban area "the size of a box and that no one knows his name," as he puts it. However, society and those in his peer group know the value of the ballers. This includes male friends, girls, and the overall perception that ballers are cool people with privileges. Skee-Lo continues throughout the song to wish he was a baller because this, in his mind, would lead to material things such as a nice car with all the accessories. Second, Skee-Lo feels that he is invisible and ignored because he is short, not tall and not a very good basketball player. In his mind, being a baller would allow him to be more visible to everyone important to him in his urban world. Third, Skee-Lo's self-esteem is impacted by his lack of identity formation as a baller in terms of his self-perception. It is important in any cultural studies and content analysis approach to examine what is absent from the text and discourse, as much as what is being said. Skee-Lo never mentions other options for success in terms of other sports or intellectual pursuits related to education in terms of forming his own identity. Narrow identities, particularly from urban areas, have been at the forefront of the discussion of helping urban and other youth dream beyond sports. As Professor Gary Sailes (1997) stated, too many black youth are "betting against the odds" when it comes to their future. Fourth, Skee-Lo desires to be fresh and cool, which is normal for any teenager or young adult. The challenge is that if he redefined what being a baller meant in a broader context (education, business, et cetera), his identity, self-esteem, and self-worth would be healthier as a young person. The next section discusses some practical strategies to address how to impact the identities of youth related to education, sport, and entertainment. Specifically, the Jordan Brand cultural sneaker will be the platform for this influence and impact.

Best Strategic Practices: Ballin, Ball, and Ballers = Education and Sport

An alternative identity model fits the scope and focus of this essay, in that the existing influence of J's can be tweaked to tackle the new "trick" of educational integration, as we have articulated throughout this essay. Hence, below are touch points of this reality being implemented, not just theorized.

Retail Stores

This will be maximized through a similar concept of J's for A's. In other words, students in elementary and high school receive Jordan sneakers for achieving the highest grades each year in school. This concept can be raised to another level, with special event planning that launches the Scholar-Baller J's at local Foot Locker's, Dick's Sporting Goods, and other footwear providers. The goal is to have youth and young adults lined up with their report cards, ready to purchase their unique J's with the educational connection.

Branding Student Athletes and Professional Athletes (and Celebrities)

There are numerous cultural identities in sport and entertainment that could be co-branded as Scholar-Ballers and draped in Jordan Brand apparel, sneakers, and so on. These Scholar-Baller candidates include Michael Jordan (of course), geography major and University of North Carolina graduate; Tim Duncan, psychology major and Wake Forest University graduate; and any of the over 90 percent of WNBA players who have their bachelor's degree. Women and men with elite athlete status, nationally and abroad, representing the Scholar-Baller/Jordan Brand partnerships, is culturally powerful.

The Role of Social Media

The tag line "Where are your J's at today?" has the potential to have student athletes across the world utilizing Twitter, Facebook, Instagram and Snapshot to highlight their Scholar-Baller/Jordan Brand status and creating an entirely different conversation about what is perceived as cool. Connecting social media followers to these cultural identities on their way to class, the library, and study groups is a potential game changer.

The Role of Higher Education

Intercollegiate athletics and higher education has a history of coexisting, for better or for worse. However, this is an opportunity for every institution to participate—at least the schools that are Nike. Scholar-Baller currently collaborates with over fifty schools each year through curriculum and instruction, incentives for those with a 3.0 grade point average or higher, and the Academic Momentum Award sponsored by Scholar-Baller and the National Consortium of Academics and Sports.

Analytics of Cultural Practice and Measuring the Impact of the Jordan Brand/Scholar-Baller Partnership

The experiences, perceptions, and responses by those participating in this cultural movement (mostly student athletes) will be systemically analyzed through surveys with both qualitative and quantitative data.

Conclusions and Some Global Thought(s)

In the final analysis, this essay has attempted to demonstrate that identity through popular culture can be shaped in an educational way that is cool. John Lennon's famous song "Imagine" is relevant to these final comments. Imagine millions of African American youth sporting J's co-branded with Scholar-Baller, which represents at least a B average in school, coupled with athletic participation from elementary school all the way to the professional ranks. Imagine a culture where the meaning of looking cool includes identities of substance, and instead of the "Triple Tragedy" (obsessive pursuit of sports goals, personal and cultural underdevelopment, and cultural institutional underdevelopment) that Dr. Edwards put forth as a framework about black athletes decades ago, we might just flip this paradigm into a *triple triumph*. Shifting cultural attitudes about education, sport, and entertainment through a sneaker known as J's might evolve as sheer irony. Ballers become Scholar-Ballers and scholars become ballers. This has the potential to ripple across many generations to come.

References

Drake. 2013. Nothing was the same (Album).

Sailes, G. 1997. Personal communication.

Skee-Lo 1995/1996. I Wish (Song).

Wilson, B., and R. Sparks. 1996. "'It's gotta be the shoes': Youth, race, and sneaker commercials." *Sociology of Sport Journal*, 13: 398–427.

Chapter 3

Myth, Stereotypes, and Images of the African American Athlete

The African American Athlete
Social Myths and Stereotypes

Gary Sailes

THE SUCCESS AND POPULARITY OF THE AFRICAN AMERICAN ATHLETE IN the past three decades is unprecedented. African American athletes dominate the popular sports of professional football (60%), baseball (30%), and basketball (85%) in the United States today. African American athletes dominate the headlines of today's sport pages and are at the core of interest in American television sports programming. The accomplishments of the African American athlete have become an accepted facet of American culture. However, in an attempt to explain that athletic success, racial attitudes emerge which further polarize the two dominant ethnic groups in the United States today, African Americans and whites.

The myths and stereotypes which attempt to explain the phenomenal success of the African American athlete are an indication of the deeply rooted divisions that exist in a racially segmented society. Consequently, they also perpetuate the development of structural barriers to entry into management and coaching positions in college and professional sport. This essay will examine the development and perpetuation of racial myths and stereotypes about the African American athlete and present the social conditions that rationalize his rise to prominence in contemporary American sport. American sport is a $200 billion industry with unprecedented interest from fans and active participants in a global market (Coakley, 1994). No social institution in American culture receives the media attention generated by sport. American sport is currently televised worldwide into hundreds of international markets. The most widely and internationally viewed American sport event is the Super Bowl (Coakley, 1994). Millions of viewers worldwide tune into college sports in

March to watch the NCAA (National Collegiate Athletic Association) basketball tournament, affectionately coined "March Madness!" The success of the 1996 women's Olympic teams, particularly the basketball team, has spurred the growth of interest in women's athletics. Title IX lawsuits and NCAA enforcement have guaranteed women a place in college athletics. Two women's professional basketball leagues have emerged and Nike has taken the lead in promoting interest in women's athletics through their commercial spots. Sport is big business and there is enormous interest. Virtually no one in the United States today is untouched by sport.

History

Concurrently, American college sport plays a significant role in popularizing sport in the United States. It has gained enormous popularity since the first collegiate event in 1852, a rowing race between Harvard and Yale Universities. Most early college sports were nothing more than extra-curricular contests organized and controlled by students (Coakley, 1994). The "Golden Age of Sport," 1919–1930, set the stage for the commercialization and rise of college sport as we know it today. During that period in our history, American technology advanced and, consequently, so did American college sports.

A new invention, the assembly line, created jobs and enabled the mass production of goods which created wealth. As a result, there was a mass migration of Americans from rural areas of the country to major urban centers like New York, Chicago, and Detroit. Inventions like the radio, printing press, and wire service spurred the growth of the mass media. As an outgrowth, the mass media began to write about American sport and sports stars, creating interest among the American public. Huge stadia were built, advances in travel (railroad) allowed schools to travel and compete against other schools, creating rivalries. Consequently, conferences were established, and, finally, the NCAA and other college sports organizations were established to control this tremendous growth (Coakley, 1994).

The media played a major role in the rise of American college sports. Coverage increased, leading to the emergence of sports heroes who later became professional athletes and sports legends. Collegiate rivalries were fueled in the press adding to the popularity of this American pastime. The college All-American was established and today March Madness, the televised presentation of the NCAA basketball tournament, has become the symbol of college basketball's emergence as one of the most popular sports on television (Leonard, 1993).

The Integration of American Sport

American college sport was a "whites only" institution with only a few African American athletes participating on teams at predominantly white colleges and universities until as late as the 1960s.

African Americans played college sports at historically black colleges and universities located primarily in the South. By the time Jackie Robinson broke the color barrier in Major League Baseball in 1947, African American athletes were being recruited to play on American college sports teams in relatively small numbers, particularly in football, basketball, and baseball. It was not uncommon for a team to have only one African American player on their college baseball, track and field, basketball or football teams (Ashe, 1993). Today, however, African American athletes account for 67% and 44% of the athletes playing NCAA Division I basketball and football. Moreover, 100% of NCAA Division I football programs and 98% of NCAA Division I basketball programs have integrated teams (Coakley, 1994).

The success of Jackie Robinson in Major League Baseball spurred the recruitment of African American talent from the Negro Baseball Leagues. Professional basketball and football emulated the trend and American colleges followed suit. By the late 1960s, nearly every major American collegiate and professional basketball, football, and baseball team was integrated (Ashe, 1993). As African Americans integrated American sport, they brought their special style of play that distinguished them from their white counterparts. For example, basketball was forever changed in its configuration when African American males began to dominate the sport with their numbers (George, 1992; Sailes, 1996). The "whites only" style of play was slowed down and consisted mostly of ball movement and outside shooting. Individual skills were sometimes sacrificed to augment team-oriented play. However, African American athletes played with a more athletic and aggressive game which highlighted individual skills like improvisational movement to the basket, slam dunking, improvisational dribbling and passing skills, and aggressive rebounding (George, 1992; Sailes, 1996). For a lot of inner-city athletes, these skills were developed in the parks and playgrounds of America's African American ghettoes and have become the standard by which basketball is currently defined.

Racial Stereotypes

African Americans are also breaking ground in sports other than basketball, football, and baseball. African Americans have kept the doors of opportunity open in professional sports like tennis (i.e., Venus Williams, Lori McNeil, Zina Garrison, Chandra Rubin), golf (i.e., Tiger Woods), swimming (i.e., Anthony Nesty), ice skating (i.e., Debbie Thomas), and gymnastics (i.e., Dominique Dawes). Consequently, however, the success of the African American athlete spurred the evolution of specific sports stereotypes and myths in an attempt to explain their success and subsequent attack on the "white status quo." These stereotypes elevated the physical prowess of the African American athlete, but attacked his intellectual capabilities. Simply put, the African American athlete was a spectacular physical phenomenon but still a "dumb jock" (Sailes, 1993b).

The historical origins of the dumb jock stereotype can be traced to 500 B.C. when Greek athletes were criticized for the inordinate amount of time they spent in preparation for competition and for neglecting their intellectual development. Greek athletes were characterized by some philosophers of the period as useless and ignorant citizens with dull minds (Coakley, 1994).

Media attention challenging the scholarship of college athletes, particularly in the revenue-producing sports of basketball and football, has tainted the academic credibility of college student athletes (Sailes, 1993a). Reports of high school student athletes not meeting NCAA minimum academic standards to establish college eligibility, accounts of college student athletes failing their courses, and the particularly low graduation rates among major college basketball and football programs foster the belief that anti-intellectualism exists among college student athletes (Sailes, 1993a, 1996). Unfortunately, Hollywood movies (the character Org in the film Revenge of the Nerds) and television situation comedies (the character Coach in the program "Cheers") facilitate the perpetuation of the dumb jock stereotype through the characterizations of unintelligent sports figures.

Sailes (1993b) found that the typical college student felt that college athletes could not compete with them in the classroom. They felt they could earn higher grades and had higher graduation rates when compared to student athletes. It was also felt that college athletes received unearned grades from their professors and took easy courses in order to maintain their athletic eligibility. This, they felt, accounted for any measure of success obtained by student athletes in the classroom.

While these perceptions were disclosed, most traditional college students were reluctant to reveal that they felt that student athletes typified the "dumb jock" stereotype. Moreover, traditional college students felt that African American athletes were least qualified to attend college and probably were admitted chiefly for their athletic talent. In addition, they felt that the typical African American student athlete was not sufficiently prepared to attend college and was least likely to be successful in the classroom. The negative stereotype of academic incompetence was perceived to be higher among African American athletes when compared to their white counterparts. In conclusion, Sailes (1993b) asserted that college students felt that if the typical student athlete was a "dumb jock," the African American athlete was the dumbest of all.

Beezley (1983) studied the development of the dumb jock stereotype traditionally associated with college football players. Although the dumb jock stereotype was prevalent in American sports culture, no substantiation could be generated to confirm its origin or its validity. Similarly, Nixon (1982) found no evidence to support the stereotype of the dumb jock. In a comparison of grade point average, graduation rate, and student perceptions, no significant statistical differences were found between typical college students and student athletes. McMartin and Klay (1983) had similar findings and also reported that positive and favorable attitudes were held about students who were also athletes. Regardless of the low graduation rates of football (53%) and basketball players (46%) that can be attributed to the time demands of these primary revenue-producing sports, the overall graduation rates for college student athletes (58%) were slightly higher than for the ordinary college student (56%) (NCAA, 1996). Although a prevalent stereotype, there appears to be no scientific basis for generalizing that the college student athlete is a "dumb jock."

It is plausible to assume that the retention of unsubstantiated stereotypes about student athletes emanates from a variety of circumstances. It is likely that most college students have very little, if any, contact with college student athletes upon which to draw factual information about student athlete academic competence. Second, if generalizations about student athletes are continually perpetuated by the mass media in fictionalized depictions (television, movies, books), it is likely that those generalizations will continue. In addition, it is doubtful that the general public reads scientific journals which clearly illustrate that student athletes generally hold higher academic grade point averages and graduate in higher percentages then the traditional college student. Sailes (1993a) attributed this to tighter academic restrictions and requirements on student athletes to maintain their eligibility to compete in college athletics.

Steele (1990) argued that one particularly sensitive race-oriented component of white superiority and African American inferiority is intelligence. Support for the physical superiority myth indirectly contributes to the belief that the African American athlete is mentally and intellectually inferior to the white athlete (Davis, 1991; Hoose, 1989; Sailes, 1991, 1993b). Conceptions about the "dumb jock" stereotype targeted at African American athletes are therefore related to racial stereotyping. This racist attitude contributes to the discriminatory practice of channeling African Americans away from the central (leadership and/or decision-making) positions in college and professional sport (Coakley, 1994; Eitzen & Sage, 1996; Leonard, 1993; Schneider & Eitzen, 1986).

Whites are reluctant to hire African Americans into management and head coaching positions in professional and major college sport because they do not have confidence in the intellectual capabilities of African Americans to manage or coach professional or major college ball clubs. Former executive for the Los Angeles Dodgers, Al Campanis, illustrated this practice when he exposed racial stereotyping in sport on national television. He made the assertion that African Americans may not have the "necessities" to be managers in professional baseball (Hoose, 1989). Positional segregation (often referred to as stacking) is prevalent among college baseball, volleyball, and football teams (Coakley, 1994; Jones et al., 1987; Schneider & Eitzen, 1986). African Americans are systematically channeled away from the team leadership positions in favor of white players. Coaches are reluctant to entrust the leadership of the team to African Americans because they believe African Americans are not intelligent enough to be successful team leaders. This is characterized by the dearth of African American pitchers in professional and college baseball and quarterbacks in college and professional football (Coakley, 1994; Leonard, 1993).

Lombardo (1978) noted two distinct stereotypes which emerged regarding African American males. Known as "the brute" and "the sambo" stereotypes, they were developed by whites to maintain their superior position in society and to denigrate African American males, keeping them subordinate. The "brute" stereotype characterized the African American male as primitive, temperamental, over-reactive, uncontrollable, violent, and sexually powerful. This stereotype intentionally separated the African American from intellectualism and mental control. White society placed importance on intellectualism and subsequently removed the African American from equal status by characterizing him with primitive physical attributes. This stereotype has been popularly used to explain the dominance of the African American athlete in football, basketball, baseball, and boxing (Sailes, 1996, 1993b, 1991). Consequently, the belief that intellectualism does not exist among African Americans has kept management and coaching positions in Division I college and professional sports mostly white (Coakley, 1994; Leonard, 1993).

The "sambo" stereotype depicted the African American as benign, childish, immature, exuberant, uninhibited, lazy, comical, impulsive, fun-loving, good-humored, inferior, and lovable. These typecasts about African Americans have historical roots in American slavery. It was felt that these characterizations relegated African American slaves to inferior status. Lombardo criticized the performance of the Harlem Globetrotters for their continued perpetuation of the "sambo" stereotype in sport and for compromising the integrity and positive image of African Americans in general and African American athletes in particular.

Other unsubstantiated race-oriented sports myths have evolved in an attempt to explain the success and over-representation of African American athletes in certain American sports. Most myths attempting to rationalize the apparent dominance of African American athletes in specific sports generally have little scientific credibility. For example, there remains the popular belief that African American athletes are physically superior to white athletes, and that their superior body build is genetically determined, giving them an advantage over their white counterparts. Many believe this advantage accounts for the success among African American athletes in football, basketball, baseball, track and field, and boxing (Coakley, 1994; Leonard, 1993).

A 1988 investigative report by the Philadelphia Inquirer sought to answer the question: "Are African Americans better athletes than whites?" (Sokolove, 1988). Similarly, a 1989 NBC special program hosted by Tom Brokaw entitled "The Black Athlete: Fact or Fiction" focused on the question: "What accounts for the success of African American athletes in American sports?" These two reports supported the theory of the physical or genetic superiority of the African American athlete. While some physical differences are apparent between African Americans and whites as a whole, it remains to be demonstrated that anatomical, genetic, and/or physiological differences between African American and white athletes contribute significantly to the dominance of either over the other in sports competition (Coakley, 1994; Eitzen & Sage, 1996; Leonard, 1993; McPherson et al., 1989; Sailes, 1987, 1991, 1993b, 1996; Sokolove, 1988).

Davis (1991) argued that the need to analyze African American success in sport is a racist preoccupation emanating from fear generated within the white status quo. It was felt that white fear of loss of control of American economic, political, and educational institutions was the catalyst for investigating the so-called athletic superiority of the African American athlete. Historically, African Americans were barred from competing against whites in sport for two reasons: (1) the country practiced segregation between whites and African Americans; and (2) it was believed that African Americans were inferior to whites and posed no significant challenge on the athletic field. When African Americans integrated American sport and began to dominate in basketball, football, and baseball, whites precluded that it was the natural physical and/or genetic superiority of the African American that enabled them to dominate those sports. Consequently, the stereotype that African Americans were naturally physically superior to whites precluded the racist notion that they are intellectually inferior and cannot compete with whites in America's corporate boardrooms. This stereotype facilitates the maintaining of white superiority and the white status quo.

Sports Myths

Many of the myths regarding African American athletes suffer from scientifically unacceptable assumptions and are not substantiated by research. Moreover, the variables impacting on the sport socialization and sport participation patterns of African American athletes in American sport emanate from the social constraints placed upon them by the dominant culture and their determination to overcome them (Coakley, 1994; Eitzen & Sage, 1996; Leonard, 1993; McPherson et al., 1989; Sailes, 1987, 1991; Sokolove, 1988).

This author compiled a list of the prevalent myths held by college students about African American college student athletes. While this was informal qualitative research at best, the information gathered was collected every semester over a period often years in a university elective course entitled 'The African American Athlete in American Sport." Each semester, class enrollment was approximately thirty students with one third African American and two thirds white. Students completed a course assignment which required them to list and explain every myth they heard and/or believed about the African American athlete. The assignments were maintained and organized for inclusion in a book. What follows is a summary of those assignments. It was interesting to note that most of the stereotypes attempted to answer two questions: "Is the African American physically superior to the white athlete?" "Why does the African American athlete dominate American sport?"

Matriarchal Theory

Many students believed that most African American athletes came from a single parent household consisting of an absent father and with the mother as the head of the household. Sailes (1984) found that this was the case for a majority of the African American athletes participating in his socialization study. It was also believed that because of the absent father, the African American athlete was uncontrollable, hostile, and unfocused. He channeled his hostility into the sports area where he excelled. In addition, the absent father caused the African American athlete to seek and establish a bond with the coach. A paternalistic relationship developed and the African American athlete became a better performer as a result of that special relationship. Evans (1978) and Anshel and Sailes (1990) found that most athletes, and the African American athlete in particular, was suspicious and distrusting of the motives of their coaches. At best, the relationship between the head coach and the African American student athlete was distant. The literature refutes the notion that a special relationship exists between the coach and African American athlete because of an absent father at home and that relationship motivated the African American athlete to excel on the athletic field.

Mandingo Theory

Jimmy 'The Greek" Snyder popularized this theory with his candid remarks on national television. His remarks led to his termination as an ABC sports analyst. It was believed that the physical superiority of the African American athlete emanated from the days of slavery. This theory holds that slave owners intentionally bred their slaves requiring physically large and muscular male slaves to mate with physically large and muscular female slaves. The offspring were physically superior to the commonly reproduced slave child. This physically superior child, it was felt, would grow up to be a better laborer in the fields.

"The Greek" asserted this type of selective breeding caused the thighs and gluteal muscles in African Americans to become superior. This, he felt, accounted for their superior jumping and sprinting abilities over their white counterparts. Common sense dictates that even if this were true, there is no possible way this could account for the physical development of 34 million African Americans today. White slave owners had slave concubines, slave women were raped by white overseers, free Negroes could choose their own mates, most slaves were unrestricted in their choice of mates (Bennett, 1996; Franklin, 1994), and foreign immigration to the United States probably took their toll on this so-called selectively bred gene pool. Interracial marrying and miscegenation were and are too prevalent in the United States for that gene pool to have survived and eventually account for any physical difference that would predispose itself in the contemporary athletic arena (Sailes, 1991).

History showed that large slaves were used as fighters and heavy gambling took place on those fights by whites. In fact, two slaves, Bill Richmond and Tommy Molineaux, were early fighters who won their owners enough money to earn their freedom (Ashe, 1993). It is quite possible that slaves were used as breeders in isolated instances, but there were too many uncontrollable social variables in early and contemporary American society to give substance to this theory. Additionally, many African Americans lived with Native Americans and intermarried with them. Common sense dictates that in all likelihood, the gene pool from slave breeding was lost prior to the beginning of the twentieth century.

Survival of the Fittest Theory

It was felt that the physical superiority of the African American athlete was incidentally created by the survivors of the "middle passage" of African slaves to the Americas. The trip from Africa to America took several months. During that time, slaves were laid on their backs and chained together by hands and feet. They assumed this position for several days at a time except for brief exercise periods on the deck of the slave ships. They were barely fed, became ill, and sometimes over 65% of the slave cargo was lost to dysentery, suicide, or murder (Bennett, 1996; Franklin, 1994). It was felt that those who survived the middle passage were physically superior beings compared to those who perished.

Today's 34 million African Americans are supposedly the descendants of that superior gene pool and this accounts for their physical superiority on the athletic field. As indicated in the Mandingo Theory, immigration, miscegenation, and interracial marrying between African Americans, whites, and individuals from other ethnic groups, especially after the end of slavery, would most assuredly have caused the dilution of any special gene pool supposedly created by the middle passage.

Genetic Theory

This theory assumed that African Americans had more white fast twitch muscle fibers and whites had more red slow twitch muscle fibers which precluded their potential in athletics. White muscle fibers were power oriented and were better able to liberate greater force over a short period of time. White fast twitch muscle fibers would be most beneficial for sports activities which required agility, speed, quickness, jumping, lifting, and throwing. This explanation was used to justify African American dominance in sports activities like the jumping and sprint events in track and field, basketball, baseball, football, and boxing. One of my white students believed that African Americans were able to run faster and jump higher than whites because African Americans had an extra muscle in their legs. He asserted he was told this by a college professor/athletic trainer who held a Ph.D. from a predominantly white medium-sized midwestern college. There is no available data or research to confirm this belief.

The Genetic Theory also assumed that whites had a preponderance of red muscle fibers which are better suited for endurance events. Red muscle fibers are better able to liberate oxygen from the blood stream to replenish the muscles for long distance activities. This was why whites dominated the middle and long distance endurance sports. Examples are middle and long distance events in track and field, swimming, cross-country skiing, cross-country running, marathons, and skating.

This theory was debunked when West Africans began and continued to dominate the marathons and middle and long distance events in track and field. Olympian Kip Keno of Kenya and others who followed him have won international marathon competitions every year. In addition, no scholar or researcher was willing to step up and confirm through scientific research the claims made by this myth. There is overwhelming evidence which supports the conclusion that social variables such as the sport opportunity structure, social and cultural norms about sport, personal aspirations, economic factors, coaching, and available facilities and programs have a greater impact in explaining the recent success of the African American athlete in American sport. Perceived closed doors to opportunities in mainstream American society and peer pressure not to pursue mainstream opportunities channeled African Americans into the only avenues they felt were open to them, in entertainment, in sports, (Sailes, 1987) or through the underground economy where they engaged in a life of crime (Oliver, 1994).

Psychological Theory

This theory presumed that African Americans were incapable of leadership in positions like quarterback in football, pitcher in baseball, or point guard in basketball. Moreover, as was discussed earlier, Al Campanis reiterated the belief of management in Major League Baseball on national television when he said that African Americans may not have the "necessities" to become managers and field coaches in Major League Baseball.

This theory also claimed that African Americans did poorly under pressure and were not good thinkers which was why they were under-represented in individual sports such as tennis, golf, skiing, skating, gymnastics, and swimming. However, when given the opportunity, African Americans have excelled in individual sports and in leadership positions in team sports for decades. There are several African Americans participating in professional tennis and golf, and who serve as head coaches in Division I and professional basketball, football, and baseball. Several of these coaches and athletes have won national titles.

The National Brotherhood of Skiers, the American Tennis Association, and the National Golf Association are all African American national organizations. The American Tennis Association is the oldest African American sports organization in the United States today (Ashe, 1993). There are African American swimming and gymnastics programs and clubs across the United States providing programs and instruction and which have produced several national amateur champions (Hoose, 1989).

African American athletes in leadership, management, and coaching positions have won national championships and titles in the United States. For example, John Thompson of Georgetown University and Nolan Richardson of the University of Arkansas have won NCAA basketball titles. Cito Gaston, general manager of the Toronto Blue Jays, and Bob Watson, general manager of the New York Yankees, have both won World Series titles. Doug Williams was a winning quarterback in the NFL's Super Bowl. Tina Sloane Green of Temple University won two NCAA lacrosse championships. However, the Psychological Theory is the primary reason many African Americans are not given management and/or coaching positions in professional and college sports today. White fear of

African Americans invading the white status quo and prejudicial attitudes about African American competence are nothing new and continue to create barriers to African American success in the administration of American sports. Given the opportunity, African Americans can excel and have proven themselves worthy of inclusion in the sports market place as on-field leaders, managers, and coaches.

Dumb Jock Theory

A corollary of the Psychological Theory, this theory challenges the academic competence of student athletes. It was generally felt that student athletes could not compete with traditional students in the classroom. In addition, it was felt student athletes took easy jock courses and majored in eligibility (general studies) rather than a legitimate academic subject.

The stereotypes against African American student athletes were even more denigrating. It was generally felt that African American athletes did not belong in college. Students felt it was the African American's athletic talents, and not his intelligence, which provided him admission to college. They felt that if athletic departments did not have special admission policies, most African American athletes could not get into college. While this may have been the practice of athletic departments in isolated instances in the past, this is less possible today. The NCAA has minimum academic requirements for student athletes to establish eligibility to participate in college athletics. Specifically, a graduating high school senior must score a minimum of 900 on the SAT and have a grade point average of 2.5 in order to receive an athletic scholarship and participate in Division I college athletics. Furthermore, the grade point averages and graduation rates of student athletes are slightly higher than their nonathletic counterparts (Sailes, 1993a). The myth of the dumb jock is unfounded and most of the literature indicates that student athletes are doing better in school than traditional college students.

Concluding Discussion

Racial myths and stereotypes are born out of ignorance. Lack of contact with different social and/or ethnic groups create ideologies that are generated from social dissonance and are founded on subjective observations. Our interpretations of other cultures are filtered through our own life experiences. To define others and to derive meaning about others based on our own cultural values, without the benefit of personal contact with those other indigenous cultures, leads to conjecture, myths, stereotypes, and inaccurate depictions of what we see.

In extreme cases, inaccurate depictions can generate fear, prejudice, and misunderstandings which can lead to confrontation. Myths and stereotypes are damaging in that respect. Until we are ready to step up and reintroduce ourselves to one another, social myths and stereotypes will continue to fuel the fires of racial hatred and bigotry that currently polarize American society.

The fears and anxieties of whites in America cause them to subjugate other cultures and ethnic groups within this country to inferior status and to create the caste system of inequities that have kept us apart for decades. It is time to pursue the truth, to interact with one another, and to have meaningful dialogue about who we are. W. E. B. DuBois suggested that the greatest problem that will face America in the twentieth century will be the race problem. Current researchers forecast that this problem will continue into the twenty-first century. It is time to learn to respect one other, to dispel the myths and stereotypes that keep us hanging onto the dark past. We must shield ourselves from the blatant negative media depictions of African American athletes portrayed as mindless physical specimens whose success is predisposed by their genetic and physiological superiority to whites. If we continue on the present journey of distrust, fear, and confrontation which is fueled by our unfounded mythological and stereotypical beliefs about one another, Americans will never reach the peace and harmony that are the rewards of enlightenment.

References

Anshel, M., and Sailes, G. (1990). "Discrepant attitudes of intercollegiate athletes as a function of race." *Journal of Sport Behavior*, 13(2), 87–102. The African American Athlete: Social Myths and Stereotypes 197

Ashe, A. (1993). *A Hard Road to Glory: A history of the African American athlete*. New York: Amistad Press.

Beezley, W. H. (1983). "Images of the student athlete in college football." In *The University's Role in the Development of Modern Sport: Past, Present, and Future*, edited by S. Kereliuk. Proceedings of the FISU Conference-Universiade '83 in association with the Tenth HISPA Congress. Edmonton, Canada: University of Alberta, (July 2–4), 447–461.

Bennett, Jr., L. (1996). *Before the Mayflower: A history of black America*. Chicago: Johnson Publishing.

Coakley, J. J. (1994). *Sport in Society: Issues and controversies*. Boston: Times Mirror/Mosby.

Davis, Laurel R. (1991). "The articulation of difference: White preoccupation with the question of racially linked genetic differences among athletes. *Sociology of Sport Journal*, 7(2), 179–187.

Eitzen, D. S., and Sage, G. H. (1996). *Sociology of North American Sport*. Dubuque: Wm. C. Brown.

Evans, V. (1978). "A study of perceptions held by high school athletes toward coaches." *International Review of Sport Sociology*, 13, 47–53.

Franklin, J. H. (1994). *From Slavery to Freedom*. New York: McGraw-Hill.

George, N. (1992). *Elevating the Game: Black men and basketball*. New York: HarperCollins.

Hoose, P. (1989). *Necessities: Racial barriers in American sports*. New York: Random House.

Jones, B., Leonard, W., Schmitt, R., Smith, D., and Tolone, W. (1987). "A log-linear analysis of stacking in college football." *Social Science Quarterly*, (March), 70–83.

Lederman. D. (1990). "Athletes in division I found graduating at higher rate than other students." *The Chronicle of Higher Education*, July 5.

Leonard II, W. M. (1993). *A Sociological Perspective of Sport*. New York: Macmillan Publishers.

Lombardo, B. (1978). "The Harlem globetrotters and the perception of the black stereotype." *The Physical Educator*, 35(2), 60–63.

McMartin, J., and Klay, J. (1983). "Some perceptions of the student athlete." *Perceptual and Motor Skills*, 57(3), 687–690.

McPherson, B., Curtis, J., and Loy, J. (1989). *The Social Significance of Sport. Champaign: Human Kinetics*.

NCAA Report. (1996). 1996 NCAA Division I Graduation-Rates Report. Overland, Kans.: The National Collegiate Athletic Association.

NCAA Report (1989). The Status of Minority Participation in Intercollegiate Sports. Washington, DC: American Institute of Research.

Nixon, H. L. (1982). "The athlete as scholar in college: An exploratory test of four models" In *Studies in the Sociology of Sport*, edited by A. Dunleavy, A. Miracle, and C. Rees. Fort Worth: Texas Christian University Press, 239–256.

Oliver, W. (1994). *The Violent Social World of Black Men*. New York: Lexington Books: New York.

Sailes, G. A. (1996). "An Examination of Basketball Performance Orientations Among African American Males." *Journal of African American Men*, 1(4), 37–46.

——— (1993a). "An Investigation of Academic Accountability Among College Student Athletes." *Academic Athletic Journal*, Spring, 27–39.

———. (1993b). "An investigation of campus typecasts: The myth of black athletic superiority and the dumb jock stereotype." *Sport Sociology Journal*, 10, 88–97.

———. (1991). 'The myth of black sports supremacy." *Journal of Black Studies*, 21(4), 480–487.

———. (1987). "A socioeconomic explanation of black sports participation patterns." *The Western Journal of Black Studies*, 11(4), 164–167.

———. (1984). "Sport socialization comparisons among black and white adult male athletes and nonathletes." *Doctoral Dissertation*, University of Minnesota.

Schneider, J., and Eitzen, S. (1986). "Racial segregation by professional football positions, 1960–1985." *Sociology and Social Research*, 70, 259–262.

Sokolove, M. (3988). "Are blacks better athletes than whites?" *Inquirer: The Philadelphia Inquirer Magazine* (April 24), 16–40.

Steele, Shelby. (1990). *The Content of Our Character*. New York: St. Martin's Press.

6

"White Men Can't Jump"
Evidence for the Perceptual Confirmation of Racial Stereotypes Following a Basketball Game

Jeff Stone
Zachary W. Perry
John M. Darley

A N EXPERIMENT WAS CONDUCTED TO DEMONSTRATE THE PERCEPTUAL confirmation of racial stereotypes about Black and White athletes. In a 2 × 2 design, target race (Black vs. White) and target athleticism (perceived athletic vs. unathletic) were manipulated by providing participants with a photograph of a male basketball player. Participants then listened to a college basketball game and were asked to evaluate the target's athletic abilities, individual performance, and contribution to his team's performance. Multivariate analyses showed only a main effect for target race on the measures of ability and team performance. Whereas the Black targets were rated as exhibiting significantly more athletic ability and having played a better game, White targets were rated as exhibiting significantly more basketball intelligence and hustle. The results suggest that participants relied on a stereotype of Black and White athletes to guide their evaluations of the target's abilities and performance.

The title of the popular Ron Shelton film illustrates a common stereotype about racial differences in athletics: White males do not possess the physical capabilities that Black males possess, and therefore, are not as skilled in sports (Biernat & Manis, 1994; Craighead, Privette, Vallianos & Byrkit, 1986; Edwards, 1973; Felson, 1981; Nation & LeUnea, 1983). Like many stereotypes, the beliefs underlying the athletic superiority of Blacks in basketball may well have a factual basis: More than 75% of the players in the National Basketball Association (NBA) and 64% of collegiate basketball players are Black (Hoose, 1989). However, the history of professional basketball makes clear the danger in predicting athletic success based solely on race: Many White men have not

Jeff Stone, Zachary W. Perry, and John M. Darley, "White Men Can't Jump: Evidence for the Perceptual Conformation of Racial Stereotypes Following a Basketball Game," *Basic and Applied Social Psychology*, pp. 291-306. Copyright © 1997 by Taylor & Francis Group. Reprinted with permission.

just played, but excelled in the NBA (e.g., Bob Cousey, Jerry West, Gail Goodrich, Larry Bird, John Stockton, Toni Kukoc, just to name a few). Thus, race accounts for only part of the variance in basketball performance and explains still less variance in athletic performance when all professional sports are taken into account (e.g., Samson & Yerles, 1988). As we describe in the next section, racial stereotypes about athletes appear to be complex and include negative beliefs about Blacks and Whites alike. The purpose of this study is to document the existence and use of racial stereotypes when assessing athletic performance, in this case, as the stereotypes were applied to the game of basketball.

Stereotypes are incomplete and overgeneralized beliefs a person holds toward a particular social group (Allport, 1954). When a person who subscribes to a stereotype observes or interacts with members of a target group, stereotypic beliefs act as expectancies during the interaction (e.g., Hamilton, Sherman, & Ruvolo, 1990; see Hamilton & Sherman, 1994). That is, the stereotype leads the perceiver to expect specific behaviors from the target, such as "If this player is White, he probably can't rebound." Once activated, expectancies can guide the interpretation of the target's behavior (Duncan, 1976; Sagar & Schofield, 1980), especially when the behavioral information is ambiguous (Bodenhausen & Wyer, 1985). Stereotypes often confirm their own veracity and may do so implicitly such that perceivers are unaware of the stereotype's activation or use (e.g., Banaji, Hardin, & Rothman, 1993; Devine, 1989; Gilbert & Hixon, 1991).

Racial stereotypes that might apply specifically to Black and White athletes in a sports context have not received much empirical attention. For example, Devine and Baker (1991) found that the attributes assigned to the social category of "Black athlete" included "unintelligent" and "ostentatious," but their study was not designed to examine attributes about White athletes. Biernat and Manis (1994) reported that Black men were perceived to be more athletic than White men, however, the ratings were made outside of a specific sports context. Other studies have failed to find evidence of stereotyped perceptions of minority athletes (e.g., Harris & Ramsey, 1974) or reported stereotyped perceptions that did not include ethnicity as a variable (e.g., Cxizma, Wittig, & Schurr, 1988; Sadalla, Under, & Jenkins, 1988). Last, in one study that examined the relation between race and basketball performance, Sapolsky (1980) compared the evaluations made by Black and White perceivers of the baskets made by Black and White basketball players. Although differences were found between Black and White perceivers, the primary measures did not include ratings of the attributes of the Black and White players themselves. In sum, few studies have examined the specific racial stereotypes that might underlie the belief "White men can't jump."

Racial stereotypes about athletes, however, have received attention in the sports media. According to the observations made by sports writers and commentators, racial stereotypes about Black and White athletes involve two general beliefs: that Blacks are physically better athletes than Whites and that Black athletes are intellectually inferior to White athletes. These assertions were brought to national attention in the late 1980s by two prominent figures in the world of sports. First, former CBS commentator Jimmy "The Greek" Snyder was videotaped suggesting that Black players were bred in slavery to be better athletes than Whites (Craig, 1989). Shortly after Snyder's comments, then-Los Angeles Dodger General Manager Al Campanis announced to a national television audience that although Blacks are "fleet of foot," they may lack some of the necessities to succeed in management positions in professional baseball (Cornwell, 1993). The truth behind these beliefs about race and athleticism has since been explored and criticized in contemporary sports publications, such as USA Today (Meyers, 1991), in a number of stories written for The Sporting News (e.g., Craig, 1989; Kindred, 1995), in two editions of Sports Illustrated ("The Black Athlete," 1968; and "The Black Athlete Revisited," 1991), and in recent books on basketball (e.g., The Selling of the Green, Araton & Bondy, 1992). The sports media provides illuminating commentary on the "possibility" that Black athletes are physically superior to Whites, but that White athletes are intellectually superior to Blacks.

It also appears that the discussion of racial stereotypes in the sports media centers around the game of basketball. For example, noted sports columnist David Halberstram made the following observation about racial stereotypes in a Sports Illustrated (Halberstram, 1987) article published after the 1987 NBA championship series, during which the Celtics, led by Larry Bird, lost to the Lakers, led by Magic Johnson:

> Yet, if there is one thing that enrages the better Black athletes ... it is the contemporary White perception, both in the media and among fans, that Black athletes are natural athletes, doing night after night what comes quite readily to them. This is an ironic update to an earlier myth, which was that Blacks were faster than Whites but could not play in difficult positions ... because they lacked both guts and talent. Whites, by contrast, are seen as less gifted but headier athletes who practice and perfect their skills better because they have ... better work habits. (p. 38)

Halberstram's observation aptly illustrates how racial stereotypes about basketball players maintain themselves: When a White man such as Larry Bird does perform skillfully, perceivers account for the unexpected performance through existing beliefs such as Whites are smarter or more hard working than stupid and lazy Blacks (see also Mead, 1985, for an example of how these stereotypes were applied to the heavyweight fight between Joe Louis and Max Schmelling). These examples from the sports media serve as evidence for a widely held belief about success in basketball: Black male athletes have more natural physical ability than do White athletes, but White male athletes are intellectually superior and have a better work ethic than do Black male athletes.

We believe it is important to document racial stereotypes about athletes because they have the potential to cause discrimination. The problem is not that there are racial differences in athletic performance; indeed, the fact that Blacks are overrepresented in professional sports such as basketball indicates that there is a relationship between race and athletic performance. The problem arises when people go beyond the relationship and infer that some characteristic about race causes the differences in athletic performance. According to our earlier discussion, one popular explanation for racial differences in athletic performance is that Black athletes are more physically skilled than Whites, but that Whites are more intelligent and diligent than Black athletes. To the degree these beliefs form stereotypes, they can influence perceptions of athletic performance. That is, racial stereotypes ascribed to athletes may serve as heuristics in information processing and lead to inaccurate evaluations of Black and White athletes who attempt to play outside of the limitations supposedly imposed by their ethnic heritage.

Perceptual Confirmation Paradigm

If people hold racial stereotypes about basketball performance, and the stereotype has an influence on how Black and White basketball players are perceived, then it should be possible to demonstrate this through the well-documented procedures used to study perceptual confirmation effects (see Hamilton & Sherman, 1994, for a review). In these studies, an action is committed by a stereotyped or nonstereotyped individual, and it is shown that perceivers evaluate its meaning differently, depending on to whom the behavior was attributed. In one classic demonstration, Duncan (1976) showed that an ambiguous shove was rated as more violent by White participants if a Black target ostensibly did the pushing compared to if a White target did the pushing (see also Bodenhausen, 1988; Darley & Gross, 1983; Sagar & Schofield, 1980). Perceptual confirmation procedures provide a useful strategy for examining whether stereotyped expectations about a target significantly alter a perceiver's interpretations of the target person's behavior.

Research on perceptual confirmation of a stereotype, however, has shown that use of a stereotype can sometimes be attenuated when individuating information about the target is available (e.g., Locksley, Borgida, Brekke, & Hepbrun, 1980). When highly diagnostic information concerning personal behaviors or attributes of a target are known, stereotyped beliefs may not influence perceptions of a target person. In contrast, if the individuating information is not useful for generating judgments about the target, stereotypes are more likely to dominate subsequent processing of a target's behavior (e.g., Krueger & Rothbart, 1988).

This suggests that racial stereotypes about race and basketball may not operate if perceivers have individuating information about a Black or White player, such as diagnostic information about the target's athletic abilities (e.g., Locksley et al., 1980). In fact, the availability of individuating information such as athletic ability may override the utility of race in evaluating the ambiguous performance of a basketball player. Perceivers may see an athletic White man as having more basketball ability than an unathletic Black male, contradicting the stereotype that "White men can't jump." Of course, if individuating information concerning the athleticism of a Black and White player was available but race still accounted for most of the variance in performance evaluation, then fairly clear evidence of stereotypic processing would emerge (e.g., Nelson, Biernat, & Manis, 1990). It may be that even when individuating information is available, perceivers believe that race is a more reliable predictor of basketball performance.

Overview

The purpose of this experiment was to investigate perceptual confirmation of racial stereotypes concerning basketball players when information about the player's race and athleticism was available. Participants were asked to rate the attributes and performance of a basketball player after listening to a radio broadcast of a collegiate basketball game. For half the participants, the player was depicted as White; for the other half, the same player was depicted as Black. This was crossed with information about the perceived athleticism of the target: Half the participants viewed a picture of a relatively unathletic target; the other half viewed a picture of a relatively athletic target. Participants were then asked to provide estimates of the target's athletic abilities, individual performance, and contribution to his team's performance.

Based on the racial stereotypes described elsewhere (Brinson & Robinson, 1991; Edwards, 1973;) and on the documented effects of individuating information (i.e., Locksley et al, 1980), we predicted that one of three patterns would emerge from the data: First, if the target's perceived athleticism influenced the perceiver's evaluations, we expected main effects for perceived athleticism on the dependent measures. Specifically, independent of the target's race, the athletic targets would be rated as possessing more athletic ability and as having played a better game overall, relative to the unathletic targets.

In contrast, if athletic stereotypes were activated by the target pictures, we predicted that participant's expectations created by the ethnicity of the targets would effect how they perceived the target's athletic attributes and performance. Specifically, we expected that stereotyped processing would lead to one of two possible patterns across the measures. First, Black targets would be rated as possessing more general physical ability than the White targets. In contrast, the White targets could be seen as more intelligent, more team-oriented, and could be seen as players that can think on their feet and hustle to make up for their lack of physical talent. Such a stereotyped response might indicate a "compensatory" set of beliefs that allows for White men to make a contribution in basketball, but only because they make up for their lack of physical ability through intelligence and diligence. Alternatively, another stereotype dictates that Black athletes are simply more talented at all aspects of sport, including those requiring intelligence and effort, relative to White athletes. As a result, the Black targets would be perceived not only as possessing more physical skill, but also as possessing more team-oriented ability, such as "court-smarts" and "stamina." This pattern would suggest a general athletic stereotype whereby White men are perceived as generally inferior to Black men in a sports context.

Methods Evaluating the Target Stimuli

The race and perceived athleticism of each target was manipulated by presenting participants with a color photograph extracted from a high school yearbook. Photos of two Black and two White men were carefully selected such that one photo in each race pair depicted an "athletic" target (i.e., broad shoulders and a relatively thick neck) and two photos within each race pair depicted a relatively "unathletic" target (i.e., thinner in the shoulders and neck than the athletic targets). The initial choice of the photos was conducted by the authors.

To test the perceptual information afforded by our selection of the target pictures, a sample of college student participants (N = 21) were recruited at a campus restaurant. Participants were asked to complete a short questionnaire study for which they would be paid $4. Interested participants were then presented the target pictures and asked to rate each for 10 relevant attributes. They were told that the pictures were experimental stimuli and that their ratings would assist the researchers in determining how the stimuli were perceived.

The target pictures were rated along attributes drawn from a modified version of the Self-Attributes Questionnaire (SAQ: Pelham & Swann, 1989), a questionnaire designed to measure self-descriptions among college students. The SAQ was adapted for the current purposes by asking participants to rate the targets in the pictures along each dimension "relative to other people the target's own age." The ratings were made along a 10-point scale for the attributes of intellectual ability, social competence, work ethic, athletic ability, physical attractiveness, leadership, common sense, likability, luck, and discipline. To avoid suspicion, participants were randomly assigned to rate either the two Black or the two White target pictures. The order in which participants rated the pictures in each pair was manipulated, but subsequent analyses showed that the order had no effect on the ratings.

The ratings were analyzed using a race (Black vs. White) x perceived athleticism (high vs. low) × attribute mixed analysis of variance. The results revealed a significant interaction between perceived athleticism and the attribute ratings, $F(9, 162) = 15.50$, $p < .0001$. The mean ratings for each target by attribute are presented in Table 1. Protected univariate tests showed that within the pictures of the Black and White players, the athletic targets were perceived to be more athletic but also more socially competent, more physically attractive, and to have more leadership ability compared with the unathletic targets, all $ps < .05$. The ratings of perceived common sense, likability, and luck, and discipline did not co-vary with the perceived athleticism of the targets.

TABLE 1   Pretest Attribute Ratings for Each Target Picture

| | Target Picture | | | |
| | Black | | White | |
Attributes	Unathletic	Athletic	Unathletic	Athletic
Athletic ability	5.00b	8.25a	4.82b	7.91a
Intellectual ability	6.63ab	6.50a,b	7.46b	6.10a
Social competence	5.88b	7.75a	6.46b	7.82a
Work ethic	7.00a	6.63a	6.73a	5.55b
Physical attractiveness	4.63b	7.88a	5.73b	7.73a
Leadership ability	5.50b	7.13a	5.91b	7.00a
Common sense	6.38a	6.63a	6.27a	5.91a
Likeability	6.88a	7.00a	6.82a	6.55a
Lucky	6.00a	6.75a	6.09a	6.81a
Disciplined	6.62a	6.75a	6.45a	5.82a

[a-b]   Higher numbers indicate the target was rated as possessing more of the attribute. Comparisons with different superscripts are significantly different at the .05 level using Fisher's LSD protected t-tests.

In sum, the ratings appeared to confirm our perceptions of the athletic and unathletic targets. Across race of target, the differences between the athletic and unathletic targets were comparable with two exceptions: The athletic–unathletic differences for the White targets was significant for intellectual ability and work ethic, but these differences were not significant for the Black targets. It should be noted that perceived athleticism also correlated with other attributes such as physical attractiveness and social competence, an issue we address in the next section.

Perceptual Confirmation Experiment

Participants. Participants were 51 (32 men and 19 women) undergraduates at Princeton University who were recruited through sign-up sheets posted on the university campus. The sample was predominately White; only three Black, two Asian-Americans, and two Hispanics participated in the study. Of the 51 participants, 31 reported that they had played basketball at the high school level, and most reported that they follow either NBA or National College Athletic Association basketball. Only seven participants claimed to have "very little" knowledge of basketball. All participants were paid $4 for their participation.

Materials. The experiment was conducted in a large rectangular room. In each corner of the room was a seat and a tape recorder with headphones. All of the recorders contained a 20-min tape recording of a Division I college basketball game. The tape was made from a radio broadcast of a University of California, Santa Barbara (UCSB) versus University of Nevada, Las Vegas basketball game, played in mid-December of 1994. The cassette featured sections of the game in which a student named "Mark Flick" played power forward for UCSB. To create an ambiguous performance for the target from the taped broadcast, all evaluative comments by the announcers and all exemplary plays by Flick were edited from the tape.

FIGURE 1 **An example of the profile information presented to participants while they listened to the taped radio broadcast of the basketball game.**

RECORDING INFORMATION
UC Santa Barbara Gouchos vs. UN Las Vegas Rebels

Player: Mark Flick #44
Class: Junior
Height:6-8   One of the
Major: Business   four pictures
Home Town : Serrito, California   was placed here.
High School; Serrito HighSchool

Tape may seem a little choppy because time-outs and lulls in the action were cut out to save time. Also, different sections of the game are used to focus on Mark Flick (Flick plays more than what is covered by the recording.). Note: When sections of the game are skipped there is a one second blank spot in the tape.

19 Minute Tape
Section 1:
Start - Beginning of the first half.
2:00 into half time-out Rebels
End - 5:41 into the first half - Hick leaves the game.

Section 2:
Start: Middle of the first half- Flick returns
End: Approx. 6 min. left in first half 23 - 19 UCSB (Flick still in game.)
Half Time Score 36 - 30 UCSB

Section3:
Start - 2 min. into the second half. 42 - 34 UCSB
End - 9:10 into the second half 49 - 40 UCSB - Flick leaves game

Key Players:
UCSB: Madden, McDougal, Butz, Muse, Flick, Carter
UNLV: Thomas, Manual, Kebu Stewart,Savoy, Johnson, Smith

Nearby each recorder was an orange folder that contained a profile of the player named Flick. All the folders contained the same player profile information including demographic information about the player's life (see Figure 1). The file also included the text of the audiotape so that participants could read along with the audio presentation.

To manipulate target race and perceived athleticism, the folder included one of the pretested pictures just described. The target pictures crossed race (Black vs. White) with perceived athleticism (athletic vs. unathletic), thus creating four different profiles (none of the pictures were the real Mark Flick). The folders were randomly distributed to each station before each trial.

Procedure. The sign-up sheets described the study as an experiment on the differences between information processed from a radio broadcast compared with a television broadcast. The task was described as "listening or watching a 20 minute excerpt of a basketball game and answering a 5 minute questionnaire." Participants were run in groups of between two and five, but each was seated at separate stations to prevent interaction during the procedures.

On arrival, the experimenter explained that participants would listen to an 18- to 20-min tape of one of four basketball games. Participants were told to use the folder by their recorder to help them follow the recording because they were only hearing certain sections of the game. Participants were also told that the file contained a player profile and that their task was to listen for that player because they would be asked to evaluate him later. Participants were then randomly assigned to an isolated listening station.

After they had listened to the game tape, participants were asked to complete a questionnaire. The questionnaire was designed to measure the participants' backgrounds in basketball and their evaluations of the target's basketball abilities and performance. Specifically, the primary measures were assessments of the target's natural ability (i.e., individual ratings of physical ability and "basketball" ability), objective estimates of his personal performance (i.e., the number of points, rebounds, and assists attributed to the target), and evaluations of his contribution to the team's performance (i.e., individual evaluations of the target's "team-play," "hustle," "court-smarts," and "position-play"). The evaluations of ability and team contribution were collected on 9-point rating scales with descriptions of the scale endpoints included at the end of the question (e.g., 5 = average for a collegiate ballplayer, 9 = great, 1 = poor). After the completed questionnaires were collected by the experimenter, participants were paid $4 for their participation and fully debriefed about the true purposes of the research.

Results

Preliminary inspection of the data revealed that participant sex, self-reports of experience playing basketball, and knowledge of college and professional basketball did not correlate significantly with the target ratings. As a result, the participant variables were dropped from any further analyses. The experimental data were analyzed using multivariate analysis of variance (MANOVA) in which the measures of basketball ability, performance, and team contribution were analyzed separately.

A Race (Black vs. White) × Perceived Athleticism (athletic vs. unathletic) MANOVA across the ability measures revealed only a significant multivariate main effect for the target's race, Wilks's Λ, $F(2,46) = 3.89$, $p < .03$. As predicted, when they thought he was Black, participants rated Mark Flick as having more physical ability ($M = 6.19$, see Table 2) and more basketball ability ($M = 5.50$) compared with when they thought Flick was White ($M = 5.48$ and $M = 4.88$, respectively). This finding supports what we take to be one core of the stereotypes, that Blacks have more of the physical skills required for playing basketball.

A similar analysis of the performance measures did not reveal any effect for the target's race or perceived athleticism, all Wilks's Λ, < 1. As seen in Table 2, the Black players were rated as having performed slightly better in points and assists, but were not perceived to have rebounded more shots compared with the White players. Generally, participants were fairly accurate in their perceptions of the target's offensive performance: In the edited radio broadcast, Mark Flick scored four points, made two rebounds and one assist. Their relative accuracy is not an unexpected finding given the objective nature of Flick's game statistics and the emphasis placed on evaluating the target's game performance.

TABLE 2 **The Ratings of Natural Ability, Individual Performance, and Team Contribution for Each Target**

	Target Picture			
	Black		**White**	
Ratings	Unathletic	Athletic	Unathletic	Athletic
Natural ability				
Basketball ability	5.28	5.75	4.75	5.00
Physical ability	6.53	6.50	6.64	5.23
Individual performance				
Points scored	4.79	4.83	4.42	3.69
Rebounds	2.57	2.33	2.17	2.23
Assists	1.50	1.75	1.33	1.23
Team Contribution				
Team play	6.53	6.50	6.64	5.23
Position play	6.23	6.08	5.91	4.92
Court smarts	5.46	5.75	6.64	5.46
Hustle	6.31	6.42	7.45	6.31

For the measures of team contribution, the Race x Athleticism MANOVA revealed only a significant multivariate effect for the target's race, Wilks's Λ, $F(4, 42) = 3.02$, $p < .03$. When Mark Flick was thought to be Black, he was perceived to be a better team player ($M = 6.52$) and his position play was rated better (M = 6.16) compared with when Hick was thought to be White (M = 5.88 and M = 5.38, respectively). In contrast, when depicted as White, Flick was perceived to have more basketball intelligence (i.e., "court-smarts," M = 6.00) and more "hustle" (M = 6.83) compared with when he was depicted as Black (M = 5.60 and M = 6.36, respectively). This set of findings supports our prediction concerning the particular nature of the racial stereotype about basketball players. Specifically, Black targets were rated as making more of a contribution to the game through better team and position play, suggesting that Blacks athletes are perceived to be generally better at playing the game of basketball. Alternatively, White targets were perceived to make more of a contribution to the team through basketball intelligence and effort. This provides evidence of the belief that Whites compensate for their lower athletic abilities in basketball through court smarts and hustle.

Univariate tests suggested that perceived athleticism may have contributed to some of the ratings concerning team contribution. For example, univariate analyses of the team-play measure revealed a significant main effect for athleticism, $F(1, 45) = 4.02$, $p < .05$, and a marginally significant interaction between athleticism and race, $F(1,45) = 3.61$, $p < .06$. The means in Table 2 show that whereas unathletic targets were perceived to contribute more to the team's overall play compared with athletic targets, the athletic Black target was rated as contributing significantly more to the team than the athletic White target, Fisher's LSD $= 2.01$, $p < .05$. Furthermore, univariate analysis of the measure of basketball intelligence (i.e., "court-smarts") revealed a marginally significant interaction between race and athleticism, $F(1, 45) = 3.15$, $p < .08$. In this case, the unathletic White target was rated as possessing more court smarts (M = 6.64) compared with the other targets as a group (M = 5.59 combined, Fisher's LSD = 1.04), $p < .05$. Thus, there was some indication that individuating information had an influence on the attributions made about the team contribution of the players. The data suggests that athletic White basketball players are perceived to be less team oriented, whereas unathletic White players are perceived to be among the more intelligent players on the court.

Discussion

The results of the multivariate analysis provided support for the hypothesized use of racial stereotypes when assessing the basketball performance of a Black or White athlete. As predicted, there indeed was a stereotype concerning the superior abilities of the Black athlete in basketball. The core component of the stereotype, we suggested, centered around the superior physical abilities of the Black athlete, and we found reasonably strong evidence that a basketball player identified as Black was perceived as having superior physical and basketball abilities. In contrast, the White targets were rated as possessing significantly less physical and basketball talent, which offers some insight into the beliefs underlying the assertion that "White men can't jump." We thus documented a claim that is frequently made about race and athletics in the sports media.

The ratings of team contribution also provided evidence of racial stereotypes about athletes. On the questions that tapped the dimensions of team play and position play, the Black targets were more highly rated than were the White targets. These attributions may reflect the general belief that Black athletes are better at all aspects of the game of basketball. However, a general stereotype about Black athletes would not explain why the White targets received higher ratings of their basketball intelligence and effort. This finding supports what we referred to as the compensatory stereotype ascribed to White men on the basketball court—if they play well in spite of their inferior physical talent (although Flick's game statistics were not exceptional), they are perceived as possessing more "court smarts" and more "hustle." Overall, the pattern of attributions observed across the ability and team contribution measures was remarkably consistent with the stereotypes discussed in the sports media: Perceivers reported that Black men have more athletic ability and are better at playing the game of basketball, but White men can contribute because they are more intelligent and make up for their lack of physical ability through effort.

Although we in no way think these results are conclusive, the data appear to challenge some current thinking about the types of attributions made to ingroups and outgroups for successful outcomes. For example, the ultimate attribution error (Pettigrew, 1979), which predicts that successful outgroup events will be attributed to relatively unstable causes, would not seem to predict the positive stable attributions of physical ability to the Black ballplayers. It also does not seem to predict the attribution of effort, a compensatory unstable explanation, to the ingroup in the study (i.e., the White athletes). That this pattern of attributions was made by the majority group (i.e., the perceivers were predominately White) is also surprising given other models of intergroup attributions (e.g., see Islam & Hewstone, 1993). Although we do not view this experiment as a test of any particular attribution model, the data imply that stereotyped attributions made about athletes might operate differently than do stereotyped attribution about other subtype categories (Devine & Baker, 1991). Uncovering the attribution processes that contributed to our findings is an important direction for future research.

At the univariate level, there was some evidence that the use of the compensatory White stereotype may be a function of the perceived athleticism of a White player. For example, the unathletic White player was thought to possess more knowledge of the game and to exhibit somewhat more hustle relative to the athletic White target. We note that applying a compensatory stereotype in this case is to some extent an accurate appraisal: If one is not perceived to be athletic, he or she would have to be smart or hustle or both to contribute to the team's success. But the overall accuracy of the compensatory stereotype is questioned when one considers that the unathletic Black target was not rated similarly—he was perceived as less intelligent and exerting less effort than the unathletic White target. In fact, perceived athleticism had no effect on any of the ratings of the Black targets, suggesting that the present manipulation of perceived athleticism might have been processed inconsistently across the race of the targets.

There are a number of factors that may have contributed to the weak and inconsistent effects obtained for the manipulation of individuating information. One is that participants were exposed to other individuating information such as the target's school, college major, and information about his position on the basketball team. It is possible that this profile information was perceived to be more diagnostic of basketball performance relative to what his apparent athleticism conveyed. This suggests that if less information were held constant across the targets, perceived athleticism may have exerted a greater influence on the evaluations of the target's performance and basketball attributes.

Another possibility is that the manipulation of perceived athleticism with photographs may not have been highly diagnostic of basketball performance (e.g., Krueger & Rothbart, 1988). A more concrete indicator of individual basketball performance, such as previous game statistics, may have had more of an effect on perceptions. Making previous performance information available would also reduce the potential for confounds that arise when photographs are used to provide individuating information—in this study, perceived athleticism was confounded with perceived attractiveness and leadership ability. Although other studies have documented the use of stereotypes when target information was presented in photographs (and participants were instructed not to rely on a stereotype to make their judgments; see Nelson et al., 1990), the presence of other information in the photographs may interfere with processing of the relevant individuating information. Nevertheless, we do note that a photograph, if it is taken as a proxy for what one learns from observing an athlete, closely approximates the type of information available in real life and thus has high ecological validity when used in perceptual confirmation research.

Another limitation to the research presented in this article was that the attribute ratings of the Black and White target pictures were not collected from the same participants who made the ratings of the basketball performance. Although the pretest and experimental participants were drawn from the same college sample, it is conceivable that the experimental participants did not perceive the photographs during the experiment in the same way as the pretest group. It should also be noted that the perceived athleticism ratings of the targets could have been affected by the fact that the ratings were made within race. Participants did not make explicit comparisons for the trait attributes across racial categories because pilot research revealed that participants resisted making cross-racial comparisons. Despite the potential difficulties in conducting such comparisons, this research does not directly address the perceptions that might emerge when Black and White athletes compete in the same basketball game.

Sometimes stereotypes are discussed as if they completely obscure any accurate perceptions of the actions of the stereotyped individuals. This is not the case in general and it was not the case in this study. On the questions that most directly related to the objective specifics of basketball performance, those questions involving points scored, assists made, and rebounds made, the perceivers were quite accurate and did not see significant differences between the Black and White players. One explanation for this result may be instructional—participants were explicitly asked to evaluate the player's performance, which may have motivated them to process the individual performance information accurately (e.g., Kunda, 1990). Another possibility is that assessing abstract concepts such as athletic ability or intelligence are more subject to the influence of stereotypes, whereas more concrete assessments, such as game statistics, are less prone to biased evaluations (e.g., Gollwitzer & Moskowitz, 1996; but see Biernat & Manis, 1994, for a potential exception to this rule). Although it is not clear why the individual performance statistics were processed accurately, the finding suggests that there may be limitations to the type of evaluations that are influenced by racial stereotypes of athletes. In conclusion, the data demonstrate that the general process of perceptual confirmation of stereotypes extends to the domain of athletic performances. To what extent these effects would perseverate following performance observations of a less ambiguous or longer duration are important questions for future study. It is also important to consider to what extent racial stereotypes can influence the perceptions of coaches or anyone who makes decisions about an athlete's future. For example, when decisions are made under time pressure or cognitive load (e.g., Macrae, Milne, & Bodenhausen, 1994), it seems possible for perceptual confirmation effects, encoded as first impressions of an athlete's potential, to influence subsequent processing of performance information (see Fiske, Bersoff, Borgida, Deaux, Heilman, 1991, for a similar analysis of how gender stereotypes can influence evaluations of performance in the workplace). It also seems possible that these stereotypes would persist because of their subtlety—racial stereotypes about athletes do not deny that either Whites or Blacks can perform successfully on the basketball court, they simply assert that the underlying causes for success in either case are different. It is important to examine whether attributions about the relation between race and athletic performance cause discrimination against Blacks who are more intelligent or Whites who are more physically talented than athletic stereotypes predict.

Acknowledgments

Jeff Stone is now with the University of Arizona.

This research was based, in part, on Zachary W. Perry's senior thesis, presented in partial fulfillment of the requirements for the degree of Bachelor of Arts in Psychology at Princeton University.

We would like to thank Kim Barletto for her help in collecting the attribute ratings and Gordon Moskowitz for his comments on previous drafts of this article.

References

Allport, G. W. (1954). *The Nature of Prejudice*. Reading, MA: Addison-Wesley.

Araton, H., & Bondy, F. (1992). *The Selling of the Green*. New York: HarperCollins.

Banaji, M. R., Hardin, C, & Rothman, A. J. (1993). Implicit stereotyping in person judgment. *Journal of Personality and Social Psychology*, 65, 272–281.

Biernat, M, & Manis, M. (1994). Shifting standards and stereotype-based judgments. *Journal of Personality and Social Psychology*, 66, 5–20.

Bodenhausen, G. V. (1988). Stereotypic biases in social decision making and memory: Testing process models of stereotype use. *Journal of Personality and Social Psychology*, 55, 726–737.

Bodenhausen, G. V., & Wyer, R. S., Jr. (1985). Effects of stereotypes on decision making and information processing strategies. *Journal of Personality and Social Psychology*, 48, 267–282.

Brinson, L., & Robinson, E. L. (1991). The African-American athlete: A psychological perspective. In L. Diamant (Ed.), *Psychology of sports, exercise, and fitness: Social and personal issues* (pp. 249–259). New York: Hemisphere.

Cornwell, R. (1993, December 5). Racism in Sports. *The Independent*, p, 8.

Craig, J. (1989, May 8). NBC deserves credit for tackling controversy. *The Sporting News*, p. 8.

Craighead, D. J., Privette, G., Vallianos, F., Byrkit, D. (1986). Personality characteristics of basketball players, starters and non-starters. *International Journal of Sport Psychology*, 17,110–119.

Csizma, K. A., Wittig, A. F., & Schurr, K. T. (1988). Sport stereotypes and gender. *Journal of Sport and Exercise Psychology*, 10, 62–74.

Darley, J. M., & Gross, P. H, (1983). A hypothesis-confirming bias in labeling effects. *Journal of Personality and Social Psychology*, 44, 20–33.

Devine, P. (1989). Stereotypes and prejudice: Their automatic and controlled components. *Journal of Personality and Social Psychology*, 56, 5–18.

Devine, P. G., & Baker, S. M. (1991). Measurement of racial stereotype subtyping. *Personality and Social Psychology Bulletin*, 17, 44–50.

Duncan, B. L. (1976). Differential social perception and attribution of intergroup violence: Testing the lower limits of stereotyping of Blacks. *Journal of Personality and Social Psychology*, 34, 590–598.

Edwards, H. (1973). The Black athletes: 20th century gladiators for White America. *Psychology Today*, 7(6)43–52.

Felson, R. B. (1981). Self- and reflected appraisal among football players: A test of the Meadian hypothesis. *Social Psychology Quarterly*, 44,116–128.

Fiske, S. T., Bersoff, D. N., Borgida, E., Deaux, K., Heilman, M. E. (1991). Social science research on trial: Use of sex-stereotyping research in Price Waterhouse v. Hopkins. *American Psychologist*, 46, 1049–1060.

Gilbert, D. T., & Hixon, J. G. (1991). The trouble of thinking: Activation and application of stereotypic beliefs, *Journal of Personality and Social Psychology*, 60, 509–

Gollwitzer, P. M., & Moskowitz, G. B. (1996). Goal effects on thought and behavior. In E. T. Higgins & A. W. Kruglanski (Eds.), *Social Psychology: Handbook of basic principles* (pp. 361–399). New York: Guilford.

Halberstam, D. (1987, June 29). The stuff dreams are made of. Sports Illustrated, p. 38–40.

Hamilton, D. L., & Sherman, J. W. (1994). Stereotypes. In R. S. W. & T. K. Srull (Eds.), *Handbook of Social Cognition* (pp. 1–68). Hillsdale, NJ: Lawrence Erlbaum Associates, Inc.

Hamilton, D. L., Sherman, S. J., & Ruvolo, C. M. (1990). Stereotype-based expectancies: Effects on information processing and social behavior. *Journal of Social Issues*, 46(2), 35–60.

Harris, M. B., & Ramsey, S. (1974). Stereotypes of athletes. Perceptual and Motor Skills, 39,705–706. Hoose, P. M. (1989). *Necessities: Racial barriers in American sports*. New York: Random House.

Islam, M. R., & Hewstone, M. (1993). Intergroup attributions and affective consequences in majority and minority groups. *Journal of Personality and Social Psychology*, 64, 936–950.

Kindred, D. (1995, October 2). You can't be colorblind. *The Sporting News*, p. 8.

Krueger, J., & Rothbart, M. (1988). Use of categorical and individuating information in making inferences about personality. *Journal of Personality and Social Psychology*, 55,187-195.

Kunda, Z. (1990). The case for motivated reasoning. *Psychological Bulletin*, 108, 480-514.

Locksley, A., Borgida, E., Brekke, N., & Hepbrun, C. (1980). Sex-stereotypes and social judgment. *Journal of Personality and Social Psychology*, 39, 821-831.

Macrae, C. R., Milne, A. B., & Bodenhausen, G. V. (1994). Stereotypes as energy-saving devices: A peek inside the cognitive toolbox. *Journal of Personality and Social Psychology*, 66, 37-47.

Mead, C. (1985, September 23). Joe Louis part 2: Triumphs and trials. *Sports Illustrated*, p. 74.

Meyers, J. (1991, December 17). Positions a Black and White issue. *USA Today*, p. 6C.

Nation, J. R., & LeUnea, A. (1983). A personality profile of the Black athlete in college football. Psychology—*A Quarterly Journal of Human Behavior*, 20,(3-4), 1-3.

Nelson, T. E., Biernat, M. R., & Manis, M. (1990). Everyday base rates (sex stereotypes): Potent and resilient. *Journal of Personality and Social Psychology*, 59, 664-675.

Pelham, B. W., & Swann, W. B., Jr. (1989). From self-conceptions to self-worth: On the sources and structure of global self-esteem. *Journal of Personality and Social Psychology*, 57, 672-680.

Pettigrew, T. F. (1979). The ultimate attribution error: Extending Allport's cognitive analysis of prejudice. *Personality and Social Psychology Bulletin*, 5, 461-476.

Sadalla, E. K., Under, D. E., & Jenkins, B. A. (1988). Sport preference: A self-presentational analysis. *Journal of Sport and Exercise Psychology*, 10, 214-222.

Sagar, H. A., & Schofield, J. W. (1980). Racial and behavioral cues in Black and White children's perceptions of ambiguously aggressive acts. *Journal of Personality and Social Psychology*, 39, 590-598.

Samson, J., & Yerles, M. (1988). Racial differences in sports performance. *Canadian Journal of Sports Science*, 13, 109-116.

Sapolsky, B. S. (1980). The effect of spectator disposition and suspense on the enjoyment of sport contests. *International Journal of Sport Psychology*, 11, 1-10.

––––. The Black athlete. (1968, July 1). Sports Illustrated, p. 21.

––––. The Black athlete revisited (1991, August 5). *Sports Illustrated*, p. 38.

African Americans in Sport:
The Theory and Uncivil Politics of Sport Recognition

Doris R. Corbett
Michelle Cook

THE SPORTING ESTABLISHMENT HISTORICALLY HAS TREATED THE MALE African American athlete as if they are solely a monetary commodity to be utilized and discarded should physical skills and talent fail to yield lucrative results for team owners and collegiate athletic programs. Through sport, young African American athletes have generally sought to achieve the American dream, but have done so at great personal and professional cost. The behavior demonstrated on and off the playing fields and courts by African American athletes often elicits unfavorable responses from both fans and the media. This essay examines the social constructivist theoretical framework in relation to the African American athlete, and explains the politics of sport recognition and media images that influence public perception. The essay will close depicting the social constructivist theoretical framework through the lens of selected outstanding African American athletes displaying their legacy and philanthropy, and highlighting their contributions to the community and society as a whole.

Social Constructivist Theoretical Framework and African American Athletes

The social constructivist theoretical framework examines "the importance of culture and context in understanding what occurs in society and constructing knowledge based on this understanding" (Kim 2001, n.p.). Social constructivist inquiry describes how people view the world in which they live, with the understanding that they are part of the larger world (Gergen 1985, 266). Social constructivists attempt to make sense of the world and how knowledge is formed. Influenced by culture and history, people make assumptions about the world. "These underlying assumptions about the world are unconscious and taken for granted" (Mills, Bonner, and Francis 2008, 26).

Social constructivism highlights the importance of culture and context in acknowledging what occurs in society and constructing knowledge based on this understanding (Derry 1999). Social "constructivism is based on specific assumptions about reality, knowledge, and learning" (Kim 2001). Social constructivists believe in the concept that reality is constructed through social activity or how human beings interact together and that these interactions determine how one learns.

Learning takes place in the dynamic relationship between human beings (McMahon 1997). "Meaningful learning occurs when individuals are engaged in social activities" (Kim 2001). All human beings are "influenced by history and cultural context, which, in turn, shape our view of the world, the forces of creation, and the meaning of truth" (Bonner, Mills, and Francis 2006). While the assumptions may not be at the forefront of one's thinking, they are still molded into our cognitive behavior. "Constructivism is a research paradigm that denies the existence of an objective reality, asserting instead that realities are social constructions of the mind, and that there exist as many such constructions as there are individuals" (Guba and Lincoln 1989, 43). In times past, it was commonly accepted that through the medium of sport, societal racial barriers could be reduced, resulting in a reduction in the promotion of stereotypical racial myths associated with black athletes.

There are several factors that contribute to understanding African American athletes' experiences and how what may be considered uncivil behavior is portrayed. One must consider how social interactions occur and whether they influence the perspectives of a person's reality. With African American athletes, there may be factors research scholars could examine to determine whether unfavorable behavior deemed uncivil determines public and media perceptions about the African American athlete. Grounded in theory, the social constructivist approach might allow the researcher to better understand why African American athletes' behaviors, which represent the intricate complexity of their role in the community and society, may be partially incorrectly defined by the media.

Social constructivism can be described as socialization, or an opportunity for the individual to learn cultural norms and to be able to assimilate in their society. It is important to scrutinize if there is a preconception about African American athletes and if this preconception develops from the mystique of sport in society. The sports kingdom, "with its obvious meritocratic orientation, prides itself on the degree to which one's social origins are of no importance on the field or court" (Washington and Karen 2001, 190). The monumental rise of many black athletes, who proportionally represent a small segment of the population, can alter the perception of opportunity for black athletes, and cause the false pretense that African Americans no longer face discrimination in sport in society (Washington and Karen 2001).

The oppressive boundaries placed on African American athletes and the uncivil politics (punitive conduct rules, rules governing celebratory behavior on/off the playing field, and the promotion of negative stereotypes) directed at African American athletes serve to diminish their value, self-esteem, and character.

In today's sporting marketplace, black players are "more likely to be punished for their demonstrative celebrations, dress code violations, and other non-conformist conduct unbecoming to what is considered a representation of American values. Behaviors such as dancing in the end zone, chest pumping, and other ethnic sport rituals are seen as arrogant or self-promoting rather than humble and self-depreciating." From a social constructivist point of view, such perspectives about African American athletes are socially established in the human consciousness (Hall and Livingston 2012, 900). The research literature demonstrates that race is a social construct (Andreasen 2000, Thompson 2006, Smedley and Smedley 2005, Ferguson 2013). "Race as a social construct is a way of grouping people into categories on the basis of perceived physical attributes, ancestry, and other factors" (APA Presidential Task Force on Evidence-Based Practice 2006). Race is also universally associated with power, status, and opportunity. A preconceived notion may exist that African American athletes focus on "sport participation as a mechanism for social mobility" (Shakib and Veliz 2012, 297). In relation to social constructivism and the treatment of African American athletes, the "discovered reality arises from the interactive process and its temporal, cultural, and structural contexts" (Charmaz 2000, 524).

The Social Constructivism of Sport in the African American Community

"Beginning in the 1900s, African Americans' triumphs in sport are said to have led to the lasting and unrealistic view that sport was a promising route to social mobility for many African Americans" (Shakib and Veliz 2012, 297). When examining African American sport socialization, it is important to consider the significance of sport in the African American community. The feeling of belonging to a community or developing social capital is important to all human beings. Social capital can be defined as "features of social organization such as networks, norms, and social trust that facilitate coordination and cooperation for mutual benefit" (Putnam 1995, 67).

The "development of identity is a socialization process shaped by experiences with one's family, community, school, group and social affiliations" (Harrison, Harrison, and Moore 2002, 122). Participation in sports has a strong impact on the development of African American youth. "Involvement in supervised and organized activities during the after school hours is associated with positive outcomes, while participation in unsupervised and/or unstructured contexts is related to less favorable adjustment" (Frederick and Eccles 2008, 1031). Conversely, there are more risky and unfavorable activities where youth can spend their time, and organized activities such as sports are a vehicle for African American youth to form positive relationships with peers and non-family members in the community, and develop skills and feelings of competency.

There are unique experiences in childhood that lead to socialization and development of identity. "Because of the abundance of negative stereotypes imposed on African Americans, the influence of perceived positive racial stereotypes have a refreshing influence on the development of Black adolescent's racial identity" (Harrison, Harrison, and Moore 2002, 124). Racial identity can lead to higher self-esteem. The concept of racial centrality, which "refers to the extent to which a person normatively defines herself or himself with respect to race" is significant in understanding the importance of youth development (Rowley, Sellers, Chavous, and Smith 1998). Furthermore, racial centrality is related to the importance of discovering one's identity. For African American youth, the greater the feeling of belonging to or identifying with their race, the greater the self-esteem of the individual.

African American youth need to have racial centrality in an effort to combat negative cultural and societal expectations. Historically, one of the most compelling ways to develop a positive identity for African American youth has been to participate in sports. Youth from African American communities see many examples of African American athletes who are successful in the sporting world. In this regard, it can help them to develop a positive racial identity. However, popular culture and organized sports can have both a positive and negative impact on the developmental process (Gaston 1986).

Sports sociologists have long considered how significant participation in athletics is to black youths and to the African American community. Through the process of socialization, one is able to determine their status and role in a community. Parental and community member influence and environmental factors can impact the development of youth within the social structure of their community. Parental influence is powerful in all communities; however, black parents face unique challenges that "create a dilemma for inculcating a positive group identity in their children" (Thornton, Chatters, Taylor, and Allen 1990, 401). The process of "socialization is considered to be both reactive, in response to racism, and proactive, as an effort to promote positive identity development" (McKay, Atkins, Hawkins, Brown, and Lynn 2003, 108).

It can be argued that society and the media contribute to the "cultural myth that [African American] athletes are more naturally gifted at sports and should go" all out to achieve the dream (Shakib and Veliz 2012, 298). Perhaps a more objective observation is the recognition that white society throughout history has been unable to accept the idea that African American athletes are superior, unless there is something to attribute to their success. "To counter what could be construed as a threat to the social superiority of Whites, African Americans achievements were framed in the media and in popular discourse as unrelated to the intellect, and a product of biological advantage" (Shakib and Veliz 2012, 298). This is a significant concept in the double-edged sword of success of African American athletes in sport. "Racial and gender bias (or prejudice) arises from overgeneralization about the characteristics or behaviors of whole groups of people applied wholesale to individuals within those group" and it is clear that there is bias when considering the successes of African American athletes and the recognition they receive (Billings and Eastman 2001, 184).

Myths, Stereotypes, and Media Images that Influence Public Perception

In American society, there are many talented athletes, both black and white. However, many talented whites who are equally as skilled as black athletes opt out, due in part to the belief that sport is a domain dominated by the African American athlete, particularly in basketball and football. Black youth often see popular culture as an alluring lifestyle that is glamorized by the media. However, the system of collegiate and professional sports can be "exploitative and both socially and politically damaging in that it implicitly underscores individualistic ideologies or success narratives that take racism off the hook by demonstrating that 'hard work' in the realm of sports or entertainment is all that one needs to escape the ghetto" (Andrews, Mower, and Silk 2010, 74).

Also repressive is the lack of recognition of the African American athlete. There is a body of literature that has historically promoted the notion "that Blacks are perceived as being more athletically-skilled than Whites" (Hall and Livingston 2010, Stone, Lynch, Sjomeling, and Darley 1999, Kane 1971). In 1987, basketball great Isiah Thomas maintained that the perpetuation of stereotypes about blacks must cease. Thomas contended that "when Larry Bird makes a great play, it's due to his thinking and his work habits. It's all planned out by him. It's not the case for Blacks. All we do is run and jump. We never practice or give a thought to how we play. It's like I came dribbling out of my mother's womb" (Wiggins 1994). Hall and Livingston reference the "Social Identity Theory," which argues "for the existence of social creativity which allows minorities to attain positive distinctiveness by outperforming majority group members in specific domains (e.g., sports), even though they are subordinate to minorities in more general domains" (Hall and Livingston 2010, 900). The "distinctiveness" may come in the form of celebrations performed after an athletic success, which Hall and Livingston (2010) describe as a perceived sign of arrogance that is tolerated for whites but not for blacks (p. 900).

Sports sociologists argue that the coverage and reporting of the natural black athlete in the media constructs many adverse consequences for African Americans (Shakib and Veliz 2012). The idea that African American athletes are genetically superior takes away from the recognition African American athletes deserve for being successful in their sport. Additionally, this myth impedes the African American athlete from achieving success in other aspects of life, because there may be the feeling that athletic success is the only important determinant for a successful life. Many other factors determine the success of an athlete, including intelligence, motivation, self-determination, commitment, drive, and determination. To theorize that African American athletes are genetically gifted dismisses all of the other characteristics that make an athlete successful.

Incivility towards African American athletes is seen frequently in the media. Examples of incivility include rude comments, discourteous behavior, and disrespectful treatment. Incivility portrayed by the media and community members towards African American athletes is common, and it is a behavior that dishonors the athletic achievement and does not contribute toward a positive relationship between races. African American athletes are seen as superior performers and attempts to explain their success polarize the black and white communities (Sailes 1998).

An example of the media depicting the political and social complexities of African American athletes' daily experiences includes the controversy that occurred when NBA player LeBron James announced that he was leaving the Cleveland Cavaliers. He was called ungrateful and arrogant and the media's questions included, "Does LeBron have the right to leave the Cavaliers?" (Hall and Livingston 2012, 899) Would this have been the headline if it were a white athlete?

Uncivil political, socioeconomic, and social complexities are present in the discourse surrounding the African American athlete. One example are the remarks of former LA Clippers owner Donald Sterling. For more than ten minutes, Sterling was recorded making racist remarks about African Americans. While talking about retired NBA player Magic Johnson to his African American girlfriend, Sterling stated, "Don't bring him to my games, ok?" He went on to say that he did not want her to associate with black people, and not to bring any of them to his (NBA) game" (Shreffler, Presley, and Schmidt 2015). In the late 1980s, major league baseball official Al Campanis declared that "[blacks] performed well on the field but [fell short] of the 'necessities' to occupy managerial positions or places of responsibility and authority in the front offices of sports organizations" (Miller 1998). Cincinnati Reds baseball team owner Marge Schott's beliefs and behaviors were often called into question. She praised Hitler, was known to be anti-Semitic, and held unfavorable views about African Americans and Asians. In 2004, "she described two of her players as 'million dollar niggers.' Schott was fined, suspended, and eventually forced to sell all but a minority interest in the Reds" (King and Schott 2004).

Stereotypes can significantly impact the way the community views African American athletes. Also referred to as social categorization, stereotyping can lead to examination of one's self concept. "The process of self-stereotyping and producing psychological groups are meshed in the development of social identity" (Harrison, Harrison, and Moore 2002, 126). This process of social identity allows one to "maintain an optimistic view of the self through identifying with or establishing favorable comparisons between one's own group and other groups" (Harrison et al. 2002, 126). "In African American culture, the overwhelming success of African American athletes [could propel the evolution of increased] collective self-esteem and perpetuate positive self-stereotypes in the realm of sport" (Harrison 2001). There are many philanthropic initiatives underway that seek to pave the way to make a difference in the manner in which African American youth are socialized into sport.

Social Constructivist Theoretical Framework Through the Lens of African American Athletes, Their Legacy, Philanthropy, and Highlights of their Contributions to the Community

Social constructivism is a subjective concept that defines humans as "cultural beings endowed with the capacity and the will to take a deliberate attitude towards the world and to lend it significance" (Ruggie 1998, 856). When constructing truth in social relationships and culture, we must consider how we are influenced by history and cultural context (Mills, Bonner, and Francis 2006). Constructivism relies on a subjective frame of mind. To understand the themes in social constructive theory related to race and African American athletes, it is important to understand that history and cultural differences come into play. Constructivism "should be understood in its conventional and critical variants, the latter being more closely tied to critical social theory" (Hopf 1998).

The concept of equality can be achieved in the sporting world if "each individual in a society enjoyed the right to compete in a contest unimpaired by discrimination of any kind" (Conley 1999). Race is a social construct "that develops out of group struggles over socially valued resources" (Weber 1998, 18). Race in the current cultural climate is an idea that can restrict some members of a society while privileging others. African American athletes who are striving to develop an identity can be hindered from doing so due to influences from other cultures. Sport themes and styles "have soaked into the fabric of African American life, as black identity is athleticized through ubiquitous role models who stimulate wildly unrealistic ambitions in black children" (Hoberman 1997, 4). The "need to analyze African American success in sport is a racist preoccupation emanating from fear generated within the white status quo" (Sailes 1993, 90).

An example of race as a social construct is the way Venus and Serena Williams are characterized when competing on the tennis court. Often, their physicality is described in terms that are not unusual when used to describe African American athletes. Black athletes are often revered for their physicality and presumed to possess an innate athleticism. A "problem arises when this occurs to the exclusion of recognizing the role played by intelligence and/or hard work" (Fordham and Ogbu 1986). The media "often downplays or obscures direct discussions of race, however, the process of differentiation used to represent Serena Williams are located within racialized media discourse" (Schultz 2005, 339).

The media plays a significant role in promoting incivility towards African American athletes. According to Buffington and Fraley, in "men's sports Black and White athletes are often presented in a diametrically opposed manner, creating a black brawn vs. white brains distinction" (2008). It can be argued that the media often fails to recognize African American athletes for their skill and knowledge of the game, but will devote a great deal of commentary addressing their sport celebrations, dress or other black cultural norms. The athletic skills of African American athletes is often "lost in the din of a media-driven sports world that manipulates the images of black athletic stars for the benefit of television networks and corporate sponsors" (Hoberman 2000, 50).

In relation to social construct theory, recognition of African American athletes is hindered by political incivility and an absence of respect for African American social norms. African American athletes are not recognized for their athletic ability should they fail to adhere to white cultural norms. What is emerging in the literature is a "discourse which depicts a White hegemonic concept of sports-person-ship to which Black athletes must adhere" (Cunningham 2009, 49).

The flaws in this concept are obvious even before one considers this perspective. The "cultural normative White hegemonic" concept of sports-person-ship does not take black cultural practices into consideration. Richard Majors and Janet Billson described the "cool pose" as "the construction of unique, expressive, and conspicuous styles of demeanor, speech, gesture, clothing, hair styles, walk, stance and handshake" that is part of black American culture (1993). Celebrations when succeeding in an athletic event are not seen as cultural, but more as showboating. However, these celebrations are a cultural norm in the African American community. African American athletes practicing cultural norms are typically not recognized for their athletic achievement, but rather for their display of celebration. Some studies have shown that white athletes are more strongly associated with the category "American," an athletic focus that suggests a patriotic American allegiance, than black athletes (Devos and Banaji 2005).

In the United States, sport can be a vehicle for African American athletes to "provide educational opportunities and social mobility both individually and collectively" (Donnor 2005, 47). Sport can be a mode for community building, a source of racial pride and mutual recognition. There are many positive role models among African American athletes who are actively engaged in good works. A number of legendary giants in sport have devised an approach and strategies designed in part to deal with the oppressive boundaries placed on African American athletes. Uncivil politics (punitive conduct rules, rules governing celebratory behavior on/off the playing field, and the promotion of negative stereotypes) directed at African American athletes serve to diminish the value, self-esteem, and character of black athletes. The philanthropic actions by some African American sporting giants emphasizes the importance of defining a positive cultural context to understand what occurs in the black community. Selected African American sport legends provide a variety of social programs that seek to dispel biased assumptions about the reality of being black. These legends provide proactive initiatives to promote positive identity development and community, and socially create and construct social institutions that provide a system that educates, embraces, and builds support processes that will make a difference.

TABLE I. **The Legacy of Selected African American Athletes: Philanthropy and Community Service**

Athlete and sport affiliation	Philanthropy and community service	Social constructionist theory in action
Jim Brown NFL football	The Black Economic Union helps cultivate African American entrepreneurship with the assistance of athletes and business professionals.	As a part of the Amer-I-Can foundation, Jim Brown works with inner-city kids, gang members, and prisons to assist at-risk and incarcerated youth and adults with gaining life management skills.
Bill Russell NBA basketball	The Bill Russell Legacy Project was established to commemorate Bill Russell's achievements as the greatest champion in the history of professional sports. As a national leader in human rights, his contributions and impact as a mentor to youth in the community have been substantial.	Bill Russell partners with Mass Mentoring of Boston, Massachusetts, mentoring youth in the community, networking with schools, religious organizations, and workplaces serving 5- to 18-year-old children.
Muhammad Ali Boxing	The Muhammad Ali Parkinson Center was established in 1997 by Muhammad Ali, philanthropist Jimmy Walker and Dr. Abraham Lieberman.	The Muhammad Ali Parkinson Center combines clinical and research expertise with community support and emotional care. The Center offers community integration and outreach through engaging recreational therapy programs and informative educational offerings for patients and caregivers.
Earvin "Magic" Johnson Jr. NBA basketball	The Magic Johnson Foundation works to develop programs and support community-based organizations that address the educational, health, and social needs of ethnically diverse, urban communities.	The core programs at the Magic Johnson Foundation include HIV/AIDS awareness and prevention; the Taylor Michaels Scholarship Program, which recognizes minority students with outstanding academic achievements, leadership, and commitment to serve their communities; and Community Empowerment Centers providing ethnically diverse communities with access to resources and programming that educate, empower, and strengthen individuals through the use of technology.

TABLE 2. The Legacy of Selected African American Athletes: Philanthropy and Community Service

Athlete and sport affiliation	Philanthropy and community service	Social constructionist theory in action
Arthur Ashe Tennis	Arthur Ashe founded the Arthur Ashe Foundation for the Defeat of AIDS in 1992. He addressed the United Nations General Assembly, urging for an increase in funding for AIDS research.	Arthur Ashe's Children's Program services children in second through eighth grades in their communities, at their schools. The Children's Program is an effective afterschool program that combines academics, and tennis, and life skills activities to help at-risk youth.

Sport sociologist and social justice scholars have become more sensitive to and aware of the disparaging climate that exists in the social institution of sport, and its impact on the African American male athlete. Greater awareness and understanding of the racial complexities associated with sport for people of color is essential. Researchers must commit long term to defining effective resolutions to the many issues confronting the black male athlete. The socialization processes that drive African American males to over emphasize sport require deliberate action by the community, families, schools, and sporting authorities at all levels. The bottom line is that too many blacks are lost striving to achieve a level of success in sport that is a dream unlikely to come true.

References

Andresen, R. O. 2000. Race: Biological Reality or Social Construct? Philosophy of Science.

Andrews, D. L., R. L. Mower, and M. L. Silk. 2010. "Ghetto Centrism and the Essentialized Black Male Athlete." *Commodified and Criminalized: New racism and African Americans in contemporary sports* : 69–93.

APA Presidential Task Force on Evidence-Based Practice. 2006. "Evidence Based Practice in Psychology." *American Psychologist* 61 (4): 271–85.

Banet-Weiser, S. 1999. "Hoop dreams: Professional basketball and the politics of race and gender." *Journal of Sport & Social Issues* 23 (4): 403–20.

Billings, A., & S. T. Eastman. 2001. "Biased voices of sports: Racial and gender stereotyping in college basketball announcing." *Howard Journal of Communications* 12 (4): 183–201.

Billson, J. M. 1993. *Cool Pose: The dilemma of black manhood in America.* Simon & Schuster.

Buffington, D., and T. Fraley. 2008. "Skill in Black and White negotiating media images of race in a sporting context." *Journal of Communication Inquiry* 32 (3): 292–310.

Charmaz, K. 2003. "Grounded Theory. Objectivist and Constructivist Methods." In *Strategies of Qualitative Inquiry*, edited by N. K. Denzin and Y. S. Lincoln, 249–91. London: Sage Publications.

Conley, D. 1999. *Being Black, Living in the Red: Race, wealth, and social policy in America*. University of California Press.

Cunningham, P. L. 2009. "'Please don't fine me again!!!!!' Black athletic defiance in the NBA and NFL." *Journal of Sport & Social Issues* 33 (1): 39–58.

Derry, S. 1996. "Cognitive schema theory in the constructivist debate." *Educational Psychologist* 31 (3–4): 163–74.

Devos, T., and M. R. Banaji. 2005. "American = White?" *Journal of Personality and Social Psychology* 88 (3): 447.

Donnor, J. K. 2005. "Understanding racism through the eyes of African American male student-athletes." *Race Ethnicity and Education Race Ethnicity and Education* 8(1): 45–67.

Ferguson, J. 2013. "Declarations of dependence: Labour, personhood, and welfare in Southern Africa." *Journal of the Royal Anthropological Institute* 19 (2): 223–42.

Fordham, S., and J. U. Ogbu. 1986. "Black students' school success: Coping with the burden of 'acting White.'" *The Urban Review* 18 (3): 176–206.

Fredricks, J. A., and J. S. Eccles. 2008. "Participation in extracurricular activities in the middle school years: Are there developmental benefits for African American and European American youth?" *Journal of Youth and Adolescence* 37 (9): 1029–43.

Gaston, J. C. 1986. "The Destruction of the Young Black Male: The Impact of Popular Culture and Organized Sports." *Journal of Black Studies* 16 (4): 369–84.

Gergen, K. J. 1985. "The Social constructionist movement in modern psychology." *American Psychologist* 40 (3): 266–75. doi:10.1037/0003-066X.40.3.266

Hall, E. V., and R. W. Livingston. 2012. "The Hubris penalty: Biased responses to "Celebration" displays of Black football players." *Journal of Experimental Social Psychology* 48 (4): 899–904.

Harrison, L. 2001. "Understanding the influence of stereotypes: Implications for the African American in sport and physical activity." *Quest* 53 (1): 97–114.

Harrison, L., C. K. Harrison, and L. N. Moore. 2002. "African American racial identity and sport." *Sport Education and Society* 7 (2): 121–33.

Hoberman, J. 2000. "The price of 'Black dominance.'" *Society* 37 (3): 49–56.

Hopf, T. 1998. "The promise of constructivism in international relations theory." *International Security International Security* 23 (1): 171–200.

Kane, M. 1971. "An Assessment of Black is Best." *Sports Illustrated* 34 (3): 78–83.

Kim, B. 2001. *Emerging Perspectives on Learning, Teaching and Technology*. http://projects.coe.uga.edu/epltt/

King, C., and M. Schott. Apologies and apologists: The disavowal of racism and the abjuration of anti-racism in the contemporary United States.

Lincoln, Y. S., and E. G. Guba. 1994. "Competing paradigms in qualitative research." *Handbook of Qualitative Research* 2: 163–94.

McKay, M., M. S. Atkins, T. Hawkins, C. Brown, and C. J. Lynn. 2003. "Inner-city African American parental involvement in children's schooling: Racial socialization and social support from the parent community." *American Journal of Community Psychology* 32 (1–2): 107–14.

McMahon, M. 1997. "Social constructivism and the World Wide Web: A paradigm for learning." Paper presented at the ASCILITE conference, Perth, Australia, December.

Miller, P. B. 1998. "The anatomy of scientific racism: Racialist responses to Black athletic achievement." *Journal of Sport History* 25 (1): 119–51.

Mills, J., A. Bonner, and K. Francis. 2006. "The development of constructivist grounded theory." *International Journal of Qualitative Methods* 5 (1): 25–35.

Putnam, R. D. 1995. "Bowling alone: America's declining social capital." *Journal of Democracy* 6 (1): 65–78.

Ruggie, J. G. 1998. "What makes the world hang together? Neo-utilitarianism and the social constructivist challenge." *International Organization* 52 (04): 855–85.

Sailes, G. A. 1993. "An investigation of campus stereotypes: The myth of black athletic superiority and the dumb jock stereotype." *Sociology of Sport Journal* 88 (97): 88–97.

Sailes, G. A. 1998. *African Americans in Sport: Contemporary themes.* New Brunswick, NJ: Transaction Publishers.

Schultz, J. 2005. "Reading the catsuit: Serena Williams and the production of blackness at the 2002 U.S. Open." *Journal of Sport & Social Issues* 29 (3): 338–57.

Sellers, R. M., M. A. Smith, J. N. Shelton, S. A. Rowley, and T. M. Chavous. 1998. "Multidimensional model of racial identity: A reconceptualization of African American racial identity." *Personality and Social Psychology Review* 2 (1): 18–39.

Shakib, S., and P. Veliz. 2012. "Race, sport and social support: A comparison between African American Perceptions of social support for sport participation." *International Review for the Sociology of Sport* 48 (3): 295–317.

Shreffler, M. B., G. Presley, and S. Schmidt. 2015. Case 5: Getting clipped: An evaluation of crisis management and the NBA's response to the actions of Donald Sterling.

Smedley, A., and B. D. Smedley. 2005. "Race as biology is fiction, racism as a social problem is real: Anthropological and historical perspectives on the social construction of race." *American Psychologist* 60 (1): 16.

Stone, J., C. I. Lynch, M. Sjomeling, and J. M. Darley. 1999. "Stereotype threat effects on Black and White athletic performance." *Journal of Personality and Social Psychology* 77 (6): 1213.

Thompson, E. C. 2006. "The problem of 'race as a social construct.'" *Anthropology News* 47 (2): 6–7.

Thornton, M. C., L. M. Chatters, R. J. Taylor, and W. R. Allen. 1990. "Sociodemographic and environmental correlates of racial socialization by Black parents." *Child Development* 61 (2): 401–09.

Washington, R. E., and D. Karen. 2001. "Sport and society." *Annual Review of Sociology* 187–212.

Weber, L. 1998. "A conceptual framework for understanding race, class, gender, and sexuality." *Psychology of Women Quarterly* 22 (1): 13–32.

Wiggins, D. K. 1994. "The notion of double-consciousness and the involvement of black athletes in American sport." *Ethnicity and Sport in North American History and Culture* 133–56.

Chapter 4

Performance Differences

8

An Examination of Basketball Performance Differences Among African American Men

Gary Sailes

HISTORICALLY, THE RACIAL PREJUDICE, DISCRIMINATION, AND SOCIAL stereotyping practiced by the dominant culture precipitated the construction of social barriers to preserve the culture, status, and privilege of white society. Many whites felt their culture was distinct from and superior to African American society (Hacker, 1992; Bell, 1992). Consequently, the distinct negative perceptions and definitions of African American culture precipitated social estrangement from white society. However, this compelled African Americans to develop positive and more accurate images of their culture. The outcomes of that effort are apparent in the diverse contributions of African Americans to North American art, music, literature, and sports. Much of African American culture is rooted in its historical and contemporary response to the racism, discrimination, and social stereotyping practiced by the dominant culture (Staples, 1982; Asante, 1988; Bell, 1992; Hacker, 1992). The inferior status relegated to African Americans emanated from the dominant culture's preoccupation with maintaining its status quo and strengthening its position of status, power, and privilege (Davis, 1990; Hacker, 1992). Inferior status was relegated to African American males, in particular, who symbolically represented the greatest threat to the dominant culture (Staples, 1982, Madhubuti, 1990).

Racism, discrimination, and social stereotyping manifested themselves in sport as in other American social institutions. The dominant culture held negative stereotypical beliefs regarding African American male athletes (Hoose, 1989; Davis, 1990; Sailes, 1993). The utilization of genetic definitions to rationalize African American domination in amateur and professional sports was socially stigmatizing and undermined the efforts of African American athletes to be successful (Worthy & Markle, 1970; Bledsoe, 1973; Jones & Hochner, 1973; Phillips, 1976; Hoose, 1989; Davis, 1990; NBC, 1990). The negative stereotypical beliefs about African American male athletes were manifested through stacking, the practice of racial positioning which was prevalent in professional baseball and football (Coakley, 1994; Eitzen & Sage, 1993; Leonard, 1993). The absence of African Americans in professional and intercollegiate sports ownership, management, administration, and coaching further exemplified the racism, discrimination and stereotyping prevalent in American sports institutions (Coakley, 1994; Eitzen & Sage, 1993; Leonard, 1993).

The African American male response to racism, discrimination, and social stereotyping was socially discernible. This coping skill was developed subliminally through the socialization process and displayed to balance or nullify the negative stigma associated with perceived inferior status (Staples, 1982; Majors, 1990; Steele, 1990). Moreover, responses to racism among African American males were a much valued and unifying component of African American male bonding (Madhubuti, 1990; Majors, 1990; Akbar, 1991;). Some African American athletes reacted to the racism, discrimination, and social stereotyping they experienced through performance on the playing field. The performance orientations among African American athletes were noticeably distinct from their white counterparts (Worthy & Markle, 1970; Axthelm, 1971; Bledsoe, 1973; Jones & Hochner, 1973; Phillips, 1976; Greenfield, 1980; Carlston, 1983; Majors, 1990; NBC, 1990; George, 1992).

Style variations in sports performance orientations among African American athletes, that were distinct from white athletes, had early origins. Historically, African Americans were denied participation in organized American sport. Except for a few token members on predominantly white college athletic teams, African American athletes were barred from participating in professional and amateur sports (Rust & Rust, 1990; Ashe, 1993). In response to the dominant culture's strong inclinations against African American participation in organized sports, African Americans established their own professional and amateur sports leagues. Further, Historically Black Colleges competed against one another in a variety of sports prior to the twentieth century (Rust & Rust, 1990; Ashe, 1993). Distinct individual expression or "style" was important among early African American athletes. Individual style was the norm and was practiced regularly by early Negro athletes (Peterson, 1984; Miller, 1986; PBS, 1988). Style is still evident and an important psycho-social mechanism among contemporary African American athletes (Majors, 1990; NBC, 1990).

Self-expression was an important coping mechanism among African Americans in combating the racial inferiority anxiety that generally accompanied the racial prejudice, discrimination, and social stereotyping experienced through social contact with the dominant culture (Majors, 1990; Steele, 1990). Self-expression manifested itself in the performance of many African American athletes and accounted for the individual orientation over the team orientation found among many African American athletes in team sports, most notably in basketball (Jones & Hochner, 1973; Phillips, 1976; Greenfield, 1980; Miller, 1986). These points were further exemplified by

Julius "Dr. J" Erving when he asserted "Style counts among inner-city basketball players" (NBC, 1990). Examples of these phenomena were in-zone displays by athletes after scoring a touchdown in football (currently banned by NFL league rules) and the individual fakes and moves of some African American basketball players.

Some African American basketball players tended to engage in "electric" self-expression, possessed the need to prove oneself, and to overcome obstacles with finesse and body control (Greenfield, 1980). Style and self expression were more important than success, fundamental technique, or performance. The power orientation of the African American athlete was personal and individual, and sometimes, it had more importance than team winning. Moreover, black athletes established personal empowerment, a sense of masculinity, and personal identity through their sports participation and performance on the playing field (Majors, 1990).

Distinct social constraints also accounted for the performance orientations among contemporary African American athletes. Limited facilities in the sports opportunity structure restricting opportunities to participate in a wide variety of sports channeled African Americans into few sports (Carlston, 1983; Sailes, 1984). Moreover, limited facilities created overcrowding and consequently generated a more aggressive competitive performance orientation, particularly in basketball (Carlston, 1983).

The barriers to participation in college and professional basketball eventually fell, creating opportunities for African American athletes (Rust & Rust, 1985). Their participation increased dramatically and their presence literally transformed the game to its present model (George, 1992). African American participation in college and professional basketball is seven times higher than their current representation in the American census (Sailes, 1984; Coakley, 1994; Leonard, 1993). The fast paced and aggressive style of current American basketball is in stark contrast to the slower, methodical game of past decades. These factors were attributed to the distinct playing style and talent of African American athletes (George, 1992).

Apparent social factors account for the participation and performance orientations among African American athletes. Those distinct performance and participation patterns are discernible in college and professional basketball. The performance orientation of the African American basketball player is the foundation for the creation of America's greatest contemporary African American basketball folk heroes (Julius Erving, Michael Jordan, Magic Johnson). The thrilling performance orientation of African American basketball players is used in the marketing of basketball licensing merchandise and is a highlight in the promotion of the game itself.

Conceptual Model

It was the intent of this inquiry to confirm the specific patterns of play that were evident among African American basketball players. The premise that African American performance orientation might have been created within a sport socialization context distinct from that of white players served as the determining factor in formulating this inquiry, thereby positioning race as the independent variable.

The literature supports the assumption that African American basketball players would be more individually oriented, more aggressive, and more expressive thereby creating more improvisational situations than their white counterparts. Utilizing a multivariate approach, these components were conceptualized in the current investigation, which attempted to quantify and extend the work of Jones and Hochner (1973), Carlston (1983), and George (1992).

Methodology

Upon studying informal (pick-up) basketball play at a large predominantly white midwestern university during the indoor basketball season, it was determined that distinct social norms regulated play. The best players, assessed by preliminary observations of skill orientations, congregated on two specific basketball courts at the primary recreational facility on campus. Varsity basketball players would join in some games when their sport was not in season. Mediocre players generally shied away from occupying the two courts during peak recreational periods.

Play was governed by a fixed set of rules. Games were over when a team scored 15 points and was ahead by two points. A basket was worth one point. Winning teams remained on the floor to play against new challengers. Teams were selected by an individual player who called "winners" on a first-come-first-play basis.

A total of fifty informal (pick-up) basketball games were observed over a period of ten weeks. Only racially isolated (all white or all black) teams were observed to preserve the homogeneity and continuity of the cultural paradigms that governed play among players of the same race. Some games contained two all-white or two all-black teams while other games included an all-black versus an all-white team.

Informal play was preferred over interscholastic, intercollegiate, or professional basketball games to ensure freedom of movement and decision making among the participants. Coaches inculcate restrictions on play through the implementation of coaching philosophy, discipline, and strategy. The success of this inquiry was dependent on the freedom of movement and decision making among the participants.

Observation teams consisted of two individuals who were not visible to the players. Game statistics were recorded by race on the following variables: shooting percentages, three-point attempts, forced shots, assists, number of passes before a shot, defensive rebounds, offensive rebounds, turnovers, steals and improvisational play. Shot charts were utilized to determine patterns of attempts at the basket.

The data recorded under improvisational play were pooled. This category included between the legs dribble, behind the back dribble, reverse pivot dribble, single or double pump before a shot, behind the back pass, between the legs pass, no-look pass, reverse lay-up, shake-and-bake moves, and other miscellaneous fakes and moves as they appeared. Each time a player attempted an improvisational move, a single point was scored.

One factor that could not be controlled by this investigation was the repeated involvement of some players or teams. Some teams were very good, defeated new opponents, and played two or three successive games. On other occasions, individual players would reappear randomly. This lack of control over repeated measures undoubtedly affected the results of the statistical procedures employed in this investigation.

However, it is felt that pick-up basketball games are governed by powerful cultural factors and norms that would confound any different theoretical approach. In retrospect, the intent of this investigation was to support a behavioral orientation among African American men rather than make any initial theoretical assumptions about specific race-based behaviors among African American and white males in informal pickup basketball games.

Results

Shooting

The data demonstrated that the African American players had lower shooting percentages than their white counterparts. Overall, whites made 54.8% of their shots while African American players made only 43.9% of their shots. The reasons for this disparity were apparent. Even though shooting outside the three-point line scored only one point, African American players made more attempts from beyond the three-point line than white players (AA = 3.70, w = 2.60). In addition, African American players took more forced shots (defender present) than white players (AA = 4.10, w = 2.70).

The African American players averaged fewer assists (AA = 0.56, w = 2.65) and fewer passes before each shot per game than their white counterparts (AA = 1.80, w = 3.40). All of the results in this category were statistically significant (F = 3.90, p < .05).

Rebounding

There was no significant difference between the two groups on the offensive rebounding variable. However, the African American players out-bounded their white counterparts on defensive rebounding by almost two to one (AA = 7.60, w = 3.90). This result was also statistically significant.

Improvisational Play

The African American players engaged in improvisational play (style) almost twice as often as the white players (AA = 6.32, w = 3.36). This finding was statistically significant. Although it was not reflected in the data, it was observed that improvisational play contributed to turnovers for African American players. There was no significant difference between the two groups on the average number of turnovers and steals per game.

TABLE 1   **Comparisons of Patterns of Play**

	Blacks	Whites
Shooting %	43.90	54.80*
3-Point Attempts	3.70	2.60*
Forced Shots	4.10	2.70*
Assists	0.56	2.65*
# Passes Before a Shot	1.80	3.40*
Defensive Rebounds	7.60	3.90*
Offensive Rebounds	5.20	5.40
Turnovers	3.90	3.89
Steals	2.90	2.80
Improvisational Play	6.32	3.36*

*Statistically significant (F = 3.90, p ≤ .05)

Discussion

The literature clearly established that African American males played basketball differently than white males for the most part. This investigation was able to support that assumption. Moreover, the data contained in this investigation suggests the rationalizations of Greenfield (1980), Jones & Hochner (1973), Carlston (1983), and Majors (1990) are valid.

The data suggests African Americans were more concerned about individual play and self-expression than were their white counterparts. The African American players had lower shooting percentages because they took more shots that were more difficult to make (three-point shots, defender present). However, those same shots generated the greatest amount of personal prestige if made. In addition, the African American players had fewer assists per game and passed less often, highlighting that an individual orientation was present. On the other hand, white players had more assists and initiated more passes per shot than their African American counterparts, suggesting a team orientation.

The data also revealed that African American players engaged in improvisational play (style) which was not specifically or directly related to shot making. Moreover, their engagement in improvisation sometimes led to turnovers. These findings further suggest the African American players were more concerned about individual self-expression (style) compared to white players. Consequently, the individual orientation for African Americans versus the team orientation for whites was present.

There were other components of this investigation which suggested that self-expression was more of an important factor to the African American players. The initial data collections in this investigation were made courtside. The recorders were not only visible to the players, but dialogue took place between the recorders and some players. However, only the African American players appeared to be curious about the presence of the recorders. When they learned that game statistics were being recorded on their pick-up games, they insisted the recorders watch closely as they played. Although the white players did make curious glances at the recording team, no verbal discourse took place at any time. It became necessary to discard the original data and to observe the games from a position not visible to the players.

It was anticipated that support for Carlston's (1983) rationalization for aggressive play among African American basketball players would appear in the data. It was forecasted that if this rationalization were valid, the African American players would lead in most or all statistical categories. The raw data validated Carlston's claim that African American players were more aggressive than white players. The African American players in this investigation took more three-point shots, took more forced shots, had more defensive rebounds, and averaged slightly more turnovers and steals per game. It would appear that Carlston's (1983) rationalizations are valid. In addition, it is plausible that African Americans play harder at sports, and basketball in particular, because it is a more important component of masculine role identity for African American males (Majors, 1990; Sailes, 1993).

Summary

It was the intent of this investigation to examine distinct patterns of play among African American athletes in basketball, a topic which is the focus of much discussion in popular sports culture, and to dispel some of the myths that permeate sport. It was not the intent of this investigation to determine one race's intellectual or physical superiority over the other. In fact, this investigation was able to support the contention that social and cultural variables were probably the primary reasons for the performance orientations of African American athletes. Current trends in sports commercialism suggest that African American performance orientations are the accepted norm for play among contemporary amateur and professional athletes. As such, they serve as the model for the development of future basketball players irrespective of race or gender.

Distinct patterns of play were evident in this investigation. While it is sometimes the popular belief that stellar performances by African Americans in sport can be attributed to genetic or physical differences from whites, this investigation was able to support the social rationalization that different environmental variables led to the development of divergent norms for sports performance orientations. More specifically, the sport socialization process generally has a greater impact in formulating athletic performance orientations than genetic or physical differences between African Americans and whites (Sailes, 1984).

While this investigation focused on the sport of basketball, its implications are far-reaching and have tangible meaning for other sports. There is clearly a need for more empirical research to understand and objectively interpret the relationship between race, culture, and sport participation.

References

Akbar, N. (1991). *Visions for Black Men*. Nashville: Winston-Derek Publishers.

Asante, M. (1988). *Afrocentricity*. Trenton, NJ: Africa World Press.

Ashe, A. (1993). *A Hard Road to Glory: A history of the African American athlete*. New York: Amistad Press.

Axthelm, P. (1971). *The City Game*. New York: Simon & Schuster.

Bell, D. (1992). *Faces at the Bottom of the Well: The permanence of racism*. New York: Basic Books.

Bledsoe, T. (1973). "Black Dominance of Sports: Strictly from Hunger." *Progressive* (June), 16–19.

Carlston, D. (1983). "An Environmental Explanation for Race Differences in Basketball Performance." *Journal of Sport and Social Issues*, 7, 30–51.

Coakley, J. (1994). *Sport in Society: Issues and controversies*. St. Louis: Times Mirror/Mosby.

Davis, L. (1990). "The articulation of difference: White preoccupation with the question of racially linked genetic differences among athletes." *Sociology of Sport Journal*, 7, 179–187.

Eitzen, S., and Sage, G. (1993). *Sociology of North American Sport*. Indianapolis: Brown & Benchmark.

George, N. (1992). *Elevating the Game: Black Men and Basketball*. New York: Harper/Collins.

Greenfield, J. (1980). "The Black and White Truth about Basketball: A skin-deep "theory of style." In Stubbs and Barnet (eds.), *The Little, Brown Reader* (2nd ed.). Boston: Little, Brown.

Hacker, A. (1992). *Two Nations: Black and White, separate, hostile, unequal New York*: Charles Scribner & Sons.

Hoose, P. (1989). *Necessities: Racial barriers in American sports*. New York: Random House.

Jones, J., and Hochner, A. (1973). "Racial differences in sports activities: A look at the self-paced versus reactive hypothesis." *Journal of Personality and Social Psychology*, 27, 86–95.

Leonard, W. (1993). *A Sociological Perspective of Sport*. New York: Macmillan Publishers.

MacDonald, W. (1981). "The Black sthlete in American dports." In W. Baker and J. Carroll (Eds.), *Sports in Modern America* (88–98). St. Louis: River City Publishers.

Madhubuti, H. (1990). *Black Men: Obsolete, dingle, dangerous*. Chicago: Third World Press.

Majors, R. (1990). "Cool pose: Black masculinity and dports." In M. Messner and D. Sabo (Eds.). *Sport, Men, and the Gender Order: Critical feminist perspectives* (109–114). Champaign, IL: Human Kinetics.

Miller, P. (1986). "The early Afro-American experience in sports." *Proteus*, 3, 60–66.

NBC Special Documentary Program. (1990, Spring). *The Black Athlete: Fact or fiction.*

Peterson, R. (1984). *Only the Ball was White.* New York: McGraw-Hill.

Phillips, J. (1976). "Toward an explanation of racial variations in top-level sports participation." *International Review of Sport Sociology*, II, 39–55.

Public Broadcasting System Documentary Film (1988, Fall). *Black Champions: A history of the Black athlete.*

Rust, E., and Rust, A. (1990). *Art Rust's Illustrated History of the Black Athlete.* Garden City, New York: Doubleday & Company.

Sailes, G. (1984). "Sport socialization comparisons among Black and White adult male athletes and non-athletes." Unpublished doctoral dissertation, University of Minnesota.

——— (1993). "An investigation of campus stereotypes: The myth of black athletic superiority and the dumb jock stereotype." *Sport Sociology Journal*, 10, 88–97.

Staples, R. (1982). *Black Masculinity: The Black male's role in American society.* San Francisco: Black Scholar Press.

Steele, S. (1990). *The Content of Our Character.* New York: St. Martin's Press.

Worthy, M., and Markle, A. (1970). "Racial differences in reactive versus self-paced sports activities." *Journal of Personality and Social Psychology,* 16, 439–443.

9

Perceptions of Athletic Superiority
A View from the Other Side

Louis Harrison, Jr.
Laura Azzarito
Joe Burden, Jr.

IN PHYSICAL EDUCATION CLASSES ALL LEARNING THAT OCCURS DOES not fall under the carefully planned and structured lessons presented by teachers (Kirk, 1992). Physical education and athletics are inextricably related by teachers who often serve as coaches of athletic teams. These teacher/coaches often unconsciously transmit values from the athletic realm to physical education classes. This unplanned and unrecognized transmission of values and beliefs is known as the 'hidden curriculum' (Fernandez-Balboa, 1993, p. 233). Often entrenched in this hidden curriculum are race-based stereotypes that provide students with distorted perceptions of physical abilities based on race. This qualitative study seeks to examine this phenomenon from the European American perspective. European American former and present athletes were interviewed regarding their sports experiences and views. Results indicate that European American athletes in this study appeared to be steered away from developing lofty athletic aspirations. This appears to be a consequence of strong race-sport stereotypes.

Introduction

Schools are presumed to be centers for learning concepts, skills, and techniques that will improve the quality of life for students. It has long been recognized that all learning that occurs in schools does not fall under the carefully planned and structured lessons presented by teachers. Students

Louis Harrison, Jr. and Joe Burden, Jr., "Perceptions of Athletic Ability: A View from the Other Side," *Race, Ethnicity and Education*, pp. 149-166. Copyright © 2004 by Taylor & Francis Group. Reprinted with permission.

glean a wealth of information informally during interactions with other students, teachers, coaches, administrators, and support personnel. Though often the information may be unintentionally transmitted during these interactions, they are no less important in developing the student's perception of the immediate setting, and the school environment. The student must then meld this with previous information gathered from their home and other environments to generate their own worldview. This informal unintentional learning that occurs in schools is socially constructed and has been labeled the 'hidden curriculum' (Fernandez-Balboa, 1993; Kirk, 1992).

Many middle and high school physical education teachers assume dual roles of teachers and coaches. As teachers, they endeavor to provide students with meaningful movement experiences that will facilitate the development of movement skills. These movement activities, more often than not, include the learning of sport skills and providing opportunities for learning and testing of skill acquisition through competition. Quite often this occurs under the supervision of a teacher/coach or in the presence of members of athletic teams. The attraction to and acquisition of sport skills is mediated by a number of factors including the social context in which the skills are presented, and the student's perception of the appropriateness of the skills (Harrison et al., 1999a, 1999b). The social context provided by the teacher/coach is inherently influenced by the ideas and attitudes emanating their social outlook and perspective. All of this information derives from socially constructed ideas and information found in abundance in the school environment.

Social Constructivist Theory

The process of acquiring knowledge, skills, and values leading to participation in various sports and physical activities could be explained within the conceptual framework of social constructivism. Social constructivist theory maintains that an individual's knowledge and meaning are culturally and socially developed (Vygotsky, 1978; Hollins, 1996). Formal or informal knowledge is formed and individual meanings are produced because of the interconnection between the context and individuals (Prawat, 1996). From a social constructivist perspective, context plays a powerful role in influencing understanding. Individuals' practice and attitudes are shaped or reinforced through the exchange of cultural ideas, information and actions embedded in specific contexts (Hollins, 1996). Perhaps, this suggests that unwritten ways of understanding and their actions contribute to forming dominant cultural knowledge and values, and therefore strengthen individuals' dominant stereotypical views. For example, the notion of race is still a pervasive stereotypical construct that functions to discriminate against African Americans in work places, schools and society. In fact, Ladson-Billings (1998) argues that race continues to be a powerful social construct in American society in general and specifically in school. African Americans encounter stratified educational barriers that are often difficult to overcome. The burden of history and its implications for political and social inequality are limiting factors in providing educational access and quality education among African Americans across the nation (Kozol, 1991).

Historical–Social Context

Historical and social factors that have constrained African Americans' access to education are intertwined with stereotypical views of African American's abilities in the classroom as well as in the realm of sports. Implicit and explicit messages, perceptions or values reflecting the dominant culture are transmitted through the hidden curriculum of physical education, and thus students' and teachers' ways of knowing and practices formed. Stereotypical messages implicit in physical education curricula are thought to be constructed to maintain positions of privilege, and enforce discrimination against individuals' participation in specific sports practices or physical education classes. Because schools are sites of acculturation, students, teachers and coaches often promote stereotypical views of racialized physical education and sports activities, reinforcing African Americans' perceived physical superiority and consequential intellectual inferiority when compared to European Americans. Because of prevalent stereotypes, many African American students may be channeled into pursuing athletic careers or steered away from academic careers, while European American students may be encouraged to pursue educational goals.

Critical Race Theory

Ladson-Billings (1998) argues for the employment of a critical race theory to explore these educational inequities. Critical race theory was developed to examine racial and social issues. Much of this theory is concerned with the role of the participants' voice in determining power in the discourse of racial justice. Critical race theory aids in constructing social reality by the use of the participants' experiences in social situations.

In the field of research in physical education, MacDonald et al. (2002) also suggests a socially critical perspective to understand issues of social justice, inclusivity and equality in sports and physical education classes. A critical examination of stereotypes of African American's physical superiority and intellectual inferiority is necessary to further understand how this stereotype functions as a limiting factor to African Americans' educational achievement. Similar to MacDonald et al. (2002), Sage (1997) urges educators and researchers to employ a critical social constructivist perspective to reflect on racialized discriminatory pedagogical practices occurring not only in educational classroom, but also specifically in gym and on the sports fields. These socially critical perspectives would allow researchers to examine teachers' or students' assumptions in sports and explore how stereotypes may contribute to students' experiences of racial discrimination in school settings (Fernandez-Balboa, 1997). By critically examining how students construct stereotypes, researchers and educators may provide insights into pedagogical practices in sports arenas and physical education classrooms and enhance equality and social change.

Findings have confirmed that preferences for, and active involvement in, specific sports, athletic competition, and physical activities differ according to gender, social and economic status, ethnicity and race (Greendorfer, 1994; Harrison, 1999; Harrison et al, 1999a, 1999b). However, while there has been considerable attention given to gender and socio-economic status, race continues to be a rather under-researched variable.

Need for Examination of Racial Issues

In an attempt to display racial neutrality and avoid the pitfalls of race research, many professionals have chosen to ignore race as an important variable in physical education research. Apple (1999) notes the conspicuous absence of race in education reform literature. In physical education and sport where the over and under representation of people of different races is so glaringly obvious, frank discussion is strikingly absent. While it may be politically correct and morally acceptable to exhibit behaviors and attitudes that espouse racial neutrality, many theoretical and philosophical views indicate that 'race matters' (see Coakley, 2001, pp. 242–278; Eitzen & Sage, 2003, pp. 285–306). It is important to note here that the notion of race is not based on mere hair texture, skin color, or anatomical features, but the shared experiences and background that bind those with similar features. It is the opinion of these authors that race as a social research variable in sport and physical education is often neglected, glossed over, or diluted with other concepts such as multi-cultural issues or diversity. We know that racial opinions, feelings, and beliefs operate in both subtle and powerful ways even when there is no explicit intention. Unfortunately, racial discourse in education is curiously absent or under-discussed in the academic arena (Apple, 1999). In the academic domain where the quest for knowledge is at the core of our mission, the discourse on race is conspicuously absent. This topic is long overdue for frank, constructive, and productive discussion (Carter & Goodwin, 1994).

Recent attempts to investigate the psychosocial influence of race in sport and physical activity have yielded interesting, though not surprising results. In a recent survey (Harrison, 1999) respondents overwhelmingly indicated that certain racial groups were more likely to participate in particular sports and physical activities. Harrison et al. (1999a) demonstrated in their study that adolescents' development of sport specific schemata, perceived competence, and future aspirations for sport involvement varied by race and gender. Because athletic competition, sport and physical activity are strongly impacted by social influences, youth may be channeled into different athletic teams, sports and physical activities based on different racial groups. Harrison (2001a) also suggested that perceived abilities in particular sports may vary by both the race of the participant, and the race of whom the participant was compared.

The study of race as an important factor in sport and physical activity is spurred by the obvious over-representation of African Americans in particular sports. Even casual observation of televised sport displays the noticeably disproportionate number of African Americans in particular sports.

For example, while African Americans comprise approximately 12% of the country's population, they make up 78% of the National Basketball Association, 67% of the National Football League, 63% of the Women's National Basketball Association, 13% of Major League Baseball (Lapchick & Matthews, 2001), and are prominent in boxing and track and field competition. Because African Americans appear to be the dominant participants in these widely televised and popular sports, the prevailing but often unspoken stereotypes of African American athletic superiority has permeated American society (Stone et al., 1997).

The idea of suggesting athletic superiority based on race is by no means a new concept. Many researchers have postulated physiological (for a review see Samson & Yerles, 1988), psychological (Worthy & Markle, 1970), and anthropometric (Meredith & Spurgeon, 1976, 1980; Spurgeon & Meredith, 1980) theories of African American sport and physical activity superiority. These theories directly or indirectly attribute exceptional sport performance by African Americans to innate abilities. While differences between African Americans and European Americans, with regard to anthropometric and physiological variables have been studied, it has been pointed out that the differences are relatively small and do not account for the immense disparity observed in professional and collegiate sports (Hunter, 1998).

A host of sport sociologists (see Carlston, 1983; Majors, 1990; Harrison, 1998; Coakley, 2001) propose views that dispute the above mentioned assertions. These authors postulate that any real differences between African American and European American sport performances are predicated on the differences in the social environments and influences that impact our lives. These sociologists contend that the differences observed are a function of the social forces that shape us, not the genetic or biological materials that make us.

Sport and physical activity represent one of the infrequent examples of a domain in which African Americans are stereotyped as superior in terms of performance. It also represents one of the few areas in which European Americans are stereotyped as inferior (Stone et al., 1991; Stone et al., 1999). These stereotypes about athletes are over-generalized views that one's racial group affiliation is the cause of athletic success or failure.

For young people, schools are the most common place to receive and exchange social knowledge. Therefore schools probably are the place where much stereotypical knowledge and ideas are exchanged and consumed. Athletic practices and events, physical education classes and unstructured sport participation are fertile venues for the formation and cultivation of stereotypes. These stereotypic ideas can be exchanged, absorbed, and reinforced by both nonmembers and members of stereotyped groups. Oakes et al. (1994) point out the propensity to identify with a salient group is known as self-stereotyping. This self-stereotyping is particularly potent when attributes of one's own group are viewed as desirable (Biernat et al., 1996). It has been shown that subtle activation of positive stereotypes enhances academic performance in both adults (Shih et al., 1999) and children (Ambady et al., 2001). The impact of negative intellectual stereotypes has been shown to be detrimental to academic performance (Steele & Aronson, 1995; Steele, 1997). While the pervasive stereotypes of athletic superiority in African Americans have been studied to some degree (Stone et al., 1997; Stone et al., 1999), the research in this domain is far from exhaustive.

Interestingly, a preponderance of the research in this domain has focused on the African American athlete. Hunter (1998) reviews the physiological literature with reference to race differences and concludes that the studies that describe quantitative physiological differences between the races report relatively small differences that do not account for the racial disparity observed in the major sports. Furthermore, small differences in anatomy, physiology, genetics, or biomechanics are not necessarily analogous to superior sport performance.

As with most phenomena, the reason for African American sport participation and performance is probably not as unidimensional as some suggest. Many factors have been cited that give logical explanations for the racial disparity in sport. But again, to this point the vast majority of research and theoretical reasoning has focused on the African American athlete. Implicit in this point of view is that European Americans are neutral or passive spectators that have little or no impact on the obvious racial disparity in the major sports. But how can one come to any reliable conclusions on this subject without first examining all of the variables from all perspectives?

A View from the Other Side

To this point no known research has investigated this phenomenon from the European American perspective. Lee (1983) found that European American youth and African American youth's sport aspirations at the high school level were significantly different. Harrison et al. (1999a) also found evidence that the sport aspirations of African American and European American junior high school students were significantly different. In this study African American males had loftier sport aspirations than European American males and aspirations of African American females were also higher than that of European females. Coakley (2001, p. 255) reports the response of an athletically involved European American sixth grader when asked if he would try out for track and basketball when he went to junior high school. The student was from a predominantly European American elementary school and had no previous experience competing against African American children. His response was 'I won't have a chance because all the black kids at the junior high will beat me out.' Coakley suggests that often European Americans avoid participation in sports where there is a preponderance of African American participation. Washington Post writer, Michael Wilbon (2002), recalls an incident:

> Fifteen years ago when I was still playing pickup basketball, a white kid in upper Northwest was the best ball handling guard in the neighborhood. He probably was one of the best in the city, and he was 13. Suddenly and inexplicably, he stopped showing up to play. I ran into his parents one evening at the grocery store and asked why he had stopped coming to the playground. And the father

said, 'He's just a skinny white kid. Why should he waste his time playing against all those black players?'

Could there be something in European American culture that steers these athletes from aspiring to collegiate and professional careers in sport? If so could this be an important component of the disparity observed in participation patterns in particular high school, college and professional sports? Could there be something in European American culture that steers these athletes away from, or dampens their collegiate and professional sport aspirations? Are there overlooked factors in European American social development that stifles the desire to seek higher level sport participation? If so, could this be an important component of the disparity observed in particular college and professional sports? Could this be an overlooked variable in this line of research? In an attempt to answer these questions we propose a qualitative analysis of interviews of several European American former high school athletes.

The Present Study

The purpose of this study was to investigate European American students' experiences in high school sports, and the impact of their culture on athleticism in high school and aspirations in college. Specifically, this research focuses on understanding (a) to what extent participants in this study were steered away from participating in high school sports and aspirations for collegiate and professional careers in sports; and (b) which overlooked factors in European American social development stifle the desire to participate in high school athletics and higher level sports.

Data Collection and Analysis

A qualitative approach was used in this study to investigate the participants' perspective on the phenomenon of athletic superiority based on race. This research took place in a public university in the southeastern United States. A sample of 25 participants were selected based on the following characteristics: (a) the participants were European American college students; (b) all the participants were former high school athletes; and (c) the participants had experiences playing or competing on a high school team with African American students/teammates. While the number of African American teammates were not specified, all participants indicated a significant number of African American teammates. All of the participants signed informed consent documents agreeing to participate in the study.

The data collection process included a formal interview and was conducted by a research staff of three African American and two European Americans collaborators (graduate students). Each interview was 45–75 minutes long. The collaborators that conducted the interviews were carefully trained to enhance trustworthiness of the interview procedure and resulting data. In particular, interviewers were instructed on how to pose questions in a neutral manner, how to ask probing questions to advance the richness of the data, and how to increase data validity by limiting data contamination through their own subjective perspectives. The collaborators were chosen to conduct the interviewees with the intention of ensuring interviewees' confidence in discussing discrimination and preserving their perspectives on racial issues in sports. The training of staff prior to and during the data-collection procedure lasted for 4 weeks, for a total of 12 hours. Though the race of the collaborators were of initial concern, data analysis revealed no recognizable differences in the responses with regard to the race of the collaborators.

The formal interviews in this study used an open-ended question approach. A sample of the questions that guided the interviews follows:

1. Were you ever in a situation in which you perceived that there was racial discrimination while participating in high school sports? Explain.
2. Were there any people in your life that appeared to steer you away from aspiring to participate in collegiate/professional sports? Who? How did they do this?
3. What did you think about this situation? How did this influence the way you felt about sport participation?
4. How has this experience affected your life?
5. Explain if and how race influences sports performance.

The interviews were conducted in a quiet area to ensure that participants felt comfortable. All the interviews were audio taped, transcribed verbatim and analyzed. Member checks were performed by having transcriptions reviewed and verified by interviewers and interviewees for accuracy and preservation of meaning. An inductive data analysis was conducted to identify categories and themes emerging from the data collected. All the data were reduced and organized by using the NUDIST qualitative data software. By using constant cross-comparison of differences and similarities of the data collected from the interviews, the researchers organized the data in categories (Patton, 1990). NUDIST qualitative software was useful in organizing and reducing data into categories by inductive content analysis. To identify and group categories with NUDIST, researchers utilized inductive questions based on the social critical perspective and the purpose of the research project. For example, throughout the NUDIST content analysis, researchers asked, how did students experience racial privilege or discrimination in their sports or physical education experiences? How did students perceive educational or sports careers? Were they encouraged to pursue educational or sports careers? How did the participants construct racial stereotypes? How did the participants perceive race as an influential factor in sports performance? After the inductive analysis, data organization and reduction into categories, researchers discussed the categorization process and emerging themes. The multiple analyst approach was used to check a reliability of the researcher that conducted the initial categorization of the data, and to ensure validity of the data (Patton, 1990; LeCompte & Preissle, 1993).

Results and Conclusions

Results of data analysis revealed two dominant emerging themes. The themes were reviewed and verified by the authors and research staff to bolster validity. In the first theme, participants indicated they were steered away from participating in specific sports by coaches and parents. In the second theme, findings identified participants' racial stereotypes as an influential factor in their participation and aspects of perceptions that contributed to the formation of those racial stereotypes. All names used in this manuscript are pseudonyms.

Steered Away!

Coaches believed blacks are better!

Of the 25 participants, only five gave no indication that they had been steered away from high-level sport participation. Some participants cited multiple reasons but most explanations seemed to fit into three basic categories: coaches, parents, and themselves. Many of the participants in this study perceived that they had been the objects or knew of others who had been targets of racial discrimination against European American athletes. They identified their coaches or parents as major agents in discouraging their participation in school athletics. In most cases they reported that coaches, both Black and White, gave preferences to African American athletes, particularly in basketball. Responses like the following typified this idea. Mark said:

> ... but when I tried out for basketball, granted I was small, I felt I did not get
> looked at by, I believe his name was coach Alvin. And I think he really looked at
> the Black athlete, didn't even [pause] ... nobody white played on his team.

Although Mark recognizes his height as a physical limitation compared to other basketball players, he noticed and reported the complete absence of white players on the high school basketball team. According to Mark, players' darker skin was an automatic device, a green card, adopted by coach Alvin to identify and select the most gifted athletes on the high school team.

Another participant, Jack, said of his basketball team: ' ... the coach was White and he tended to play the Black people more and I actually think he was scared to them is why.' Similar to Mark, Jack also believed his white coach was responsible for racial discrimination on the basketball team. Interestingly, Jack interpreted the coach's decisions as based on feelings of white fear or intimidation toward blacks. Pinar (2001) suggests that white male fear of blacks is due to a 'crisis of white masculinity'. According to Pinar, as a result of the white 'crisis of masculinity', blacks are often depicted by mass media and the public as aggressive and violent.

In several cases the discrimination was not considered overt, but implied in the language of the coach. The following statement, quoted by a participant, was made of a European American coach in humor, but portrays a pervasive attitude in this realm. The participant recalls the coach's speech:

> ... I remember one instance, our head football coach was talking to us, and he was going about, saying how you're man enough to ask the question but are you man enough to hear the answer? And then he looked at one of our White players and told him, he was like Mike, if you come to my office and ask why can't I play DB (defensive back)? Well I'm going to tell you that you are white and slow. So there were generalizations made that the more skilled positions would be played by African Americans.

This coach's response may have been an attempt at humor, but it carries a powerful and potent message to both African American and European American athletes. It would seem to indicate that the position of defensive back is and will be closed to European American athletes. According to many participants, coaches were not only responsible for steering white players away from playing on basketball teams, but also tended to racialize players' positions on the teams in which certain positions were often given to African Americans.

In middle and high schools, physical education teachers often hold most coaching positions. Therefore attitudes and actions in the athletic realm can easily spill over into physical education classes. Participants in this study viewed their athletic experiences in high school as limited by coaches' decisions about who could play on the teams. Race appeared to be a major selective factor. Because their racial beliefs and attitudes are perceived as having an impact on promoting and encouraging players, coaches may be important agents in producing and reproducing racial discrimination in school systems through athletic participation.

Parents said strive for academic and career success!

Students enter schools with a wealth of prior knowledge, experiences, and beliefs constructed within their social environments, and families. Often students' perceptions of schooling and sports may be influenced by their family's attitudes, and their experiences constrained by racialized views of academics and athletics. Several participants (10) indicated that their parents placed much more emphasis on academia than on sports. When asked if anyone steered them away from aspirations of becoming a college or professional athlete, Mike said:

> My mom did. When I was in high school I got recruited by some junior college to go play football. And she said well (Mike) are you going to make a career out

of this? And I said probably not you know. And she said do you think that you can play division one? I was like definitely not, I would play two years of Ju-Co and that would be it. And she was like, why waste time and abuse on your body if you can go to the school that you want to go to for academics and go ahead and get on with what you want to do with your life.

Obviously, sports participation was not a priority for this mother. Mike's mother perceived participating in sports as a waste of time and an abuse of the body, and schooling as a place for the exercise of the mind; his mother connects academic success with career and future success. The mind and the body are therefore viewed as split, a production of body-mind dichotomy. Specifically, this response echoes the common Eurocentric view of the body-mind dichotomy in which the mind is superior and the body is inferior (Bordo, 1993). Apple (1999) argues that this notion is pervasive in American society, particularly the educational system. This body-mind dichotomy can also be explained in racialized terms in which the mind is constructed around whiteness, and the body or the physical around blackness.

Another participant, Ken, who seemed to be influenced by a combination of his parents and peers, responded:

> ... my parents kept me grounded. They would always get on me about my grades and say well you know hopefully you play college football one day. If you really truly work, but you got to keep your grades up so you can have other options. But like people would say, sometimes like well why your playing basketball? You know you will never, you know, you don't jump high enough, you cannot run fast enough in high school.

This response indicates a multi-level affront to the participants' aspirations to further his sports participation. Again, the parents view sport as a subordinate to the primary goal of increasing academic performance. In this case, one way to discourage white students from participating in athletics and striving for sports success was to underline their limited physical skills. Ken's parents, while insisting that his academic endeavors should take priority, may be implying that their son's physical skills are inferior. His friends indicate that there are bodies capable of such performance, but that his body (a white body) is not one. This conception can be understood as part of constructed racial stereotypes of students' physical skillfulness or academic success. They use sport as a motivation to improve academic performance, while the participant's peers decompose his efficacy by disparaging his sport skills.

Several participants (12) indicated that their own perceptions of their athletic ability was the deciding factor. One response that was rather typical was: ' ... just my ability. Limiting myself. Nobody steered me away, I knew that I would never play college sports, I did athletics for fun and I did it just for something to do ...'

This suggests that the participant's self evaluation of his sports skills, however accurate, may have limited his sport participation aspirations. Similar to Ken's friends' conception of his limited physical performance, students themselves may believe they are not skilled or good enough. In summary, parents' and participants' self-perceptions of their physical abilities raises questions, to be further researched, about the extent to winch the white students' self ability concept in athletics is influenced by Eurocentric culture in American sports.

Stereotypical Perceptions

Many of the participants in this study communicated directly or indirectly their harboring of stereotypical perceptions. Stereotypical perceptions are socially constructed notions, often based on fallacious or limited information that can possibly have detrimental consequences or reproduce maladaptive stereotypical behavior (Harrison, 2001b). In this case, pervasive racial stereotypes were apparent in many responses of the participants. One participant, Robert, indicated that: 'There are more Blacks that play sports than Whites, well there is in basketball ... seems like white guys coach and ownership and all that.' Similar to Robert, another participant said:

> I think the predominant Black sports are football and basketball. I think Whites
> predominantly run baseball, which is the other top sport. And in the smaller
> sports, I think it is just performed ... well, I guess, ice hockey and lacrosse, I think
> those are predominantly white sports. Asians got ping-pong, that's for sure!

Both participants considered professional athletes in 'top sports' as predominately African American, especially in football and basketball. Robert even referred to Blacks as more active in playing sports than Whites, and noted the numbers of Whites predominant in coaching positions. The response reflects the powerful influence of racial stereotypes in sport and physical activity. Often efforts to appear politically correct or inoffensive may mask these stereotypes, but recent literature (Stone et al., 1997) attests to their pervasiveness. These authors demonstrated that participants listening to a broadcast of a college basketball game relied on socially pervasive stereotypes in assessing the abilities of players based on their perceived racial affiliation. Players identified as African American by the researchers were perceived as possessing better physical skills, while players perceived as European American were rated as having less talent. While political correctness and efforts to project racial neutrality form the facade of many people, the underlying reality is that these longstanding and potent stereotypes remain entrenched and strongly influence how we view the athletic performance.

A participant commenting on how African Americans and European Americans are different, alluded to how career opportunities varied by race.

I believe a Black man's way out is to go into sport. That is his ticket to college and hopefully as a career. But only 1% make it. Whereas I think more white guys with the exception of offensive linemen, pursue other things. Whether it is getting a job out of high school or furthering their education ... and I think it is two different cultures even though you grow up in the same country. And that's just the facts.

This participants' response reinforces the stereotypical notion that the only way to achieve success for African Americans is through sport performance. The converse of this theme also emerged. Participants in this study perceived that they were steered away from aspirations of participation in collegiate and professional sport and directed and motivated toward academic pursuits by coaches and parents. This notion, espoused by the coaches and parents of the participants in this study, reinforces the predominate stereotype of European American intellectual superiority. In our society it is easy to find evidence to reinforce this stereotype. With the exception of a relatively small number of academicians, few consider that the causes reside in inequitable educational opportunities and access to educational institutions. While improvement in race relations have taken place in recent years, true equal opportunities in all facets of life remain evasive.

Another participant, Leonard, indicated a similar response when he responded: 'Maybe just because they (African Americans) are better athletes. Maybe because more White people focus on being smart, succeeding, and making a lot of money in business. Black people mostly focus on sports and stuff.'

These responses reflect the depth and pervasiveness of racial stereotypes in the realm of sport. Race is so often stereotypically associated with different ethnic groups' performance of specific sports, that quite often this stereotypical thinking can mislead people to believe that those racial differences in sports participation are 'biological' or 'natural'. Leonard believed African American's higher rate of participation in sports could be explained by a biological difference, a physical superiority, compared to whites. At a time when espousing such ideas is deemed unpopular or politically incorrect it appears the suppression of overt expression of stereotypical beliefs does little to extinguish them.

Factors that Influenced Racial Stereotypes

In response to question five, (explain how race influences sport performance.) of the 25 participants, only four responded that they didn't believe race influenced sport performance. The participants yielded abundant and interesting but a varied array of responses. Those that responded in the affirmative gave multiple explanations for their responses that included socio-economic (15), genetics (16), culture (19), intelligence (5), psychological (17) and media influences (8).

One insightful and complex thinking participant, Greg, gave a rather detailed multiple categorical response:

> You know what, I don't know. I hear a lot about it and I hear it debated all the time and I think it does, not so much color of skin but what's happened throughout time and discrimination that's gone on in this country for so long has basically made the white socio-economic towards academics and making money and the African American has been so long considered the hard laborer of America and the country basically built on the backs of African American workers. You know, they're strong, big and aggressive people. You know they know what they want to get and when they go into sports they excel at it. I mean you see so many soft non-athletic white males that are great in school, my gosh I mean they can crunch numbers with the best of them but if you give them a baseball or anything else athletic that they can't do it because they've never been introduced to manual labor.

Apple (1999) explains how the educational system creates and reproduces racial relationships by privileging whiteness. As Apple argues 'for black male students, their supposedly "lesser ability" is tacitly assumed. "Valuable" students, then, are not usually Black' (p. 11). In contrast to understanding race as a social construct, Greg views race as a natural or essentialist category in which African Americans are associated with athletic prowess and whites with intellectual performance. Genetics is often used as a scientific explanation to construct the racial stereotypical view of Africans Americans success in sports. Greg continued:

> ... when you see black youth growing up they are constantly playing outdoors and their parents have hard jobs that they have to go and work everyday, and do physical things, so they are brought up with having to be very physical and I think that in itself has a correlation whether its scientific or not is a correlation to their excellence in manual jobs such as sports. There is a lot of people you see everyday that are the size of African Americans in the weight room and on the football field and in baseball. I mean you see that in the white population but not to the level that you see with black people. I think that whether it is genetic, socio-economic conditions, or attitude about sports between cultures; I'm not going to sit here and say that we're all the same because I think everyone knows that we're a little different. We grow up differently and that has an affect on sports.

Another factor that emerged from the interviews was the idea that African Americans are superior in sport activities due to their socioeconomic status. Greg's assumption underlines a generalization that African Americans' upbringing is more difficult because of economic disadvantages. Therefore, because of their low-socio economic status, the physical labor blacks are submitted to can play an important role in explaining African Americans' participation in sports. Greg sees blacks' upbringing as poorer than that of the average white person; sports, not academics, is therefore a chance for African Americans to gain economic success and recognition in society.

Another participant, Paul, attributed blacks' superiority in sports to genetic racial differences. Paul stated:

> I think it is just mainly those are more explosive sports. You need explosion to break through that line, vertical jump ... that's genetically [italics added] ... it's been proven blacks have more explosive type muscles than whites do or Asian. It has something to do with it that their power is a little bit better so when you get up into the upper echelon of professional sports. They are the ones that are going to have the extra little burst, extra power for them to break through that line quicker, rebound quicker.

The idea that race is a biological factor that influences sports performance is overwhelmingly embedded in and outside of the realm of sports. In this case., Paul's response reveals the stereotypical view of African Americans' innate athletic superiority. Similar to other participants, Paul views Blacks as 'naturally' physically skilled, confirming a pervasive stereotype of black physical superiority; the body-mind dichotomy underlying this belief, reproduces racial stereotypes. This stereotype also produces an educational and social system within a 'politics of whiteness' (Apple, 1999) in which African Americans are channeled into the realm of sports and whites into academic pursuits.

Differently from Paul, John perceived race as an influential psychological factor in the realm of sports performance, explaining:

> I don't think it necessarily influences performance as much as it influences perceptions of performance. Because like I know a lot of guys who would line up on the line of scrimmage and see a white guy across from them it would be one thing. But if they saw a black guy, they would be kind of intimidated by it. I was never personally like that until you play them you can't tell who is better anyway. But some guys may automatically be like this guy is big and black and I can't handle him. I think it influences performance that way because you are already at a disadvantage mentally so you are not playing your best so that guy will get the better of you because mentally you are not ready to go.

John's comments may lead one to believe that many white athletes may be so profoundly influenced by the race of their opponents that they may prime candidates for the self-fulfilling prophecy. Robert Merton (1948) originated the idea of the self-fulfilling prophecy, which is the tendency for one's expectations to elicit behavior that will confirm the expectation (Hamilton & Trolier, 1986; Myers, 1993). Edwards (1973) applies this self-fulfilling prophecy to the sport realm, using race as the source of performance expectations. Gilovich (1991) cites two types of self-fulfilling prophecies, the true self-fulfilling prophecy and the seemingly-fulfilled prophecy. The true self-fulfilling prophecies are those in which the person's expectation invokes the very behavior that was anticipated. As John suggests, a European American football athlete who anticipates superior athletic skills from an African American opponent and therefore acquiesces to defeat psychologically. The opponent sensing this acquiescence responds by performing with confidence and the prophecy is fulfilled. The acquiesce of the European American in this case causes superior performance in the African American opponent.

The seemingly-fulfilled prophecy refers to expectations that alter or limits another's responses in a way that it is difficult to disconfirm previous expectations. If a European American athlete believes that African American athletes are superior they may choose not to compete against them at all, thus the European American athlete has no chance to disconfirm the expectation.

Educational Implications

The school context is a rich amalgamation of beliefs, perceptions, and ideas that interact with society in general to exert an important influence on the content and context of student learning. In physical education classes and sport teams, the prevailing conceptions and stereotypes exert a notable influence on the participation patterns and aspirations of young people. It appears from this study the prevailing stereotypes regarding sport and physical activity are strongly perpetuated in the school environment from the viewpoint of both African American and European American students. While previous theoretical perspectives and research have studied this phenomenon from the viewpoint of African Americans, the outlook from the European American view is under-investigated. Some researchers suggest that the study of whiteness is an essential, but missing aspect of the study of race and racism in sport and physical education (Long & Hylton, 2002). The prevailing stereotype regarding the superiority of African Americans in sport and physical activity, coupled with the idea of European American intellectual superiority appears to be well entrenched in the lives of these participants. Some suggest that this notion is certainly not confined to the borders of the United States (Gilroy, 2000; Carrington & McDonald, 2001) but does appear to have firm grip in the realm of sport. This is apparent in the responses of the participants and is seemingly reinforced by those who influence the participant's lives. The responses from the participants imply that they are steered away from athletic pursuits and toward academic performance.

Many physical education candidates choose the profession based on their own experiences in sport and as a means of continuing that experience. Studies like this highlight some of the subjective experiences that need to be addressed during the teacher education process by teacher education programs. Students who have not brought the forefront of their conscious (and unconscious) perceived failures and negative experiences can not facilitate the dreams, desires and potential possibilities of their future students.

The results of this study point out the dire need for physical education teacher educators and practitioners to include the investigation and discussion of racial stereotypes in the content of their courses. Instructional strategies to reduce the negative effects of race-based competency perceptions should be developed. Frank discussions are needed to help dispel the racial myths and stereotypes that prevail in our society. As in sex education, if we evade the discussion of the facts, our students are vulnerable to the influence of misinformation myths, and stereotypes that permeate our society.

As renowned curriculum theorist William Pinar (1994) contends, 'we say we are what we know. But, we are also what we do not know. If what we know about ourselves—our history, our culture is distorted by delusions and denials, then our identity—as individuals, as Americans—is distorted' (p. 245).

References

Ambady, N., Shih, M., Kin, A. & Pittinsky, T. L. (2001) Stereotype's susceptibility in children: effects of identity activation on quantitative performance, *Psychological Science*, 12(5), 385–390.

Apple, M. W. (1999) The absent presence of race in educational reform. *Race, ethnicity and education*, 2, 9–16.

Biernat, M., Vescio, T. K. & Green, M. L. (1996) Selective self-stereotyping, *Journal of Personality and Social Psychology*, 71, 230–245.

Bordo, S. R. (1993) *Unbearable weight. Feminism, western culture, and the body* (Berkeley, University of California Press).

Carlston, D. E. (1983) An environmental explanation for race differences in basketball performance, *Journal of Sport and Social Issues*, 7, 30–51.

Carrington, B. & McDonald, I. (2001) 'Race', sport and British society, in: B. Carrington & I. McDonald (Eds) *'Race', sport and British society* (London, Routledge), 1–26.

Carter, R. T. & Goodwin, A. L. (1994) Racial identity and education, in: L. Darling-Hammond (Ed.) *Review of research in education* (Washington, DC, American Educational Research Association), 291–336.

Coakley, J. J. (2001) *Sport in society: issues and controversies* (Boston, McGraw-Hill).

Edwards, H. (1973) *Sociology of sport* (Homewood, IL, Dorsey Press)

Eitzen, D. S. & Sage, G. H. (2003) *Sociology of North American sport* (Boston, McGraw-Hill).

Fernandez-Balboa, J. M. (1993) Socio-cultural characteristics of the hidden curriculum in physical education, *Quest*, 45, 230–254.

——— (1997) Introduction: the human movement profession—from modernism to postmodernism, in: J. M. Fernandez-Balboa (Ed.) *Critical postmodernism in human movement, physical education and sport* (Albany, State University of New York Press), 3–10.

Gilovich, T. (1991) *How we know what isn't so* (New York, Free Press).

Gilroy, P. (2000) *Against Race: imagining political culture beyond the color line* (Cambridge, Harvard University Press).

Greendorfer, S. L. (1994) Sociocultural aspects of kinesiology, in: E. F. Zeigler (Ed.) *Physical Education and Kinesiology in North America Professional and Scholarly Foundations* (Champaign, IL, Stipes Publishing), 99–123.

Hamilton, D. L. & Trolier, T. K. (1986) Stereotypes and stereotyping: an overview of the cognitive approach, in J. F. Dovidio & S. L. Gaertner (Eds) *Prejudice, Discrimination, and Racism* (New York, Academic Press), 127–163.

Harrison, C. K. (1998) Themes that thread through society: racism and athletic manifestation in the African American community, *Race, Ethnicity, and Education*, 1, 63–74.

Harrison, L., Jr. (2001a) Perceived physical ability as a function of race and racial comparison, *Research Quarterly for Exercise and Sport*, 72, 196–200.

——— (2001b) Understanding the influence of stereotypes: implications for the African American in sport and physical activity, *Quest*, 53, 97–114.

——— (1999) Racial attitudes in sport: a survey on race-sport competence beliefs, *Shades of diversity: issues and strategies: a monograph series*, 2.

Harrison, L. Jr., Lee, A. & Belcher, D. (1999a) Self-schemata for specific sports and physical activities: the influence of race and gender. *Journal of Sport and Social Issues*, 23, 287–307.

Harrison, L. Jr., Lee, A. & Belcher, D. (1999b) Race and gender differences in the sources of students' self-schemata for sport and physical activities, *Race, Ethnicity and Education*, 2, 219–234.

Hollins, E. R. (1996) *Culture in School Learning* (Mahwah, NJ, Lawrence Erlbaum).

Hunter, D. W. (1998) Race and athletic performance: a physiological review, in: G. A. Sailes (Ed.) *African Americans in Sport* (New Brunswick, Transaction Publishers), 85–101.

Kirk, D. (1992) Physical education, discourse, and ideology: bringing the hidden curriculum into view, *Quest*, 44, 35–56.

Kozol, J. (1991) *Savage inequalities. Children in America's schools* (New York, Crown Publishers).

Ladson-Billings, G. (1998) Just what is critical race theory and what's it doing in a nice field like education? *Qualitative Studies in Education*, 11, 7–24.

Lapchick, R. E. & Matthews, K. J. (2001) *Racial and Gender Report Card* (Boston, MA, Northwestern University Center for the Study of Sport in Society).

Lecompte, M. & Preissle, J. (1993) *Ethnography and Qualitative Design in Educational Research* (Boston, MA, Academic Press).

Lee, C. C. (1983) *An Investigation of the Athletic Career Expectations of High School Athletes.*

Long, J. & Hylton, K. (2002) Shades of white: an examination of whiteness in sport, *Leisure Studies*, 21, 87–103.

MacDonald, D., Kirk, D., Metzler, M., Nilges, L. M., Shempp, P. & Wright, J. (2002) It's all very well, in theory: theoretical perspectives and their applications in contemporary pedagogical research, *Quest*, 54, 133–156.

Majors, R. (1990) Cool pose: black masculinity and sports, in: M. A. Messner & D. F. Sabo (Eds) *Sport, Men, and the Gender Order: Critical feminist perspectives* (Champaign, IL, Human Kinetics), 109–114.

Meredith, H. V. & Spurgeon, J. H. (1976) Comparative findings on the skelic index of black and white children and youths residing in South Carolina, *Growth*, 40, 75–81.

Merton, R. K. (1948) The self-fulfilling prophecy, *Antioch Review*, 8, 193–210.

Myers, D. G. (1993) *Social psychology* (New York, McGraw-Hill).

Oakes, P. J., Haslam, S. A. & Turner, J. C. (1994) *Stereotyping and Social Reality* (Cambridge, Blackwell).

Patton, M. Q. (1990) *Qualitative Evaluation and Research Methods* (Newbury Park, Sage Publications).

Pinar, W. (1994) *Studies in the Postmodern Theory of Education* (New York, Peter Lang).

——— (2001) *The Gender of Racial Politics and Violence in America* (New York, Peter Lang).

Prawat, R. S. (1996) Learning community, commitment and school reform, *Journal of Curriculum Studies,* 28(1), 91–110.

Sage, G. H. (1997) Sociocultural aspects of human movement: the heritage of modernism, the need for postmodernism, in: J. M. Fernandez-Balboa (Ed.) *Critical Postmodernism in Human Movement, Physical Education and Sport* (Albany, State University of New York Press), 11–26.

Samson, J. & Yerles, M. (1988) Racial differences in sports performance, *Canadian Journal of Sport Science*, 13, 109-116.

Shih, M., Pittinsky, T. L., & Ambady, N. (1999) Stereotype susceptibility: identity salience and shifts in quantitative performance, *Psychological Science*, 10(1), 80–83.

Spurgeon, J. & Meredith, H. V. (1980) Secular change of body size and form of black American children and youths living in the United States, *Anthrop Kozl*, 24, 237–240.

Steele, C. M., & Aronson, J. (1995) Stereotype threat and the intellectual test performance of African Americans, *Journal of Personality and Social Psychology*, 69, 797–811.

Steele, C. M. (1997) A threat in the air: how stereotypes shape intellectual identity and performance, *American Psychologist*, 52(6), 613–629.

Stone, J., Lynch, C. I., Sjomeling, M. & Darley, J. M. (1999) Stereotype threat effects on black and white athletic performance. *Journal of Personality and Social Psychology*, 11, 1213–1227.

Stone, J., Perry, Z. W. & Darley, J. M. (1997) 'White men can't jump': evidence for the perceptual confirmation of racial stereotypes following a basketball game, *Basic and Applied Social Psychology*, 19, 291–306.

Vygotsky, L. (1978) *Mind in Society: The development of higher psychological processes* (Cambridge, MA, Harvard University Press). 166 L. Harrison, Jr. et al.

Wilbon, M. (2002) To NBA's European stars, 'bid white stiff doesn't translate. *Washington Post.* Available online at: www.washingtonpost.com/wp-dyn/articles/A33377-2002May4.html.

Worthy, M. & Markle, A. (1970) Racial differences in reactive versus self-paced sports activities, *Journal of Personality and Social Psychology*, 16, 439–443.

10

Talented Genetics or Genetically Talented
The Historical Rationale for Black Athletic Success

Tina Hunt
Isaac Ivery
Gary Sailes

THERE HAS BEEN A LONG ENSUING DEBATE REGARDING TALENT AND whether or not it truly exists, or if it is a manifestation of environmental influences. Proponents of natural talent believe that some individuals are simply gifted and are more adept at performing certain activities than others. However, how can it stand that an individual is a 'natural' at something? One does not excel at swimming, for example, right from birth, or even one's very early years. It stands to reason that learning takes place, and advocates of the environmental influences and learning side believe that it is through practice, specifically deliberate practice, that provides for an individual to acquisition expertise. Arguers of genetics say that an individual who inherits genes from an athletically capable mother and father are much more likely to become athletically advanced. Well, if the child has received two recessive genes with athletic ability being the dominant genes, then that athletic capability of the parents means nothing, as the offspring has not inherited it. Even so, the supposed 'talent' the child has inherited will not manifest itself if practice and learning does not take place; sitting on a couch all day will not bring out the ability in this supposedly 'talented' athlete.

In considering genetic and environmental influences, one cannot ignore the social aspects of the environment as well, which are now becoming paramount in how sports participation and ability are perceived. Consider such sports as basketball and football, which dominate American sports media. Then consider the athletes that are the focus of the media's attention, the athlete's that dominate their respective sports: the athletes who are taller, faster, bigger, stronger ... and quite often Black. Black athletes grace newspaper and sports magazines covers; they are featured in television highlights of the day's game, and are talked about over radio broadcasts. These athletes dominate sports. Not to say that their White counterparts are inferior nor do not have their own share of media dominance, as they certainly do. People speak of these Black athletes and their impressive sports performances with regards to the individual athlete, all the while unknowingly conversing about the dominance of the Black athlete. It is as if people are afraid to talk about it, and they are. It is a taboo subject for some, but why? Have not America and the world come a long way since the days of slavery, segregation, and prejudice? These athletes are awesome, powerful, and 'talented' human beings, and that ability and 'talent' had to come from somewhere, just like everyone else. Is it a genetic advantage? Are they physiologically superior to other athletes? Or is it a question of mere talent; is it something that is unexplainable and natural? Consider genetics and innate talent, and also consider practice and the environment. Combine that with the social influences experienced by each individual on a daily basis, and an equation that can result in failure or success emerges. It is a matter of perception and knowledge, and what the individual chooses to do with it.

Referring back to the acquisition of elite performance, and the notion that it is learned, one must make note that learned movements, often termed skills, are part of two classes of movements. The first class may be regarded as genetically defined, being inherited or self-differentiated, and pertain to the way in which one controls one's limbs, as well as reflexive actions. The second class can be thought of as the learned movements (Schmidt & Lee, 2005), such as learning to write and performing the triple lutz in figure skating. Therefore, can it not be said that when an individual has acquired the ability to write, and even to write in a neat and legible manner, that they have acquired expert performance (with regards to writing)? The same goes for performing the triple lutz in figure skating events; the skater performs various routines and progressions to get to that point, which quite often takes several years to achieve.

Going back to the discussion of the Black athletes and their dominance in the sporting arena, many raise the point of education and availability of practice times and facilities, as well as quali-fied individuals to coach and instruct. The belief that these athletes often come from homes and schools where education is at subpar levels, and sports teams were clubs after school just to keep kids off the street, is a bit of a stretch. It certainly lends its hand to the advocates of innate talent, because if these athletes have no place to learn, how did they ever become so good? However, this may be where media influence emerges and instills images of duress and hardship in our minds when associating with the Black athlete (after all, consider it preposterous that these athletes live similar lives to their White counterparts and came out better).

With this paper, it is the goal of the authors to explore and analyze the current research on the topics of genetics and talent, and combine it with the sociological influences relating to athletic success. By uncovering aspects related to human biology, physiology and anatomy, as well as the sociologically driven aspects of human behavior, one hopes to reveal new correlations among the aforementioned, and possibly a new argument for the talent debate. Granted, not everyone can achieve high levels of performance, but as seen with elite performers, they have overcome many obstacles and practice significantly more than those individuals who do not perform at the elite level. It is the goal of this paper to investigate why.

Learning of a Task

Individuals seeking to perform at the elite level, and for those that already do, consider practice to be of utmost importance. Research has shown that the superior performance of experts and elite individuals and the characteristics of these performances are attributable to the experience and time allocated to the desired activity, with usually a ten year minimum (Ericsson, Krampe, & Tesch-Römer, 1993). There is a difference between practice and deliberate practice, however, as deliberate practice is inherently less enjoyable, and involves specific tasks to overcome weakness whereby individuals constantly work towards improvement. Some individuals, however, may enjoy deliberate practice because of the successful outcome. Engaging in deliberate practice requires a great deal of motivation and effort, and individuals working towards expertise and elite performance must keep that end result in mind. In essence, they are planning for the long-term and working in the short-term. In a survey of NCAA Division I athletes, it was found that they attributed more successful athletes as having benefited from more experience and training, as well as athletic talent, when compared with less successful athletes (Hyllegard, McElroy, & Krejca, 2003). In other words, even the athletes themselves, whether the more or less successful, recognize the importance of training and experience. With training, there is no question that techniques and methods have greatly evolved over the years, contributing to greater amounts of success, and possibly contributing a hastening affect on the ten year minimum in the deliberate practice theory. As a hypothetical proposition, one may take note that innovations in training techniques enhance the ability of an individual to place greater demand on the body during a single training session. This may increase the rate of neuromuscular adaptation, and therefore the rate at which learning may occur, as an individual may be allowed to progress through the stages of training more quickly. This area warrants further investigation.

When analyzing population data, it may be noted that as a whole, each generation is taller, heavier, and markedly more skilled because of these increases than the generation before (Rowland, 2002). These are reflections of evolution. Every race and every life form evolves over time; it is unavoidable. Needless to say, the evolution of the human population has contributed to increased ability of experts. With this, however, comes athlete selection, which lends itself to youth being selected due to differences in height and perceived ability at an early age to being selected for more specialized training, which transfers into deliberate practice. This athlete selection, per se, can also lead to a socialization aspect, in which the young athlete will gravitate towards participation in activities that are best suited for his or her height and maturity status, and be selected for more advanced training from there.

A model for youth's socialization into sport was proposed by Côté and Hay (2002) that follows a progression through what they termed the 'sampling phase', to the 'specializing years', to the 'investment/recreation phase'; the model also acknowledges that participants may drop out at any time. Beginning with the sampling phase, children take part in a wide variety of activities, with their key motivation being fun and enjoyment and the emphasis being structured or deliberate play as opposed to deliberate practice. As the child becomes older and progresses with their activities, they may choose to move on to the specializing phase, where deliberate practice begins to take on a key role. Beginning deliberate practice at this age correlates with the research carried out by Ericsson, Krampe, and Tesch-Römer (1993), whereby experts began deliberate practice at an early age and continued to do so until expert performance was achieved, on average ten years after commencing deliberate practice. After the specializing phase, the individual can choose to drop out (as the case with any phase), enter into the recreational phase to play for fun, or to enter the investment phase. By entering into the investment phase the individual has decided to commit more seriously to his or her choice activity, with more intensive training and competitive success. The focus here is on Long-Term Athlete Development (LTAD), which progresses athletes from the early stages of fun and play, to the more advanced stages of intensive training and deliberate practice. In the MacPhail and Kirk study (2006), some of the athletes commented on the change in difficulty from the sampling phase, to the specialization phase, to the investment phase, stating that the introductory group (as was termed by the Forest Athletic Club where the study was taking place) had involved "'doing lots of drills and short things' and that the more specialised group entailed 'running around the track' and 'the coach timing you' (65)." As evidenced by this study, deliberate practice begins at an early age, and individuals make the choice to continue. There were some contrary findings to the Ericsson, Krampe, and Tesch-Römer (1993) study, however, as some of the athletes commented that they enjoyed deliberate practice; some because they were becoming more successful, and others enjoyed the more structured and intense training.

Socialization

How do the theories of deliberate practice and Côté and Hay play in to the success of the Black athlete? Consider the sports that Black athletes dominate and excel in: basketball, football, and track and field. When these athletes are young, they group together and play unorganized pick-up basketball games and football games. They head down to the local courts, join local clubs (namely track and field), and/or stay after school to play some ball. They socialize together, and begin playing for fun at a young age (sampling phase). As they grow older and join teams in high school, practice sessions become more involved (specializing phase). By this time, many of them have had nearly ten years of experience in their respective sports, and are near entrance of the investing phase, which they may begin late in their high school or early collegiate years. They have quite unknowingly set themselves up for success by commencing participation in these sporting activities at such an early age. This concept of course applies to those individuals who did not drop out during any of the phases.

Exposure to deliberate practice is also evidenced in team sports, such as those the Black athlete commonly participates in. Though practices may be viewed differently, experts in team sports still have gone through approximately ten years of training before achieving the expert level (Helsen, Starkes, and Hodges, 1998). Another question must be drawn from this data, however, and that is, why these sports? What draws Black athletes to football, basketball, and track and field? Yes, they begin early, but there is a socialization aspect unique to how Black athletes enter sport. An argument quite often made is that of the economic status of Blacks; that they have lower-income jobs and paying for tennis lessons or swimming lessons is not within their budget, but going out to the local courts and playing a game of basketball or heading to the track to run some laps is, as doing so does not require a fee. Geography also may contribute, as Blacks live in urban areas where there is not as much space allocated to aquatic and tennis facilities. It is difficult pinpoint, however, the exact sociological mechanism that drives the young Black athlete toward a certain sport. Media images no doubt play a large role, as an aspiring youth sees images of a Black athlete slam-dunking the basketball during a televised basketball game, that elite player becomes that child's hero, and that young athlete gravitates towards that sport. Again, however, success and/or talent is not manifested unless learning and training (deliberate/intensive) takes place, which is touched upon by Sailes in his paper, The Myth of Black Sports Supremacy (1991):

> The research appears to support the contention that the Black athlete may enjoy physical advantages over his White counterpart, but these advantages are insignificant unless they are fully developed through vigorous training and by participating in a nurturing and competitive environment that creates an opportunity for athletic success (485).

Here again, one is drawn back to the theory of deliberate practice. Socialization contributes to deliberate practice because it brings in the participants. Athletes will come together to work together; they will push each other through hard practices and performances so that they can prove to themselves, and everyone else, that they are capable of achieving the best. It is also possible, however, that this drive for top performance combined with the effects of socialization may solidify athletic skills and techniques at a faster rate. Therefore, the Black athlete who achieves athletic expertise at an age that is seemingly earlier than usual, even when the deliberate practice theory is applied, may have matured athletically more quickly due to these effects.

Another factor in the success equation that cannot be left out is the media. As a contributor to the socialization effects, the media can be very influential when it comes to promoting the images of African American athletes. Whether positive or negative, the fact that Black and White athletes are treated differently by the media affects the way that they are viewed by the public (the "if he's White, put him in the spotlight; if he's Black, but him in the back" attitude). Children identify with athletes of the same race and desire to mimic their favorite athlete's style of play. In such an aspect, the media becomes a very powerful tool that gives today's youth a chance to see their favorite players and learn their favorite moves. This goes against the fact that Black athletes have had their success in sport attributed to their 'natural' abilities. The media has portrayed reoccurring images that have furthered the stereotypes that the Black athlete is characterized as having "natural athleticism," which is consistent with racist theories that insinuated that Black athletes possess physiological characteristics that contribute to them having superior speed, reflexes, and jumping ability (Wilson, 2001). With the media constantly portraying these stereotypes, children are learning each day that they are supposed to perform a certain way just because of their race. Former NBA star Danny Ainge was actually considered to be among the naturally elite players in the mid 1980s because he had the widest range of athletic skills. Ainge was actually considered to be a better all-around player than Michael Jordan, but his talents were minimized by his coach who insisted that "he was not the most gifted," but he got the most of what little he had. Ainge could actually touch the top of the square of the backboard in high school, but this conflicted with the expectations of white basketball players so he was never acknowledged for it (Hall, 2002). White children that watch basketball will see Ainge's style of play and try to adopt that style, all the while unaware that he has other abilities that are not recognized by the media. They will learn to be complacent and, as a result, they will fall into the stereotype of the typical White basketball player. On the other side, Black children will learn the opposite style of play by watching a player like Michael Jordan. Michael Jordan has what is considered an "above the rim" game, which contributes to the stereotype of the Black athlete and their athleticism by referring to the idea of the Black athlete's natural talent and jumping ability.

Sport commentators contribute to the perceived differences between Black and White athletes with the way in which they describe the athletic skill and the highlights of the players in the game. When a commentator is talking about a Black player, they use phrases such as "look at his leaping ability" or "he is such a great athlete." If the commentator is talking about a White athlete, the phrases compliment the hard work the individual has put in to the game, and how that individual uses his head to play the game (YAAAMS, 2001). This contributes to the way that children learn how to play specific sports. Watching others play is a form of visual learning, which helps children understand how to play sports better without having to practice every day. This raises the question, can one attribute the athletic ability of the Black athlete to 'natural ability,' or does one acquisition these skills through different forms of learning? Media influence can contribute to the way today's youth learn how to play a sport. The images on television and the internet lead people to believe that Blacks and Whites are supposed to play sports a certain way. Such descriptions and perceptions perpetuate a stereotype that Black athletes have natural athletic ability, when in fact, some of their athletic skill can be attributed to what they have learned by viewing sports, whether on the television or in person.

Genetics

The theories behind genetics have been another stereotype that has contributed to why people believe that Black athletes are so successful in sports. It is said that Black athletes possess certain genes that make them better for certain sports because it gives them the physical ability that is needed to be better players. Black athletes are considered to have 'natural athleticism' because the arguments that support this theory are based on observable and measureable physical and physiological genetics. The suggestion is that physical characteristics such as body size, physiological facts of muscle differences, enzymes, and cell structure is the basis for why black athletes have an advantage in athletics (St. Louis, 2003). As mentioned previously, Black athletes have been considered to have better jumping and sprinting abilities. Black athletes are not typically given credit for the work that is put in to their athletic ability. Stating that an individual is 'naturally talented' is comparable to passing off the work that individual has put in, and in the case of Black athletes, it may be considered a way to avoid admittance that they do put their fair share of work in.

Practice is important in developing the 'natural' skill and techniques applicable to sports and it is one of the deciding factors in whether or not a Black athlete will make it in the professional league. Harvard psychiatrist Alvin F. Poussaint refers to the success of Black athletes with his opinion. Poussaint attributes the success of Black athletes to the fact that they want to "outclass whites on the ballfield, on the dance floor, and in the boxing ring." The desire to be the very best leads to more practice which helps the athlete increase their overall skill level. Once again, a reference to deliberate practice may be applied. The Black athlete's desire to become the best fuels their drive to practice harder and more often, giving them a playing advantage.

Legrand Clegg (1980) published an essay in pertaining to Malachi Andrews study in which Andrews and his researchers "discovered" that melanin, rather than being a fairly inert pigment, was important for its ability to protect the skin from harmful effects of the sun. This was believed to be important in the athletic success of Black athletes because it meant that they were able to absorb a lot of energy (solar) which in turn could be used to achieve superior speed in running events (Wiggins, 1989). Clegg may have been in accord with Andrews, but much of the information has been accounted to a sense of ethnic pride and the rather symbolic importance that athletic success played in the Black community. The misinformation with Andrews research is quite palpable, as human beings are not capable of absorbing solar energy and using that energy for their own expenditure; humans are not capable of photosynthesis and therefore that statement cannot be true. It is just another example of how stereotypical statements have influenced the perception of Black athlete's success. The study was another example of how society used the genetics of Black athletes to attribute their abilities to factors outside of meaningful practice and hard work, which are words that commentators often use to describe their counterparts. Another concept that may be taken from this study is one that has been previously mentioned: evolution. Constant exposure to the sun darkens one's skin. When an individual resides in an area that experiences greater amounts of sun exposure and is considered to be a warmer climate, that individual's skin will be darker as a result. Individuals from warmer climates (consider the terminology African American descent) had to adapt to the demands of the climate by developing darker skin tones. Evolution favoring the dominant trait, the individuals with the darker skin survived, evolved, reproduced, and became the human beings we recognize today.

It has been suggested that Black athletes excel in sports that require more physical prowess such as sprinting and jumping because sport scientists believed that they possessed more fast-twitch muscle fibers, which are critical for explosive physical activities and movements (St. Louis, 2003). Most Black athletes are not given the credit that they are due because society has stereotyped them as being only 'natural athletes.'

In the book *Taboo* by Jon Entine, it states that Black infants are born more mature than White infants. According to Michigan State's Robert Malina, "Black infants tend to have somewhat advanced skeletal development. They also tend to be somewhat more neurologically, or what we call neuromuscularly, alert." Malina has found that the faster maturation of Black infants continues throughout their life regardless of what social class they may belong too. In Malina's research it was discovered that African Americans demonstrate superior eye-hand coordination, hold their necks erect as well as walk earlier, and enter puberty earlier (Entine, 2000). Here again, one may consider the effects of learning on athletic maturation. If Black individuals' neuromuscular systems develop and mature at a faster rate than a White individual's neuromuscular system, then that may give them a predisposition to learning and reaching expert levels. But then again, however, this learning curve can only be manifested if it is acted upon in an environment that is conducive to nurturing those athletic skills necessary for excellence in sport. If the stimulus is not there, the reaction cannot happen.

With that said, are Black babies born athletically superior to White babies, and if so, is that the reason why Black athletes dominate certain sporting events? The truth is that this connection cannot be made without the proper research, and it does not take into account other factors outside of genetics that may assist the athlete and help that athlete become successful. Blacks and Whites develop different body types early in life. A wide range of studies have found that by age five or six Black children consistently excel in the dash, long jump, and the high, which all require short bursts of power and speed. When they hit their teens Blacks demonstrate a significantly faster patellar tendon reflex time, as well as an edge in reaction time over Whites (Entine, 2000). Genetic influences are important, but they cannot be the determining factor of the success of

Black athletes. Athletic skills must be honed and these genetic factors may act as catalysts to assist the athlete in his or her practice.

History and the Theories Behind It

It has been purported by some that the dominance of Black athletes in sports has ties dating to the times of slavery. The strength and speed of Black athletes, as believed by some, is a trait that has been passed down through the generations and is the reason that Black athletes have been able to be so successful in sports that require an abundance of physical ability. In 1988, on Martin Luther King Day in Washington D.C., Jimmy "the Greek" Snyder gave his insight on one of the theories that is believed to contribute to why the Black athlete is so successful in certain sports. Snyder's opinions were directly related to the issue of slavery and the genetic implications that has created today's Black athlete. Jimmy Snyder's comments were similar to ideas expressed by others, such as: "On the plantation, a strong black man was mated with a strong black woman. Blacks were simply bred for physical qualities," and:

> The Negro was brought to this country as a physical specimen, a physical thing, to work the land. He was right away involved in physical labor: And he was involved in sports by the white slave owner: One owner might say to another, 'My nigger can outrun you nigger,' or 'My nigger can beat up yours.' This started a pattern of physical excellence. … Competitions gave him an out, and it has continued that way through the years.

By fostering the competitive desire in one's slaves in order to maximize physical ability and strength, a road was laid out for Black athlete physical excellence. This was an environment, however, that subjected the Black individual/athlete to deliberate practice through continuous hard work in the fields and around the plantations; this environment nurtured these abilities and allowed the Black individuals to become stronger, faster, and better than those who were not subjected to the same forms of stimuli. One may consider that the Black athlete has been subjected to more evolutionary stimulus for athletic excellence than the White athlete; while the Black individual was working hard in the fields, slaving away, essentially developing strength, power, speed, and even endurance, the White individual did no work of the sort. In essence, Black athletes have come to excel to such an extent because they have had more deliberate practice when looked at in an evolutionary perspective. If the White man had been a slave, he just might be where the Black athlete is now. For, as Entine stated, "Think of what the African slaves were forced to endure in this country merely to survive. Black athletes are their descendants." (2000, 72)

Referring back to Snyder, he made a comment about Black athletic superiority, which is as follows: "The Black athlete is a better athlete because he's been bred to be that way. … During slave trading, the slave owner would breed his big woman so that he would have a big black kid, see. That's where it all started." Snyder also stated that Black athletes could jump higher and run faster because they had the high thighs and big size that gave them the advantage over their white counterparts (Entine, 2000, 72). This "breeder" theory is also related to a second theory that involves slavery and the passing of genetic athletic dominance. The survival of the fittest theory, as proposed by Sailes, states that the physical dominance of the Black athlete was incidentally created by the survivors of the "middle passage" of the slaves on the way to America (Sailes, 1998, 192). The trip took several months, and during those months the slaves were poorly nourished and suffered physical damage to their bodies. In order to survive the trip the slaves had to be physically superior in order to survive. History has shown that slaves were bred and chosen selectively to make sure that the strongest and most fit slaves were able to survive and work under the harsh conditions. However, interracial marrying and miscegenation are much too prevalent throughout history in the United States for that gene pool to have survived the years and account for any physical difference in today's athletes (Sailes, 1998, 192). History has had too many uncontrollable variables in American society to prove that the athletic success of today's Black athlete is positively correlated to slave breeding. The physical prowess would have been diluted as the years passed, which means that it cannot account for the success of Black athletes. According to these theories, genetics is not as important as deliberate practice and hard work, therefore once again lending belief to learning adaptations.

Another theory was also proposed by Jimmy "the Greek" Snyder, which had not been well recognized before his career ended. When he was explaining his previous theory, which has become known as the "breeder" theory, Snyder noted that Black athletes are successful because "they practice and they play and they practice and play. They're not lazy like the white athlete" (Entine, 2000, 73). Perusal of these comments refers one back to the deliberate practice and learning concept. Snyder may not have known about deliberate practice, but his comments demonstrate that he was aware of something other than genetics that contributed to the success of the Black athlete. Snyder's comments demonstrate that genetics may play a role, but practice and repetition is more important and a better determinant of success in sport. Snyder also notes that Black athletes are not "lazy like the white athlete." Working hard is a statement that is typically assigned to White athletes because the Black athlete is supposed to be 'naturally talented.' Although Snyder's comments were not appropriate at the time, they do bring up a good point, how much of the Black athlete's success can be attributed to genetics?

The aforementioned genetic theory is directly related to the difference between Black and White athletes. According to this theory, Black and White athletes are born with genetic differences that allow them to excel at specific sports. The theory states that Black athletes have more red fast twitch muscle fibers, also known as Type II fibers, and White athletes have more white slow twitch fibers, also known as Type I fibers, which decreased the White athletes potential in athletics (Sailes, 1998, 193). Type II muscle fibers are directly related to power and strength generation, and are better for generating greater force for a shorter period of time. They are most beneficial for sports that require speed, agility, quickness, jumping, lifting, and throwing (Sailes, 1998, 193). The sports that are best for displaying these physical characteristics are basketball, baseball, football, boxing, and sprinters in track and field events. The Type I fibers that are most commonly attributed to White athletes are said to be better suited for endurance events, as these fibers have a higher aerobic capacity, due to the increased mitochondrial density, and are better suited to liberate oxygen from the blood stream to replenish the muscles when exercises for extended periods of time. The white slow twitch fibers (Type I) were attributed to the success White athletes experienced in middle and long distance events in track and field, swimming, cross-country, and marathons. (Sailes, 1998, 193)

The genetic theory takes all of the credit away from the athlete and gives it to factors that are not under human control. To what extent is this true and why is genetics given more attention than the amount of work that the athlete puts into his or her sport? The fact that West Africans have been dominating middle distance, long distance, and marathon events disproves the genetic theory and gives more power to the concept of deliberate practice. Kenyan, Ethiopian, and others athletes of African descent have been winning international marathon competitions more each year (Sailes, 1998, 193). Athletic skill is composed of more than just genetics; it is a mixture of the work and resources that are available that contribute to athletic success in sports.

A second theory is the matriarchal theory which is tied to the fact that most Black children are born and raised in single parent households, often without a father figure. According to Gary A. Sailes, it is believed that Black athletes were uncontrollable, hostile, and unforced and they channeled this hostility into sports. Also, the lack of a father forced the Black athlete to find another role model and in most cases the coach became the new paternal figure in the athlete's life. This theory was put to the test and it was found that most athletes are suspicious and distrusting of their coach's motives (Sailes, 1998, 191). The relationship between the coach and athlete could either positively or negatively affect the athlete which could push them towards excellence in sport or not push them at all. Either way, there is more behind the success of the Black athlete than genetics alone, and this study concludes that one must consider a number of different perspectives before one may determine why Black individuals have become so successful in sport.

People were once convinced that Black athletes were incapable of being in leadership positions such as quarterback, pitcher, or point guard. Al Campanis, a baseball commentator, reiterated the psychological theory on national television when he said that Black athletes may not have the "necessities" to become managers and field coaches in Major League Baseball (Sailes, 1998, 194). The reason for the birth of this theory is that it is believed that Black athletes worked poorly under pressure and were not good thinkers; therefore, Black athletes could not lead a team by using their minds; Black athletes were only good for the raw athletic talent the athlete possessed. The psychological theory states that Black athletes are underrepresented in individual sports like tennis, golf, skiing, skating, gymnastics, and swimming because they do not have the thinking power that White athletes use to excel in those sports. Although, when compared to their counterparts it does not seem like there are many African Americans in leadership positions, the fact is, however, that African Americans have had success in leadership positions. Doug Williams broke a number of records on his way to winning a Superbowl as a Black quarterback for the Washington Redskins, during a time when people thought that a Black quarterback could not lead his team to victory in a game of such large significance. According to Gary A. Sailes in The African American Athlete: Social Myths and Stereotypes, White fear of African Americans invading the white status quo is nothing new and it continues to create barriers to African American success in the administration of American sports (1998, 195). It has been proven that given the opportunity, African Americans have the potential to excel in positions of intellect, and should be included inside the offices as administrators and coaches, as well as on the playing field.

In connection to the psychological theory is the dumb jock theory. The dumb jock theory challenges the academic competence of Black student athletes. The theory refers hypothesizes that athletes do not have to work hard in school because they are given the easy route. They take the easy classes and are given good grades simply because they are athletes. The stereotypes classifying Black student athletes were more denigrating. It has been purported that Black athletes did not belong in college because one could only get there by using his or her athletic prowess not using actual intelligence (Sailes, 1998, 195). Several individuals felt that institutions gave Black athletes a free pass to college without actually earning the right. The NCAA's grade requirements help combat the dumb jock theory because the requirements state that high school athletes must at least have a 2.5 grade point average and a minimum of 900 on the SAT in order to receive an athletic scholarship to any Division I institution. In addition, the grade point average and graduation rates of student athletes are slightly higher than their nonathletic peers; in fact, much of the literature indicates that student athletes are doing better in school than most traditional college students (Sailes, 1998, 195). The dumb jock and psychological theories fail to give Black athletes credit for having intelligence and only attributes the athlete's successes to natural skill. It takes away from the fact that it requires a certain amount of intelligence to be able to read playbooks and develop an effective practice strategy that would ultimately increase the athlete's skill level in a given sport whether it is an individual or team sport.

Discussion

Theories and scientific research abound with regards to the Black athlete in sport, and the success the Black athlete has experienced. The media and the oftentimes sensationalist perceptions it presents can no doubt serve as a useful sociological motivator, to any individual of any gender and any race. But why here, and why now? Other countries certainly have their share of biases and rifts, but none so strongly as the dissention between Blacks and Whites in America. One should question this, as the dissention may lend itself towards the opinions and views the media and other individuals currently hold towards Black athletes, the success of these athletes, and how they compare with White athletes. These perceptions can be, and quite often are, beyond unreasonable and can furnish an array of emotions ranging from anger to pride. Such feelings can lead an individual, and particularly youths, to associate strongly with what they see and hear. As was previously mentioned, youths see images of their favorite player and model that players form, style, and techniques. The youth models this behavior in hopes of essentially becoming their favorite player. In turn, this may lead the youth to engage in play, which becomes practice, to eventually becoming deliberate practice, all which may be traced back to sociological, media, and stereotypical influences.

Conclusion

Talent or genetics? Learning or naturally occurring? One may continue to argue the points and lean towards genetic inclinations, but what it all comes down to is learning and deliberate practice. Talent, abilities, speed, power, endurance and strength cannot manifest themselves; an individual must put forth effort and have the desire to learn in order to reach the level of an expert. Race, gender, or ethnicity do not have significant effects on athletic success, so in the case of the Black athlete it is the result of the time and effort any given individual has put in to his or her respective sport. The media has worked as a sociological printmaker of stereotypes and hubris in attempts to rationalize the reason why Black athletes are so successful. It is not because of superior genetics, skin color advantages, or any of the other stereotypes that have become so engrained in American sports media. The theory of deliberate practice holds true to them; they begin practicing at an early age, go through the stages, and come out on top. People keep striving to find reasons that are not there, nor will ever be there, to explain the success of Black athletes. Why are Black athletes so successful? Because they have the desire and motivation to learn, practice, and achieve success in their sport, just like anyone else, but they have to overcome the stereotypes and challenges put before them by a White male dominated society. Therefore, when they achieve success, it seems like such an unbelievable feat that they had to have some sort of advantage. Their advantage? The challenges placed upon them that make achieving success that much more difficult, that requires that much more deliberate practice, that they overcome.

References

Côté, J. & Hay, J. (2002). Children's involvement in sport: a developmental perspective, in: J.M. Silva & D. Stevens (Eds) *Psychological Foundations of Sport*, 484-502 (Boston: Merrill).

Clegg, L. H. (1980). Why Black athletes run faster. *Sepio*, 29: 18-22

Entine, J. (2000). *Taboo: Why Black athletes dominate sports and why we're afraid to talk about it.* New York: Public Affairs.

Ericsson, K.A., Krampe, R. Th., & Tesch-Römer, C. (1993). The role of deliberate practice in the acquisition of expert performance. *Psychological Review*, 100, 363-406.

Hall, R. E. (2002). The Bell Curve: Implications for the Performance of Black/White Athletes. *The Social Science Journal*, 39, 113-118.

Helsen, W.R., Starkes, J.L., & Hodges, N.J. (1998). Team sports and the theory of deliberate practice. *Journal of Sport & Exercise Psychology*, 20, 12-34.

Hyllegard, R., McElroy, L., & Krejca, W. (2003). Perceptions of the importance of training, experience, and athletic talent for achievement in sports. *Perceptual and Motor Skills*, 96, 379-380.

MacPhail, A., & Kirk, D. (2006). Young people's socialisation into sport: experiencing the specialising phase. *Leisure Studies*, 1, 51-74.

Rhoden, William C. (2006). *$40 Million Slaves*. New York: Crown Publishers .

Rowland, T. (2002). The ascendancy of the modern athlete: a virtual roundtable. *Pediatric Exercise Science*, 14, 111-117.

Sailes, G.A. (1991). The myth of black sports supremacy. *Journal of Black Studies*, 21, 480-487.

Black Athletes and the Media. (2001). YAAAMS. Retrieved May 8, 2008, from Young African-Americans Against Media Stereotypes Web site: http://www.yaaaiiisrorg/editQrials/articles/blackathletes.php

Sailes, G. A. (1998). *African Americans In Sport*. New Brunswick, New Jersey: Transaction Publishers .

Schmidt, R. A, & Lee, T.D. (2005). *Motor Control and Learning: A behavioral emphasis* (4th ed.). Champaign: Human Kinetics.

St. Louis, B. (2003). *Sport, Genetics and the 'Natural Athlete': The resurgence of racial science*. Sage Publications. Body Society: 9-75.

Wiggins, D. K. (1989). "Great Speed But Little Stamina:" The Historical Debate Over Black Athletic Superiority. *Journal of Sport History*, 16.

Wilson, B. (2001). Impacts of Black Athlete Media Portrayals on Canadian Youth. *Canadian Journal of Communication*, 24 [Electronic version]. Canadian Journal of Communication Corporation.

chapter 5

African American Women and Sport

11

Invisible Pioneers
Exploring the Experiences of
African American Female Athletes

Emily J. Houghton
Jennifer A. Bhalla

Authors' Note

THIS RESEARCH WAS PARTIALLY SUPPORTED BY THE EDITH MUELLER Endowed Fund for Graduate Education-University of Minnesota Tucker Center for Research on Girls and Women in Sport.

Historically, race and sport research in the field of sport sociology has tended to focus primarily on African American male athletes (Birrell 1989). While a great deal of knowledge has been generated about men, with the exception of several studies (Bruening, Armstrong, and Pastore 2005, Bruening, Borland, and Burton 2008, Carter 2009, Green, Oglesby, Alexandra, and Franke 1981, Smith 1992, Vertinsky and Captain 1998, Withycombe 2011), the sporting experiences of African American women have largely been neglected.

For a number of years, research dedicated to African American female athletes has primarily consisted of biographies of professional athletes that highlighted sport as upward mobility (Corbett and Johnson 2010) or focused on media depictions of African American female athletes in televised or print coverage (Cooky, Wachs, Messner, and Dworkin 2010, Douglas 2002, Hardin, Dodd, Chance, and Walsdorf 2004, Spencer 2004). This focus on elite professional athletes, such as Wilma Rudolph, Althea Gibson, and Serena and Venus Williams, while significant, may obscure the experiences of other African American female athletes for whom sport played an important role in their lives, but who did not make it to the professional level.

Further contributing to the marginalization of African American women is the restricted way in which dialogues about race and gender have been constructed—meaning that a discussion of African American people meant a discussion of African American men, and a discussion of women really meant a discussion of white women (hooks 1981). Bruening (2005) pointed out that this construct has carried over into present-day sport scholarship, and has contributed to the erasure of women of color. For example, research has often explored female athletes as a homogenous group, not taking into account the impact of race or social class on their experiences (Bruening et al. 2005). This approach fails to provide a complete picture of the experiences of African American female athletes. As a result of the incomplete and lacking analyses, we know little about the role sport has played in the lives of African American women who participated at the high school or collegiate level.

The overall lack of research on African American female athletes is problematic for several reasons. First, African American women are overrepresented in collegiate track and field and in collegiate basketball, yet, they are severely underrepresented in positions of leadership as coaches. Even fewer African American women are athletic directors in National Collegiate Athletic Association (NCAA) institutions (Acosta and Carpenter 2014, Lapchick, Fox, Guiao, and Simpson 2014) Subsequently, the lack of African American women in leadership positions means that there are fewer administrative role models or mentors for female athletes (Abney, 1998). We know little about their experiences (social support, academic and athletic achievement, and barriers) as student athletes or sport managers. Finally, the dearth of scholarly research on African American female athletes contributes to the perception that their experiences are not valued in academia, as well as in society at large (Bruening et al. 2005, Collins 2000). Conducting research that examines experiences of African American female athletes from the early Title IX era will provide a greater understanding of the role sport plays in the lives of these understudied women.

Thus, the purpose of this study is twofold: 1) to gain valuable knowledge about an underrepresented group of women; and 2) to provide an opportunity for African American female athletes to tell their stories.

Theoretical Framework

This paper is guided by a multiracial feminist framework, specifically Collins's (2000) work on intersectionality, as a way in which to understand the black female experience. Intersectionality examines the ways in which race, gender, and social class contribute to oppression. These intersecting forms of oppression simultaneously subordinate some groups while privileging others, so while one group is disadvantaged the other gains unearned benefits (Zinn and Dill 1996). Within this context, Collins (2000) encapsulates this as the matrix of domination, which is a "historically specific organization of power in which social groups are embedded and which they aim to influence" (p. 246). People experience these intersecting forms of oppression and the matrix of domination differently based on their social location. An intersectional approach that takes into account race, social class, and gender is key in understanding the experiences of African American female athletes.

Another important component of intersectionality, specifically black feminism, relates to the fact that black women have historically been excluded from mainstream institutions and their ideas suppressed. The silencing of black women positions them as "the other" and has rendered them invisible, thus keeping inequitable relationships intact. This has led black feminist theorists to liken the act of speaking to an act of resistance (hooks 1989). Discussing the concept of "coming to voice" for women of color, hooks (1989) eloquently states, "Speaking becomes both a way to engage in active self transformation and a rite of passage where one moves from object to subject" (p. 12). As discussed previously, African American women have fundamentally been silenced in sport sociology literature due to a lack of representation (Bruening et al. 2005, Green et al. 1981). In order to combat the silencing of African American female athletes, it is important to provide an avenue where underrepresented populations utilize their "voice" to share their stories of the ways in which sport has impacted their lives. Consequently, this research attempts to share the stories of African American female athletes through an intersectional framework.

While a shared history of oppression within the matrix of domination may produce similar experiences among black women, historical conditions are fluid and may change a connection to a shared consciousness (Collins 2000). As such, it is important to acknowledge the potential for the divergent experiences of black women. Jarvie and Reid (1997) also caution against the tendency towards "universality" of theories of race relations, black feminism, and black identity, due to the complexity and shifting contextual nature of race and racism in society. Researchers should not utilize a "one theory fits all" approach to analyzing experiences of black female athletes. Despite the academic history of black feminism, scholars posit that the use of an intersectional approach to understanding African American female experiences in sport is relatively new (Bruening et al. 2005). Essentializing African American female athletes by gender or race will fail to provide a holistic understanding of the ways in which their sporting experiences intersect race, gender, and social class.

Intersectionality and Sport

Recently, researchers of sport have utilized an intersectional theoretical framework to examine the nuanced experiences of African American female collegiate athletes (Bruening 2005, Bruening et al. 2005, Bruening et al. 2008, Carter 2009, Withycombe 2011). Bruening and colleagues (2005) examined the silencing of African American female athletes. They found that the women felt silenced, marginalized, and racialized, which in turn led to feelings of powerlessness. Silence stemmed from a lack of media coverage of African American female athletes, an administration and coaching staff that participants felt was not adequately recruiting and retaining African American female student athletes, and sexist treatment by support staff and male student athletes (Bruening et al. 2005). Carter (2009) found similar results in a study of African American female athletes at an NCAA Division I Predominantly White Institution (PWI). Athletes reported feeling alienated and isolated based on highly racialized interactions with peers and faculty. As the results suggest, despite their elite status as Division I athletes, these African American women faced many barriers based on race, gender, and social class that were both institutional and individual.

Withycombe (2011) examined African American female athletes' experiences with stereotypes. Similar to Bruening et al. (2005), Withycombe found that some African American participants felt that coaches treated them differently based on the stereotype that black athletes were naturally athletic. Participants also felt that others perceived them as unintelligent because they were African American. Though, in contrast to Bruening et al. (2005), participants did perceive sport as a meritocracy, free from racial and gender issues.

In addition, Bruening and colleagues (2008) examined factors that influenced sport participation patterns of African American female athletes. Socialization agents such as mentors, family, and peers played a large role in their sport experiences. Participants noted that socioeconomic status also impacted access sport participation, as well as the types of sports they chose. Some participants who lived in metropolitan areas had limited access to certain sports and played basketball or track, while other participants who lived in suburban areas and were bi-racial participated in perceived "white sports" like soccer. Bruening et al. (2008) noted that the varied experiences of participants in the study speaks to the idea that there is not one universal African American female experience.

Within an intersectional framework, the results of these studies provide insightful information about the experiences of present-day African American collegiate athletes, in that participant experiences varied based on factors like race (bi- or multiracial), sport type, and social class. Despite the contributions the previous studies provide, there is still very little literature regarding African American female athletes from the early Title IX era. The collaborative approach, with the emphasis on sporting experiences of African American female athletes, seeks to fill the gap in the literature by exploring the role sport played in the lives of six women who participated in high school or collegiate sport in a large metropolitan area before and during the early stages of Title IX; and also to enable their stories to be heard.

Method

Participants

Six women aged 49 to 64, who competed in high school or collegiate sport in the same metropolitan area in the United States during the 1960s and 1970s, participated in this study. Participants were recruited from a panel that researchers attended. The panel focused on women's sport experiences in this area before Title IX. It was open to the public, and was held at a well-known local historical building. These women had interconnected stories, and were a purposeful sample—they were asked to participate because of their unique and connected experiences. They have familial and friendship ties that span five decades; they felt comfortable with one another, and supported and fed off of each other when sharing stories.

All participants competed in basketball. Other sports played included softball, track, flag football, volleyball, gymnastics, speed skating, hockey, skiing, baseball, table tennis, and karate. All of the participants competed in one or more sports at the high school level, and four competed at the intercollegiate level.

Design

Researchers used a qualitative research design to emphasize the experiences of participants. Using this research method allowed researchers to understand the meaning participants gave to sport participation, and explore participants' experiences in sport from childhood to adulthood. A semi-structured interview format was used in the focus group and the individual interviews. Pre-determined, open-ended questions were asked of all participants (see Table 1). Clarification and elaboration probes were used to help understand the meaning behind the response and reduce personal and methodological bias (Patton 2002). The focus group and interviews were conducted at times and locations that were convenient to the participant. Individual interview schedule protocol was based on focus group answers—some questions posed were the same for all participants, some were unique to the individual based on her responses. The focus group lasted approximately 120 minutes, and the individual interviews were between 45 and 155 minutes.

TABLE 1. SAMPLE INTERVIEW QUESTIONS FROM THE FOCUS GROUP AND INDIVIDUAL INTERVIEWS

Section I: Background information

1. What types of sports did you play while growing up?
   Probe: Why would you say you played those sports in particular instead of other sports?

Section II: Main questions

2. What were your experiences at [name] playground?
   Probe: What sports/activities were offered there?
3. What have your sport experiences meant to you?
   Probe: What do you think you have learned from participating in sport?

For a particular individual (individual interview):

4. In the group interview, you said that, "I'm looking at being an athlete, and being a woman-of-color athlete in [state] in a full-time job." What did you mean by that?

Section III: Wrap-up questions

5. Is there anything else that you would like to share about your experiences that we haven't talked about today?

Procedure

Institutional Review Board consent was attained before participants were recruited.

Data analysis

Participants completed one focus group and one individual interview. Interviews were transcribed verbatim and transcripts were coded using inductive content analysis. The focus group and all interviews were analyzed using inductive and deductive content analyses, similar to previous research (Bruening et al. 2008, Patton 2002). Inductive analyses allowed researchers to uncover new themes, while researchers used deductive analyses to identify themes that supported theoretical suppositions. Focus group data were analyzed as one unit. Additionally, information focused on the research questions that were specific to each participant was pulled out and used in the subsequent individual interview. Interviews were analyzed as their own unit.

For the analysis, after the interview was transcribed, both researchers independently read and coded the transcripts. Each researcher identified raw data points (representative quotations), and these points were used in subsequent analyses. Coders then discussed each raw data point and included it if there was consensus. In the case of a disagreement, coders discussed reasons for inclusion or exclusion and did not move on until consensus was attained. Similar raw data units were grouped into lower-order themes and named accordingly. Similar lower-order themes were grouped into higher-order themes and named to capture their meaning. Once consensus was reached, similar higher-order themes were grouped into two dimensions that captured their overall meaning. Finally, an external reviewer who was familiar with the field of sport sociology, but not with the results of this study, coded lower-order themes into higher-order themes.

Several steps were taken to enhance the trustworthiness of the data collection and analysis. Both researchers have an extensive background in sport and physical activity. Both played sport at the intercollegiate level and played multiple sports in their youth. Both researchers have been trained in and have completed previous research using qualitative methodology (Bhalla and Weiss 2010, Stanec and Bhalla 2015). Additionally, researchers conducted a member check by emailing the transcription of the focus group and the individual interview to each participant. They were able to add or change anything on the transcription, and only transcriptions approved by the participants were used in analysis. Finally, researchers used an external reviewer to reduce potential bias.

Results

Inductive content analysis revealed seven higher-order themes that fit within two overriding dimensions—individual and relational. Under the individual dimension are the higher-order themes of pioneer, diverse identities, and lasting impact of sport experiences. For the relational dimension, the higher-order themes of racism, respect for their relationships, importance of a support system, and lack of social support emerged (see Table 11.2). Each higher-order theme will be defined and discussed, with a quotation or two provided to add clarity. The themes related to the individual dimension will be explained first, followed by the themes under the relational dimension.

TABLE 2. EMERGENT DIMENSIONS AND HIGHER-ORDER THEMES

Individual	Relational
Pioneer	Racism
Diverse identities	Respect for their relationships
Lasting impact of sport experiences	Importance of a support system Lack of social support

Individual

Pioneer

Lower-order themes included fighter, activism, competitive with boys, and collegiate athletes. These women felt that they were pioneers in the sense that they had to fight to participate in something that was not clearly open to them. They saw this fight as a form of activism and took on that role. These women also felt that being a mentor would serve as activism. One woman stated, "We all had a vision that we wanted to continue to help female athletes become successful, not only in basketball, but in general in all sports." Additionally, these women were competitive with the boys and saw that as a constant fight as well. One woman said, "I had to sit in the middle of the court and boycott in order to play with the guys ... and then when you went out there, you better be tough 'cause you're gonna get your teeth knocked out." Finally, some of these women knew and embraced their role as pioneering women participating in collegiate sport, and beyond. One woman said, "She was one the first black athletes from [state] to play for the [professional basketball league] back in 1979." These women knew they were the first to play in certain leagues or at particular levels, and self-identified as (one of) the first to do this at that time.

Diverse identities

This higher-order theme included a variety of ways in which the women identified themselves within the sport domain. Lower-order themes included high-level athlete, committed to physical activity, tomboy, supporter of women's sports, feminine and sporty, giving back to the community, sport as self-worth, and having an understanding of the historical context and the importance of their contributions to their sport community. One woman said,

> You know, I know, I had to go to street school to help some young ladies doing the same things and I still go back to my community and help them. They struggle in several areas and to help them tap into their potential that they could be good athletes, business women, whatever it is.

These women saw themselves as mentors to the younger generation and this is how they could support women's sports and help them grow.

Lasting impact of sport experiences

The lower-order themes of learning life skills and developing friendships show the understanding of these women that sport has the ability to teach a person more than physical skills, and that what is fostered in the sport environment can have a lasting effect on the life of a person once the engagement in that sport is over. One woman confidently said,

> It's [sport] just an invaluable experience just to be able to play on a team with a common goal and sort of transcending that now in the work place. I have a team right now of six people and they're, I probably have the most diverse team, in all of [job] in terms of age, gender, race and I've tried to bring some of those skills that we learned in terms of working with, playing with individuals at the [university].

Skills learned many years ago transcended sport and moved into the workplace—something that proved valuable for achieving goals and developing healthy relationships. A different woman talked about sport providing a path for her to learn skills. She said,

> I honestly don't know what the road would have been because I can't think of anything else that would have provided me with the type of experience and all the life lessons that sport has. ... I mean, I know I could probably get it from some of the fine arts, music, speech and debate, but I am still not sure it can be delivered as well as it has been delivered through sport.

Finally, in terms of developing friendships, another woman said, "I find that our relationship, they've never faltered, never diminished; we still have them."

Relational

Racism

Participants experienced racism in two forms: institutional and individual. Racism played out in different forms, including not being recruited to play a sport at the collegiate level (when peer Caucasians were) and being made to feel *other* when playing sport the collegiate level. One woman stated,

> I'm back here in the 60s and I'm looking at being an athlete and being a woman of color athlete in [state] is a full-time job because all of the institutions that are around here don't cater to us and we're a secondary thought as you were saying

about you know, somebody had to from here [their community] initiate the contact with the [university].

The two-pronged attack on these women emphasized that racism was prevalent in the sport and physical activity realm, as well as other domains during this time.

Respect for their relationships

Lower-order themes include reverence for each other, respect for other female athletes, and reverence for the other women in the study. They understood that they were not alone in the fight to participate, and looked to each other, peers they were competing against, and other strong women they felt were fighting for justice in other domains for reassurance and camaraderie. One woman said, "I can kind of look at it as you know we all played on separate teams but in reality we are our own team. ... We can not see each other for years on end and when we come back it's like we never missed a step." Additionally, participants appreciated the longevity of relationships fostered by playing youth sport. One woman added, "I was going to say you know even though I don't see these young ladies very often but it's like when I see them it's like we've never left. It's wonderful."

Importance of a support system

Several lower-order themes emerged to explain the higher-order theme of social support, including mentors, family support, family socialization, peer support, peer socialization, community support, and role models. These women acknowledged and valued the support of many significant others, ranging from individuals to the community. One woman highlighted the positive impact of a mentor on her team's ability to participate in sport:

> It was really hard on the families because a lot of the families didn't have transportation. And so with all the games being away all I remember is [mentor's] red 1954 Ford station wagon. He'd throw all of us kids into that wagon and take us over to the east side or wherever we played and we'd get out and we'd play and usually beat everybody.

Another woman credited others for her ability to play. She said, "I had to keep explaining to them [teammates], if it wasn't for them being my teammates, I wouldn't be standing on the court by myself *period.*"

Some participants felt a lack of parental, peer, and community support for their sport participation. One woman said, "It wasn't sit me down and explain to me the potential that I had, nobody could create a mental picture for me that was a vision that gave me hope because the focus was on my behavior." She knew she was in charge of her participation and she would not be getting help from her family in regards to succeeding in the physical activity domain.

The themes and dimensions highlight the importance of individual and relational factors in the ability of these women to participate in sport. Lessons learned and friendships made when young perpetuated throughout their lifetime, and participants referred back to their youth playing days with admiration for themselves and others.

Implications

Intersectionality theorizes that oppression is intertwined through various social locations, such as race, class, and gender. The history of African American female athletes, particularly those who competed during the early implementation of Title IX, has rarely been explored, thus rendering them invisible. Thus the purpose of this research was twofold: 1) to gain valuable knowledge about an underrepresented group of women; and 2) to provide African American female athletes an opportunity to give "voice" to their stories.

The results from the focus group and individual interviews illustrated that these women sought opportunities to compete in organized and informal sports against both boys and girls at a young age. While two women had limited access to organized sport (one due to living in a rural area and the other due to lack of programming for girls), they all shared a passion for competition that eventually propelled them into organized activities. According to Corbett and Johnson (2010) and Hall (2001), African American communities often supported athletic endeavors for female athletes. Several of the women in the study, who grew up in the same community, cited that support as a reason for their continued participation through high school and, for several of them, college. When the opportunity arose to compete against white female athletes, one participant faced racism by being denied access to a prestigious sporting club. This visibility within their own communities, yet exclusion and thus invisibility in white communities, as well as academia, highlights the importance of understanding the historical context of African American female athletes' sporting experiences.

In speaking to the visibility/invisibility paradox, many of these women discussed the importance of being role models and mentors to younger African American women. Recognizing the lack of African American women in leadership positions within society, they felt it was important for them to give back and mentor younger generations. Research from Bruening et al. (2005), and Carter (2009) found similar results in the contemporary collegiate population. Those athletes felt it was important to be seen as positive role models for African American female athletes, and several of the participants intended to pursue mentoring others, as they found mentors had helped them be successful. Carter and Hart (2010) found that African American female athletes sought the characteristics of being a guide and a role model, having relational attributes, and providing constructive criticism within their mentorships. These features are not necessarily unique to African American female athletes, but they are what these athletes are seeking when identifying a mentor. Furthermore, Corbett and Johnson (2010) also noted that it is important to have African

American women in positions of leadership to serve as role models for others, as that provides a vision for younger people to strive towards.

Results elucidate how African American women may experience and maneuver sport, and operate within an overall structure that potentially, often successfully, limits options and forces negative participation outcomes (e.g., Bruening et al. 2008). Much of the architecture of sport is built to create opportunities for males, especially in the late–civil rights era, but these women chose to participate and made that happen. How these women perceived their experiences is important in understanding how participation was viewed within their historical and cultural context. Understanding the lived experience provides valuable contextual and factual information to create a more comprehensive understanding of the research interest (e.g., Smedley 2012). This type of information also provides contextualized meaning about sport participation, and this is something that can be used in the future creation of physical activity programs, especially for African American girls. The blatant expression of pride and enthusiasm towards themselves and others demonstrates that participation in sport was an acceptable and valued activity within their community. Social relationships in sport and physical activity are important motivators to participation (e.g., Ullrich-French and Smith 2008), and the longevity of relationships identified in this study supports the continued importance of social engagement within the physical domain.

Results give voice to the pride these women felt about their accomplishments and the enduring relationships that developed from their sport participation. The current study should serve as a springboard for more research on the experiences of diverse populations within the realm of sport and physical activity. Although opportunities for participation have grown in recent decades (Acosta and Carpenter 2014), it is important to consider and understand diverse needs of different populations. Future research should continue to explore firsthand accounts of African American female athletes, as well as athletes from varying ethnic and cultural backgrounds, as this is an important step in collecting authentic historical representation, which may be used as a basis for current and future programming.

Sport can be a vehicle to teach physical skills, but the literature is now supporting the idea that sport can also help teach life skills to participants (e.g., Gould and Carson 2008). However, much of the information related to life-skills learning in sport is concentrated on how adolescents and young adults have learned life skills through participating in sporting experiences (e.g., Danish and Nellen 1997). While it is important to understand how life skills are learned through sport, it is also imperative that we understand how these life skills are used later in life, outside of the sporting context. Results from this study provide some insight into how former sport participants used skills learned in adolescence later in life. Additionally, many studies do not specially address the African American experience, so this study may serve as a foray into gaining new information. The experiences of life-skills learning with diverse populations is an area ripe for further research, and will provide researchers and practitioners valuable information to guide educational sessions and future programming. The current study supports previous research, but also extends our knowledge to a marginalized population.

A final implication is the salience of social support, including peer relationships in sport. Previous research has shown that peers (among other social agents) are important motivators for sport and physical activity participation (e.g., Ullrich-French and Smith 2008). However, there is a dearth of research on the impact of long-standing peer relationships developed through sport participation. The current study was not centered on this, but the theme of the importance of the social system highlights the need to research this line of inquiry further. Additionally, practitioners must realize that social systems are integral to the sport experience, and must work to foster and promote social support systems that encourage continued participation. Thus, social support is an essential component and must be considered and planned for when organizing an activity or developing a new program.

Conclusion

There are some limitations within the framework of this research. Participants had overwhelmingly positive experiences in sport and physical activity. There is a need for a larger sample size to attain a more complete view of the opportunities and challenges for African American women in sport during the early Title IX era. Thus, future research can and should explore the experiences of African American women around roughly the same age from differing geographical regions, to see how access to opportunities compared. This would provide important historical data on African American participation in sport and ideally would make the experiences African American female athletes visible to others.

Participants in this study bonded through participation in sport and their friendships have endured for decades. This encourages women of today to value their sports experiences for more than the physical activity it provides. With the obesity epidemic and a greater understanding of the positive outcomes of sport and physical activity participation, it is imperative that the voices of diverse individuals are heard and understood within their contextual viewpoint. Results from this study have the potential to be used as inspiration for future generations of African American females to participate in sport and physical activity. Additionally, results can help practitioners design physical activity programs based on the experiences of these individuals. Culturally competent sport and physical activity programs are needed to support continued participation for all individuals.

References

Abney, R. 1999. "African American women in sport." *The Journal of Physical Education, Recreation and Dance* 70 (4): 35.

Acosta, R., and L. Carpenter. 2014. "Women in intercollegiate sport: A longitudinal, national dtudy thirty-seven year update, 1977-2014." http://acostacarpenter.org/2014%20Status%20of%20Women%20in%20Intercollegiate%20Sport%20-37%20Year%20Update%20-%201977-2014%20.pdf.

Birrell, S. 1989. "Racial relations theories and sport: Suggestions for a more critical analysis." *Sociology of Sport Journal* 6: 212–27.

Bruening, J. E. 2005. "Gender and racial analysis in sport: Are all the women White and all the Blacks men?" *Quest* 57 (3): 20.

Bruening, J. E., J. F. Borland, and L. J. Burton. 2008. "The impact of influential others on the sport participation patterns of African American female student-athletes." *Journal for the Study of Sports and Athletes in Education* 2 (3): 379–417.

Bruening, J. E., K. L. Armstrong, and D. L. Pastore. 2005. "Listening to the voices: The experiences of African American female student athletes." *Research Quarterly for Exercise and Sport* 76 (1): 82–100.

Carter, A. R. 2008. "Negotiating identities: Examining African American female collegiate athlete experiences in predominantly White institutions." Unpublished doctoral dissertation, University of Georgia, Athens.

Carter, A. R., and A. Hart. 2010. "Perspectives of mentoring: The Black female student-athlete." *Sport Management Review* 13 (4): 382–94.

Collins, P. H. 2000. *Black Feminist Thought: Knowledge, consciousness, and the politics of empowerment.* New York: Routledge.

Cooky, C., F. L. Wachs, M. Messner, and S. L. Dworkin. 2010. "It's not about the game: Don Imus, race, class, gender and sexuality in contemporary media." *Sociology of Sport Journal* 27 (2): 139–59.

Corbett, D., and W. Johnson. 2010. "The African American female in collegiate sport: Sexism and racism." In *Modern Sport and the African American Experience*, edited by G. Sailes, 181–216. San Diego, CA: Cognella.

Danish, S. J., and V. C. Nellen. 1997. "New roles for sport psychologists: Teaching life skills through sport to at-risk youth." *Quest* 49: 100–13.

Douglas, D. D. 2002. "To be young, gifted, Black and female: A meditation on the cultural politics at play in representations of Venus and Serena Williams." *Sociology of Sport Online* 5 (2): 1–23.

Green, T. S., C. Oglesby, Alexandra, and Franke. 1981. *Black Women in Sport.* Reston, VA: American Alliance for Health, Physical Education, Recreation and Dance.

Gould, D., and S. Carson. 2008. "Life skills development through sport: Current status and future directions." *International Review of Sport and Exercise Psychology* 1: 58–78.

Hardin, M., J. E. Dodd, J. Chance, and K. Walsdorf. 2004. "Sporting images in Black and White: Race in newspaper coverage of the 2000 Olympic Games." *Howard Journal of Communications* 15: 211–27.

hooks, b. 1981. *Ain't I a Woman: Black women and feminism.* Boston: South End Press.

hooks, b. 1989. *Talking Back: Thinking Feminist, Thinking Black.* Boston: South End Press.

Jarvie, G., and I. Reid. 1997. "Race relations, sociology of sport and the new politics of race and racism." *Leisure Studies* 16 (4): 211–19.

Lapchick, R., J. Fox, A. Guiao, and M. Simpson. 2014. "The 2014 Racial and Gender Report Card: College Sport." http://www.tidesport.org/2014%20College%20Sport%20Racial%20and%20Gender%20Report%20Card.pdf.

Patton, M. Q. 2002. *Qualitative Research and Evaluation Methods* (3rd edition). Thousand Oaks, CA: Sage.

Scraton, S. 2001. "Reconceptualizing race, gender and sport." In *'Race', Sport, and British Society*, edited by B. Carrington and I. McDonald, 170–87.

Smedley, B. D. 2012. "The lived experience of race and its health consequences." *American Journal of Public Health* 102: 933–35.

Smith, Y. R. 1992. "Women of color in society and sport." *Quest* 44 (22): 228–50.

Spencer, N. 2004. "Sister Act IV: Venus and Serena Williams at Indian Wells: 'Sincere Fictions' and White Racism." *Journal of Sport and Social Issues* 28 (2): 115–35.

Ullrich-French, S., and A. L. Smith. 2008. "Social and motivational predictors of continued youth sport participation." *Psychology of Sport and Exercise* 10: 87–95.

Vertinsky, P., and G. Captain. 1998. "More myth than history: American culture and representations of the Black female's athletic ability." *Journal of Sport History* 25: 532–61.

Withycombe, J. L. 2011. "Intersecting selves: African American female athletes' experiences of sport." *Sociology of Sport Journal* 28 (4): 478–93.

Zinn, M. B., and B. T. Dill. 1996. "Theorizing difference from multi-racial feminism." *Feminist Studies* 2: 321–31.

12

The African American Female in Collegiate Sport
Sexism and Racism

Doris Corbett
William Johnson

THE SUBJECT OF RACISM AND SEXISM IN COLLEGIATE SPORT CONTINUES to be a complex issue that causes Americans to be particularly sensitive. The fact that there have been too few African American sportswomen celebrated as role models is a reflection of the problems in this area. Even as we swiftly approach the 21st century, the American society is vaguely aware of the sporting experience of the African American sportswoman. This essay addresses the cultural milieu of the African American sportswoman from a herstorical and sociological perspective: noted African American athletes are profiled; the cultural inclusiveness of the African American woman in sport is discussed; the impact of Title IX on women of color in the historically Black institutions of higher learning is evaluated; special attention is given to the unsung African American basketball-coaching heroines who have been historically overlooked in the sporting community; and an overview of Proposition 48 and Proposition 16 is presented, with a view on the effect they have had on African American sportswomen. In addition, a review of prominent African American women in sport who are in athletic administration or related fields is featured; racial and sexual barriers women of color face in sport are discussed; and last, the media's attitude toward the African American sportswoman is examined.

A Herstorical and Sociological Perspective
of the African American Female

The concern regarding women in sport has brought with it a focus on African American women in particular. A new scholarship about women of color has been strengthened by the growing acceptance of African American and women's studies as distinct areas of inquiry.

In order to better understand the psychological and sociological nature of the African American woman in sport, the cultural milieu of the African American woman in society must first be reviewed.

Society viewed and treated African American women differently from White women in the United States. African American women have suffered many hardships and have not been treated as status symbols of their spouses or placed in a protected position in society.

Although the women's liberation movement focused on a number of theories regarding female inequality, very few models have examined in depth the constraints of both racism and sexism. It is a herstorical fact that African American women were excluded and denied mainstream participation in the political-economic development of the larger society until the Civil Rights movement of the 1960s. Prior to that time, the law denied African American people normal adult prerogatives. Widely sanctioned acts such as rape, sexual exploitation of African American women, low wages, menial jobs, and substandard educational programs all functioned as stringent barriers to participation in the political and economic process.

Like the African American woman, the White woman has also been victimized. However, the stereotypic traits differ and are quite often the very opposite. For example, almost without exception, African American women have been portrayed as aggressive, whereas White women were pictured as passive or nonassertive. The stereotypic African American/White opposites include (a) independent–dependent, (b) loud–coy, (c) dominant–submissive, and (d) castrating–seductive (Gump, 1975).

The herstory of the African American woman has shaped concepts of her identity as well as her ideals, attitudes, behavior, role, and responsibilities. The African American female is believed to be instilled with skills essential to her maintenance and conducive to her survival. Bonner (1974), Lewis (1975), and Staples (1973) have suggested that young African American women have not been socialized to conform to stereotypic behavior patterns. Instead, African American women have continually challenged the system to define and maintain their own personal being.

There are herstorical differences between the African American women and White women that tend to create a different social milieu that surrounds each race. Although the United States is ethnically diverse, the standard of feminine beauty has tended to be defined by European history and European literature. The standard for assessing feminine beauty has been, until recently, described as light complexion, golden hair, and fragile build; and she is soft, small, and delicate. White women have been portrayed as the ideal housewives and symbols of love and motherhood.

The antithesis of this standard is dark complexion, kinky hair, and sturdy build. The Black woman was considered to be tough and a hard-working matriarch in the home (King, 1973).

Cultural and ethnic conceptions of masculinity and femininity, the degree of sex-typing according to class, and the dominant/submissive relationship between the sexes tend to vary within and among all the various ethnic groups. As individuals and families adopt the mores and folkways of the United States, each generation will tend to erase ethnic differences as their members are absorbed into the urbanized, industrialized culture. First-generation Americans and first-generation migrants from rural areas are usually more patriarchal and traditional in their conceptions of masculinity and femininity. This pattern varies according to the cultural heritage, the unique herstorical experiences of the group, and the current availability of educational and economic opportunities to various ethnic groups (Yorburg, 1974).

For the African American woman, there was the general presumption by society that because she represented an "inferior status" in society (not limited to, but featured as, a tough, hardworking domestic or working-class individual), the roughness and toughness of the sporting world would only be a natural and an acceptable place where she would be competent.

In an era when minorities have been vocal relative to a wide range of social issues, African American women have been relatively salient with respect to their status in athletics:

> The Black woman's role in sports in the so-called Golden Era of sports in the 1930's and 1940's was nearly non-existent. The shackle of segregation handi-capped the Black female in sport, but a few did excel in several sports including basketball, tennis, track, and golf. (Pinkey, 1975, p. 58)

Women in general have protested the lack of attention, respectability, and professional opportunities available to them in sport that the male athlete has traditionally enjoyed. The African American male has aggressively sought leadership roles and careers in athletics beyond his active years of competition. The African American female has not been proportionately represented in athletics at all levels, such as interschool competition, coaching, officiating, administrating, policy making, and league work (Houzer, 1971).

Houzer (1971) reported that African American women appeared to be moving toward a position of lesser interest and involvement in sport and athletics. Her findings reflected a decline in interest and sport involvement by African American women due to socially based factors. Similarly, Alexander (1979), in a study of the status of minority women in the Association for Intercollegiate Athletics for Women (AIAW), suggested that various factors account for the underrepresentation of minority women in athletics: (a) lack of money for lessons and equipment, (b) availability and rental of facilities, (c) lack of racial role models, (d) time commitments for child care, study responsibilities, and wage-earning responsibilities, and (e) available opportunities in geographic areas of minority population concentration.

In spite of segregation and racism, many African American women had the opportunity to participate in sports through clubs organized especially for that purpose, such as the Alpha, Physical Culture Club, Smart Set, and St. Christopher (Young, 1970). African American women have been participating in sports and athletics for many years. During the years of Black-White segregation, however, they were forced to compete only against other Black women in tournaments that, to the country as a whole, "did not count." One of the most widely held myths about the African American woman in sport is the belief that African American women favor track and field, in light of their successes in these events.

According to Houzer (1971), there is no substantial evidence that African American women favor participation in track and field. A 1969 study sampled 265 women students enrolled in five predominantly Black colleges in the state of South Carolina. From data collected, it was found that the subjects were generally negative in their attitudes toward track and field. The sports and activities of softball, volleyball, basketball, modern dance, and bowling were identified as the top five preferences. The subjects also indicated significant interest in tennis, badminton, swimming, gymnastics, square dance, soccer, and archery. Metheny (1972) argues that participation in track and field was more related to limited opportunities than to individual preferences.

With an increase in interest and support in general for women in sport, particularly post-Title IX, more and more women are not only being physically active, but they are also more inclined to participate in sport competitively. Although the African American culture has traditionally embraced the Black sportsman, Hart (1974), after discussing the plight of the woman in sport, commented,

> In startling contrast is the Black woman athlete. In the Black community, it seems a woman can be strong and competent in sport and still not deny her womanliness. She can even win respect and status. Wilma Rudolph is an example. (p. 441)

Hart (1980) suggests that within the Black culture, sport involvement provides women of color status and prestige. Coakley (1982) has supported the notion that the African American community places few constraints on the Black sportswoman. If this is true, then it might be suggested that gender-role expectations for African American women are less constraining in the Black culture than they are for White girls and women in White culture. For example, Black women more often have traditionally been represented in the sports of basketball, softball, and track and field. For the White sportswoman, public acceptance toward participation in these sports has not been encouraged (Del Rey, 1977; Snyder & Kivlin, 1975; Snyder & Sprietzer, 1975). White women are most represented in the individual sports of tennis, swimming, and gymnastics. These sports still remain as the most acceptable sports for White women (Metheny, 1965). Metheny (1965) found that sports that require application of force to a heavy object, body contact, or hard running and throwing are generally discouraged for the White female.

Oglesby (1981), in her writings, "Myths and Realities of Black Women in Sport," differs with Coakley (1982) and Hart (1974). Oglesby (1981) submits that the socioeconomic, political, and psychological environment in the United States has not been supportive of the advancement of the Black woman in sport. Oglesby (1981) argues that Black women have been a casualty to the double affliction of racism and sexism. The fact that Black women have systematically been neglected in the research literature simply supports this point of view. Further, Oglesby (1981) reports that most of the investigations on minorities and women have examined the sporting experiences of the Black male and the White woman in sport, without exploring the sport experience with regard to the Black woman.

In our view, the limited number of studies that have been conducted are tainted in their findings because they do not examine the sporting experience of Black women in its context. Not only do the few studies that exist neglect the sporting activities of the African American woman, but they also fail to depict how African Americans perceive women of color participating in sport. Much of the literature documents the achievements of a select group of African American women in primarily one or two sports. For example, the struggles and accomplishments of Wilma Rudolph in track and Althea Gibson in tennis have been reflected as the norm for women of color in sport. Their stories are used to reaffirm the myth that sport is a mobility escalator, and therefore, the existence of racism and discrimination in sport and society becomes disguised. Their experiences reflect their fight to compete with Whites and to gain recognition from Whites. By focusing on the few available, highly acknowledged examples of African American athletes, such as Althea Gibson and Wilma Rudolph, the authors believe the stereotypes and myths regarding the African American sportswomen are reaffirmed. Although many African American women competed and contributed to sport before and after Althea Gibson and Wilma Rudolph, these two women are considered the most significant athletic forces among African American women in sport history. The reality that the participation of African American women has been restricted to just a few sports is an issue that has caused considerable discussion (Boutilier & SanGiovarmi, 1983,).

African American women have shown courage and determination in sport and have been instrumental in playing an important role in breaking down color and gender barriers in society. There have always been great African American athletes, but awareness of the African American female athletes has changed dramatically in the last 50 years, primarily because of television. Cheryl Miller, in a 1995 Ebony magazine article, states that her father told her that

> ... if a White coach had to choose between a Black athlete and a White athlete of similar skills, he would choose the White athlete. Every time. The moral therefore was that it was not enough for us to be good—we had to be flat out better. (quoted in "Slap," p. 25)

Miller (quoted in "Slap," 1995) goes on to point out that

Being a Black woman athlete, I have personally seen a lot of racial and gender bias. I was 13 years old, for example, when I tried out for an all-male basketball team. The coach, who was White, told me that if I could beat his son in a one-on-one game to 11 points, I could play on the team. I trounced him, 11 to 1, and asked the coach when I should report to practice. He looked me straight in the eye and said, "Miller, the only court I'll see you in will be a court of law. No girls will ever play on my team." I ran home crying and told my dad that I was quitting and that I never wanted to play basketball again. He sat me up straight and said: "I didn't raise any quitters. Tomorrow you will try out for the girls team and become the best who ever played . ..." This was a turning point in my life. From that moment on, I never accepted being second best. (p. 25)

The achievements of African American women in the areas of law, politics, science, medicine, education, religion, the military, business, the arts, and sports have been impressive. The following provides an inventory of just some of the many great African American athletes who excelled in sport despite racial and gender barriers.

Outstanding African American Women in Sport

Evelyn Ashford (Track)—Broke Wilma Rudolph's 20-year-old in the 100 meters. In 1979 was considered the top sprinter in the world. In 1984 achieved an Olympic record and received a gold medal in the women's 100-meter run. In 1984 received the gold medal in the women's 4x100-meter relay. In the 1988 Olympics, won a gold in the 400-meter relay and a silver in the 100-meter dash. Selected as one of the 100 Golden Olympians.

Tai Babilonia (Ice Skating)—First African-American woman to make the U.S. ice-skating team and compete in world-class competition.

Camille Benjamin (Tennis)—Outstanding professional tennis player.

Renee Blunt (Tennis)—Outstanding professional tennis player.

Surya Bonaly—Five-time European skating champion.

Valerie Brisco-Hooks (Track and Field)—Set Olympic and American records in all her finals; in the Los Angeles Olympics she won three gold medals for the 200-meter, the 400-meter and the 166-meter sprint relay; in 1988 she won a silver medal in Seoul as a member of the 2nd-place, 1600-meter relay team. Selected as one of the 100 Golden Olympians.

Lillian R. Greene-Chamberlain (Track)—Was the first U.S. national champion in 800m long before it became an Olympic event, and the first African American to represent the United States in 400- and 800-meters in international competition. A three-time member of the United States women's All-American Track and Field Team, she set national and world records in women's middle-distance running events. Gold medalist in the 1959 Pan-American Games.

Alice Coachman (Track and Field)—Listed among the 100 Golden Olympians. Alice Coachman's high jump of 5-feet-6 and one-fourth inches earned her a gold medal at the age of twenty-six. Nearly fifty-one years ago, in 1948, Alice Coachman from Tuskegee Institute became the first Black female Olympic gold medalist when she placed first in the high-jump competition at the XIV Olympiad in London, England.

Cherly Daniel (Bowling)—Champion bowler.

Dominique Dawes (Gymnastics)—Competed in her second Olympics (1996) to help the U.S. women's gymnastic team to win its first gold medal in Olympic history. She won a bronze medal in individual competition. Dominique Dawes was the top U.S. overall scorer on the night the U.S. women's gymnastic team won its first gold medal in Olympic competition. Without her, there would have been no celebration, no gold medal.

Anita DeFrantz (Rowing)—A bronze medalist and captain of the U.S. rowing team at the 1976 Montreal Olympic Games, and a member of the 1980 Olympic Rowing Team, DeFrantz also won a silver medal at the 1978 world championship before taking up posts on the National Rowing Association and National Olympic Committee in the United States.

Gail Devers (Track)—Gold medal winner in the 1992 Olympics in the 100-meter sprint. Member of the women's 4x400 Olympic Relay Team; 1996 USOC Athlete. Three-time Olympic gold medalist sprinter. Listed in the Jan./Feb. 1997 edition of the Olympian as one of the top 10 sportswomen. She claimed the 100 meters in Barcelona in the 100-meter hurdles.

Carla Dunlap (Bodybuilding)—Accomplished and nationally acclaimed bodybuilder.

Diane Durham (Gymnastics)—Outstanding, nationally recognized gymnast.

Teresa Edwards (Basketball)—Member of the U.S. 1996 Olympic and National Basketball Team. Listed in the Jan./Feb 1997 edition of the Olympian as one of the top 10 sportswomen. Is also listed among the 100 Golden Olympians.

Nikki Franke (Fencing)—1975 National Fencing Champion, 1975 Pan-American Team (second place), member of the 1976 Olympic Team.

Chryste Gaines (Track)—Member of the U.S. women's 4x100 relay team for the 1996 Centennial Olympic Games in Atlanta, receiving a gold medal

Zina Garrison (Tennis)—Was the first Black player to win the junior singles championship at Wimbledon. At the XXIV Olympiad in Seoul, Korea, she won a gold medal for doubles tennis and a bronze medal in singles tennis. She was the first African-American woman to play at Wimbledon since Althea Gibson in 1958, and in 1988 was a member of the first U.S. Olympic tennis team since 1924. Zina became the first Black to rank in the top 10 since the women's pro tennis tour began in 1971. Selected as one of the 100 Golden Olympians.

Althea Gibson (Tennis and Golf)—Champion at Wimbledon and Forest Hill. First Black to win at Wimbledon and the U.S. Open. Outstanding golfer and a member of the LPGA.

Tina Sloan Green (Field Hockey and Lacrosse)—U.S. Women's Field Hockey Squad in 1969; U.S. Women's National Lacrosse team in 1968 and 1972.

Traci Green (Tennis)—Member of the U.S. National Tennis team, 1995 and 1996.

Florence Griffith Joyner (Track)—World record holder in the 100- and 200-meter events. She brought fashion, flair, and high finance to women's track; at Seoul Summer Olympics in 1988, she won three gold medals in the 100- and 200-meter races and the 400-meter relay, and a silver medal in the 1600-meter relay; she surpassed Wilma Rudolph's record. Selected as one of the 100 Golden Olympians.

Lucia Harris (Basketball)—Three-time All-American. Player averaged 31 points per game at Delta State; she dominated the 1976 Olympics and was later elected to the Hall of Fame. She is the 1977 Broderick Cup Winner.

Flo Hyman (Volleyball)—First-team All-American to the United States Volleyball Association (USVBA). Flo Hyman led the rise of United States women's volleyball. She became the most recognized, most influential, and most dominant player on the best U.S. women's team ever, the 1984 Olympic Team. The 6' 5" Hyman led the U.S. team to a fifth-place finish at the 1978 World Championships, the best performance for the United States in a major international competition.

Nell C. Jackson (Track)—American record 200-meter; member U.S. Olympic Track and Field Team, 1948; member U.S. Pan-American Track and Field team, 1951, in 400-meter relay.

Cheryl Jones (Tennis)—Outstanding professional tennis player.

Mamie "Peanut" Johnson (Professional Baseball) —She was one of only three women to play in the Negro leagues, and the only one who pitched. At 63 years old, she is the only one of the three still alive. Johnson posted pitching records of 11–3,10–1, and 12–4 in 1953, 1954, and 1955 with the Indianapolis Clowns of the Negro American League. She played with Henry "Hank" Aaron and against Leroy "Satchel" Paige.

Jackie Joyner-Kersee (Track)—At 34 won a bronze medal at the 1996 Olympic Games. She has won three golds, a silver, and two bronzes since 1984 in the long jump and heptathlon. Holds the world record in the seven-event heptathlon. She is a trustee, Women's Sports Foundation. Selected as one of the 100 Golden Olympians. She has signed a one-year contract, with a one-year option, to play for the Richmond Rage of the American Basketball League. She plans to compete in track after the ABL's season concludes in March.

Stacy Martin (Tennis)—Highly ranked doubles professional tennis player.

Mildred McDaniel (Track and Field)—In 1956 became the first American female to set an Olympic and a world's record in the high jump. At the XVI Olympiad in 1956 in Melbourne, Australia, she won a gold medal in the high jump.

Lori McNeil (Tennis)—One of the highest ranking professional players; often played as Zina Garrison's doubles partner,

Cheryl Miller (Basketball)—Former star, University of Southern California women's basketball team; won 1982 national championship. Gold medal winner as a member of the U.S. Women's Basketball Olympic team in 1984. Selected as one of the 100 Golden Olympians. A Wade Trophy Recipient.

Inger Miller (Track)—Member of the U.S. Women's gold medal 4x100 relay team for the 1996 Centennial Olympic Games in Atlanta.

Madeline Manning Mims (Track)—Member of four Olympic Teams—1968, 1972, 1976, and 1980; in 1968 became the first American woman to win a gold medal in the 800-meter ran. Gold medalist in 800-meter ran and set an Olympic record of 2:00.9.

Sharon Monplaiser (Fencing)—Olympic fencer at the 1996 Centennial Olympic Games in Atlanta.

Renee Powell (Golf)—The second African American female to tour the professional golf circuits since Althea Gibson; has been with the LPGA since 1967.

Wilma Rudolph (Track)—Was the first African American woman to win three gold medals in track at a single Olympics. At the XYEE Olympiad in 1960 at Rome, Italy, she dominated the Olympics by winning three gold medals.

Chanda Rubin (Tennis)—Turned pro at age 15. Won a Grand-Slam event in 1995, the French Open; has reached the semifinals of the Australian Open; outstanding performance at the 1995 Wimbledon, playing the longest match of Wimbledon history, Has been ranked as high as number 10.

Kim Sands (Tennis)—Outstanding professional tennis player,

Leslie Allen Selmore (Tennis)—Turned pro in 1977 and won the women's singles at the ATA (American Tennis Association) National Championship, which earned her a wild-card into the U.S. Open. She was the 1981 Avon champion. Her last appearance at the U.S. Open was in 1986. She owns her own tennis academy in Jacksonville, FL.

Brianna Scurry (Soccer)—U.S. Women's soccer team member for the 1996 Centennial Olympic Games that won the gold medal game against China.

Debi Thomas (Ice Skating)—Became the first Black to win an Olympic medal (bronze) in figure skating on February 27, 1988. She was also the first Black skater to win both the U.S. and World Figure Skating championships, both in 1986. Thomas retired from skating in 1992 to enter medical school, and graduated from Northwestern University Medical School.

Verneda Thomas (Volleyball and Track and Field)—Member of the 1964 Olympic volleyball team; Member of the 1956 track and field team for the Pan-American Games.

Gwen Torrence (Track)—In 1992, won two gold medals and one silver medal at the XXV Olympiad in Barcelona, Spain. A world-champion sprinter and member of the U.S. Women's gold medal 4X100 relay team for the Centennial Olympic Games in Atlanta in 1996.

Wyomia Tyus (Track)—Gold medal in the 1964 Olympics for the 100-meter and a silver medal for the 400-meter relay; 1968 Olympics, won a gold medal for the 100-meter and another gold medal for the 400-meter relay. Selected as one of the 100 Golden Olympians.

Marian E. Washington (Basketball)—United States Women's National team—1969, 1970, 1971; and AAU All-American team—1972 and 1974

Ruth White (Fencing)—In 1969 first African-American and youngest to ever win the national fencing title; won five major fencing titles.

Willye White (Track)—Considered the grand old lady of track; silver medal in the long jump; silver medal on the 400-meter relay team; and won four medals in the 1959, 1963, and 1967 Pan-American Games; 17 national indoor and outdoor track titles.

Lucinda Williams-Adams (Track)—Olympic gold medalist in track and field; the third runner on the 1960 Olympic relay team with Wilma Rudolph. They called her "Lady Dancer." At the Pan-American Games in 1959, with 33 countries competing, she won the 100- and 200-meter races.

Venus Williams (Tennis)—Seventeen-year-old Venus Williams has been playing tennis for 12 years. Williams has been the most heavily recruited and richly reimbursed American prodigy since Jennifer Capriati. She made her Grand Slam debut at the 1997 French Open. She has played on the WTA Tour since turning pro in 1994. She made it to the final round of the 1997 U.S. Open in Flushing Meadows, NY, inaugurating the newly renamed Arthur Ashe Stadium by being the first African American to play in the finals of the U.S. Open under the new stadium name. Venus became only the second unseeded female finalist in the history of the U.S. Open in 1997. In the spring of 1998, Venus made it into the WTA Top Ten, winning her first WTA Singles title at the IGA Tennis Classic in Oklahoma City. She is currently ranked number seven and is the first American-born woman to win the Lipton Championship in Key Biscayne, FL, since Chris Evert in 1986. She has been named to the U.S. Federation Cup team. In 1996 and 1997, Venus was ranked 204 and 25 respectively and with a prize-money earning from $12,750 in 1996 to $460,536 in 1997. In 1997, she earned Tennis magazine's Most Improved Female Pro award. Venus Williams and fellow American Justin Gimelstob defeated Serena Williams and Argentina's Luis Lobo to win the 1998 French Open Mixed Doubles title.

Serena Williams (Tennis)—Younger sister to Venus Williams and is expected to become a world-class tennis star herself. Serena is currently ranked number 27. Teaming with her sister Venus, she captured the doubles crown at the IGA Tennis Classic in Oklahoma City in the Spring of 1998.

Lynette Woodard (Basketball)—Had an enormous impact on women's basketball by becoming the first female to play with the Harlem Globetrotters. A Wade Trophy recipient

These briefly profiled African American women have pushed and persevered to make a difference. As African American sportswomen, they represent a selected few of the noted and outstanding women of color who have excelled in basketball, fencing, golf, bowling, lacrosse, rowing, field hockey, ice-skating, tennis, figure skating, track and field, soccer, gymnastics, bodybuilding, baseball, and volleyball (Boutilier & SanGiovanni, 1983; Corbett, 1987; Green, Oglesby, Alexander, & Franke, 1981).

In the past two decades sport sociologists and other social scientists have challenged the fairness and objectivity of those who report the sport experience in American society. As we seek to know more about the sporting experience of African American women within the Black culture, icons such as Althea Gibson have made it clear that they did not perceive themselves as Negro champions, even though society perceived them as a model for Negroes. Gibson commented that she saw herself as a tennis player and that she "never set herself up is a champion of the Negro race" (Gibson, 1958, p. 35). Similarly, Venus Williams has stated that "we just want to get out there and play like the rest. We've shown that we can play just like any one else. We want to be a champion for people of all color of skin" (quoted in Leand, 1998, p. 10).

Oftentimes White America holds a different interpretation of the role and function of sport in the Black community, and as a consequence, ideological generalizations, stereotypes, discrepancies, and contradictions are promoted in society and in the research and popular literature. White America, for the most part, is unaware and perhaps even uninterested in the realities of the sport experience for the African American sportswoman.

Cultural Inclusiveness of the African American Woman in Sport

Researcher Terese M. Stratta (1995) conducted an ethnographic study on the relevance of intercollegiate sports to African American women athletes. Stratta (1995) attempted to understand and describe the cultural reality of African American female athletes. Her findings suggest that many of the White athletes viewed and interacted with people from other cultures on the basis of stereotypes and that many Whites were unaware of the cultural impact their actions and words had on people of color in general, and on African American female athletes in particular. For example, Stratta (1995) points out that when attempting to lead teammates, White athletes would frequently disregard the historical, cultural relations between White and Black people. White athletes failed to realize that traditionally, Black people have been "told" by White people what to do, how to do it, and in general, what constitutes reality. Given these types of historical tensions, African American athletes admitted that at times they were treated "like slaves" rather than as teammates. White athletes generally are unaware of the fact that White people have historically had the "power" to define contextual relations that resulted in cultural group tensions on the team when African American athletes attempted to offer alternative perspectives (Stratta, 1995).

Other important examples of racial tension are reported in Stratta's (1995) study, which speaks directly to some examples of subtle racism. She reports that White teammates ignored/disrespected the cultural existence of African American athletes and were unaware of their own White privileges. For example, when socializing before or after a sport event, African American athletes were expected to enter "all-White" contexts; however, White athletes would not consider entering a racially mixed or Black context because of the "inherent dangers" associated with these social settings. In addition, whenever the parents and fans of White athletes formed cliques and socialized before, during, and after sport contest, many times they failed to invite the families of African American athletes to participate in these activities. As one athlete noted:

> "When I come off the field, the parents of my teammates kind of shy away from me and don't speak to me. And they speak to everyone else's parents, even if they don't know them, but they don't speak to my parents." (quoted in Stratta, 1995, p. 54).

Unfortunately, this and similar behavior is too often found as the normative experience for African American athletes at majority-White institutions of higher learning. When White athletes, spectators, and sporting administrators do not support African American teammates and fans in settings outside of the playing field, African American athletes feel "used" for their athletic prowess with little or any regard for their cultural existence. In short, the cultural consciousness of those concerned with sport must be raised.

Twenty years after the passage of Title IX, the federal regulation prohibiting discrimination on the basis of sex in college education has gone a long way to enhance sporting opportunities for women in general, but particularly the African American woman in the historically Black institutions of higher education. Title IX has played an important role in the creation and development of program opportunities for the Black sportswoman.

The Impact of Title IX at Historically Black Institutions of Higher Education

Title IX assures everyone (regardless of sex) an equal chance to learn skills, choose an area of study, partake of an opportunity for advancement in status, participate in sport, receive a scholarship, or otherwise benefit from the contributions of any institution supported by federal aid (United States Commission on Civil Rights, 1980). The regulations apply in three main areas: admission of students, treatment of students, and employment in the institution. Treatment of students is related to access to and participation in course offerings and extracurricular activities including student organizations and athletics. It is the area of intercollegiate athletics that provoked bitter discussion and controversy. Compliance is determined by the elimination of discrimination in athletic programs. Title IX does not require equal aggregate expenditure for male and female athletics. Some of the provisions of Title IX regarding sports programs are summarized as follows (United States Commission on Civil Rights, 1980):

1. All physical education classes in elementary, secondary, and postsecondary schools must be offered to both sexes.
2. There shall be no discrimination in competitive athletics. The act allows, but does not require, separate teams for members of each sex; the "nature" of the particular sport should be taken into account. Contact sports need not be open to both sexes; however, institutions are required to open intramural and club teams to members of both sexes.
3. Males and females must receive equal opportunity in selection of sport, levels of competition, provision of equipment and supplies, scheduling of games and practices, coaching, academic tutoring, practice and competitive facilities, publicity, and athletic scholarships.

Despite the fact that some negative attitudes toward women in sport persist, major changes in the level and patterns of participation for women have occurred. Since the implementation of Title IX in 1975, the opportunity for female athletes to participate in intercollegiate sport has increased substantially. For example, in 1977, one year before the Title IX compliance date, the number of sports offered women was 5.61 per school. In 1980, the number had grown to 6.48; in 1986, to 7.15; and in 1988, to 7.31. The number for 1990 dropped slightly, to 7.24 (Acosta & Carpenter, 1990).

Title IX has been beneficial to African American women in sport, for it has indeed stimulated some changes in the way African American women sport teams have been treated by largely male-dominated and controlled athletic administrators. Title IX has increased the participation opportunities at historically Black colleges and universities (HBCU). In 1993, for example, there were 1,012 Black women participating as athletes in intercollegiate athletics out of 17,298 women in some 213 colleges and universities surveyed by Blum. Another study found 2,760 Black women on athletic scholarships in National Collegiate Athletic Association (NCAA) Division I institutions in the 1990–1991 academic year (Abney & Richey, 1992). It would appear, however, that the power of Title IX to remedy the historical position or status of African American women in sports is limited.

Because most universities tend to provide more sporting opportunities for men than for women, Title IX requires colleges and universities to increase the opportunities available for, and the resources expended on, women in their intercollegiate athletic programs. As a result, many colleges and universities have sought to comply with Title IX by adding more sports to the women's program. The National Collegiate Athletic Association (NCAA), which originally opposed the enactment of Title IX, has now made gender equity a major concern, which has resulted in the formulation of the National Collegiate Athletic Association Gender-Equity Task Force, which has identified several sports for women that universities may consider for compliance purposes. These sports include ice hockey, rowing, synchronized swimming, team handball, water polo, archery, badminton, bowling, and squash. Unfortunately however, African American women from the inner city and from low-income backgrounds do not have ready access to the training and development necessary to compete for scholarships and collegiate opportunities in these sports.

The enforcement of Title IX has suffered setbacks in recent years. The 1984 U.S. Supreme Court Grove City decision effectively denied the application of Title IX to non-federally funded programs, such as college departments of physical education and athletics. In March 1988, however, Congress enacted, over a presidential veto, the Civil Rights Restoration Act, which effectively renewed jurisdiction of Title IX over college departments of physical education and athletics. The period of 4 years without Title IX were years in which athletic scholarships for women were reduced and other negative changes were made in some women's intercollegiate athletic programs (Acosta & Carpenter, 1990).

African American sportswomen and their athletic programs have also experienced the evils of sexism in the historically Black institutions of higher education. Male athletic directors at historically Black colleges and universities (HBCU) have been reluctant to share revenue with the female athletes. The enforcement of Title IX has posed some hardships for most institutions. Eliminating sexism, like eliminating racism, is not an easy goal.

According to Howard University's head women's basketball coach, Sanya Tyler, historically Black universities are very much a part of the core of collegiate athletics and do not escape the responsibility for compliance with Title IX. Howard University, a historically Black University, has long been a pioneer in matters of civil rights, but was thrust into the national spotlight when a six-person, D.C. Superior Court jury ruled in favor of the Howard University head women's basketball coach, Sanya Tyler, by awarding an unprecedented $2.4 million which was later reduced by the presiding judge to $1,454,000. The jury found that the university violated the D.C. Human Rights Act by discriminating and by retaliating against Tyler once she filed suit; and that the university violated federal Title IX statutes by discriminating against Tyler (Blum, 1993; Hente, 1993). According to Tyler, Howard University found itself having to defend itself against sexism and discrimination in the 1991 SANYA J. TYLER (Plaintiff) v. HOWARD UNIVERSITY, et al. (Defendants) Civil Action (No. 91–11239) only because it chose to believe that the university was exempt from federal law. Black schools because they are historically Black are not excluded from having to comply with Title IX regulations (Tyler, 1998). This judgment now rests as the cornerstone of current litigation and has, it is hoped, moved fair-minded individuals to make fair-minded and equitable decisions within their institutions. Tyler points out, however, that "many institutions are still slow in putting in place functional plans to provide equal opportunity to women through athletics" (S.J. Tyler, personal communication, September 2, 1998).

Historically, Black male athletic programs have functioned as second-class citizens striving to emerge into a National Collegiate Athletic Association (NCAA) Division I program. The majority of the athletic programs in the Black institutions of higher learning have not been able to produce revenue at a level that would qualify them to be major players in the big league. Athletic administrators in these institutions have witnessed the success of the athletic programs in the major White institutions and have observed their White colleagues as they enjoy the financial rewards that come with bowl games and media coverage, as well as other lucrative benefits. Many of the males responsible for the implementation of athletic programs have taken the position that selected male sport programs, especially football and basketball, should not have to suffer in order to support the female programs (Alston, 1980). In reality, however, this concern is not a legitimate one. Very few football or basketball athletic programs generate sufficient revenue to support themselves (Begly, 1985). This is true also for not only the women's athletic programs, but even the minor male sport programs in the historically Black institutions. The majority of the money spent for intercollegiate athletics for both male and female programs is still derived from student fees.

Not until recently have many of the athletic programs in historically Black institutions sought to achieve Division I status. Because a commitment to achieve Division I status is a costly one, many of the Black institutions experienced difficulty in adhering to the Title IX mandate while at the same time building or rebuilding their programs with limited funds. Consequently, the decree to provide resources fairly has not received a warm reception in the Black institutions of higher learning (Simmons, 1979). The idealist, however, might argue that a minority institution's athletic program would be more receptive to providing equitable opportunities to women for moral and ethical reasons.

Unfortunately, Black institutions have attempted to take as long as they can to do as little as possible to comply, even today, with the inherent principles of Title IX. On the 25th anniversary of Title IX on June 23, 1997, only a few Black institutions could boast that they had moved ahead to comply with the letter and the spirit of the law of Title IX. In the area of scholarship, often no systematic approach to the financial-awards process has ever been used. For the most part, the commitment to equitable opportunity in the area of scholarships is no more than a paper commitment. Improvements have been found in travel and per diem as well as in dining and training facilities. The worst news, however, is in coaching. Fewer women are coaches, hold leadership positions, or have an opportunity to make important decisions regarding their athletic programs. Female coaches have to work longer hours with less pay and with a shorter contract term than do their male coach counterparts (Alston, 1980).

Although the African American sportswoman has tired of second-class status both in society and sport, she has long become accustomed to discrimination due to race and gender and, therefore, holds little expectation that equity in sport will exist for her. There is no doubt that the problems encountered at the historically Black institution are any different from the problems that exist at predominantly White institutions of similar size. Regardless, the historically Black institutions must seek to train, identify, and employ minority female coaches and administrators who are sensitive to the problems and are willing to stand tall to address the inequities, in order to enhance the welfare of the next generation of sportswomen of color.

Although Title IX has served to improve the status and program opportunities for women, racial and sexual barriers continue to exist and must be addressed.

Racial and Sexual Barriers in Women's Collegiate Sport

Racial and sexual barriers surrounding the involvement of the African American woman in athletics include:

1. Limited financial support. The lack of funds diminishes the opportunity for the minority female to receive quality training and have access to the best equipment for use.
2. Physical education teachers often are lacking in the background to coach competitive teams. The success of African American women in the sports of basketball and track and field has real implications for the physical education teacher who is socialized to emphasize these activities as she prepares for her professional career. Myths and stereotypes continue to exclude and serve as barriers to the African American woman who wishes to develop coaching and teaching skills in the individual sports of golf, tennis, gymnastics, and swimming. The success of Black women in track and field and basketball has led many individuals to believe that these activities are the only ones in which Blacks are better prepared to teach, train/coach, and officiate.
3. Lack of administrative support where competitive programs and interest exist. The major problems surrounding involvement of African American women in sport include limited financial support for athletes and athletic programs; lack of encouragement and support to attend and participate in workshop and training programs; and, with the increase in the numbers of African American women entering collegiate sport programs with undeveloped skills, greater coaching attention.
4. Lack of positive opinion leaders as role models who are African American sportswomen. It is difficult for a minority to select to enter an organization that is 90% White male.
5. Tendency of White coaches to associate the Black female athletes with only certain sports (i.e., basketball and track and field). The high participation in track and field by Black women is probably more related to limited opportunities than to individual preferences. The commonly accepted belief that women of color are naturally gifted athletes in some sports and totally inept in others creates a barrier for them to be accepted in other sports. The result is a limitation in the variety of sports offered to them. Opportunities must be provided to African American women who can derive benefits from athletic programs other than basketball and track and field.
6. Discrimination in team selection, particularly in the sports of volleyball and basketball. Racial stacking is also evident for the Black female in sport. In volleyball, Blacks are

underrepresented at the setter position, and they are overrepresented as hitters, a position requiring jumping, agility, and reaction—all physical characteristics. Whites are found in positions high in interaction, coordinative tasks, leadership, and outcome control. Blacks, in contrast, are found in peripheral positions where these traits are low and physical skills are paramount. Stacking is found to be stronger in volleyball than basketball (Eitzen & Furst, 1989; Furst & Heaps, 1987; Kanter, 1977; Simmel, 1950; Yetman, Berghorn, & Thomas, 1982).

7. Discrimination in hiring. Women of color are less likely to be recruited as coach, athletic director, or official. Therefore, too few African American women are actively involved in preparing for careers in coaching, officiating, or athletic administration.

8. Limited skill-development opportunities. African American women athletes are underrepresented in such sports as tennis, gymnastics, and swimming. Minority women are nearly absent in these sports because they do not have access to both the human and financial resources to develop these skills. Special training, facilities, and equipment are essential in the development and maintenance of skills for these activities.

9. Coaches' hours. Female coaches have to work longer hours with a more difficult goal to attain, have fewer financial rewards, and have a shorter term of contracts than do male coaches. Coaches are required to take too many hours away from their family. All too often, the female coach, and particularly the African American female coach, is without coaching assistants, which would enable coaches to have more time to spend with their families. Long coaching hours and the lack of coaching assistants also deter many capable minority women from pursuing a coaching career.

10. Officials. Many women are not motivated to be officials because of the perception that officiating is considered something that men do, and not girls, ladies, or women. Officiating is also less appealing to some women because of the amount of road time required to travel to officiating sites.

11. Intimidation from male coaches and fans. Support systems must be developed and maintained that will provide the African American woman with the confidence that she can do the job. There is an unspoken message conveyed by the "majority society" that she is not qualified, will never be qualified, and will never be as competent as a male coach.

12. Unwillingness to travel. The demands to travel are greater for the African American coach, who must often function without assistants and, therefore, must also serve as a coach, scout, recruiter, trainer, and counselor.

Understandably, the solutions to eliminating these barriers are not simple. Institutions must first develop a nurturing and supportive environment where concerns can be acknowledged, and admit that racism and sexism are legitimate issues and that there are problems to be solved. Professionals who express concern about both racism and sexism should be supported, not discouraged.

Denying that the barriers exist only hampers progressive behavior by everyone. Administrators must closely examine their own programs and define avenues by which:

1. A much greater number of African American women will hold positions of authority as athletic directors, coaches, athletic trainers, and officials. Role models in these positions are essential to the successful recruitment and retention of African American women in these roles.
2. Adequate financial resources are in place to develop, support, and maintain quality athletic programs.
3. Female coaching salaries must be comparable to the male coaches' salaries in the same sports.
4. African American women must be encouraged to participate in a variety of sports without being singularly directed into the sports of basketball and track and field.
5. Institutions can expand and provide locker-rooms and other facilities, including training facilities, to accommodate increased female participation. In many instances in the historically Black institutions, the male athletes and coaches have not been willing to share these facilities.

Propositions 48 and 16: Is It Double Jeopardy—A Race and Class Bias?

Another barrier to participation in sport has been the institution of Propositions 48 and 16. At least this is the position of many African American college presidents, athletic directors, coaches, and some civil rights leaders (Johnson, J.B. & H.W. Lundy, 1988). These leaders strongly believe that Propositions 48 and 16 reduce participation opportunities for African American athletes.

Proposition 48, the predecessor of Proposition 16, requires student-athletes to have a minimum SAT score of 700 (ACT score of 17) and a minimum GPA of 2.0 in at least 11 courses in core subjects. The core course requirements include 3 years of English, 2 years of math, 2 years of natural or physical sciences, 2 years of social sciences, and 2 additional academic courses. Under Proposition 16, course work requirements increase from 11 to 13 courses with the additional stipulation that the number of English classes be increased to 4, the 2-course mathematics requirement include algebra, geometry, or a higher level mathematics course, and 1 additional academic elective. A student-athlete with an SAT score of 700 (ACT, 17) must have a minimum GPA of 2.5; alternatively, a student-athlete with an SAT score of 900 (ACT 21) must have a minimum GPA of 2.0.

The storm surrounding Propositions 48 and 16 has been over those provisions specifying minimum test scores as a condition for sports participation. The critics have argued that these tests are culturally biased. The fundamental arguments against Proposition 48 and 16 are that (a) the minimum SAT score requirement is arbitrary and (b) the SAT and the ACT are racist diagnostic tests that only display a cultural bias that favors Whites. It is argued that the SAT and ACT score requirement is punitive for the African American student-athletes because statistics show that under Proposition 48, 55% of Black students generally score lower than 820 on the SAT, and 69% score lower than 15 on the ACT (Chu, Segrave, & Becker, 1985).

Certainly, one could argue that Propositions 48 and 16 force the interscholastic athlete to take seriously the whole notion of being a student first and an athlete second. The controversy continues, and although there is some empirical evidence to show the impact Proposition 48 has had on the Black athlete, there are no data to date to show its effect specifically on the African American sportswoman. Generally speaking, the female athlete is more successful academically.

It has been argued that women of color and women from a low socioeconomic background are penalized due to their socioeconomic status and ethnicity on the standardized SAT and ACT tests. Because income level is a strong indicator of SAT and ACT test performance, average scores on standardized tests increase steadily with increases in family income. Research findings indicate that minority-group members score lower than Whites on both the SAT and ACT, but graduate at a higher rate than do White athletes who score low on standardized tests.

A study conducted by the Educational Testing Service found that the SAT underpredicts the academic performance for African American women more than for women of any other race (Final Report of the NCAA Gender-Equity Task Force, 1993). Because of these factors, African American female student-athletes who are poor or are from working-class families are less likely to meet the National Collegiate Athletic Association (NCAA) minimum eligibility requirements. In the end, African American student-athletes must meet the standards. They may not like these standards, but they will have to rise to the challenge despite any real or imagined race and class or gender bias inherent in such standardized exams.

The Overlooked Stars: African American Women Basketball Coaches

Many of this country's best college and university basketball coaches are African American women. These women build winning teams, but must deal with sexism and racism in a male-dominated institution of higher learning. African American female collegiate coaches are not bringing in the highest salaries in coaching, and their talents have not earned them the public recognition and respect they deserve. Yet, despite the double whammy of sexual and racial prejudice and discrimination, African American women are among the leading basketball coaches at predominantly White and historically African American colleges and universities.

Some of the Top 10 leaders in the National Collegiate Athletic Association (NCAA) Division I include C. Vivian Stringer, who coached more than 11 years at the University of Iowa and earned her 500th career victory at that university. Stringer is now the head basketball coach at Rutgers

University; and Marian Washington has been head coach at the University of Kansas for more than 21 years and is the first African American woman to ever coach women at a predominantly White institution.

Although historically Black institutions do not break into the Top 25, veterans like Shirley Walker, head basketball coach at Alcorn State University, is one of the game's most accomplished coaches, with 200-plus wins. Howard University's Sanya Tyler has on three occasions gained entrance to the National Collegiate Athletic Association (NCAA) Championship play-offs; Patricia Bibbs of Hampton State University has acquired over 160 career wins; and Bessie Stockard of the University of the District of Columbia is renowned for her historic winning teams.

With the inspiring performance of the U.S. Women's national basketball team in the 1996 Olympic Games, and their winning of the 1996 Olympic gold medal, women's professional basketball became a reality. The recent formulation of the two women's basketball leagues, the WNBA (Women's National Basketball Association) and the American Basketball League (ABL), which is two more than there were in 1996, will lead to greater leadership opportunities for many of the outstanding African American ABL and WNBA players (such as Sheryl Swoopes, Lisa Leslie, Teresa Edwards, Teresa Weatherspoon, Trena Trice, or Andrea Congreaves) who are destined to become primary candidates for coaching and senior-level athletic administration positions in the future.

Just as there have been many impressive achievements made by African American women athletes, and their story has been underreported in the media, it is equally important for the media to report the achievements of the African American leadership in the field of sport and physical activity. What follows is a bird's-eye view of the many accomplishments of role models who are carving their own place out at the top of their profession in the area of sport leadership in the academy, professional educational, and sport associations and organizations.

—

Selected African American Women Sport Leaders and Educators of Health, Physical Education, Leisure, and Dance

Lucinda Williams Adams—Former president of the National Association for Sport and Physical Education (NASPE); supervisor of health, physical education, and drivers' education, Dayton Public Schools, Dayton, OH.

Robertha Abney—Former president of National Association for Girls and Women in Sport (NAGWS); associate athletic director Slippery Rock University, Slippery Rock, PA.

Alpha Alexander—Director of health promotion and sports advocacy, YMCA, New York; vice chair, USOC Member Services Committee; member, USOC Board of Directors throughout the

1997–2000 quadrennium; recently awarded the 1996 Olympic Shield presented in recognition and appreciation for outstanding service to the organization. She is only the second woman in history to receive the honor.

Gwendolyn Calvert Baker—Member, USOC International Relations Committee; member of the USOC Board of Directors throughout the 1997–2000 quadrennium; president/CEO, U.S. Committee for UNICEF; past president of the YWCA.

Beth Bass—Women's Basketball Coaches Association.

Renee Brown—Director of player personnel for the Women's National Basketball Association; former Olympic coach; as one of five WNBA Directors, Brown is the highest ranking African American on the League's administrative staff.

Lillian Greene-Chamberlain—First and only woman and American to serve as director of the Physical Education and Sport Program for the 161 member nations of the United Nations Educational Scientific and Cultural Organization (UNESCO), headquartered in Paris, France (1978–1988); only woman to serve on the Board of Trustees of the American University in Paris, France (1979–1989); first and only woman to announce a major sporting event in Madison Square Garden in New York City, as the official announcer of the Colgate Women's Games, the largest (approximately 10,000 registrants annually) and longest running (21 years) all-female athletic competition in America (1989–present); International Committee chair and Vice President of Athletes on the Women's Sports Foundation (WSF) Board of Trustees; Board of Directors, National Fitness Leaders Association; Board of Maryland Special Olympics; Maryland Governor's Council for Physical Fitness; Board of Directors, the American Running and Fitness Association.

Carla Coffey—Head, track/field. Cross-country USA T and F Committees Smith College.

Rochelle Collins—National Collegiate Athletic Association (NCAA) assistant director of Youth Sports.

Doris R. Corbett—Professor of sport sociology, Howard University; member of the International Olympic Committee (IOC) Sports for All Commission; president, International Council for Health, Physical Education, Recreation Sport, and Dance (ICHPBR.SD); former president, American Alliance for Health, Physical Education, Recreation, and Dance (AAHPERD); first African American president of the National Association for Girls and Women in Sport (NAGWS); former Association for the Intercollegiate Athletics for Women (AIAW) board member; initiator/facilitator of the Howard University Women's Varsity Sport Program (1973), having formulated and framed the Howard University Varsity Proposal for Women's Athletics, and acted as its first women's basketball coach.

Charlene Curtis—Assistant basketball coach, University of Connecticut, Storrs, CT.

Anita DeFrantz—Attorney and director of the Amateur Athletic Foundation of Los Angeles. On September 4, 1997, at the International Olympic Committee's (IOC) 106th Session in Lausanne, Switzerland, Anita DeFrantz again made history. She became the first woman in the 103-year history of the IOC to be elected to serve as one of the organization's vice presidents (the IOC is the supreme authority of the Olympic Movement); became a member of the IOC Board of Directors in 1992; member of the USOC International Relations Committee; member of the U.S. Rowing Board of Directors; current president of the Amateur Athletic Foundation of Los Angeles; member of the Executive Committee of the U.S. Olympic Committee; trustee of the Women's Sports Foundation; vice president of the 1984 Los Angeles Olympic Organizing Committee; awarded the bronze Olympic Order by IOC in 1980.

Evie Dennis—USOC special assistant to the president; member of the USOC Executive Committee, USOC International Relations Committee, and Minorities in Sports and Women in Sports Task Forces; assistant chef de mission for the XIIIth Pan-American Games in Winnipeg, Canada, in 1999; USA chef de mission for 1991 Pan-American Games; Technical Commission member for Association of National Olympic Committees; jury of appeal/running referee for USA Track and Field at 1996 U.S. Olympic Trials; recipient of the Olympic Order in 1992; 1976 and 1980 Olympic head women's track and field team manager; USOC vice president, 1985–1988; USOC chef de mission, 1988 Seoul Olympic Games delegation; retired superintendent of Denver Public Schools.

Kathy Ellis—First African American woman president of NDA (National Dance Association) 1980, 1990.

Vivian L. Filler—Former director of intercollegiate athletics, Tennessee State University, Nashville; former director of intercollegiate athletics at Northeastern Illinois University, Chicago: former associate director of intercollegiate athletics at Indiana University of Pennsylvania.

Linda S. Green—Lawyer, administrator and professor; vice chair, USOC Audit Committee; member, Black Women's Sport Foundation, University of Wisconsin Law School.

Tina Sloan Green —Member of the board of directors for the National Collegiate Athletic Association (NCAA)—NYSP (National Youth Sport Program), Founder and Executive Director, Black Women's Sports Foundation.

Gwen Harris—Head track and field coach, James Madison University.

Wendy Hillard—Past president, Women's Sports Foundation; television sports commentator, coach, and former elite-level rhythmic gymnast.

Barbara Jacket—Head track and field coach, Prairie View A and M.

Sharon Jones —Former outreach director of the Oakland A's, which made her the highest ranking woman in baseball with the Oakland A's World Series team in 1990; executive director of College Relations at Mills College, Oakland, CA.

Cheryl Littlejohn—Head women's basketball coach, University of Minnesota.

Sadie Magee—Senior woman administrator, Jackson State University.

Cheryl Miller—Sports announcer; former player and coach at the University of Southern California; named general manager and head coach of the Phoenix Mercury.

Benita Fitzgerald Mosley—1984 Olympic gold medalist hurdler; director of the ARCO Training Center; president, Women's Sports Foundation.

Camille O'Bryant—Sport sociologist, Ohio State University.

Bev Oden—USA Volleyball board of directors.

Lynette Overby—NDA (National Dance Association) past president; professor, Michigan State University, East Lansing, MI.

Marcia Oxley—Programme manager, Eastern Caribbean Community, Sport Development Programme.

Violent Palmer—First African American NBA basketball official.

Dorothy Richey—Former president, National Association for Girls and Women in Sport (NAOWS); first woman to be named athletic director of both men's and women's athletic programs at Chicago State University; chairperson, Department of Physical Education, Spelman College.

Robin Roberts —Television sportscaster and host of In the SportsLight, ABC's Wide World of Sports, and co-host of Good Morning America/Sunday. Roberts has also been a correspondent for ESPN's NFL PrimeTime (1990–1994); correspondent and then anchor for ESPN's SportsCenter (1990); host of ESPN's Sunday SportsDay, (1990–1995).

Yevonne Smith—Sport sociologist, Michigan State University, East Lansing, MI; 1995 NASPE Sport Sociology academy chair; Women's Sports Foundation Advisory and Research Council member; North American Society for Sociology of Sport Executive Board; co-chair of the Inclusion and Diversity Committee; member of the editorial board of the *Sociology of Sport and Quest Journal.*

Sonja Steptoe—Senior editor, Sports Illustrated.

Vivian Stringer—Head basketball coach, Rutgers University, NJ.

Demise Taylor—Head women's basketball coach, WNBA—Utah Starazz.

Delores "Dee" Todd—Assistant commissioner, Atlantic Coast Conference; co-chair, USOC Minorities in Sports Task Force, National Collegiate Athletic Association.

Sanya Tyler—Head women's basketball coach, Howard University, Washington, D.C.

Kathy Richey-Walton—Head basketball coach, Spelman College, Atlanta, GA.

Marian Washington—Head basketball coach, University of Kansas; an NACDA (National Association of Collegiate Directors of Athletics) and U.S. Olympic Committee Collegiate Olympic Coaches medal winner for the sport of basketball.

Willye White—USOC—USCSC committee; chair USOC Women in Sports Committee USA Track and Field.

Barriers can be overcome, and the media make a significant difference in determining the degree of public support in the promotion of African American women in sport at all levels of involvement.

Media Attitude Towards the African American Sportswoman

Too often the media serve to reinforce previously existing attitudes and behaviors rather than to introduce new ones. This view casts the media as preservers of the status quo rather than agents of social change (Rintala & Birrell, 1984). It has been well-documented that Blacks have made tremendous strides in American sport, but little research has examined the extent of media coverage highlighting the African American sportswoman.

The media coverage that women of color receive in the leading magazines reflects our public awareness and says a great deal about our level of acceptability for the sportswoman of color. What the leading magazines report serves as a medium to illustrate our cultural values and stretches our definition of excellence beyond just public recognition of one's success. The media's portrayal of the African American sportswoman serves as a mirror of society, and it is our truth teller.

If, for example, we reflect on our expectations before the 1984 Olympic Games began in Los Angeles, the majority of sport fans and athletes felt that the Games would serve as the impetus to lift the Black gold medalist into the world of commercial endorsements, unlimited exposure, and infinite respect. However, 48 gold medals and 14 years later, most of the Black Olympic heroes and heroines from the 1984 Games are still waiting to be celebrated. There has been a general lack of recognition and respect for even the latest group of African American Olympians from the 1996 Atlanta Games.

Since the 1996 Olympic Games have ended, it appears that an outpouring of affection and adoration, media exposure, and commercial endorsements has been directed at the United States swimming and gymnastic teams, whereas African American gold medalists who excelled in track and field and basketball have remained essentially on the sidelines. Williams, Lawrence, & Rowe (1985) explain this phenomenon by stating that women's increased participation is severely impeded by social inequities in society. One must remember that a considerable number of Whites perceive African Americans as natural athletes, and Whites therefore expect African Americans to excel in sports. Consequently, when women of color perform well, as they did in the 1984, 1988, and 1996 Olympic Games, there is often a feeling among the majority (primarily White America) that the sport achievement of Blacks, regardless of how exceptional, does not deserve special acclaim in the form of special recognition and awards. Edwards (1969) explains that:

"Many Black athletes have felt at one time or another that they were discriminated against. Aside from the money, prestige is the greatest incentive to professional sports participation. In amateur athletics, it is the main incentive, along with love of the game. Prestige is typically accrued and measured by the frequency and general tone of publicity that an athlete receives in the various reporting media. Black athletes as a whole feel many sports reporters have not always given credit where credit is due." (pp. 9–10)

Because the mass media are recognized as among the most powerful institutions in our society, the mass media serve as an important vehicle for communicating social values and identifying role models. Consider the fact that African Americans in general now outnumber Whites on the playing field and are beginning to rise in numbers in coaching and executive positions. Thus, it seems peculiar that White reporters still dominate sports journalism. It can be argued and reasoned that different sensibilities and insights are warranted in today's modern sports reporting given the racial and ethnic dynamic present on the playing fields. The extent to which women of color in sport are invisible in the media suggests a symbolic annihilation of them. The African American sportswoman's perspective in sport is lost to the public for examination.

Corbett (1987) investigated the portrayal of African American sportswomen in 14 leading magazines (Cosmopolitan, Glamour, Good Housekeeping, Ladies Home Journal, Ms, Redbook, Women Sport and Fitness, Woman's Day, Working Woman, Black Family, Crisis, Ebony, Essence, and Jet) for a 2-year period (1985 and 1986) immediately following the 1984 Olympic Games. Only 20 African American sportswomen were identified in the review of 286 magazines. Corbett's (1987) findings clearly indicated that sportswomen of color are underrepresented in the popular literature reviewed. The pattern of coverage revealed that the African American sportswoman is essentially invisible and more likely to participate in very specific individual sports; and the sports that she most often represents are the least costly sports. Athletes participating in basketball and track and field received more attention. The White female Olympian received considerable attention in the media and was represented in a variety of sports.

Although the media have the power to act as agents of social change and can impact on society's attitude toward the African American sportswoman, they have not done so in a positive and progressive way. It is revealing to note that Corbett (1987), in her 2-year study of the portrayal of sportswomen of color, reported that Ms magazine featured only one Black sportswoman (Lynette Woodard—basketball) in the 2-year period investigated. During this same time frame, three White women (Diana Nyad, swimmer; Greta Waitz, runner; and Beverly Francis, bodybuilder) were featured. Similarly, Essence magazine in May 1985 did a celebration of Black women without any mention of an African American sportswoman. Ebony magazine in its November 1985 edition depicted Black women in history who have made outstanding contributions to society. However, no mention or recognition was given to the African American sportswoman. Valerie Brisco-Hooks said it best in an interview in 1985 when she commented, "I'm still waiting for some good things to happen" (Ebony, 1985).

The pathetic reporting by the media on the achievements of women of color in sport and particularly on the African American woman in sport is reflective of the limited gains made by African American women not just as athletes, but also in the area of sport management.

African American (Black) women represent 15.5% (see Table 1) of the collegiate athlete population, yet they are significantly under-represented at all other levels of sport leadership and administration.

TABLE 1   Percentage of College Student-Athletes

Females: Division I			
Black Women	Latino Women	White Women	American Indian/Alaskan/American Women
15.5%	2.2%	82.1%	0.5%

Source: 1997 Racial Report Card (Adapted and reprinted with permission)

Across all of the divisional levels (Division I, Division II, Division III) of sport, African American women hold few leadership positions (i.e., as a college head coach, associate or assistant athletic director, athletic director, or even as the college faculty representative to the National Collegiate Athletic Association [NCAA]). The percentage of African American women who have been included in the culture of sport as athletic sport leaders and administrators is limited as depicted in the following tables compiled by the Northwestern University's Center for the Study of Sport in Society in its 1997 Racial Report Card (Lapchick & Matthews, 1997). Tables 2, 3, and 4 reflect the extent to which African American women are included in the sport culture in leadership positions.

TABLES 2 AND 3   A Percentage Status Report on College Sport Leadership

DIVISION I

Racial group	College Head Coaches Women's teams	College Assistant Coaches	College Athletic Directors	College Associate/ Assistant Athletic Directors	College Senior Women	College Faculty Rep. Admin.
Black Women	2.1%	7.7%	1.0%	1.8%	8.4%	1.3%
White Women	40.3%	46.9%	63%	27.8%	89.8%	. 15.4%
Other Women	0.5%	1.8%	0.3%	0.1%	13%	0.3%
Black Men	3.2%	4.8%	9.1%	7.5%	0%	6.1%
White Men	52.1%	35.7%	82.2%	61.7%	0.4%	76.2%
Other Men	1.8%	3.0%	1.0%	1.1%	0%	0.6%

Source: 1997 Racial Report Card (Adapted and reprinted with permission)

DIVISION II

Racial group	College Head Coaches	College Assistant Coaches	College Athletic Directors	College Associate/ Assistant Athletic Directors	College Senior Women	College Faculty Rep. Admin.
	Women's teams					
Black Women	1.6%	3.9%	0.8%	3.5%	16.7%	2.2%
White Women	35.7%	48.6%	10.6%	31.4%	80.2%	12.6%
Other Women	0.9%	2.0%	0.4%	0.9%	0.6%	0.9%
Black Men	2.9%	3.8%	9.8%	4.4%	0%	7.4%
White Men	56.2%	38.7%	77.7%	58.8%	2.5%	75.2%
Other Men	2.8%	3.1%	0.8%	0.9%	0%	1.7%

Source: 1997 Racial Report Card (Adapted and reprinted with permission)

The evidence as reported in the 1997 Racial Report Card (Lapchick & Matthews, 1997) clearly shows that African American women are underrepresented in college sport leadership positions. Only in Division II do Black college senior women administrators, at 16.7%, even come close to the percentage of Black women athletes represented in college sport, at 15.5%. At all divisional levels (Division I, II, and III), in each of the leadership positions (college head coach, assistant coach, athletic director, assistant athletic director, college senior women administrator, and/or college faculty athletic representative), the African American woman is significantly underrepresented.

DIVISION II

Racial group	College Head Coaches	College Assistant Coaches	College Athletic Directors	College Associate/ Assistant Athletic Directors	College Senior Women	College Faculty Rep. Admin.
	Women's teams					
Black Women	1.0%	2.7%	0.3%	1.7%	2.8%	0.4%
White Women	46.2%	52.1%	24.4%	42.4%	90.3%	22.1%
Other Women	0.9%	1.0%	0.5%	0.3%	0%	0%
Black Men	2.3%	3.5%	3.4%	3.7%	6.9%	1.8%
White Men	47.6%	38.7%	70.9%	50.8%	6.9%	75.4%
Other Men	2.0%	2.0%	0.5%	1.0%	0%	0.4%

Source: (Adapted and reprinted with permission)

Summary

The experience of the African American female in society, and particularly in sports, has been different from that of the White female. For the Black woman, the Black community has played an instrumental role in protecting the self-esteem of the African American woman by functioning as a buffer to the negative influences of the larger society. The African American community provides a sense of personal security, identity, and belonging and a different criterion for self-assessment. The stage has been set for a workable solution to improve the status and overall conditions of athletic programs in the historically Black institutions. Title IX has made a difference. Although all is not well, significant changes have occurred post-Title IX. African American sportswomen have become more vocal about the issues of racism and sexism. There are supportive and caring networks of professionals who want to make a difference and are willing to provide a supportive sport environment. Society needs to know about the African American sportswoman's achievements and how her experiences compare with and/or relate to those of other women of color and cultures. The public must know that there are many African American sportswomen other than Althea Gibson and Wilma Rudolph who have made significant contributions. The attitude of the media towards the African American sportswoman continues to be an issue in that the nature and degree of coverage are primarily based upon economic considerations and the prevailing interest of "majority members" of society. The struggle continues as more media attention is expected and demanded. Similarly, more support and media coverage are expected and demanded from within the historically Black colleges and university sport programs for women. The recent successful litigation by Howard University's Sanya Tyler points the way for other Title IX complaints to be levied and successfully litigated. Administrators must now think harder and longer about whether they are willing to spend more dollars on women's athletic programs or take the risk of facing a lawsuit and a long judicial process.

Suggested Readings

Birrell, S., & Cole, C. L. (1994). *Women, sport, and culture.* Champaign, IL: Human Kinetics.

Corbett, D. R. (1997). *Outstanding athletes of Congress.* Washington, DC: United States Capitol Historical Society.

Dealy, F. X. (1990). *Win at any cost: The sell out of college athletics.* Secaucus, NJ: Birch Lane Press.

Funk, G. D. (1991). *Major violation: The unbalanced priorities in athletics and academics.* Champaign, IL: Leisure Press.

Gibson, A. (1958). *I always wanted to be somebody.* Philadelphia: Harper & Row Publishers, Inc.

Lapchick, R. E., & Matthews, K. J. (1997). *1997 racial report card.* Boston: Northeastern University Center for the Study of Sport in Society.

Nelson, M. B. (1991). *Are we winning yet?* New York: Random House.

Plowden, M. W. (1996). *Olympic Black women.* Gretna, LA: Pelican Publishing Company, Inc.

Ryan, J. (1995). *Little girls in pretty boxes.* New York: Doubleday.

Sperber, M. (1990). *College sports inc: The athletic department vs. the university.* New York: Henry Holt and Company.

Study Questions

1. Describe and contrast the cultural and herstorical milieu associated with the African American woman in society with that of the White woman.

2. Identify and discuss the achievements of five contemporary African American sportswomen who have excelled in sport.

3. Identify five contemporary and prominent African American women who hold or have held significant leadership or administrative positions in sport or related areas.

4. What has been the impact of Title IX for the African American sportswoman in the Historically Black Colleges and Universities?

5. Discuss what is meant by culture inclusiveness as it relates to the African American woman in sport.

6. Identify and discuss the racial and sexual barriers many African American sports women experience.

7. Show how Proposition 48 and Proposition 16 may discriminate against the African American female student-athlete from a low socioeconomic background.

8. Discuss the role of the media in acknowledging the contributions of the African American female athlete.

References

Abney, R., & Richey, D. L. (1992, March). Opportunities for minority women in sport—The impact of Title IX. *Journal of Physical Education, Recreation and Dance, 56.*

Acosta, R. V., & Carpenter, L. J. (1990). Women in intercollegiate sport: A longitudinal study thirteen year update 1977–1990. Unpublished manuscript, Brooklyn College, Brooklyn, NY.

Alexander, A. (1979). Status of minority women in the Association on Intercollegiate Athletics for Women. Unpublished master's thesis. Temple University, Philadelphia.

Alston, D. J. (1980, January). Title IX and the minority women in sport at historically Black institutions. Paper presented at the National Minority Woman in Sport Conference, Washington, DC.

Begly, G. (1985). The current economic status of intercollegiate sport. In D. Chu, J. O. Segrave, & B. J. Becker (Eds,), *Sport and higher education* (pp. 287–297). Champaign, IL: Human Kinetics Publishers, Inc.

Berghorn, F. J., Yetman, N. R., & Hanna, W. E. (1988). Racial participation and integration in men's and women's basketball: Continuity and change, 1958–85. *Sociology of Sport Journal* 5, 107–124.

Blum, D. E. (1993, April 7). Forum examines discrimination against Black women in college sports. *The Chronicle of Higher Education*, p. A39.

Blum, D. E. (1993, July 7). Howard basketball coach wins $1.1 million in sex-bias lawsuit. *The Chronicle of Higher Education*, p. A45.

Bonner, F. B. (1974, Summer). Black women and white women: a comparative analysis of perceptions of sex roles for self, ideal-self and the ideal-male. *The Journal of Afro-American Issues*, 2.

Boutilier, M. A., & SanGiovanni, L. (1983). *The Sporting Woman*. Illinois: Human Kinetics Publishers.

Chu, D., Segrave, J. O., & Becker, B. J. (1985). *Sport and Higher Education*. Champaign, IL: Human Kinetics Publishers. Inc.

Coakley, J. J. (1982). *Sport in Society: Issues and controversies*. St. Louis, MO: C.V. Mosby.

Corbett, D. (1987). The magazine media portrayal of sportswomen of color. ICHPERD/CAHPER World Conference Towards the 21st Century conference proceedings. Vancouver, Canada: University of British Columbia.

Del Rey, P. (1977). In support of apologetic for women in sport. *International Journal of Sport Psychology*, 8, 218–223.

Edwards, H. (1969). *The Revolt of the Black Athlete*. New York: Free Press.

Eitzen, D. S., & Furst, D. (1989). Racial bias in women's collegiate volleyball. *Journal of Sport and Social Issues,* 13(1), 46–51.

Furst, D. M., & Heaps, J. E. (1987). Stacking in women's intercollegiate basketball. Paper presented at the annual meetings of the North American Society for the Sociology of Sport, Edmonton, Alberta.

Gibson, A. (1958). *I Always Wanted to Be Somebody* (p.35). Philadelphia: Harper & Row Publishers, Inc.

Green, T S., Oglesby, C. A., Alexander, A., & Franke, N. (1981). *Black Women in Sport*. Reston, VA: American Alliance for Health, Physical Education, Recreation and Dance.

Gump, J. P. (1975). Comparative analysis of Black women and white women sex role attitudes. *Journal of Consulting and Clinical Psychology,* 43, 858–863.

Hart, M. M. (1980). Sport: Women sit in the back of the bus. In D. F. Sabo, Jr., & R. Runfola (Eds.), *Jock: Sports and Male Identity* (pp. 205–211). Englewood Cliffs, NJ: Prentice Hall.

Hart, M. M. (1976). On being female in sport. In M. Hart (Ed.), *Sport in the Sociocultural Process* (p. 441). Iowa: Wm. C. Brown Co.

Hente, K. (1993, July 7). Tyler's shot at equity rings clear—A Title IX victory for Howard coach. *The Washington Post*, p. B6.

Houzer, S. P. (1971). The importance of selected physical education activities to women students in predominately Black South Carolina colleges. Unpublished master's thesis, Springfield College, Springfield, MA.

Johnson, J. B., & Lundy, H. W. (1990, April 27–28). The NCAA's Rule 48 and Proposition 42: An overview. The Sport Leadership Conference, Grambling State University, Grambling, LA.

Kanter, R. M. (1977). Some effects of group life: Skewed sex ratios and responses to token women. *American Journal of Sociology*, 82,965—1006.

King, M. C. (1973, March-April). The politics of sexual stereotypes. The Black Scholar.

Lapchick, R. E., & Matthews, K. (1997). 1997 racial report card. Boston: Northeastern University Center for the Study of Sport in Society.

Leand, A. (1998, July-August). Smashing success. *Olympian*, 10.

Lewis, D. (1975, Fall). The Black family: Socialization and sex roles. *Phylon*, 36, 221–237.

Metheny, E. (1965). *Connotations of Movement in Sport and Dance*. Dubuque, IA: William C. Brown.

Metheny, E. (1972). Symbolic forms of movement: The feminine image in sports. In Oglesby, C. A. (1981). Myths and realities of Black women in sport. Cited in T. S. Green, C. A. Oglesby, A. Alexander, & N. Franke (Eds.), *Black Women in Sport*. Reston, VA: AAHPERD Publications.

National Collegiate Athletic Association. (1993, July 26). Final report of the National Collegiate Athletic Association (NCAA) Gender-Equity Task Force.

Pinkey, R. (1975, June-July). Taking a sporting chance. *Encore*, 58–63.

Rintala, J., & Birrell, S. (1984). Fair treatment for the active female: A content analysis of young athlete magazine. *Sociology of Sport Journal*, 1(3), 231–250.

Simmel, G. (1950). *The Sociology of Georg Simmel* (K. H. Wolff, trans.). Glencoe, IL: Free Press.

Simmons, G. L. (1979). The impact of implementing Title IX in a predominantly Black public university. U.S. Department of Health, Education and Welfare National Institute of Education.

Slap in the face. (1985, Summer). *Ebony*, 6, p. 25.

Snyder, E. E., & Kivlin, J.E. (1975). Women athletes and aspects of psychological well-being. *Research Quarterly*, 46,191–199.

Snyder, E. E., & Spreitzer, J. E. (1975). The female athlete: Analysis of objective and subjective conflict. In D. M. Landers (Ed.), *Psychology of Sports and Motor Behavior*. University Park: Pennsylvania State University.

Staples, R. (1973). The Black matriarchy. In *Race Relations: Current perspectives*. New York: Winthrop.

Stratta, T M. (1995). Cultural inclusiveness in sport: Recommendations from African American women college athletes. *Journal of Physical Education*, Recreation and Dance, 66(7), 25–56.

United States Commission on Civil Rights. (1980). *More Hurdles to Clear.* Washington, DC: Educational Clearinghouse, #63.

Williams, C, Lawrence, G., & Rowe, D. (1985). Women and sport: A lost ideal. *Women's Studies International Forum,* 8(6), 639–645.

Yetman, N. R., Berghorn, F. J., & Thomas, F. R. (1982). Racial participation and integration in intercollegiate basketball, 1958–1980. *Journal of Sport Behavior,* 5, 44–56.

Yorburg, B. (1974). *Sexual Identity, Sex Roles and Social Change.* New York: John Wiley and Sons.

Young, V. H. (1970, April). Family and childhood in a southern negro community. *American Anthropologist,* 72.

13

Brown Sugar

Media Images of African American Female Professional Athletes

Kelli Hinton
Gary Sailes
Zayn Jenkins
Elizabeth Gregg

PAST ACCOMPLISHMENTS OF AFRICAN AMERICAN FEMALE ATHLETES have been infrequently publicized in the sports world. However, African American female athletes have been exploited for years with regard to their athletic ability and performance. The experiences of African American female athletes significantly differ from those of dissimilar races and ethnicities. Although they are women, they are not privy to the full spectrum of women's rights and as African Americans, they are subject to the consequences of racist and sexist practices (Lewis, 1995). While attending predominately white education institutions, African American female athletes face the likelihood of encountering the pressures of being an outstanding athlete due to the perceptions of African American athletes among other predominant stereotypes.

Historically, when exceptional black female athletes such as Wilma Rudolph and Althea Gibson dominated sports, African American women were particular targets of criticism because of their eccentric athletic ability. During this period in our history, whites controlled most sectors of American society including sports. African Americans were expected to fill the role of grateful, stalwart employees and entertainers (Edwards, 1999). The accomplishments of African American women athletes went unrecognized. Sport science demonstrates that women athletes will prevail at certain sports due to their biological and genetic distinction to men. For example, in events such as ultra-marathons, the Iditarod, and marathon swimming, women's naturally higher fat levels are an asset compared to the lower fat levels of men (Entine, 2000). Not only do women, specifically African American women train hard, they are also born into a culture that expects them to perform well. However, when addressing the problems and challenge of women athletes, white middle class women were the primary topic of discussion (Lewis, 1995).

Consequently, circumstances in sport which impacted the participation for women began to take place. On June 23, 1972, the U.S. Congress passed Title IX as part of the Education Amendment Act. Over three decades have passed and racial and gender inequity still exist in higher education. Title IX has benefited Caucasian women more than African American women. The discussion on women athletes typically ignored the experiences of the African American woman athlete. Historically, African American women have been excluded from the image of women as weak and frail. Being strong appeared to suggest that black women could withstand the social situations and experiences that 'other' women could not (Collins, 1990). This description is prevalent in current American society.

The percentage of African American student-athletes at predominantly white institutions has increased dramatically over the last three decades (Gaston, 2003). Racism and sexism have been a part of black women's experiences for centuries. While a great deal of research has been done in the area of 'race and sport,' it has largely focused on black men. The purpose of this study is to explore the various segments of mistreatment experienced among African American female athletes. Related issues regarding this study are (a) Title IX, (b) the media's portrayal of, (c) discrimination, and (d) the Black Family expectations of black women athletes.

Literature Review

Being African American and female would suggest that this group would experience twice the discrimination compared to a group of Caucasian women or a group of African American males. African American women have never rested on the pedestal created to protect the supposed biologically and spiritually pre-determined timidity of women. In fact, African American women are viewed as just the opposite. African American female athletes are often portrayed as animalistic and in need of male control. Women in general were steered away from sport in early years, but for different reasons than white women, African American female women often had to forgo athletic opportunities due to 'the necessity of work' (Evans, 1998).

History of Black Females in Sport

The history of sport, as is true for contemporary American sport, the focus of emphasis has mostly been on male athletes (Richardson, 2005). Men most often dominate social institutions in America. Historically, African Americans lacked the control and power to change that fact. African American women have had to overcome the experience of intersecting oppressions from being black and female. The remaining indigenous groups comprising American society are viewed as dominant groups in the eyes of the African American woman. This hegemonic ideology is a reflection of the dominant male cultural group to establish and maintain power over other groups (Pedersen et al, 2007). Whether that power is real or imagined, it is a practiced ideology of subordinated groups within this country, including among African American women. Sport is male dominated and women threaten this hierarchy. White men, white women, black men and those with higher social standing all prevail over the African American woman (Edwards, 1999).

In November of 1945, Jackie Robinson took his first-at-bat in Major League Baseball. His presence initiated the beginning of a racial transformation within sport. By comparison, there was an African American female athlete that was recognized as initiating the black female movement in sport, Althea Gibson. Gibson not only broke barriers in tennis, but she was also the first black woman on the LPGA tour. In 1951, she became the first African American to play at Wimbledon. No doubt, African American female athletes from that period in American history had to overcome insurmountable obstacles to achieve their accomplishments and change the world around them. Consequently, these opportunities of success were not without precarious social challenges and battles with the mainstream establishment in changing the consciousness of the American status quo.

Lansbury (2001) suggests that sources for news in the 1940s and 1950s contributed to the loss of at least two black women athletes from public memory, 1940s track star Alice Coachman and 1950s tennis great Althea Gibson. In short, by focusing primarily on race or gender rather than athletic talent, the white and black press constructed public identities for Coachman and Gibson that marginalized them as athletes. In the white press, gender became the essential element around which black female athletes' careers were interpreted. Not to say that race was never a factor, but it was generally secondary to gender. In the case of Alice Coachman, she received little coverage from the white press mainly because she participated in a male gendered sport, track and field (Lansbury, 2001).

While the presentation of Coachman and Gibson in the white press revolved primarily around gender, race became the focal point for constructing their identities in the black press (Lansbury, 2001). Althea Gibson was successful in a socially accepted women's sport, tennis. She was covered more by the white press because of her gender. However, she suffered from this same classification when the media began to describe her play as too masculine.

The white press focused primarily on gender while the black press focused on race and finding ways to uplift and encourage more African Americans to enter into new fields. Coincidently, white women began to leave certain sports such as track & field as black women entered and began to dominate that sport, particularly in the sprint events. More white women were concerned with the masculine aspect of the sport than excelling at their skill. In tennis, it was considered a socially acceptable feminine sport, but a sport for the elite class. The world of tennis did not openly welcome working class participants (Lansbury, 2001). Choosing to emphasize either gender or race over athletic skill and hard work, both black and white sports journalists unknowingly contributed to marginalizing and ultimately defining black female athletes to the general public.

In contemporary society, African American female athletes continue to concentrate their numbers and dominate in particular sports, specifically basketball and track. Additionally, African

American female athletes are making moves in new areas although fairly obscure (Richardson, 2005). Serena and Venus Williams continue to dominate in tennis. Ranked in the top five in the world for the past two years, the prodigal Williams sisters have stunned the world. The key to their performance is fast serves and strong returns that exhaust their opponents on the court (Biography Channel). A new arena where African American women participation is increasing is fencing. Laura Flessel-Colovic has established herself as one of the world's best (Richardson, 2005). She has won three Olympic medals, three World Championship titles, and became a positive icon within a sport usually associated with white European men.

Title IX and Race

Title IX of the Educational Amendment Act of 1972 was legislation passed to forbid gender discrimination in any educational setting that receives federal funding. Title IX states:

> No person in the United States shall, on the basis of sex (et. al.), be excluded
> from participation in, be denied the benefits of, or be subjected to discrimi-
> nation under any educational program or activity receiving federal financial
> assistance. (Title 20 U.S.C.)

Title IX has drawn the most attention in relation to its coverage of college athletics. One reason athletics has received more scrutiny than other educational programs is because the biggest discrepancy is often found in college athletic departments. Women from minority groups are underrepresented in college sports. They only compose 25 percent of female undergraduates (Chronicle, 2003). Many African American children are not able to participate in the privileged sports of soccer, golf, and lacrosse due to the extra costs and their unavailability within inner city communities. African American women are mainly seen participating in basketball and track because of their few economic requirements and availability.

The presence of African American female athletes in sports today has significantly increased over the years. But the question regarding how real the numbers are remains obscure. The NCAA Women's basketball championship in April of 2007 displayed an image of diversity in women's collegiate athletics. Eighty percent of the starters for Rutgers and Tennessee were nonwhite (Gill, 2007). However, the prevalence of African American females in Division I sports is an illusion. In actuality, the percentage of African American female athletes actively participating in college sports today is considerably lower for all sports compared to basketball and track and field due to clustering in those two specific sports. Regardless of the increased number of Title IX generated athletics scholarships across the country at various universities, African American female athletes have not been able to take advantage of them. Part of this problem is the clustering of African American women into basketball and track and those numbers not changing much since Title IX's inception in 1972. According to the NCAA, over 85% of black female student athletes compete in either basketball or track (NCAA.org, 2009).

African American female athletes have not benefited from Title IX and the expansion of women's athletics because the sports that have been added have minimal participation among African American women (Jackson, 2006). Emerging sports such as gymnastics, swimming and crew are unlikely to attract African American women because of inherent restrictive cultural norms and traditions, lack of resources, programs and opportunity and perceived social alienation generated from participation in what are typically seen as "white" sports.

Media Portrayals

As the quality and percentage of women athletes participating in American sport increased, the media coverage of their events has also grown. No doubt, the media concluded that televising or covering women's sports was profitable. The question if they were respected more for their skill or their sexual image is a topic of considerable debate among feminist scholars. The portrayal of African American women as sexual beings began in American slavery, persisted through the Jim Crow period, and continues today. It is no longer a secret or an unknown fact that African American female athletes struggle with recognition regarding playing a major factor in the sports world. In addition, they are scrutinized and discriminated against because of their color as well as gender (Edwards, 1999). The most vivid example reverts back to the racist and sexist remarks made by Don Imus in April 2007, when he called the players of Rutgers University Women's who happened to be predominantly African American, "nappy-headed hoes!" (CBSNews.com, 2007). However, the denigrations do not end there. While playing at the Australian Open, comments made by Australian tennis coach Roger Rasheed were found to be sexiest and degrading (LarryBrownSports.com, 2009). Rasheed stated, "Take a look at this now. Make or think as you will, ladies, but for me, that's a pretty good sight," referring to Serena Williams buttocks. Far too many African American female athletes are sex symbols and commentators and sports analyst tend to cross the line and make remarks that are disrespectful. When comparing African American female athletes and white female athletes, there is often a distinctive difference in the adjectives used to describe each woman's self image. Specific descriptors that involve the sports skills of African American female athletes are repeatedly replaced with typical judgmental stereotypes and sexist remarks by the media (Edwards, 1999).

As African American female athletes venture into traditional male sport territories, their status as world-class athletes traversed them to the role of celebrity. Celebrity status generated endorsement contracts for both print and television opportunities (Carty, 2005). The prevailing culture about women athletes also transformed African American female athletes into icons for sexual deviance in sport. Women's bodies were the main focus of attention. But with the eruption of extraordinary stars such as the U.S. Women's 1999 World Cup Championship Team, and tennis greats Venus and Serena Williams, there has been a slight change in the portrayal of feminism and femininity. African American female athletes are now among the few female athletes that embrace their muscles, strength, fitness, and competitiveness. Although African American female athletes are still viewed more as an object of desire, their bodies represented a new kind of discipline (Carty, 2005).

Discrimination

The issue of discrimination in sport is usually described as unequal treatment on the basis of race and gender. African American women athletes face some of the same challenges as African American male athletes. However, African American women also face gender inequities. Consequently, they face the dual challenge of coping with racism and sexism. (Coakley, 2009). Such racism is evident in sports and at all levels of participation. The sport media characterizes females differently than males, focusing on their familial relationships and their physical attractiveness rather than their performances on the field of play (Pedersen et al, 2007). When photos of female athletes appear in sport pages, they mostly depict the athlete's non-active role.

Television commentators for women's sports have in the past referred to female athletes by their first names and as "girls" or "ladies" (Coakley, 2009).

The public's perception is that sports are an equal economic opportunity for minorities. Additionally, African American female athletes do not fit the traditional notion of femininity in sport. Jenny Thompson, the greatest female swimmer ever, posed topless for Sports Illustrated. Brandi Chastain, member of the 1999 U.S. Womens World Cup Team, posed nude (except for her Nike cleats). Both Thompson and Chastain are blond, white, and physically fit females (Carty, 2005). Because they fit the traditional concept of American femininity, their muscles are not viewed as threatening. African American femininity is generally viewed differently.

The African American Family Expectations

The image of women athletes as mannish failed heterosexuals represents a thinly veiled reference to lesbianism in sport. The word homophobia has been a consistent problem in sports. It is an act of disrespect and unfair treatment criticizing an individual's sexual preference that exists outside mainstream ideology about heterosexual behavior (Cahn, 1993). Gay men and lesbians have always been and will always be a part of sports. Coakley (2009) suggests that changed ideologies rooted in education are needed. He asserts that Americans must understand that sexuality does not affect one's athletic abilities on the playing field or one's ability to be an admirable and respected person off the playing field. With the exception a few professional athletes, most lesbian and gay athletes wait until after they retire from competition to make their sexuality public. It is taboo for professional athletes to publicly-address their sexuality, in fear of being ridiculed and isolated by their counterparts (Coakley, 2009). Sheryl Swoopes was the first African-American woman athlete to come out as lesbian (WSF, 2007). In addition, former Orlando Magic center/forward John Amaechi made history as being the first African American professional NBA player to openly admit to being a homosexual (ESPN.com, 2007). The initial reaction in both cases was public shock.

African American homophobic attitudes and practices historically stem from oppression by white society. The traditional black family believes homosexuality is detrimental to the black family, an abomination, and is a "white" thing (Glaude, 2003). Most African American women deal with homosexuality by being closed off on the subject. Homophobia is a sensitive taboo subject that exists in the African American community as in white society (Brown-Douglas, K. (2003).

African American families have strong family ties and flexible gender roles. Although, the majority of African American families are Christian based and believe in the male dominated household, they are the primary social unit and source of emotional and material support for many African American lesbians (Greene, 2000). An African American lesbian is less likely to be excluded from her family than a white lesbian.

Methodology

Data for this study was acquired through a web based content analysis. Google images were obtained via the Google.com website. A total of 615 images were viewed. The sports chosen were basketball, volleyball, tennis, soccer, track & field, boxing, softball, fencing, and gymnastics. The sports were chosen based on the research team's knowledge of African American female participation. Categories were divided into (a) Sexual, (b) Athletic, (c) Feminine, and (d) Neutral. Once the information was obtained, a simple statistical test was conducted to find the percentage of female athletes that were portrayed by print advertisements. Some photos fell in multiple categories but were placed into alternating categories on a consistent basis to eliminate repeated measures.

Definition of Terms

Sexual: Revealing sexually provocative images.

Athletic: Action, sports oriented images.

Feminine: Any photo displaying a softer glamour image.

Neutral: Any non-action, non-sexual, or non-feminine intended image.

The following graphs depict the total number of photos from the nine sports considered.

		Categories			
Athlete	Sport	Athletic	Sexual	Feminine	Neutral
Lisa Leslie	Basketball	19	5	11	15
Sheryl Swoopes	Basketball	4	4	7	35
Dawn Staley	Basketball	6	3	7	34
Laila Ali	Boxing	25	7	17	8
Laura Flessel-Colovic	Fencing	11	0	5	4
Dominique Dawes	Gymnastics	25	2	11	17
Brianna Scurry	Soccer	11	0	7	32
Natasha Watley	Softball	26	0	9	9
Venus Williams	Tennis	22	6	2	20
Serena Williams	Tennis	19	10	11	10
Florence Griffith-Joyner	Track & Field	23	4	10	5
Marion Jones	Track & Field	41	3	7	17
Annett Davis	Volleyball (beach)	21	1	4	3
Totals		253	45	108	209
					615

Discussion

This study set out to examine the media's portrayal of African American female athletes. Race and popularity of the athlete and sport were important factors to consider when selecting subjects. Identical images were not considered for inclusion. Very few studies have been completed which investigated and analyzed the media images of African American female athletes. This fact established the uniqueness of this particular study.

To answer the main research question, "How are African American female athletes truly represented by media?" four categories were identified. Before the data analysis, the assumption was made that regardless of sport, all African American female athletes would have some form of sexual photo/media exposure. It was believed that African American women in general are viewed by the male dominated society as sexual objects for the most part. Our presumptions were based on the related literature.

The results of this study revealed an interesting trend. The highest percentage of images found in our investigation was categorized under Athletic (41%) images followed by Neutral (34%) images. The literature consistently demonstrated that the predominant images of African American female athletes was that they were viewed as sex symbols. However, this study showed there were few (7%) sexual images of any of the women athletes who participated in this study.

Conclusions

The results of this study demonstrated a possible shift in the images of African American women athletes. While a small percentage of the data (7%) disclosed that sexual images of African American women athletes continues to exist, it is surprising to note that the percentage is relatively small. Further examination of the data suggests a conservatism that exists among African American female athletes. Because so few images were sexual or soft feminine images (18%), perhaps a modicum of control over their social image exists among African American women athletes. While no athlete has control over the photos taken while they compete in their sport, it was suggested by the research team that athletes do have control over their images outside of sport. How they dress or pose for personal photo shoots or for product endorsements and other media opportunities is, at least in part, under their control. However, another consideration must be considered. Product endorsements opportunities are controlled by companies who are very conscious and sensitive about their product and company image. A resulting third postulation is that the media and corporate America does not embrace nor recognize the sexuality of African American athletes and view them as athletes reserving the ideology of American sexuality and femininity for white females. The only exception in this study where that sexuality was embraced was with Serena Williams who carefully scripts her public image as a professional athlete. No doubt further research is necessary to fully understand the social images of African American female professional athletes.

References

Bailey, S.M. (1993). The current status of gender equity research in American schools. *Educational Psychologist*, Vol. 28, 4, 321.

Brown-Douglas, K. (2003). Homophobia and heterosexism in the Black church and community. In Glaude, E.S., West, C, (Ed), *African American religious thought: an anthology* (pp 996–1018). Westminster John Knox Press. Louisville, KY.

Cahn, S. K. (1993). "Muscle moll" to the "butch" ballplayer: Mannishness, lesbianism, and homophobia in U.S. women's sport. *Feminist Studies*, 19, 2, 343–368.

CBSNews.com, (2007), http://www.cbsnews.com/stories/2007/04/12/national/main2675273.shtml

Coakley, Jay, (2009), *Sport in Society: Issues and controversies*, McGraw/Hill: New York.

Douglas, D.D., (2002). To be young, gifted, black and female: A meditation on the cultural politics at play in representations of Venus and Serena Williams. http://www.physed.otag.ac.nz/sosol/v5i2_3.html

Edwards, J. (1999).The Black female athlete and the politics on (In) Visibility. *New Political Economy*, Vol. 4, 2, 278.

Entire, J. (2000). Taboo: Why Black athletes dominate sports and why we're afraid to talk about it. *Public Affairs*, 387 pp.

ESPN.com, (2007), http://sports.espn.go.com/nba/news/story?id=2757105.

Evans, T.M. (1998). In the Title IX Race toward gender equity, the Black female athlete is left to finish last: The lack of access for the invisible woman. *Duke Journal of Gender Law & Policy*, HeinOnline. http://heinonline.org/HOL/Page?collection+journals&handle=hein.journals/howlj42&div=11&size=2&rot=0&typw=image

Gaston, J.L. (2003). The Impact of Title IX on group representation in athletic administration: A trend analysis of NCAA institutions. *National Association of Student Affairs Professionals Journal*, Vol. 6, 1, 79.

Gill, E. (2007). The prevalence of Black females in college sports: It's just an illusion. *Diverse Online*. Retrieved on May 14, 2008. http://www.diverseeducation.com/artman/publish/printe_7384.shtml

Greene, B. (2000). African American lesbian and bisexual women. *Journal of Social Issues*, 56, 2, 239–249.

Jackson, C.A. (2006). Measuring the impact of Title IX for women of color: The case of the University of Akron. A Dissertation presented to the Graduate Faculty of The University of Akron.

Jones, R., Murrell, A., & Jackson, J. (1999). Pretty versus powerful in the sports pages: Print media coverage of U.S. women's Olympic gold medal winning teams. *Journal of Sport and Social Issues*, Vol. 23,183.

Kane, M. J. (1996). Media coverage of the post Title IX female athlete: A feminist analysis of sport, gender, and power. *Duke Journal of Gender Law & Policy*, HeinOnline. http://heinonline.org/HOL/page?collection=journals&handle=hein.journals/djglp3&div=7&size=2&rot=07type=image

Lansbury, J.H. (2001). "The Tuskegee Flash" and "The Slender Harlem Stroker": Black women athletes on the margin. *Journal of Sport History*, Vol. 22, 8, 233.

Larrybrownsports.com, (2009)., littp://larrybrownsports.com/tennis/announcer-roger-rashed- likes-serena-williams-ass/1234.

Pedersen, M., Laucella, P., & Miloch, K. (2007). Sport sociology and media. In strategic sport communication. *Human Kinetics,* Champaign, IL.

NCAA.org., (2009), http://www.ncaa.org/wps/ncaa?key=/ncca/ncca/sports+and+championship/general+information/stats/w+basketball/index.html,

Rasheed, R. (2008). Venus Williams' bottom comments spark outrage. *The Daily Telegraph Article*. Retrieved May 16, 2008. http://www.news.com.au/dailytelegraph/story/0,22049,23059840-5001021,00.html

Richardson, D. (2005). Natural causes: Black female athletes. Black Athlete Sports Network www.blackathlete.net. Retrieved on May 14, 2008.

Schult, J. (2005). Reading the catsuit: Serena Williams and the production of Blackness at the 2002 U.S. Open. *Journal of Sport and Social Issues*, Vol. 29, 338. Venus and Serena Williams Biography. Retrieved May 21, 2008. http://www.thebiographychannel.co.uk/biography_story/960:954/1/Venus_Serena__Williams.htm

Women's Sport Foundation. (October 2007). Reflections on the significance of Sheryl Swoopes coming out as a lesbian. http://www.womenssportsfoundation.org/Content/Articles/Issue/Homophobia/R/Reflections-on-the-Significance-of-Sheryl-Swoopes-Coming-Out-As-A-Lesbian.aspx

Chapter 6

College Sports

14

College Students' Perceptions, Myths, and Stereotypes about African American Athleticism

A Qualitative Investigation

C. Keith Harrison
Suzanne Malia Lawrence

Fanciful new constructions of race aside, modern biology leaves little doubt that our classification of races is not biological at all. Blacks having dark-skin is of as much interest as blue-eyed people having blue eyes. The immense political and emotional baggage we carry with the concept of human race, despite what might seem intuitively obvious to some people, is, in fact, a consequence of our own social relations, and is simply not a biological topic. (Vandermeer, 1996, p. 125)

Introduction

ONE OF THE MOST UNRESOLVED DEBATES IN THE ACADEMY AND THE broader society is the myth of the African American athlete's superiority and dominance in a few sports. While little systematic scientific evidence confirms any genetic edge directly correlated with athletic performance, the question continues to be raised in both scholarly and public spaces. The myth of African Americans achieving in sports has been historically stagnant and has its origins with the construction and ideology of race in America. Since the latter part of the nineteenth century, professionals in fields such as coaching, athletics, anthropology, sociology, physical education, biology, medicine, and sportcasting have contributed analysis of and insight into the debate of Black athletic superiority (Wiggins, 1997). But for all that, no scientific evidence has been concluded that clearly states:

> African Americans are athletically superior because of genetic endowment.
> (Miller, 1998; Coakley, 1999)

The current study examines the perceptions of college students in regards to myths and stereotypes of athleticism. Reasons for racial disparity in sport and Black athletic superiority is explored. The 'natural' athlete myth literature (Hoberman, 1997; Entine, 2000) is investigated. The cultural and social factors involved in athleticism (Proctor & Harrison, 1999; Harrison, 2000a) lends itself to the current study as well.

Black Athletic Superiority and Perpetuated Stereotypes

The widely held belief in Black athletic superiority is actually fairly recent, arising only after barriers to Black participation in sports were removed (Hoberman, 1997). Currently, Black athletes are consistency stereotyped as being better athletes than their White counterparts. According to Edwards (1971), There are no differences that make any difference. Athletic skills are essentially culturally linked capabilities. It is racism, not genes, that explains the domination of Black athletes' (p. 38). In Hoberman's (1997) famous controversial work titled Darwin's Athletes, he addressed the stereotype of Black athletic superiority. Hoberman's (1997) main theme was that society's infatuation with Black athleticism perpetuates the negative stereotype that Blacks are physically superior and intellectually inferior compared to Whites. Hoberman (1997) reiterated the message that the celebration of athletically talented Black Americans, as played out in sports today, is harmful.

However, notions of Black athletic superiority and intellectual inferiority permeate the minds of thousands, if not millions, of American citizens. Part of the reason is that the manner in which this debate has been framed is biased, political, and limited in analysis. Davis (1990), in the article titled 'The articulation of difference: White preoccupation with the question of racially linked genetic differences among athletes', illuminates the direction of the current study:

> This paper focuses on the contemporary White public and scientific preoccupation with the question of racially linked genetic differences between Black and White male athletes. It is argued that the preoccupation itself is racist because it is founded on and naturalizes racial categories as fixed and unambiguous biological realities, thus obscuring the political processes of racial formation. The biological determinism underlying the preoccupation conceals both human agency and sociopolitical forces, including racism. (p. 179)

Individuals fail to conceptualize the gigantic array of sports that White athletes participate in such as National Hockey League (NHL), Major League Baseball (MLB), Major League Soccer (MLS), Professional Golf Association (PGA), and the Ladies Professional Golf Association (LPGA). According to some sport sociologists, racism and representation are historically linked in American society (Edwards, 1969; Harrison, 1998; Hawkins, 1998). Images that depict Blacks as childlike, lazy, and hyper-physical are the major themes of media portrayals and are present in modern day society. The media often depict Black men as brutes, athletic icons, strong, and fast but rarely, if at all, as smart. These depictions cause harmful stereotypes to be perpetuated in society (Stone et al, 1999).

Books such as Jon Entine's (2000) Taboo: Why Black Athletes Dominate Sports and Why We Are Afraid to Talk about it continue to narrow this issue and overlook social and cultural factors, other ethnic groups, and the political connection of this issue in terms of educational and occupational access, and economic attainment. A few coaches and teachers have expressed to one of the co-authors that White youth shy away from running sprints and other events because White youth claim, 'Blacks are better at this sport or that sport than we are'. Entine is partially right in the context of his title—society is afraid to discuss this issue in an overt manner. Covertly though, this discussion is taking place. As a result, cultural sound bites surface that reinforce racism such as 'White men can't jump', 'Blacks jump out of the gym', and 'speed kills'. 'Once again, research such as Entine's perpetuate the myth of the "natural" Black athlete, rather than destroying it' (Coakley, 1999, p. 4). This leads us to the cultural and social explanation of African American athleticism.

Cultural/Social Factors

Several scholars and sport sociologists (Carlston, 1983; Majors, 1990; Harrison, 1998; Coakley, 2001) maintain that differences between European American and African American athletes and their performances are due to the differences in social environments and influences that impact their lives. These sociologists argue that variables of political, social, historical, ideological, and cultural strife are much more significant than the biologically determined and/or eugenic category of race.

After 30 years of investigating, reviewing research, and thinking about the issue of race and athletic performance, noted sport sociologist Jay Coakley (1999) concluded the following: (1) there are genetic differences between individuals; (2) genetic characteristics are related to sport performance; (3) it is not very probable that one gene accounts for success across a range of sports; (4) there is no scientifically recognized biological reason to suspect a connection between skin color and genes related to sport performance; (5) the development of bodies and the development and expression of physical skills are related to cultural definitions of skin color and race; and (6) culturally based ideas about skin color influence how athlete and entertainers are watched and perceived in this society. Coakley is leading researchers away from exploring the biological reasons for athletic performance and he attributes common societal perceptions to culturally based ideas.

Cultural and social factors in the debate of Black athletic superiority need to continue to be explored. Proctor and Harrison (1999) stated, 'We are not likely to convince students, faculty, staff, or the larger community that prevailing social prejudices are wrong, if we teach them only about biological factors affecting performance and ignore cultural contributions' (p. 14). Miller (1998), a sport historian, contended the significance of history and social policy in the debate of individual abilities in his following quote:

> Since 'race matters,' as the title of one of Cornel West's noted book avows, we need to discuss why it should. It matters in our scrutiny of the contexts and remedies of present social conditions, in our concern that the long history of racial oppression be reckoned with as we debate social policy. We must also examine when it should not it should not matter in judgments of individual abilities and accomplishments. (p. 124)

Race should be disregarded in judging individual performances; however, this is very seldom the case in today's society.

The highly utilized genetic explanation for athleticism fails due to the fact that the features that are explored to make distinctions among groups are usually the product of cultural evolution. Cultural evolution is more rapid than Darwinian evolution and it is readily reversible because its products are environmentally interactive (Proctor & Harrison, 1999). Therefore, cultural evolution should prevail in the behavioral diversity displayed by human groups (Proctor & Harrison, 1999). To this end, no scholar has ever found systematic evidence that connects genetically-based, performance-related physical traits that serve as the basis for athletic performance in any or all sports (Coakley, 2001).

This investigation, through the use of an open-ended interview question, explores cultural myths and stereotypes about White American and African American athleticism. Specifically, this study utilized the Athletic Ability and Achievement Attitudes and Beliefs (AAAAB) instrument (Harrison et al, in press) which was developed in collaboration with experts in the fields of sport sociology, sport psychology, sport history, and sport management, as well as logical content from related literature. The AAAAB instrument (Harrison et al., in press) was developed to qualitatively and quantitatively determine those variables that most impact students' perceptions of Black and White athleticism and White athletic inferiority.

The scope of this inquiry explored the responses to one of the open-ended questions from the AAAAB instrument (Harrison et al., in press) (question listed in Methods section). These two questions were developed based on two common stereotypes addressed in scholarly and popular literature on race and athleticism. This refers to the stereotypical assumption that in a few high profile sports such as football and basketball White athletes are inferior and Black athletes are superior (Hoberman, 1997). As part of a larger study, the current study examines the data from one of the two open-ended questions. The remaining open-ended question and

Likert items are beyond the scope of the current study; however, they are briefly described in the Methods section of this manuscript. This explicit focus on qualitative data is due to the rich and expressive narratives by most of the participants to both open-ended questions. In terms of asking two open-ended questions, both questions were strategically positioned in the survey to avoid confusion by the respondents. This was so respondents would focus on each question separately. Both open-ended questions are proactively framed to elicit responses to the Black/White binary of athletic performance.

Theory and Central Focus

Relevant literature was synthesized to further analyze the scholarly analysis of the 'natural' African American athlete. While the current study focuses on the various scholarship and conceptions of this topical debate, theories such as Allport's (1954) noted contact hypothesis appear to be salient. Allport's major thesis is that families impact the knowledge construction of their children and themselves, and that the less interaction they have with members of other ethnic or racial groups, the less likely they will have complex understandings of their behavior. In terms of race and sport and its high visibility, it is hypothesized that perceptions will be biased and uneducated. This leads this paper to focus on the following central questions: (a) do college students believe in Black athletic superiority?; (b) which factors do college students attribute successful athletic performance to?; and (c) do college students think that race has an influence on athletic performance?

Methods

Participants
Participants include 301 college students from a Midwestern university. Participants (N = 301) are enrolled in introductory communication classes. Participants consist of 70% female (n = 211) and 30% male (n = 90). The ethnic distribution of the sample is as follows: 76.6% White, 12.7% Asian, 6.2% African American, 2.4% Hispanic and 2.1% other. The mean age of the college students is 20. Each student received regular class credit by the instructor for participation in the study (neither of the primary researchers serve as the instructor of these classes). The data collection process took approximately 25 minutes for the introductory classes to complete the survey.

Survey Instrument
There are few inventories that specifically examine perceptions of athleticism, thus the need for the AAAAB instrument (Harrison et al., in press). The survey instrument contains 53 items. Forty-five items were measured using a 5-point Likert scale. The responses were coded as follows: 1 = strongly agree, 2 = agree, 3 = neutral, 4 = disagree, 5 = strongly disagree. There are two semi-

structured questions and six demographic and control items. Reliabilities were determined for the items and alpha levels were obtained. While not the focus of the present study, the items measured students' perceptions of athletes in terms of race on four general levels:

1. athletes achieve at sports because of hard work (23 items = 0.98);
2. athletes achieve at sports because of natural ability (12 items = 0.97);
3. athletes achieve at sports because they are physically better than others (two items = 0.91); and
4. athletes achieve at sports because they are mentally better than others (two items = 0.88)

The AAAAB instrument (Harrison et al., in press) was developed to qualitatively and quantitatively determine those variables that most impact students' perceptions of Black and White athleticism and White athletic inferiority. The scope of the current study qualitatively examines participants' responses to one of the open-ended questions which is listed as follows:

> Of all the racial and ethnic groups in sports, African American athletes have been categorized and labeled as 'natural' athletes, meaning they have some superior genetic edge and dominate certain sports (i.e. football, basketball, and track and field). Explain why you agree or disagree with these notions. What are the reasons for African American athletic achievement in certain sports?

Data Analysis

Participants were presented with one open-ended question regarding African American and White American athleticism (listed above) and instructed to offer a response to the question. After the written responses to the question were collected, they were transcribed into a hard copy (text) for data analysis.2 An investigative team, which consisted of four individuals trained in qualitative research methodology, two of which were the primary researchers, was utilized throughout the data analysis process.

Hierarchical content analysis, as suggested by Patton (1990), was utilized throughout the data analysis process. Following transcription, each investigator read each of the participants' transcripts in order to get a sense of the college students' perceptions. Each investigator independently identified raw-data themes that characterized each participant's response. Raw-data themes are quotes which capture a concept provided by the participant. Then, the investigative team met to discuss the transcripts. The primary purpose of this meeting was to interpret and identify major themes. Raw data themes were utilized to conduct an inductive analysis in order to identify common themes or patterns of greater generality. Themes were derived from all of the transcripts and attempts were made to interpret commonalties among the perceptions described in each of the transcripts (Patton, 2001). Primary researchers identified major themes and subthemes across transcripts and support for each theme was located in each of the transcripts (Patton, 2001).

Finally, utilizing the themes that were previously identified, transcripts were coded and categorized by two trained researchers. Meaning units associated with each theme were identified in each of the transcripts in order to determine the number and percentage of participants that responded within each of the major themes (see Table 1).

Results

The primary focus of utilizing the open-ended question is to assess participants' perceptions of African American athletic achievement Seven major themes emerged which are descriptive of the participants' (n = 301) perceptions, thoughts, and feelings concerning the debate of African American athleticism: Black physical advantage, Black work ethic, Black cultural factors, race disregard, societal factors, Black limited opportunity, and unawareness/X factor. The following section will outline the specific themes and subthemes and give direct quotes from the participants' responses.

Black Physical Advantage

The first theme, Black physical advantage, describes participants' responses which use genetics and natural ability to explain African American athletes' dominance in certain sports (football, basketball, and track). The theme of Black physical advantage is comprised of three subthemes: biology/genetics, history/evolution, and body/ muscle structure. The subtheme of biology/genetics suggests that the African American athletes have superior physical genes and traits. The subtheme of history/evolution attributes Black athletic excellence to historical conditions. The subtheme of body/muscle structure suggests that Black athletes are successful due to the build and muscle structure of their bodies. Participants express the significance of 'God-given' talent in regards to athleticism; consider this example from a participant:

"Absolutely. People are afraid to say it because they think it will come off as racist but the key is Blacks are better athletes than Whites. It doesn't mean he does not work just as hard to develop their talents and it doesn't mean the are any less capable mentally, but what truly separates them is their God-given physical ability: the numbers don't lie; now many say Black players are in the NBA as compared to Whites. The same can be said for the NFL." (157)

TABLE 1 **Major themes: descriptive percentages of transcripts (N = 301)**

(ALL THEMES ARE INCLUDED TO DEMONSTRATE OBJECTIVITY AND NOT TRUNCATE THE MAJOR NARRATIVES VERSUS THE OUTLIER THEMES)

Theme	N	Percentage	Quotes

Black physical advantage	75	25%	I agree that many African Americans are blessed with the ability to play sports and have a number of skills. If people bring genetics into this situation:— African Americans may be taller or bigger and have an advantage in the sports category.
Black work ethic	72	24%	I disagree with these notions. I think the reasons for African American athletic achievement are: drive, commitment and interest.
Black cultural factors	57	19%	I disagree with this stereotype. I think it is completely culturally biased. We label certain sports as 'White sports', 'Black sports', 'wealthy/elitist sports' and 'common sports'. For each race, I think there is a designated 'coolness' attributed to each sport ...which is masculine, which is for the elite ... it all effects the decision.
Race disregard	41	14%	I don't think that it's correct to label a particular race as 'natural' athletes. I'm not sure if African Americans are necessarily better at certain sports despite their large numbers in them (i.e. basketball, basketball, football, etc.). There are no specific reasons for African Americans athletic achievement in certain sports. That is like asking, 'Why is Julie so smart?' It's a dumb question. Certain people are blessed with certain talents.
Societal factors	33	11%	African Americans athletic achievement is due to the encouragement they receive from others and promise of rewards and (better) opportunities (e.g. college education) that can come through athletic achievement.
Black limited opportunity	27	9%	Historically, African Americans were restricted from certain activities. They were allowed to participate in such things as boxing in order to be entertaining for the majority group in society. Blacks were not allowed to play many sports for several years because of the discrimination in the American society. It was necessary for those who wanted to play to show that they were extremely good at the sport. This high standard has continued throughout history into today.
Unawareness/ X factor	27	9%	I disagree, but I don't know why they succeed in certain sports—maybe we just see them more because of media coverage.

Note: Please keep in mind that participants wrote anywhere from two to three sentence responses to an entire paragraph. Each of the responses included several key concepts that coincide with the studies seven major themes. Very few participants' responses exclusively coincided with only one theme.

An African American participant explains the differences between races by history.

> I believe it's because of our history—we've never had anything delivered to us on a silver spoon. We work hard everyday in the struggle therefore there's more of a mean to strive for the 'good life'. (130)

Many of the participants attribute African American athleticism to their muscles and bodies, as the following comments illustrate:

> I think it definitely seems as though a lot of African American athletes have natural athletic builds—growing taller, having leaner muscles, etc. (222)

> African Americans muscles and bodies are slightly different allowing them to run faster and such. (59)

> Blacks in general I think are 'given' a natural talent for athleticism. (218)

Twenty-five percent (75/301) of participants list at least one of the following factors: biology, genetics, history, evolution, body, and/or muscle structure (see Table 1). These comments are interesting when considering that approximately 99% of the anatomical structure is the same and that out of 17 genes, there are more differences and variation within the races than between them (Vandermeer, 1996).

Black Work Ethic

The second theme, Black work ethic, is comprised of three subthemes: practice, effort, and dedication. The subtheme of practice suggests that Black athletes practice more hours than their White counterparts. The subtheme of effort demonstrates the Black athlete has determination and works hard. The subtheme of dedication consists of African American athletes' commitment to athletics. Black athletes' sheer determination and hard work is described by one participant:

> "A lot of success, historically are attributed to dedication and hard work. While many Black athletes have come from under-privileged poor families. They have fought more racial barriers to be where they are today. For some Blacks, athletics isn't their gift. For others, it is a way of life, playing pickup games on concrete urban playgrounds. Much of Black progress has been in professional sports. Give credit to their hard work and perseverance." (247)

Another participant expresses African American athletes tendency to practice long hours.

> There may be more Blacks in some sports because they practice more or because they play more as children. (224)

Participants recognize African American athletes strong work ethic, as the following comment illustrates:

"Yes, some White athletes are inferior in certain sports, not because of their color, but because of their lack of hard work in that sport. African Americans work very hard and therefore succeed in that sport." (105)

The following participant attributes Black athletic superiority to dedication:

I disagree. They try hard at the sports they play. The reason that they achieve is due to their dedication. (245)

Twenty-four percent (72/301) of the participants mention work ethic in their explanation of the difference between Europe American and African American athletes' abilities and successes (see Table 1). To date, there has been no investigation beyond anecdotal evidence of time investment by athletes and how that leads to superior athletic performance. This is a research question that should control for race, class, and gender, due to the fact that the present participants express these constructs in their responses.

Black Cultural Factors

The third theme, Black cultural factors, involves participants' thoughts that African American athleticism is due to environmental and cultural factors. The theme of Black cultural factors is comprised of three subthemes: Black focus/dreams, Black ticket out, and Black family/community. The subtheme of Black focus/dreams suggests that African American athletes have 'hoop dreams' (Sailes, 1998). The subtheme of Black ticket out consists of the idea that African Americans use sport to get out of poverty. The subtheme of family/community involves how Black athletes are encouraged by their families to play certain sports. One participant expresses the idea that African Americans have dreams surrounding their success in sports.

I think more African Americans have dreams of being a star athlete one day and so they work at it more. They use athletics as a way out of the urban areas, whereas Whites don't really have that need. So we see a larger amount of African Americans in urban sports like basketball. (221)

Some participants express the notion that Blacks utilize sports to pave their way out of poverty.

I disagree. They excel cause usually lower socio-economic are, and is only way out. May work harder. (1)

I think achievement is due to attitudes—many African Americans who happen to be living in lower income neighborhood might see sports as a way to lots of money and a way out. The Black role models they see are Michael Jordan, Tiger

Woods, so they might want to emulate those figures they see people like them have been able to achieve in that area. (177)

The following participant acknowledges family influence and encouragement in the African American community.

> I think this is untrue. One possible reason for their high achievement in sports is that their community/family may put more emphasis on that instead of school-work. (208)

This theme describes participants' explanation that athletes play certain sports based on their dreams, upward mobility, and family. Nineteen percent (57/301) of the participants recognize the differences of how the various races are raised and cultural distinctions between the two (see Table 1).

Race Disregard

The fourth theme, race disregard, depicts participants' claim that there is no evident edge in sport based on race. Participants offer several reasons for athletic prowess among both races (Whites and African Americans). The theme of race disregard is comprised of two subthemes: work ethic and talent. The subtheme of work ethic represents participants who attribute athletes success in sports primarily to hard work and time commitment. Participants also attribute athletic success in certain sports (football, basketball, and track and field) to natural talent which is evident in the subtheme talent. Participants express that African Americans do not have an advantage over White athletes based on race, as the following comment illustrates:

> Notions like 'White man's disease' just add to racism in our society and paint African Americans as savage beast capable of little more than athletics. This so-called disease is simply untrue. There are plenty of successful athletes of both races. (140)

One participant describes athletic talent regardless of race:

> While some people may have natural talent in certain sports, these talents are by no means a product of their race. Rather, the talents could belong to a person of any race. (232)

Participants simply attribute athleticism to the specific factor of hard work regardless of race as the following comments illustrate:

Although body type does play a roll in an athlete's ability, the most important part of an athlete is his dedication. (237)

I think there is also a lot of hard work put into practicing that gets all athletes, African American or White or any other race, to the high level of athletic achievements they have reached. (222)

The following comment describes athletic success to natural talent:

Yes, some African Americans are natural athletes, but then again, some Whites are natural athletes too. I cannot explain why there are more African Americans in football and basketball, and I cannot explain why there are more Whites in hockey and golf. (210)

Participants report that there are excellent athletes in all sports regardless of race. Fourteen percent (41/301) failed to buy into the myths of Black athletic superiority (see Table 1). Ninety percent of all sports have less than 1% of African American participation and presence in their sports (Lapchick, 2001), but the perception still remains that 'Black athletes dominate sports' (Entine, 2000).

Societal Factors

Another theme that emerged from participants' responses was societal factors, which holds the society and the media accountable for common societal viewpoints concerning athleticism. The theme of societal factors is comprised of three subthemes: media influence, societal encouragement/expectations, and stereotypes. The subtheme of media influence involves participants who report that the media is responsible for perpetuating stereotypes concerning African American athleticism. The subtheme societal encouragement/expectations attributes athleticism to society's specific expectations. Participants recognize the affect of racial myths and assumed racial differences which is evident in the subtheme of stereotypes. The influence of the media is described by one participant:

I feel that the way society perpetuates these stereotypical viewpoints that one race is better than the next. Through this method, the people listening to the media have a higher chance to think these are true. However, I think that the physiognomy of particular individuals are better suited for a specific sport and therefore those who just don't have the same genetic physical make-up. (252)

Some participants express the influence of society's encouragement and expectations that athletes are exposed to; for example one participant stated:

I disagree with these notions. I feel that African Americans are encouraged to practice at these sports and are expected to do well: this is why I feel that they succeed. Not because of natural ability, but because of societal expectations. (291)

The following participants explain how racial stereotyping has influenced people's opinions and expectations:

No, I do not feel White athletes are inferior in sports. I believe the reason people believe that they are is because of racial stereotyping. People have come to believe that Whites should be doctors/lawyers, etc . ... and that African Americans should be excel at sports, neither one of these stereotypes reflect true facts. (291)

African Americans seem to be able to achieve higher strength and physical superiority than Whites. My high school gym teacher once said they have different kinds of muscles ('fast-twitch' I think) that enables them to have more explosive speed and strength and that Whites have slow twitch muscles that—give them more endurance. I have no idea if this is accurate—he was a pretty stupid guy—but I think this is a somewhat widely accepted theory. (238)

Some participants (11%, 33/301) acknowledge the influence of society and express the powerful effect that the media and stereotypes can have on perceptions (see Table 1). In terms of race and perception, evidence has been found that Black and Whites see the world differently based on social issues or effigies in cinema that relate to social issues (Alderfer & Smith, 1982; Cooper, 1998; Entman & Rojecki, 2000; Hill, 2002).

Black Limited Opportunity

The sixth theme, Black limited opportunity, describes participants' recognition of the lack of resources and opportunities in certain lower class neighborhoods. The theme of Black limited opportunity is comprised of three subthemes: lack of education/resources, socioeconomic status, and discrimination. The subtheme of lack of education/resources describes participants' recognition of lack of resources and education in certain lower class neighborhoods, often Black neighborhoods. The subtheme of socioeconomic status suggests that athleticism is due to class level and family income. The subtheme of Black discrimination involves participants who report that African Americans are discriminated against in certain sectors of society. This theme depicts the relevance of opportunities towards athletic participation. Consider this example from a participant:

No: I think the prevalence of certain groups in certain sports can be explained by looking at the opportunities these groups had growing up and what they were encouraged to do. Sometimes, it has a lot to do with the neighborhoods people grow up in. Not every neighborhood has a golf course and not every neighborhood has a frozen pond or skating rink. (18)

Another participant acknowledges the lack of education for some Black individuals:

Sometimes Blacks see sports as their only way of getting out of 'the hood', sadly to say. People don't always have the same opportunities education wise, either, so sports might just be the only way some Blacks can see themselves going to college. (236)

This participant realizes the significance of socioeconomic status:

Also, some minorities grow up in low socioeconomic areas (along with Whites) but more in minority groups and sports tend to be what they do instead of joining gangs or school. Opposite goes for Whites. Many Whites are middle/ upper class. They are raised to focus more on school and not sports, so they don't practice sports as much (hard work), so they're just isn't as many Whites in some of these sports. (114)

The following participant acknowledges institutional discrimination in society toward African Americans:

Disagree, African Americans' achievement should be given the credit it deserves, but I think it has largely to do with the fact that they are not allowed to succeed in other contexts of life as easily as Whites. Sports can be an outlet, or they can be one of the few fields where they are not discriminated against (in terms of finding a position). (227)

Nine percent (27/301) of the participants recognize the differences in opportunity between the races, affirming social policy discrimination research by scholars on urban demography (see Table 1) (Wilson, 1996; Kelley, 1997).

Unawareness/X Factor

The final theme of unawareness/ X factor is a theme that emerged based on the tendency for participants to simply admit that they did not know the answer. This theme did not include any subthemes. The following responses are representative of this theme:

I disagree, I'm not sure why African Americans dominate certain sport just like I don't know why Whites achieve at other sports. (6)

I don't know if these statements are true. (42)

I don't know if it has been scientifically proven that Blacks, if more so than Whites are natural athletes. (146)

The following participant seems to express the 'X factor', in terms of not knowing what the variable is or is not in terms of certain groups dominating particular sports:

> I do not know that much about African Americans' genetic abilities or if they are better at sports than other races. Therefore I don't know for sure if I agree or disagree. I would have to say, however that I would like to disagree. I think that there are a lot of African Americans in sport mainly due to the fact that perhaps they had more exposure to sports as kids than other races. Or maybe they are very dedicated. I do not really know why they have such high achievement, though. (205)

These quotes suggest that some people (9%, 27/301) are open to being educated about this topic, and that curricular diversity with controversial issues such as the present one could prove positive for informing and shaping views (see Table 1) (Hooks, 1994). These quotes also affirm what some scholars have suggested and the empirical data indicates: that no one knows 'why' African American athletes dominate a few sports (Coakley, 2001). The discussion section that follows will enable the researchers to engage in a more in-depth synthesis of what the findings mean and imply.

Discussion

In regards to the theme of Black physical advantage, participants attribute African American athleticism to 'God-given' genes, Darwinian evolution, and muscular structure. The display of excellence in basketball, football, and track and field by Black athletes has led these college students to believe Blacks have superior genetic traits. One participant even went so far as to say that African Americans are the chosen race:

> African American athletic achievement in certain sports can be attributed to hard work, motivation, and their place as the chosen race by God for hot slam-dunking action. (229)

The physiological literature with reference to race differences was reviewed by Hunter (1998) and Harpalani (1998). Both scholars concluded that the quantitative studies of physiological differences between the races report relatively small differences and do not account for the racial disparity observed in the major sports. Furthermore, small differences in anatomy, physiology, genetics, or biomechanics are not necessarily analogous to superior sport performance (Harrison, 2001). Participant responses as presented in the Results section (Black physical advantage theme) focus on various Black body parts such as shorter tendons, longer femurs, higher levels of testosterone, and more 'fast-twitch' muscles. Miller (1998) also claimed the focus on the body when contemplating differences as his following quote illustrates:

> With regard to the historical construction of racial categories, moreover, we ought to consider that even if many social commentators argue that the most significant debate today concerns the ways test scores or the reification of diverse cultural stances can be used to fold, bend, spindle, and mutilate existing public policy, the body continues to loom large in many people's thinking about difference. Indeed, the highlights of TV sports reports often provide the most obvious, vivid markers of distinctions associated with race and ethnicity. (p. 124)

Carrington (2002) continues to highlight the focus on the body. He explains how the media focuses on Black bodies and faces in their representation of athletes, entertainers, and musicians.

Many scientists have arrived at a variety of explanations for athleticism. For example, Coetzer et al. (1993) found that the major determining factor among those assessed was in training intensities between Black and White runners. Astrand and Rodahl (1986) recognize that natural endowment (genetic factor) plays a major role in performance capacity but conclude that the most important factor that determines the individuals' response to training is their ability to be highly motivated. Findings such as these lead to the idea that work ethic plays a significant role in athletic excellence.

The theme of Black work ethic demonstrates that participants attribute Black excellence in certain sports to long practice hours, determination, and dedication. Even with evidence that support the idea of work ethic and mental excellence (Harrison et al., in press), the racial ideology that exists today often celebrates the 'natural' athlete myth. The results of the Harrison et al. study (in press) support the theme of Black work ethic in the current study. Harrison et al. utilized a survey and assessed college students' perceptions of race, athletic ability, and achievement. The investigators found that on average (based on Likert scale) African American students strongly agreed with the statement that African Americans succeed at sports because of hard work while White students reported that they agreed with this statement. Dr. Alvin Poussaint, a psychiatrist at Harvard, addressed the issue of Black athleticism and claimed that Black athletes simply work harder in this lengthy but salient quote:

In some Whites there is an unwillingness to face the fact that Black athletes work harder. Throughout the years of discrimination, Blacks began to see sport as survival. You do what you've been trained to do. But along the way, the traits which made (them) able to excel at sports—mental acuity, mental concentration, mental toughness, work ethic—the very traits which Blacks weren't supposed to have and supposedly were the reason to keep them out of sports in the first place, now those traits are given little or no credence. Why don't we look at the mental work within sport? If the attitude of the majority and minority was more open, more Blacks would become mathematicians and scientists. Right now, it's a matter of self-fulfilling prophecy. (Pouissant, cited in Wiley, 1991, p. 186)

According to Tucker (1994), the transformation of racial ideology, very much steeped in political and social forces, causes most people to disregard work ethic and mental prowess. Today, the justification for African Americans outperforming Whites in a few sports (football, basketball, track, boxing) has produced rhetoric and societal discourse that African Americans are physically superior, but mentally inferior. Any athletic talent or prowess is present because of God-given talents and 'natural' abilities, not personal industry or cognitive and psychomotor mastery of athletic techniques (Robeson, 1919).

In the theme Black cultural factors, participants attribute athleticism to specific facets of Black culture such as dreams, ticket out of poverty, and family influence. African American cultural influences on their athletic expression are best explained when sociopolitical influences are considered which involves societal influence and limits in opportunity (Gilroy, 2000). Evidence is building in the debate of the 'natural' athlete that supports variables of political, social, historical, ideological, and cultural strife being much more significant than the biological category of race.

The consideration of cultural factors has been supported by the same physiologists who claimed to properly assess and determine the physiological capacity between ethnic groups, one must consider the fact that there are very different modes of life, nutritional backgrounds, and state of physical training between, as well as within, each ethnic group (Hunter, 1998; Proctor, 1999). The way in which individuals live, what foods they eat, and which training methods they adopt are usually based on cultural factors and can have a significant impact on athletic success. Performance is not based upon a specific workout, a single technique, a feature of anatomy, or a unique trait of physiology. Instead, it is a complex accumulation from multiple experiences drawn from our culture, society, history, and geographic location (Proctor, 1999).

The major theme of race disregard involved participants who completely disregarded the issue of race in their responses. Participants specifically state race does not have anything to do with it. For these participants race does not matter in determining individual physical feats or athletic performance. Athleticism can be attained by anyone through a variety of avenues, hard work, natural talent, dedication, and determination. The Harrison et al. (in press) study parallels the current study again through the following two findings: (a) students tended to agree or agree strongly with the statement that athletes succeed at their particular sport because of hard work; and (b) on average students disagreed with the items that stated that athletes of one race achieved because they were mentally or physically better than another race. These researchers concluded that work, which is the result of motivation, is the key component for performance levels above and beyond the average.

The following results of the Harrison et al. (in press) study also coincide with the sub-theme of media influence and the major theme of Black physical advantage in the current study. Participants report that the media is responsible for perpetuating stereotypes concerning African American athleticism. And many of these stereotypes surround the notion that African Americans have some type of physical advantage over White Americans. Harrison et al. found students who watched three or more hours of TV a day in college were more likely to agree with the statement that 'African Americans achieve at football because of natural ability. They also found White students who watched three or more hours of TV in college were more likely to agree with the statement that 'basketball is mostly African American because Blacks are physically better than Whites'.

As Carrington (2002) notes, 'Mainstream media culture is dominated by Black faces and bodies, from the sports fields and fashion catwalks, to our cinematic screens and music video channels, and even (occasionally) within the high, cultural spaces of award ceremonies for novelistic and avant-garde artistic production' (p. 1). Research consistently infers that media still portray African Americans inaccurately and stereotypically (Rainville & McCormick, 1977; Murrell & Curtis, 1994; Rada, 1996). All three of these aforementioned studies confirm stagnant beliefs about Blacks: they are athletic but not intelligent; possess animal and not human characteristics; and lack positive character traits. As participants have demonstrated, culturally-based ideas about skin color influence perceptions in the debate of athleticism (Coakley, 2001). Individuals gain these ideas not only from their cultural group but also from their exposure to the media.

Historically, unequal and separate societies were created and reinforced by the mainstream media. On television, the characterizations of Black communities as excellent in athletic performance are highly representative. This is coupled with the absence of Blacks in roles of excellence in other professions (Hoberman, 1997), which serves to recreate and support the myth of genetic predisposition to high levels of athletic performance rather than attributing performance to high levels of hard work. In the long run, this has channeled Black youth into sport and away from intellectual pursuit, which is needed to achieve excellence in our society. This channeling of Black youth has created powerful stereotypes about African Americans (Wiley, 1991; Hoberman, 1997).

The subtheme of stereotypes emerged in the present study in which participants recognize the affect of racial myths and assumed racial differences. In the participants' quotes they explain how racial stereotyping has influenced people's opinions, expectations, and perceptions. Harrison (1999) surveyed 200 college students enrolled in the physical education activity program at a southeastern regional university in the United States. Respondents overwhelmingly indicated that certain racial groups were more likely to participate in particular sports and physical activities. Harrison (1999) also concluded, 'That most subjects, regardless of race, indicated that racial groups were better in sport activities that generally have been stereotyped for that group. It is interesting but ambiguous as to why African American subjects indicate European Americans are better at activities where little or no African American presence appears' (p. 8). Harrison's study parallels the current one by utilizing college students as well.

The subtheme of stereotypes also supports Hoberman's (1997) claim that society's infatuation with Black athleticism perpetuates the negative stereotype that Blacks are physically superior and intellectually inferior compared to Whites. He argues that African Americans are entrapped by the world of athleticism which involves Blacks seeking respect and opportunity and Whites seeking entertainment and profit. Both White Americans and African Americans are discouraged from challenging fundamental assumptions about racial difference, thus both tend to accept the idea of Black athletic superiority. A great example of a stereotype being reiterated and perpetuated is when Entine (2000) concluded his book with the following remark 'White men can't jump' (p. 341). These types of remarks and labels reinforce racism and perpetuate the myth of the 'natural' Black athlete, rather than destroying it (Coakley, 1999).

The first research question in the current study addresses whether college students believe in Black athletic superiority. Some college students do buy into the notion of the 'natural' Black athlete. This is evident in the theme of Black physical advantage and in the subtheme of Black physical attributes in which participants report that African Americans have a superior gene, an extra muscle, a longer femur, and are given these attributes by God. Clearly, participants are finding race to be a significant factor in athletic prowess.

The second question involves which factors college students attribute to successful athletic performance. College students in the current study attribute athletic excellence in certain sports (basketball, football, and track and field) to a variety of following factors: (a) genetics; (b) history, (c) evolution; (d) muscle structure; (e) work ethic; (f) culture; (g) dreams; (h) family, (i) natural talent; (k) media stereotypes; (l) opportunity; and (m) encouragement. Many of the participants attribute athleticism to a combination of these factors. Few participants attribute it only to one factor.

The final question addresses whether college students think that race has an influence on athletic performance. Some participants, which is evident in the theme race disregard, report that race is to be disregarded and any individuals that have work ethic and talent can be successful in athletics. However, on the other hand, there were plenty of participants as mentioned earlier that seem to buy into the idea of racially superior genes. These participants attribute excellent athletic performance to race and they strongly believe that African Americans have an advantage over White athletes in certain sports.

The myth of the 'natural' athlete, Black athletic superiority, or White athletic inferiority (whatever the preference of terminology is), still exists today, the irony being that African Americans have been historically excluded from competing in sport due to beliefs of their athletic inferiority. Carrington (2002) concludes that is it evident that colonial myths about Black power have been most clearly expressed in the discourse of the 'tough' Black athlete making the athletic Black body a key repository for contemporary desires and fears about Blackness. The power of the media, cultural stereotypes, myths, and lack of knowledge have perpetuated beliefs of a superior athletic gene that African Americans possess. Numerous public individuals and groups have internalized these myths about attributes in sport and have done little to challenge their assumptions. Who or what should be the impetus for the public to challenge and possibly even change their views of stereotyping African American and White American athletes?

Conclusions and Future Implications

Limitations
The current study was not randomly assigned and had significantly more women than men. People of color were also minimized in the participant sample. Irrespective of these shortcomings, the researchers feel that the current study may suggest a pattern of thinking and the racial knowledge that exist in American culture about Black athletes. Further, the demographics of the participants reflect the population trends of women in higher education in terms of increasing their presence in undergraduate and graduate education (Coleman, 1996).

The dearth of underrepresented ethnic groups in the current study reflects the ethnic representations on many predominantly White campuses. G.K. Harrison et al. (2002) found that in another investigation with a large communication class at the same institution in the current study, many of the students come from the suburbs, several African American students from large cities, and many White American students grew up in neighborhoods with little diversity and attended high schools with few people of color, especially African Americans. This lack of integration supports Allport's (1954) argument mentioned earlier in regards to the contact hypothesis theory.

Recommendations

Research is lacking in terms of qualitative and quantitative inquiry into Black athletes and their feelings, attitudes, and experiences about this issue, including their training methods from childhood to adulthood to achieve in sports (Lowrence, 2001; L. Harrison et al., 2002). In short, Blacks do not dominate sports; they dominate a few sports that have allowed them to compete.

The researchers see the need to pose a few significant questions. Is society afraid to attribute African American achievement to the environment, hard work, and lack of opportunities in the broader societal context and how do myths and pseudo-science affirm status quo beliefs about racist ideology? This progressive framing would move the debate forward, and the investigation of why White males exist and 'dominate' Fortune 500 companies, Chief Executive Officer (CEO) positions, front office positions, and the like would surface in terms of genetic rhetoric and 'natural' athlete propaganda (Harrison, 2000 a,b). Why are there no genetic theories recycled about White overrepresentation in boardrooms paralleling the overrepresentation of Blacks in gyms and gridirons?

In conclusion, it appears that the myth of the 'natural' Black athlete is another social excuse, both convenient and political, to attach notions, inferences, and connotations to an ethnic heritage and population that has historically been oppressed, ostracized, and exploited (Gilroy, 2000). It seems unimaginable that at the turn of the twenty-first century, African Americans are still perceived to be both sub- and super-human. This reflex and tendency to stereotype African American achievement and excellence must continue to be challenged in various scholarly disciplines and public discourses. There is a need for scholarship, as Coakley (1999) stated, that 'Destroys the myth of the natural Black athlete' (p. 4). In the final analysis, the biologist and anthropologist consider race to be a social construction and a distant category of the past when examining human behavior. Clearly, many of the college students in this study use race not only as a conduit but as a necessary cognitive process to understand African American athleticism.

One way to challenge students' views is class dialogue. Scientifically, the empirical data should be presented which examine both sides of this issue, historically and contemporary. Demonstrate to students how stereotypes and stigmas are developed in the culture by utilizing the contact hypothesis theory which transforms these views. Essentially, humanize deep-seated and engrained beliefs. Challenge the students with various literature, data, and research on the subject. The course content must be interdisciplinary: anatomy, physiology, biology, history, sociology, sport management, physical education, movement science, and art must address the issue of race and athleticism. Pedagogically, hooks' approach (1994) of teaching to transgress and lifelong critical thinking of these timely issues may cultivate a change in attitudes. Techniques and strategies in class that challenge racism and not individuals as racist would be a healthy design. College students' perceptions, myths, and stereotypes about African American athleticism are a mere microcosm and vessel to the larger society's attitudes and beliefs about this timely issue.

Acknowledgements

This research is supported by the Office of the Vice Provost for Academic Affairs, the Division of Kinesiology and the Department of Sports Management and Communication at the University of Michigan. Special thanks to Professor Travis Dixon in the Department of Communication at the University of Michigan for his assistance with this study and his students in the introductory communication classes. We would also like to thank the race, media, and stereotype research team at the University of Michigan (Susan Douglas, Nicholas Valentino, Catherine Squires, Kristen Harrison and Derrick Valiant).

Correspondence: G. Keith Harrison, The Paul Robeson Research Center for Academic and Athletic Prowess, Division of Kinesiology, Department of Sport Management and Communication, Ann Arbor, MI 98109–2214, USA. Tel: 1 734 763 9574; e-mail: (ckharris@ umich.edu).

Notes

1. Both authors contributed equally. Order of authorship is alphabetical. C. Keith Harrison is a faculty member at the University of Michigan in the Division of Kinesiology in the Department of Sports Management and Communication. Harrison studies race relations, sport and higher education, and the effects of media images on African American male student athlete career aspirations and desires. Harrison is founder and director of the Paul Robeson Research Center for Academic and Athletic Prowess. Suzanne Malia Lawrence is a faculty member at State University of West Georgia in the Physical Education and Recreation Department. Lawrence focuses her research on social justice issues in sport, career transition of athletes, and the experiences of African American athletes. Lawrence implemented a sport psychology concentration at Coker, which is unique to the southeast region on the undergraduate level.

2. All narratives by the respondents are transcribed verbatim, irrespective of grammatical syntax.

References

Alderfer, C.P. & Smith, Elk. (1982) Studying intergroup relations embedded in organizations, *Administrative Science Quarterly,* 27, pp. 5–65.

Allport, G. (1954) *The Mature of Prejudice* (Redding, GA, Addison-Wesley).

Astrand, P. & Rodahl, K. (1986) *Textbook of Work Physiology: Physiology bases of exercise* (New York, McGraw-Hill).

Carlston, D.E. (1983) An environmental explanation for race differences in basketball performance, *Journal of Sport and Social Issues,* 7, pp. 30–51.

Carrington, B. (2002) 'Race', representation and the sporting body. Paper submitted to the Cucr's occasional paper series, pp. 1–37.

Coakley, JJ. (1999) Keynote presented at the Paul Robeson Research Center for Academic and Athletic Prowess Second Annual Symposium, Ann Arbor, MI.

Coakley, J. (2001) *Sport in Society* (Boston, MA, McGraw-Hill).

Coetzer, P., Noakes, T., Sanders, B., Lambert, M., Bosch, A., Wiggins, T. & Dennis, S. (1993) Superior fatigue resistance of elite Black South African distance runners, *Journal of Applied Physiology,* 75, pp. 1882–1827.

Coleman, M.S. (1996) 'And miles to go before we sleep': the unfinished journey of women in science. Speech given to the Iowa Commission on the status of women.

Cooper, B. (1998) The White–Black fault line': relevancy of race and racism in spectators' experiences of Spike Lee's Do the Right Thing, *Howard Journal of Communications*, 9, pp. 205–228.

Davis, L.R. (1990) The articulation of difference: White preoccupation with the question of racially linked genetic differences among athletes, *Sociology of Sport Journal,* 7, pp. 179–187.

Edwards, H. (1969) *The Revolt of the Black Athlete* (New York, Free Press).

——— (1971) The sources of the Black athlete's superiority, *The Black Scholar*, 3(3), pp. 33–41.

Enttne, J. (2000) *Taboo: Why Black athletes dominate sports and why we're afraid to talk about it* (New York, Public Affairs).

Entman, R. & Rojecki, A. (2000) *The Black Image in the White Mind: Media and race in America* (Chicago, University of Chicago Press).

Gilroy, P. (2000) *Against Race: Imagining political culture beyond the color line* (Cambridge, Belknap Press of Harvard University Press).

Harpalani, V. (1998) The athletic dominance of African Americans—is there a genetic basis?, in: G. Sailes (Ed.) *African Americans in Sport* (New Brunswick, NJ, Transaction).

Harrison, C.K. (1998) The assassination of the Black male image in sport, *Journal of African American Men*, 3(3), pp. 45–56.

Harrison, C.K. (2000a) Anatomy, race and sport: cultural images and athletic performance. Lecture/paper given at Washington State University, Victor P. Dauer Distinguished Lecture in Pullman, WA.

Harrison, C.K. (2000b) What happened to the White athlete?: integration, de-segregation and ideology—empirical answers. Lecture/paper given at Oregon State University, Corvallis, OR.

Harrison, C.K., Proctor, L., Comeaux, E., Plecha, M. & Valdez, A. (2002) Sport, race and film: socio-cultural significance of media perceptions. Paper presented at American Alliance of Health, Physical Education and Dance Annual Meeting in San Diego, CA.

Harrison, C.K., Harrison, L.H., Lawrence, S.M., Proctor, L. & Love, Q, (in press) Racial knowledge about myths and stereotypes about African American male athleticism: a mixed method approach, *Journal of American and Comparative Culture.*

Harrison, L. Jr. (1999) Racial attitudes in sport: a survey on race-sport competence beliefs, in: *Shades of Diversity: Issues and Strategies a Monograph Series* Volume II (Reston, VA, American Alliance of Health, Physical Education, Recreation and Dance).

Harrison, L, Jr. (2001) Perceived physical ability as a function of race and racial comparison, *Research Quarterly for Exercise and Sport*, 72, pp. 196–200.

Harrison, L. Jr., Burden, J, Jr. & Azzarito, L. (2002) Perceptions of athletic superiority: a view from the other side. Paper presented at the American Educational Research Association Annual Meeting in New Orleans, LA.

Hawkins, B. (1998) The dominant images of Black men in America: the representation of OJ. Simpson, in: G. Sailes (Ed.) *African Americans in Sport* (New Brunswick, Nj, Transaction).

Hill, F. (2002) Contrasting perceptions of employment opportunities among collegiate football coaches: the truth and the consequences. Paper presented at the Status of Minorities in Sports: Current Issues, Problems and Recommendations, Symposium at Michigan State University, East Lansing, MI.

Hoberman, J. (1997) *Darwin's Athletes: How sport has damaged Black America and preserved the myth of race* (Boston, Houghton Mifflin).

Hooks, B. (1994) *Teaching to Transgress: Education as the practice of freedom* (New York, Routledge).

Hunter, D. (1998) Race and athletic performance: a physiological review, in: G. Sailes (Ed) *African Americans in Sport* (New Brunswick, NJ, Transaction).

Kelley, R. (1997) To *Mama's Dysfunctional: Fighting the culture wars in urban America* (Boston, Beacon Press).

Lapchick, R.E. (2001) *Smashing Barriers: Race and sport in the new millennium* (Lanham, Madison Books).

Lawrence, S.M. (2001) The African-American athlete's experience of race in sport an existential phenomenological investigation. Unpublished dissertation, Knoxville, TN, University of Tennessee.

Majors, R. (1990) Cool pose: Black masculinity and sports, in: M,A. Messner & D.F. Sabo (Eds) *Sport, Men, and the Gender Order: Critical feminist perspectives* (Champaign, IL, Human Kinetics).

Miller, P.B. (1998) The anatomy of scientific racism: racialist responses to Black athletic achievement, *Journal of Sport History*, 25(1), pp. 119–151.

Murrell, A.J. & Curtis, E. (1994) Causal attributions of performance for Black and White quarterbacks in the NFL: a look at the sports pages, *Journal of Sport & Social Issues*, 18, pp. 224–233.

Patton, M.Q. (1990) Qualitative Evaluation and Research Methods (Newborn Park, CA, Sage).

Proctor, L. (1999) Mythology: genetically based African American athletic prowess. Paper presented at the Western Society for Physical Educators Meeting in Reno, NV.

Proctor, L. & Harrison, C.K. (1999) Don't believe the hype: the mythology of African American male athletic prowess. Paper presented at the North American Society for Sport History, Pennsylvania State University, State College, PA.

Rada, J.A. (1996) Color blind-sided: racial bias in network television's coverage of professional football games, *Howard Journal of Communication*, 7, pp. 231–239.

Rainville, R. & Mccormick, E. (1977) Extent of covert racial prejudice in pro football announcers' speech, *Journalism Quarterly*, 54, pp. 20–26.

Robeson, P.L. (1919) The new idealism. Valedictorian speech, Brunswick, NJ, Rutgers University.

Sailes, G. (1998) *African Americans in Sport* (New Brunswick, NJ, Transaction).

Stone, J., Lynch, C.I., Sjomeling, M. & Darley, J.M. (1999) Stereotype threat effects on Black and White athletic performance, *Journal of Personality and Social Psychology*, 77(6), pp. 1213–1227.

Tucker, W. (1994) *The Science and Politics of Racial Research* (Urbana, IL, University of Illinois Press).

Vandermeer, J. (1996) *Reconstructing Biology: Genetics and Ecology in the New World Order* (New York, John Wiley & Sons, Inc.).

Wiggins, D.K. (1997) *Glory Bound: Black athletes in a White America* (Syracuse, NY, Syracuse University Press).

Wiley, R. (1991) *Why Black People Tend to Shout* (New York, Carol).

Wilson, W.J. (1996) *When Work Disappears* (New York, Alfred Knopf Press).

15

Short Communication
African American Athletes' Experiences of Race in Sport

Suzanne Malia Lawrence

CARRINGTON AND MCDONALD (2002: 2) SUGGEST THAT 'A "CULTURE OF racism" is deeply ingrained in sport' and a great deal of research has explored aspects of race relations and racial discrimination in sport. In recent years, sport sociologists in the US have taken an increasing interest in African American athletes, including Brown et al.'s (2003) study of the perceptions of racial discrimination among White and Black athletes. However, few scholars have undertaken qualitative investigations of the experiences of African American athletes, or given athletes an opportunity to tell their stories in their own words.

There are few studies of White and Black athletes' feelings, attitudes, and experiences about their participation in sport (e.g. Harrison et al., 2002). Anshel (1990) explored Black athletes' interactions with White head coaches, the significance of behavioral styles, the needs of Black athletes, and the effect of their environment on performance. Benson (2000) carried out a qualitative investigation of 'at risk' African American student athletes and found that the athletes' marginal academic performances were constructed in a system of interrelated practices engaged in by the members of the academic setting. And Harrison and Lawrence (2004) conducted a qualitative investigation of African American athletes' perceptions of career transition. Because of the limited research in this area, there is a special need to focus on qualitative investigations of Black athlete's experiences, specifically with regard to race.

The purpose of this study is to investigate African American athletes' experiences of race with regard to specific incidents during their athletic careers. The following research questions are addressed. a) What specific incidents are African American athletes aware of in which race played an important role in their athletic careers? b) What relationships are central for African American athletes in their sporting environments?

Methods

Because of the topic of the study, attempts to recruit participants can be challenging. Race is a volatile and very personal topic, and Coakley (2004) notes that race is not a topic that many people feel comfortable talking about. Eight African American participants were recruited employing Patton's (2001) strategy of purposeful sampling. The purpose of this strategy is to select information-rich cases for in-depth study. The size of the sample and specific cases depend on the study's purpose and the resources of the researcher.

Participants

The study was announced at the beginning of physical activity courses at a major south-eastern university in the US. Potential participants were initially asked whether they identified as African American and if they were athletes. More information about the study was presented to those answering 'yes' to both questions; and these individuals were asked if they felt able to share their experiences of race in their athletic careers. Those who agreed to participate were informed of their confidentiality rights, and signed consent forms; they were also asked to suggest additional athletes who may be interested in participating, and two professional athletes were added to the sample through these recommendations.

The participants are four female and four male African American athletes who had participated in eight different sports: baseball, basketball, boxing, dance, football, gymnastics, softball, and track. Brief descriptions of each of the participants are presented in Table 1. Participants expressed a desire to remain anonymous, and chose their own pseudonyms.

Procedure

After completion of a bracketing interview (Van Maanen, 1983), initial and follow-up (audio-taped) interviews were conducted with each participant. The initial interview lasted approximately 30–45 minutes and the follow-up interview approximately 20–5 minutes. During the initial interview participants were prompted with the following open-ended statement: Tell me about any specific episodes in your athletic career in which race played an important role. Most participants reported on more than one incident, and 22 cases were shared (see Table 2). Follow-up questions were asked in order to obtain more detailed accounts of each of the episodes. All quotes by the participants were transcribed verbatim, irrespective of grammatical syntax. Following the initial interview, a copy of the transcribed audio-tape and a return envelope was mailed to each participant. If participants felt some aspect of the contents needed revision, they so indicated and returned the transcript.

TABLE 1 **Brief description of the eight athletes**

Participant pseudonym	Gender	Sport	Current/former athlete highest level of competition	Age	Varsity team status	No. of years of competition
Christian	Female	Softball	Current/professional	21	Starter	11
Kendra	Female	Softball	Current/collegiate	22	Non-starter	13
Kim	Female	Gymnastics	Former/all state	19	Starter	11
Stacey	Female	Track/dance	Former/high school	20	Non-starter	6
Tom	Male	Baseball	Former/collegiate	31	Starter	25
Kyle	Male	Boxing	Current/professional	33	Starter	23
Willie	Male	Basketball	Former/collegiate	26	Starter	21
Jay	Male	Football/track	Former/collegiate	25	Starter	18

Themes were developed using an interpretive research group prior to the follow-up interviews (Denzin and Lincoln, 2000). During the follow-up interview, a summary description of the themes for each transcript was given to the participant. The purpose of this interview was to obtain clarification and offer participants an opportunity to add any other information (Denzin and Lincoln, 2000; Lincoln and Guba, 1985; Marshall and Rossman, 1999).

Data Analysis

An interpretive research group consisting of four individuals trained in qualitative research methodology engaged in data analysis. Initially, the group members read each participant's transcript separately. The transcripts were then read line by line to obtain a sense of the meaning units within the transcript, and a cluster of initial thematic meanings was derived using a process developed by Marshall and Rossman (1999). Following this, the separate transcripts were interpreted as one group and common thematic patterns were noted and identified.

TABLE 2 The frequency of incidents in each of the situational contexts described by athletes

	Setting/situation	Number of episodes
I	**Game/practice related**	**9**
	High school team tryouts	3
	Away games	2
	Pre-game warm ups	1
	Athlete's coach vs opponents' coach	1
	University volleyball team practice	1
	Boxing match	1
II	**School related**	**6**
	Treatment from school campus personnel	4
	Voting for high school honor awards	1
	Race riot on campus	1
III	**Hotel/restaurant setting**	**4**
	Treatment by restaurant employees	3
	Treatment by hotel employees	1
IV	**Miscellaneous**	**3**
	Contract negotiations	2
	Treatment by neighbors	1
	Total number of episodes	22

Results

The participants identified 22 different race related experiences in sport, both positive and negative, in four settings. Table 2 provides a breakdown of the frequency of these experiences. Five major themes emerged from participants' experiences of race in sport: 'being hurt', 'outrage and shock', 'team togetherness', 'being empowered', and 'differences'. These themes are taken directly from the participants' words ('in vivo coding', Ryan and Bernard, 2000).

Being Hurt
'Being hurt' involved participants experiencing heartache and sadness; they felt used, abused, and stereotyped as a result of their experiences. Participants described times when they were not given

equal opportunity or when they were treated unfairly. Kyle expressed the pain he felt when his promoter took away his opportunity to box in a championship fight.

> I'd go ahead and challenge another level of boxing and just go for that avenue. Like my youth is still there and my ability is still there, they're afraid that, you know, I may be able to beat this guy. So, they kind of protect him, and they used me along the same. So, I feel like I was, that kind of like hurt me. More or less racially toward me, I think I was just being used in that way. (Kyle)

Stacey spoke of having her feelings hurt during basketball tryouts.

> Well I remember, I was thinking, I don't know if I was mad about the time, but remember trying out for basketball team. And I was pretty good. I was pretty good. And I remember thinking I didn't get picked because they already had some Black people on the team. And I know some people that were sorry athletes that played on the team. And I told my mom and dad that I don't want to play on that team. I tried out and I worked hard. And I didn't make the team. So I just stopped playing basketball after that because it just hurt my feelings. (Stacey)

Another athlete described several experiences that were extremely tough to go through.

> Oh, they would say, some people would be like we don't want you, and this is in the 90's. This is in the late 90's and people are still calling, you know, we don't want your business here niggers, you know, and stuff of that nature. When something got tore up. When we check out of the hotel and we got on our bus, we couldn't leave. Sometimes they would call the police and say well, those niggers stole stuff from the room, you know, from an alarm clock to bed sheets. And none of that stuff happened. And we just had to pay for stuff right on the spot. (Willie)

Willie also had experiences that involved local townspeople, and one in a restaurant.

> Oh, they would say won't you city niggers go back to where you come from. We don't want you down here. We don't need you down here. You're no good to this town and stuff like that. The people in that town, most of the White people in the town. And, the town is 70% Black and 30% White. And, this was a real, it was real racial, you know. But most of the Black people, they try to, they tolerate it and they go along with it But, it was pretty rough. (Willie)

Some times, they would, they would go as far as dropping the stuff, and they would act like it was an accident. Well, you knew it wasn't an accident. You know, they knew you had a certain time to eat, you know, because you've got shoot around and you've got so long for your food to digest, you know, before you could get out there and play. And they would do stuff like that on purpose. (Willie)

Athletes were also aware of the racial stereotypes some people have about Black athletes.

But that's what we see, people look at Black athletes as being a physical specimen, but not mentally you know. I would like to see more Blacks holding down front office positions in professional sports as well as college sports where there be more head coaches in college or assistant coaches in college or trainers so be it. I think the tide is turning a little bit I still think there's a long way to go, but hopefully you know Black athletes will stop getting stereotyped as just being a physical specimen; hopefully people can start, owners can start looking at them as having the mental capacity to excel as well. (Tom)

Another athlete spoke of a difficult relationship she had with her high school softball coach. This particular athlete's father was told that she would never pitch at the local high school because she does not have blonde hair and blue eyes. She described how the coach hurt her feelings.

He had got that message from the head coach, do you know what I mean? But, that junior, that JV coach, he told me. He sat there and told me that I was not a pitcher. He told me I was a thrower. So, you're not a pitcher—you're a thrower. Well, that hurt my feelings. What is a thrower, you know? I'm a pitcher. I'm not a thrower. So, that hurt my feelings. (Kendra)

The same athlete explained being deprived of the opportunity to play softball for her high school team.

Like, it was hard, not necessarily though to give in to him, but I wanted to play with my friends, you know. I had played with them before we even, you know, got to high school. So, I wanted to continue playing. We had played summer ball all the way up, you know, starting out eight years old. So, I wanted to continue playing with them, you know. Then, to see them, you know, I went and watched them play, but that was hard too to sit there and watch them, you know, play knowing that I could have, you know, I should have been playing, but he, you know, he took that away from me in a sense. (Kendra)

Athletes also reported being aware of perceived unfairness. Christian described how she felt that the result of the voting for high school Athlete of the Year award came down to the color of a person's skin.

> But for this particular reason for whatever it may have been with my student body, you know, I wasn't voted for this. And some people could say it's all popularity, but, you know, most of the time things like that turn out pretty fair. I mean this was an obvious choice not just saying this from myself, but from others who approached me afterwards, and even some faculty people who approached me afterwards. So, I really feel like it came down to the color of skin. And even though everyone knew that it wasn't right, you know, they still allowed it to go on, and they still voted this certain way.

> But just to see how obvious something could be, and then you know people would still ignore it regardless, you know. You know, I'm sure there was other factors. But I still feel like had I been White in that same situation that that wouldn't have happened. Part of it was political, part of it was because, you know, I wasn't White. I wasn't I guess financially up with those kind of people. You know, i wasn't financially down with most of the Black people either. But, it was just the fact that, you know, I just wasn't. I wasn't a part of their group even though they had to include me because I was involved in so many things. (Christian)

Six of the eight participants experienced this type of pain, heartache, and stereotyping with regard to their athletic experiences.

Outrage and Shock

The theme 'outrage and shock' describes athletes' responses to their experiences of race and discrimination. Participants reflected on their shock and bewilderment over some of their experiences. Jay described his feelings of both shock and anger concerning racial slurs that were directed towards him following the loss of a close contest.

> We ended up losing the game, but I remember like racial slurs occurring then. That was the first time I really experienced something like that in sports. It kind of shocked me, took me by surprise, and I was upset about it. I told the coach after the game, and he was upset too, you know, and I was surprised that he was upset because he was Caucasian also. You know, he was taking a stand. I was surprised. He was more outraged. He apologized, you know, for the incident, and he was very upset, you know, that had happened especially I think not only

because it was one of his athletes, but just because of it was another person, another human being that was treated wrong I guess. (Jay)

Tom felt a great deal of rage in response to a racially motivated incident that occurred in the middle of a high school football game.

> And we were playing away once again, and I remember tackling one of their players on their sideline right in front of their cheerleaders, and as I was getting up I was on my back, and I'm getting up and one of the cheerleaders spits right in my face you know and calls me the N word once again. Obviously, I was the team captain so obviously I didn't want to lose my cool. But I can honestly say anybody that knows me knows how laid back I am, but that is the one time in my life, athletic or not athletic, that I really wanted to fight you know. But one it was a girl and I can honestly say I think if it had been a guy I would probably have punched him. But it was a girl, and we were in the 'boondocks' ... and you know it was a predominantly White school, and we had about eight or nine Blacks on our football team. (Tom)

Kim reported that she and her family were refused service at a restaurant,

> I was shocked because, you know, I remembered like everybody else eating but me not having my food yet, but I thought they were just slow, you know, with the food. So, that's what I thought it was, and then like when my mom told me, I was like oh, well, you know, it kind of makes sense why everybody else was eating and I wasn't eating. (Kim)

Kendra, in the incident described previously (when she was not considered 'blonde or blue eyed enough to pitch for the school team'), described how surprised she was when she experienced prejudice for the first time.

> I was like, because first of all, as a little girl, I'm thinking, I can't wait to play for this high school when I get older because they had, they had one of the best programs in the State. So, I was all, you know, since I was a little excited about that and then to hear that, it's just kind of like, I was, like your dreams and stuff are like crushed but then at the same time, I'm like why, because that's the first time I had ever experienced anything like that, you know, of anybody being prejudice toward me because I didn't have blonde hair or blue eyes, or. That was the first time I had ever, yea, experienced anything. I couldn't believe that. (Kendra)

Kendra also experienced her coach making derogatory remarks about her in the newspaper.

> Yea, and there was like an article on the front page of the sports section, and it
> had a mean looking picture of him, actually, mean looking. He was saying that,
> you know, he was talking about my scholarship and saying that he said, he said.
> It quoted him. It said I have no character because, he was saying because. I don't
> remember exactly what it said, but it said I had no character because I didn't
> stay, I didn't play for my high school. But, that yea, that newspaper article. He
> basically tried to, you know, bring me down to his level. I couldn't believe it. I
> couldn't believe that he even said that. First of all, I was really upset (Kendra)

Stacey expressed her bewilderment and lack of understanding when she first experienced being
classified on the basis of her color.

> We have people that just, I've never understood that people look at the colors,
> and I see people. When I went to my old school it was like everybody was, if that
> person was James then he was James. And if the person was Jane then she was
> Jane, you know. There was no definition of color. But when I moved to where I
> live now I got to realize the color definition. (Stacey)

Willie reported a racial incident that shocked him and his teammates.

> One time, we were playing this one team and the (opposing) coach spit on him
> (our coach). One of our opponents we was playing, he spit on our coach and
> called him a nigger. Our coach stared at him, and just walked away. We were
> pretty shocked. (Willie)

And Stacey described how the teachers were surprised about a race riot that occurred on her high
school campus.

> I don't know if they were expecting it, but I remember a lot of teachers were—
> some teachers were asking if everybody was okay. And I think they were a little
> surprised that it happened too. (Stacey)

Six of the participants experienced anger, rage, surprise, bewilderment, and/or a lack of understanding in relation to their experiences of race discrimination.

Team Togetherness

'Team togetherness' describes feeling a sense of camaraderie with teammates and a sense of belonging to the team. Participants also reported learning from their teammates and coaches. During these situations, participants experienced race in their sporting context without any racial problems.

> Guys was always close. We was a close team. So, whenever we went in a restaurant, the guys were always close together. (Willie)

> Really, I don't think I don't have any specific times when race played a role because I think a lot of times in team sports when you play mixed races then people are going to root for a team rather than a separate person. And so they see you as one of the team. (Stacey)

Several athletes spoke of their relationship with fellow African Americans, showing awareness of how their Black friends understood them better than White people.

> There was always that inter- or intra-racial type thing going on where some African Americans may call other African Americans, you know, the N-word where I see they, you know, we shouldn't do that. We have so much opposition and somewhat of a different racial culture that's why should we call ourselves that, you know, to each other. I think that's one thing, you know, that may have occurred. Someone called me that. (Jay)

> And a lot of times it's different too because there's just things that Black people can relate to that White people can't. So sometimes if certain things happen I mean my Black friends would understand that someone White wouldn't really necessarily understand. Because they may not know what it was like to grow up rough in their life in this little home. (Christian)

Tom felt a sense of responsibility toward his teammates.

> Obviously, I was the team captain so obviously I didn't want to lose my cool. So like I said I didn't want to cause any confusion. Like I said I am the captain and here we have underclassmen I was supposed to be setting an example for them and that would have been a bad example. So me being the captain that's what kind of motivated me to back off that situation also. (Tom)

Willie explained that observing people's reactions to a teammate, the only White kid on the team, taught him a lot.

> They would call the one White kid, the other team, they would call him a nig-ger lover and stuff, and at some times, we would have—when we were getting ready to leave, they would have the rope where you hang people with. Some of them would swing that at us, and stuff like that. It was just—it was just—it was terrible.
>
> I never seen—I had never seen or experienced anything like that, but he really matured out of it and he learned a whole lot. It taught him a whole lot. You know, he said it didn't bother him. He said it didn't bother him, but I know it probably did bother him a whole lot. At the time, he never said it bothered him, but I knew it bothered him the whole time, but you know. And the bad thing about it, the guy never got playing time, you know. You know, he never played hardly, but he just—it was a learning experience for him. He really appreciated it—you know, that learning experience. (Willie)

Willie felt he learned a lot from the way in which his coach reacted to the racial slur and act described earlier.

> Yes, because you know, he looked at it as if he would do something like that, because he don't expect, he would never expect us to act that way. So, he wasn't going to act that way. He just walked away. You know, it was, I learned a lot. It was, I think it was an experience. I learned from it. I learned a lot from it, you know. But, it was—I learned that—I feel like you can go. (Willie)

Six of the participants reported times when they learned about race relations from being on a team, and felt a sense of togetherness.

Being Empowered

The theme 'being empowered' describes circumstances where athletes learned from, or experi-enced a feeling of empowerment as a result of racial incidents.

> I think many things that I may go through like that eventually makes me a better person whether I understand it then or not. But it just shows me that I can't allow something that, you know, measured by someone else's standards I can't allow that to credit myself or discredit myself. (Christian)

And there was plenty of times that I just wanted to leave, and but I just stayed with it and toughed it out. I learned from it. I learned a lot from it, you know. But, it was, I learned that, I feel like you can go. White people can go through the majority of Black neighborhoods and probably get treated the same way, so. So, that's what I got out of it, and I just, I just learned a lot from it. It made me stronger. It made me a whole lot stronger. (Willie)

Jay spoke of feelings of empowerment after he and some other students had expressed concern over the lack of African American history in a standard history course. They formed a committee to have an African American history course approved.

That was one thing and also in high school, we had an issue about an African American history class where we would have, you know, just world history and regular history,

American history, but not an African American history class. So, I think me and a couple of my classmates were instrumental in proposing that and eventually getting that established, you know, at the high school.

I think it was empowering, you know, knowing that you can have a force, can have a say, so in influencing your academic curriculum because I guess with that, we had to talk to the principal. We had to talk to different people in the school system, like the superintendent, this and that, and it was a very invigorating and empowering experience by being able to do that. And, I think it was a blessing to be in a school or a situation that was open to your ideas and then facilitate implementing that So, it was a great experience. (Jay)

Willie took a spiritual stance with regard to how he made sense of what he had experienced.

It was a learning experience, and it was something that I feel like I needed. I felt like it is something God was taking me through that I needed to go through. You know, at times, you wanted to just like hey, I want to pack my clothes up and I want to leave. But, you know, my mom always telling me, don't run. Just stay there and battle with it. You know, she was always telling me God ain't going to put no more on you than you can bear. And I just, I stuck with it. (Willie)

And Jay described a new perspective he acquired as a result of a particular experience with race.

It was kind of a realization of how the world is and how my place or how I fit into the whole scheme, you know, race-wise. So, it made me much more aware. I think after that it changed my total outlook on everything. I became more militant, more aggressive toward racial issues as a result of that occasion, (Jay)

'Being empowered' deals with experiences that prompted participants' feelings of empowerment and improvement. Four athletes experienced a sense of strength in response to going through difficult events.

Differences

'Differences' describes incidents in which participants were very aware of differences between themselves and others, usually White people. It should be pointed out that five of the athletes experienced life as a student athlete at a predominantly White university. Participants became aware of differences in dress, speech, hair, financial status. They were also aware of differences within their race and outside their race with regard to how teammates handled racial conflict.

Teammates, I'm not real sure. They really, I think they, I don't know if they really knew a whole lot about the situation or if they did, they really didn't make, you know, much comment. I think the guys I played with, you know. We didn't have any problems as far as racial discrepancies or relations, but I think their attitude was more like probably they didn't even want to talk about it, you know, because it kind of disturbed the flow I guess that we had as far as relationship-wise. I think they probably had the attitude of let's just not talk about it. It's in the past. It happened. Let's just go on from there and not let that disturb, you know, what we have, the type of camaraderie that we have on the team. (Jay)

Stacey indicated she was aware of differences in speech and dress.

Yeah it's just my tone of voice change. I can speak—I mean sometimes I'll have to say it's slow or dull, you know. When I get home my speech relaxes because I'm around the family. But I can speak the keen language if I wanted to. I mean perfect grammar and pronunciation and all that stuff. But sometimes I can act, oh I hate that word. And I don't dress like everybody dresses. I don't dress exactly Black and I don't dress exactly White. I mean I look different. Sometimes I do my hair in braids, and when I do my hair that way I don't do a lot of styles. And I don't do anything real plain. (Stacey)

Christian noted how she was treated differently when she was with people of her own race than with people who were White.

> And now I see, I see when I go in a store with my Black friends and get followed around compared to when I was with my White friends and I didn't So there is a difference. It's not obvious to you when you're on one side or the other so I've experienced both sides. (Christian)

And Kim stated that she felt different, but not discriminated against.

> I can remember going to meets and feeling, you know, being like the only different one there and stuff like that, but other than that, they never called me out on it or I never got scored low, or at least I didn't think so because of my race or anything. (Kim)

Four participants experienced differences between 'Black and White,' which accompany their experience of race in sporting contexts.

Conclusions

Race plays a key role in the lives of the African American athletes in this study, a role that it does not play in the lives of White athletes. Participants experienced more than just race-related hassles—they experienced racial slurs and acts, such as having bottles thrown at them, being spit on, and being called a 'nigger'. In response to such acts and slurs participants experienced powerful emotions of pain and bewilderment. Some of the stories were unbelievably sad and heart wrenching and some of the more horrifying experiences affected the quality of these athletes' lives. Their stories serve as evidence to support critical race theory claims that race is vitally significant and racism is found in all sectors of society (Delgado, 2001); and Carrington and McDonald's (2002: 2) claim that 'a "culture of racism" is deeply ingrained in sport'.

Athletes in this study were continually conscious of their 'differences', they were hurt, shocked and outraged by the racial incidents they describe, but they also sometimes felt empowered by their responses to such incidents, they continually learned from the incidents, and they enjoyed the 'team togetherness' facilitated by their sport participation. The athletes were also conscious of the contradictions—in the athletic arena, teammates, fans, administrators, and coaches might express gratitude and adulation. Unfortunately, feelings of acceptance change fairly quickly when the setting changes to classrooms, restaurants, hotels, or when their athletic performance is considered to be inadequate.

The voices and experiences of African American athletes have not often been heard in research in the sociology of sport—others have usually spoken for them. This study represents a preliminary attempt to give voice to the everyday experiences of race in the lives of African American athletes. We hope that their stories will encourage sociologists of sport to continue to explore the specific experiences of athletes.

References

Anshel, M.H. (1990) 'Perceptions of Black intercollegiate football players: Implications for the sport psychology consultant', *Sport Psychologist* 4: 235–48.

Benson, K.F. (2000) 'Constructing academic inadequacy: African American athletes' stories of schooling', *Journal of Higher Education* 71(2): 223–46.

Brown, T.N., Jackson, J.S., Brown, K.T., Sellers, R.M., Keiper, S. and Manuel, W.J. (2003) '"There's no race on the playing field": Perceptions of racial discrimination among White and Black athletes', *Journal of Sport and Social Issues* 27: 162–83.

Carrington, B. and McDonald, I. (2002) 'Sport, racism and inequality', *Sociology* 11: 8–13.

Coakley, J. (2004) *Sport in Society*, 8th edn. Boston, MA: McGraw-Hill.

Delgado, R. (2001) *Critical Race Theory: An introduction.* New York: New York University Press.

Denzin, N.K. and Lincoln, Y.S. (2000) *Handbook of Qualitative Research*, 2nd edn. London: Sage.

Harrison, L. Jr, Burden, J. Jr and Azzarito, L. (2002) 'Perceptions of athletic superiority: A view from the other side', paper presented at the American Educational Research Association Annual Meeting in New Orleans, LA.

Harrison, C.K. and Lawrence, S.M. (2004) 'African American student athletes' perceptions of career transition in sport: A visual and qualitative investigation', *Race Ethnicity and Education* 6: 373–94.

Lincoln, Y. and Guba, E. (1985) *Naturalistic Inquiry.* Newbury Park, CA: Sage.

Marshall, C. and Rossman, G.B. (1999) *Designing Qualitative Research,* 3rd edn. London: Sage.

Patton, M.Q. (2001) *Qualitative Evaluation and Research Methods*, 3rd edn. Newborn Park, CA: Sage.

Ryan, G.W. and Bernard, H.R. (2000) 'Data management and analysis methods', in N.K. Denzin and Y.S. Lincoln (eds) *Handbook of Qualitative Research*, 2nd edn, pp. 769–802. Thousand Oaks, CA: Sage.

Van Maanen, J. (1983) 'Reclaiming qualitative methods for organizational research', in J. Van aanen (ed.) *Qualitative Methodology*, pp. 115–28. London: Sage.

16

Personal Troubles and Public Issues

A Sociological Imagination of Black Athletes' Experiences at Predominantly White Institutions in the United States

Joseph N. Cooper

Introduction

> Man is a social and an historical actor who must be understood, if at all, in close
> and intricate interplay with social and historical structures. (Mills, 1959: p. 158)

SPORTS REPRESENT A MICROCOSM OF SOCIETY. THIS POPULAR PHRASE refers to the fact that sports do not operate as a vacuum separate from society, but rather as one part of the whole (Coakley, 2009; Edwards, 1973a, 1973b; Sage, 1998). Often times sports reinforce the dominant power structures and social inequalities present within a society. More specifically, Black participation in sports in the United States (US) has always been a contested terrain that reflected the state of Black Americans within the broader US society. A prime example is the exclusion of Black athletes from intercollegiate athletics at predominantly White institutions (PWIs) and the concurrent exclusion of Blacks from mainstream society (e.g. politics, education, business, etc.) from the early seventeenth century through the late nineteenth century (Wiggins & Miller, 2003). PWIs did not integrate Black athletes until the early twentieth century (Wiggins, 2000). During this period, only a limited number of outstanding Black athletes (e.g. Paul Robeson, Jesse Owens, and Jackie Robinson) were admitted to these institutions primarily for their athletic abilities. Consequently, these Black athletes encountered unwelcoming environments that ambivalently applauded their athletic prowess, yet simultaneously viewed them as intellectually and socially inferior (Edwards, 1994; Hawkins, 2010; Lapchick, 1991; Sailes, 2010; Sellers, 2000).

A key factor associated with these challenges, as it relates to Black athletes, has been the historical and contemporary practice of racism in the US (Brooks & Althouse, 2000; Coakley, 2009; Edwards, 1973b; Sage, 1998; Sailes, 2010; Wiggins & Miller, 2003). In order to understand how racism operates within the US society it is important to define race and racism. Helms (1994) defined race as a "reified, socially defined categorization system that has become the basis of one form of social identity" (pp. 294–295). In the US, phenotypical features such as skin color, facial features, hair texture, and body structures have been used as social markers to label and identify people of the Black racial group. Consequently, the social practice of racism emerged through the promulgation of negative stereotypes based on racial categories. Coakley (2009) defines racism as "attitudes, actions, and policies based on the belief that people in one racial category are inherently superior to people in one or more other categories" (p. 281). Both Black athletes at PWIs and Blacks in the broader US society faced multiple levels of racism (e.g. institutional, cultural, and individual), which contributed to negative life outcomes (e.g. limited educational opportunities, lower career mobility, poorer health outcomes, higher rates of incarceration, etc. (Hawkins, 2010).

Furthermore, the practice of racism against Blacks has been commonplace in the US since 1619 when European settlers enslaved Black Africans on US soil primarily for economic exploitation (Hine, Hine, & Harrold, 2006). Consequently, racism remains deeply entrenched in US social institutions (e.g. political, economic, educational and religious) and cultural practices (e.g. sport, music, and art), thus creating a socially stratified society where Blacks are viewed and treated as inferior to Whites (Coakley, 2009; Sage, 1998; Wiggins & Miller, 2003). The pervasive racism against Blacks throughout the US has contributed to negative social experiences in various social settings including post-secondary institutions (e.g. PWIs). Thus, understanding the history of racism against Blacks in the US provides a more comprehensive socio-historical context for the critical examination and understanding of Black athletes' experiences at PWIs.

Sociological Imagination: A Framework for the Examination of Racism in the United States

According to C. Wright Mills (1959), the sociological imagination is a process of understanding the connection between biography and history. Biographies occur on an individual level whereas history involves a culmination of events on a structural level. Mills' (1959) contends biographies and history are inextricably intertwined. The link between biographies and history manifests in the emergence of personal troubles and public issues. Personal troubles are events that "occur within the character of the individual and within the range of his immediate relations with others" (Mills, 1959: p. 8). An example of a personal trouble is a Black athlete's motivation or lack thereof to be engaged academically at a PWI. Contrarily, public issues are "matters that transcend these local environments of the individual and the range of his inner life" (Mills, 1959: p. 8). An example of a public issue is the persistent academic achievement gap between Blacks and Whites within the US educational system (ETS, 2011; NCES, 2007; Nettles & Perna, 1997a, 1997b). It is the promise of the sociological imagination that enables individuals to understand the connection between personal biographies and broader socio-historical realities in order to address both problems rooted in structural arrangements (Mills, 1959).

For the purposes of this paper, the sociological imagination will be used as a critical lens to examine the history of a specific group of people (Blacks) in a specific context (US). However, the author acknowledges several scholars have different interpretations of the appropriate use of the sociological imagination in social science inquiry (Dandaneau, 2000; Denzin, 1990; Gitlin, 2000; Richardson, 1997; Spencer, 2010). For example, one interpretation suggests Mills' (1959) intention for using the sociological imagination was to focus on the structural arrangements across international societies. From this perspective, prevalent issues such as racism, sexism, and classism would be dissected and contrasted within a global context. Another view, which the author advocates, is the notion that the sociological imagination serves as useful tool to examine structural arrangements and broad social problems within a specific context. These perspectives are not inherently contradictory, rather interpreted and applied in a different fashion. This idea of multiple interpretations is consistent with the social constructivist epistemological stance held by the author (Denzin & Lincoln, 2005; Lincoln & Guba, 2000). Furthermore, this perspective supports the idea that the sociological imagination can apply to any societal context where historical events and structural arrangements influence the lived experiences of individuals within a given society.

The contextualization of Black athletes' experiences at PWIs within a broader socio-historical narrative of Blacks in the US allows for an in-depth analysis of inequitable US structural arrangements. More specifically, the comparison of the collective biographies of Black athletes and historical events associated with Blacks in the US draws attention to widespread structural inequalities pervasive throughout US social institutions (e.g. political, economic, judicial, educational, and religious). Similar to other facets of US society, intercollegiate athletics serves as a site for the reinforcement of dominant power structures (Coakley, 2009). The ability to analyze the relationship between the personal troubles of Black athletes at PWIs and the historical impact of public issues on Blacks in the US constitutes an effort to deconstruct the dominant power structure, which oppresses them (McDonald & Birrell, 1998; Spencer, 2010). The deconstruction of the dominant power structure, which in the US is rooted in the ideology of White supremacy, will enable new structures to emerge that empower those who are oppressed (DuBois, 1996).

Both Blacks with the US and Black athletes at PWIs have experienced similar challenges as result of their social status. These similar experiences stem from the fact that Blacks have historically been subject to racist beliefs, which view them as innately inferior to Whites (DuBois, 1996; Helms, 1994; Hine et al., 2006). A review of relevant literature revealed four common themes shared between both groups: 1) racial discrimination/social isolation; 2) academic neglect; 3) economic deprivation; and 4) limited leadership opportunities.

Intersection #1: Racial Discrimination/Social Isolation

A major issue facing both Blacks in the broader US and Black athletes at PWIs is the experiences with racial discrimination and social isolation. At both the macro (US) and micro (PWI) level, Blacks constitute a minority group. As minorities, Blacks have experienced environments and social norms that are constructed for the dominant White culture (DuBois, 1996). Understanding the connection between the socio-historical experiences of Black in the US and the experiences of Black athletes at PWIs provides a more comprehensive examination of public issue and personal trouble of racial discrimination/social isolation (Mills, 1959).

Public Issue

Historically, a public issue facing Blacks in the US society has been the practice of racial discrimination. Racism in the US has been used a social marker used to justify various forms of discrimination, subordination, and injustice against Blacks (Helms, 1994; Hine et al., 2006). Although other racial and ethnic minority groups have experienced similar forms of oppression, the experiences of Blacks are unique. Black Americans are the only racial group in the US to be subjected to an extended period of slavery and to have *de jure* (legalized) segregation laws passed against them that were fully supported by the Supreme Court (Bell, 1992; Sage, 2000; Wilson, 1996). In nearly every facet of American society (e.g. economic, educational, political, health, and judicial), Blacks have historically been and continue to be significantly disadvantaged (ETS, 2011; Hine et al., 2006).

Prior to 1865, Blacks were legally enslaved and disallowed citizenship under the US constitution. Blacks were enslaved solely based skin color. Following the *Emancipation Proclamation of* 1865, Blacks were liberated from legalized slavery, yet racially discriminatory practices and attitudes remained prevalent throughout the US. The idea of White supremacy was the underlying ideology rooted in these racially discriminatory beliefs, which was supported by theories of scientific racism and social Darwinism (Comstock, 1912; Jensen, 1969; Jones, 1998; Stone, 1908a; Van Evrie, 1870). This ideology purported the misconception that Whites were innately superior to Blacks, thus justifying their enslavement, mistreatment, and subjugation in all aspects of US society (DuBois, 1996; Helms, 1994; Hine et al., 2006).

Similar to racial discrimination, Blacks within the US have also been subject to social isolation (Hine et al., 2006). With no citizenship rights, Blacks were socially and politically isolated from participating in society with the exception of serving in subservient roles for Whites. The passage of the Fourteenth Amendment in 1865 mandated states to recognize all residents as citizens and protect their US constitutional rights. Although this legislation was significant, Blacks still did not own the necessary resources (e.g. land and assets) to fully integrate into mainstream US society. Blacks were regulated to substandard housing conditions both in rural and urban areas throughout the US (DuBois, 1996). Throughout the Reconstruction period (1865-1877), Blacks remained segregated from Whites, particularly in the South, because Whites still controlled a wealth of the economic, educational, and political resources (Hine et al., 2006).

Throughout the late nineteenth century through the mid-twentieth century, several factors contributed to the social isolation of Blacks in the US (Hine et al., 2006). The continued disenfranchisement of Blacks, the practice of Jim Crow laws in the South, and lynching of Blacks in the South among other factors ensured Blacks did not have equal opportunities for life, liberty, and pursuit of happiness. The milestone *Plessy v. Ferguson* (1896) ruling reinforced the legality of racial segregation between Blacks and Whites and established the 'separate but equal' standard. The judicial support for segregation further isolated Blacks from living a quality of life compared to Whites. Over fifty years later, the passage of *Brown v. Board of Education of Topeka* (1954) overturned legalized segregation in educational institutions. Additionally, the efforts of the Civil Rights movement led to passage of historic legislations such as the *Civil Rights Act of* 1964, which outlawed discrimination against people of color and women in public facilities. Other significant accomplishments associated with the Civil Rights Movement included the *Voting Rights Act of* 1965, *Executive Order* 11246 by President Lyndon B. Johnson, and the *Civil Rights Act of 1968* to name a few (Hine et al., 2006). In spite of these monumental legislations, Blacks in the post-Civil Rights era US continued to face structural inequalities related to racially discriminatory beliefs and practices.

Personal Troubles

Black athletes have a long history of experiences with racial discrimination and social isolation at PWIs (Adler & Adler, 1991; AIR, 1988, 1989; Anshel, 1990; Benson, 2000; Hawkins, 1999; Lawrence, 2005; Sailes, 1993; Singer, 2005). Since the late nineteenth century, Black athletes have been marginalized at PWIs. Famous Black athletes during this era such as Paul Robeson (Rutgers University; football), William Henry Lewis (Amherst College; football), and W.T.S. Jackson (Amherst College; football) all have documented experiences with social isolation as racial minorities in their classes as well as on their athletic teams (Wiggins, 1991). The negative stereotypes Black athletes faced at PWIs stemmed from the pervasiveness of the dumb jock myth (Edwards, 1984; Harrison & Lawrence, 2004; Hawkins, 2010; Sailes, 2010; Smith, 2009). The basis of this theory suggests Black males are innately athletically superior, yet intellectually inferior (Azzarito, Burden, & Harrison, 2004; Edwards, 1984; Harrison, 2001; Hunt, Ivery, & Sailes, 2010; Martin, Harrison, Stone, & Lawrence, 2010; Sailes, 2010). Despite the fact that the dumb jock theory has yet to be supported by scientific research, the insidious acceptance of this theory within US educational institutions has presented significant psychological and social obstacles for Black athletes (Edwards, 1984; Sailes, 2010; Singer, 2008). The prevalence of these racist stereotypes within discursive practices at US educational institutions has contributed to negative academic outcomes, limited personal development, and poor psychological adjustments for Black athletes (Benson, 2000; Comeaux & Harrison, 2007; Harrison & Lawrence, 2004; Singer, 2008). Thus, these Black athletes were victims of stereotype threat (Steele & Aronson, 1995). Stereotype threat refers to the fact that Black athletes at PWIs academically underperform due to the presence of increased psychological pressure (both consciously and subconsciously) to disconfirm the negative stereotypes associated with their academic capabilities.

Intersection #2: Academic Neglect

The second common theme present in both the literature on Blacks in the US as well as Black athletes at PWIs is the shared experience with academic neglect. Education has been considered the gateway to achieving the American Dream of economic stability and overall quality of life. However, the acceptance of racist beliefs that subordinate Blacks has created significant barriers for Blacks to attain levels of education at rates comparable to Whites (ETS, 2011).This next section outlines the history of academic neglect against Blacks in the US educational system in connection with the contemporary academic neglect experienced by Black athletes at PWIs.

Public Issue

Historically, educational opportunities for Blacks in the US have been significantly limited and often times non-existent (Gutek, 1986; Hawkins, 2010; Henderson & Kritsonis, 2007; Hikes, 2005; Palmer & Gasman, 2008; Roebuck & Murty, 1993). For example, prior to the Civil War only 28 Blacks graduated from college (Willie, Grady, & Hope, 1991). Although Blacks in the north had more opportunities to earn an education, *de jure* (legalized) racism remained a major obstacle for Blacks in their quest to acquire traditional forms of education (Hikes, 2005). In response to this *de jure* racism, Blacks were forced to establish their own educational institutions (e.g. African Methodist Episcopal (AME)), along with the assistance of a handful of White organizations such as the Quakers, Presbyterians, American Missionary Association (AMA), Christian Methodist Episcopal (CME), the Bureau of Refugees, Freedmen's societies, and Abandoned Lands (Gallien & Peterson, 2005; Hawkins, 2010; Walther, 1994). The first Black colleges were established in the north (Cheyney in 1837; Lincoln in 1854; Wilberforce in 1856) by Christian missionaries (Branson, 1978; Fleming, 1984).

Following the *Emancipation Proclamation of* 1865, which legally ended the practice of slavery in the US, the US government initiated widespread efforts to establish educational facilities for Blacks (Browning & Williams, 1978; Fleming, 1984). Many leaders in the South remained ambivalent towards granting equal educational opportunities to Blacks (Fleming, 1984). In concert with these racist attitudes, several states passed laws that alienated Blacks and restricted their educational opportunities to vocational training (Browning & Williams, 1978). The racist laws also known as Black codes were established to ensure Blacks remained subservient labor for Whites (Hine et al., 2006). In 1890, the monumental Morrill Land Grant Act was passed and all states were required to either provide separate schools for Blacks or integrate Blacks into existing institutions. As a result, 16 Black colleges were established to provide opportunities Blacks in vocational areas such as mechanical arts and agricultural sciences (Fleming, 1984). Although these educational gains were a sign of progress, these separate and *unequal* institutions reinforced the prevailing ideology of White intellectual superiority (Fleming, 1984; Hikes, 2005; Schwaneger, 1969; Wilson, 1994).

Over a century has passed since *Brown v. Board of Education of Topeka* (1954) and many Blacks still attend largely segregated and unequal primary and secondary schools. A recent study revealed that 39% of Black students attend an intensely segregated school (90 to 100% racial minority) (ETS, 2011; Orfield, 2009). Accompanying the racial segregation is the lack of qualified teachers. A recent study by Aud, Fox, and KewalRamani (2010) found that in predominantly Black high schools, 25% of the math teachers did not possess a college major or a standard certification in the main subject they taught. In comparison, predominantly White high schools, 8% of the math teachers did not have a college major or a standard certification in the main subject they taught. These disparaging statistics support the notion of academic neglect of Blacks in the US primary and secondary educational systems.

Personal Troubles

Often times Black males are marginalized by the educational system through dominant discourses on intelligence, smartness, and academic achievement (Hatt, 2007). Dominant discourses are present in institutional (e.g. culturally bias standardized tests) and cultural practices (e.g. the dearth of African and African American literature courses offered at the primary and secondary level) (Hawkins, 2010). Many Black students as early as preschool begin to be tracked into remedial or special education classes (Hatt, 2007; McBay, 1992; Wright-Edelman, 1988). Consequently, this academic stigmatizing contributes to Black students' low academic achievement, low self-efficacy, and increased likelihood of attrition (Hatt, 2007).

More specifically at the post-secondary level, Black athletes must cope with the label of being dumb jocks (Edwards, 1984; Harrison & Lawrence, 2004; Hawkins, 2010; Sailes, 2010; Smith, 2009). The acceptance of this insidious stereotype has been reinforced by previous research findings that Black athletes who participated in revenue producing sports were more likely to enter college academically underprepared (AIR, 1989; Purdy, Eitzen, & Hufnagel, 1985; Sellers, 1992; Shulman & Bowen, 2001) and less likely to achieve academic success compared to their college student peers (Ervin, Saunders, Gillis, & Hogrebe, 1985; Gaston-Gayles, 2005; Purdy et al., 1985; Shulman & Bowen, 2001). Thus, reinforcing the notion that Black males innately possess athletic talents, but intellectually they are limited (Edwards, 1994; Hawkins, 2010; Lapchick, 1991; Sailes, 2010; Sellers, 2000).

Conversely, several scholars have argued the academic performance of Black athletes' is less reflective of their individual merits, but more indicative of institutional arrangements and educational malpractice which treat them as intellectually inferior (Adler & Adler, 1991; AIR, 1988, 1989; Benson, 2000; Gaston-Gayles, 2005; Hawkins, 1999; Sellers, 1992). A few widely publicized cases of institutional neglect in regards to Black male student athletes were the cases of Kevin Ross, Dexter Manley, and Gregg Taylor (Donnor, 2005; Ferris, Finster, & McDonald,

2004; Johnson, 1985; Sellers, 2000). Each of these athletes enrolled in their respective institutions with severe academic learning disabilities. Ross was functionally illiterate after spending four years at Creighton University (Sellers, 2000). Similarly, Manley was also functionally illiterate after three years at Oklahoma State University before entering the National Football League (NFL) draft (Ferris et al., 2004). Taylor had his athletic scholarship terminated after refusing to participate in the team's practices because he felt it impeded his academic progress (Johnson, 1985). Although these Black athletes were confronted with severe learning disabilities, they share a similar experience with many Black athletes who are primarily admitted to generate revenue from their athletic abilities (Edwards, 1984, 2000; Funk, 1991; Hawkins, 2010; Sailes, 2010; Singer, 2008; Smith, 2009). Instead of providing, the adequate academic support necessary for them to develop academically these institutions primarily focused on exploiting them for their athletic abilities. These isolated cases were supported by the previous studies that suggested the academic neglect of Black male student athletes remains a major problem at many PWIs (Adler & Adler, 1991; AIR, 1988, 1989; Benson, 2000; Gaston-Gayles, 2005; Hawkins, 1999; Sellers, 1992).

Intersection #3: Economic Deprivation

Another common experience shared between both Blacks in the broader US society and Black athletes at PWIs is the experience with economic deprivation, disadvantage, and exploitation. The economic exploitation of Black athletes at major Division I institutions resembles the historical exploitation of Blacks in the broader US society. Although the conditions under which the exploitation transpired were vastly different, the stratification of power, inequitable distribution of wealth and resources, and disparate outcomes are eerily similar. In order for Blacks to attain true equality, structural policies and practices must take into account historical inequalities within the US society, and thus be sufficiently reformed to provide fair treatment of all individuals regardless of race (DuBois, 1996; Mills, 1959).

Public Issue

US capitalism operates under a class stratification system whereby three distinct classes (capitalist, middle, and working) fulfill specific economic roles (Sage, 1998). The capitalist class is typically small in number (roughly 2 percent), yet represents the wealthiest Americans who control the means of production (e.g. capital and land). The middle class consist of a group of income earners who share some power with capitalists, but remain largely dependent on the capitalist class who owns a majority of resources (e.g. wealth, assets, etc.). The working class is the lowest class with no ownership and limited economic resources. In the US, these stratifications were established along class, gender, and racial identification. Throughout history, Whites have dominated the capitalist and middle classes whereas Blacks were predominantly members of the working class.

As members of the working class, Blacks experienced various forms of oppression, discrimination, and economic deprivation (Sage, 1998).

Since the inception of slavery in 1619, Blacks were a source of labor for the economic profitability of Whites. Following the *Emancipation Proclamation in* 1865, Blacks continued to struggle with gaining economic independence because Whites retained control over the regulation of wages and prices, land, and property (Hine et al., 2006). Throughout the twentieth century, Blacks continued to experience economic deprivation. In 1959, Blacks constituted 25.1% of Americans living under the poverty line (US Bureau of the Census, 1982). Between 1979 and 1980, the number of Blacks in poverty increased from 2.5 million to 19.7 million compared to the number of Whites in poverty 530,000 to 8.6 million. In spite of the fact that Blacks only constituted 12% of the US population, they made up over 29% of the poverty population. More specifically, in 1980, the poverty rate for Blacks (32%) was over three times the rate of Whites (10%). These statistics highlight the level of economic deprivation experienced by Blacks throughout the mid-twentieth century (US Bureau of the Census, 1982). Poverty among Blacks is an intergenerational process perpetuated by structural inequalities and class stratification (Bell, 1992). In 1988-1989, Black children attended schools where over one-third (43%) of their classmates lived in poverty (Orfield, 2009). In 2006-2007, Black children attended schools where 59% of their classmates lived in poverty compared to White students who attended schools where 32% of their classmates lived in poverty. Children who grow up in poverty are more likely experience substandard educational opportunities, poor health and nutrition outcomes, residential insecurity, and exposure crime and gang activity. Poverty levels are the number one indicator of economic deprivation. Blacks' longstanding experience with poverty perpetuates the lack of economic opportunities and limits access to upward social mobility (Orfield, 2009).

Unemployment and annual income are additional indicators of economic deprivation (US Department of Commerce, 1993). In 1979, the Black unemployment rate was almost twice that of Whites. Ten years later in 1989, the Black unemployment rate increased to over twice the rate of Whites, 13% and 5%, respectively. Given that Blacks were a racial minority (roughly 12 percent) of the overall US population, yet constituted a larger percentage of those in poverty highlights the structural racism embedded in US society. Moreover, Blacks earned less income than Whites did over a 23-year span. From 1984 to 2007, the wealth gap between Blacks and Whites increased from $20,000 to $95,000. Moreover, according to the most recent census data, the household income for Blacks and Whites was $32,303 and $49,471, respectively (DeNavas-Walt et al., 2011). Considering wealth and income are the strong indicators of economic stability, Blacks remained significantly disadvantaged compared to Whites (Shapiro, Meschede, & Sullivan, 2010).

Personal Troubles

Several critics of the NCAA purported the structure of major Division I intercollegiate athletics was inherently exploitive of student athletes, particularly Black athletes (Barbalias, 2004; Byers, 1995; Edwards, 1984; Hawkins, 2010; Lapchick, 1984; Sack & Staurowsky, 1998; Smith, 2009;

Zimbalist, 2001). For years, Black athletes have been overrepresented in the two largest revenue-generating sports, football, and men's basketball, while simultaneously graduating at lower rates than their student athlete counterparts have. In 2007-2008, Black males represented 25% of all student athletes in Division I, 60.4% of Division men's basketball players and 46.4% of Black football players (NCAA, 2009). In 2008, there were 821,481 Black males enrolled in post-secondary instiutions which was roughly 5% of all undergraduate enrollment and 36.2% of Black student enrollment (NCES, 2009). As a result, several scholars have suggested Black athletes were being exploited by these institutions for financial gain (Edwards, 1985; Hawkins, 1999, 2010; Rhoden, 1989; Sellers, 2000; Singer, 2005; Smith, 2009).

Polite (2011) defines exploitation as "the unfair treatment or use of, or the practice of taking selfish or unfair advantage of, a person or situation, usually for personal gain" (p. 2). Under this definition, the NCAA and its member institutions exploit Black athletes, as well as other non-Black athletes in participating in the top two revenue-generating sports, for revenue generation without adequately compensating them for their services (Byers, 1995; Funk, 1991; Hawkins, 2010; Smith 2009; Zimbalist, 2001). The relationship between the NCAA, member institutions, and student athletes in revenue generating sports (e.g. FBS football and Division I men's basketball) is problematic on multiple levels. One, the educational missions of these institutions promotes academic excellence and personal development of its students. If Black athletes are being recruited to generate revenue for their athletic abilities, then their primary purpose is not to receive a *paramount* educational experience rather it is to excel athletically to generate revenue for the athletic departments, the institution, and other institutional stakeholders (e.g. NCAA staff, Conference Commissioners, Head Coaches, etc.) (NCAA, 2011a). Two, these student athletes in revenue generating sports are generating millions of dollars for their institutions and not receiving even a fraction of compensation for their contributions. This is not only ethically wrong, but also maybe in violation of anti-trust laws enacted by Sherman Anti-Trust Act (Acain, 1998; Davis, 1999). Therefore, the practice of athletic exploitation reveals the overemphasis of athletics over academics at a several US post-secondary institutions presents significant problems that are reflective of the broader social issue of economic exploitation of marginalized groups (Funk, 1991; Hawkins, 2010; Lapchick, 1984; Sack & Staurowsky, 1998; Smith, 2009; Wolff & Keteyian, 1990).

In 2011, the NCAA reported $845.9 million in revenue, an overwhelming amount of revenues was generated from a rights agreement with Turner/CBS Sports for coverage rights of the March Madness Men's Basketball Tournament (NCAA, 2012). Although the revenue generated on "the backs of our Black brothers" continues to increase at exponential rates, the low graduation and high attrition rates of Black athletes remained a major problem at NCAA member institutions who notably promoted the prioritization of academic excellence in their mission statements (Hawkins, 2010: p. 94). Conversely, findings from a recent NCAA study revealed the most recent graduation rates for Division I African American male student athletes was 62% which was 21 percentage points lower than the graduation rate of their White male student athlete counterparts (NCAA, 2011c). Although proponents of the NCAA proclaim these student athletes are receiving a *paramount* educational experience, these statistics suggest otherwise (NCAA, 2011a, p. 1). The inverse relationship between the money generated in sports, where Black males were overrepresented, and low graduation rates of these same students suggests these athletes were being exploited for their athletic labor. Consequently, the overemphasis on athletic performance contributes devaluation of their holistic development (Edwards, 1973a, 1973b, 1984, 1994; Hawkins, 2010; Polite & Hawkins, 2011; Sellers, 2000; Smith, 2009).

Intersection #4: Limited Leadership Opportunities

Throughout history, Blacks have been overlooked and underrepresented in various leadership roles. Similar to Blacks in the broader US, Black male student athletes experienced a lack of leadership opportunities largely based on racial stereotypes about their intellectual abilities (Steele & Aronson, 1995). These stereotypes are deeply rooted in US institutional practices (Sage, 1998). In concert with Mills' (1959) sociological imagination, the history of Black exclusion from leadership opportunities in US society along with the lack of leadership opportunities afforded to Black athletes during as well as following their athletic careers is inextricably linked. In order to address this prevailing public issue, it is imperative to understand its origins from a socio-historical context. Once this understanding is attained, then efforts to deconstruct and rearrange current structural arrangements can occur and widespread empowerment among the oppressed can manifest (Hawkins, 2010; McDonald & Birrell, 1998; Spencer, 2010).

Public Issue

Prior to the Reconstruction period (1865-1877), Blacks did not possess any citizenship rights and therefore unable to pursue leadership opportunities (Hine et al., 2006). An example of Black exclusion from leadership was evident in the lack of Black representation in the US military from the later nineteenth century through the early twentieth century. Although Blacks were allowed in the military after 1865, they were restricted to strictly subordinate roles. In 1917, there were over 5000 Blacks in the Navy, but nearly all of them were relegated to subservient roles such as waiters and kitchen attendants. In the Army, Blacks were also limited to serving as road construction workers, cooks, and bakers. During World War I, only 42,000 out of the over 380,000 Black males in the military were allowed to serve in combat. This practice was supported by fallacious studies that promoted the ideology of White supremacy. In 1925, a study conducted by the American War College reported that Blacks were physically unfit for combat, mentally incompetent, and innately inferior to Whites. Negative propaganda such as this aforementioned study influenced a majority of White military leaders, politicians, and journalists to perceive Black soldiers as inferior (Hine et al., 2006).

During the Reconstruction era, most Black males feared pursuing political offices for fear of retaliation from Southern Whites. In spite of these threats, Blacks experienced marginal progress in terms of political representation during the late nineteenth century. Between 1865 and 1877, 14 Black males served in the US House of Representatives. In response to Black progress in US politics, Whites employed several deceitful tactics to disenfranchise Blacks from voting such as the use of literary tests, poll taxes, and property qualifications. Thus, the progress made during the late 1800s was stifled by the turn of the century. In 1900, nearly all congressional representatives were White. The Fifteenth Amendment, which granted Blacks voting rights, was passed in 1869, but the aforementioned barriers limited Black participation. In 1965, the President Lyndon B. Johnson passed the Voting Rights Act, which prohibited educational requirements as qualification for voting. The passage of this law meant that Blacks could not be denied their civil right to vote based on educational attainment (Hine et al., 2006).

Political offices epitomize leadership roles in US society. Local, state, and national politicians have the ability to create laws, which govern the lives of all Americans. Throughout the mid-twentieth to early twenty-first century, Blacks continued to make strides in political representation, but remained largely underrepresented in Congress. For example, from 1969-1971, out of the 535 members of Congress there were less than 10 Black members (Amer, 2008). At the turn of the century, from 1999-2001, the number has remained between 39 and 43. Currently, African Americans account for 8.1% of the members of the 112th US Congress, which is slightly lower than the 12.6% African Americans among the total US population (Manning, 2011; US Bureau of Census, 2012). Despite progress such as the election of the first African American president, President Barack Obama, the persistent underrepresentation of Blacks in the US Congress signifies the lack of leadership opportunities available to Blacks in the nation's higher leadership positions.

Personal Troubles

A longstanding problem facing the NCAA and its member institutions has been the persistence underrepresentation of racial/ethnic minorities in leadership positions (Woods, 2011). Since the mid-twentieth century, Blacks have had a strong presence as participants in intercollegiate football, men's basketball, track and field, and women's basketball. Yet, conspicuously Blacks have been underrepresented in the leadership positions of these sports at the intercollegiate level. According to a study conducted by Harrison (2004), in 2003, Blacks made up nearly 50% of Division IA football players, but less than 1% of these schools had Black football head coaches. From 1996 to 2004, only one Black head coach had been hired as of 2004, only 21 Black males had held head coaching positions in Division IA football. These stark discrepancies between player representation and the lack of head coach representation suggests Blacks are viewed as athletic commodities, but not considered fit for head coaching positions (Brooks & Althouse, 2000).

More recently, Lapchick, Hoff, & Kaiser (2011) found that only 11.7% of the Football Bowl Subdivision (FBS) schools' athletics directors were people of color. The 2011 season started with 15% (18 out of 120) FBS head football coaches were Black. As of March 25, 2011, at the highest levels of the NCAA headquarters (EVP (Executive Vice President)/SVP (Senior Vice President)/ VP (Vice President)) Blacks made up 25% compared to 75% for Whites. In addition, 100% of the 11 FBS conference commissioners were White males. In all of Division I, excluding HBCU conferences, all 30 (100%) of Division I conference commissioners were White. The under-representation of Blacks in all levels of intercollegiate athletics suggests race and racism remain significant mitigating factors in leadership opportunities available to Blacks (Lapchick et al., 2011).

A possible explanation for the lack of Black representation in leadership positions in sport is the continued practice of racial stacking. Racial stacking is "the disproportional relegation of athletes to specific sport positions on the basis of the prescribed characteristic of race" (Leonard, 1987: p. 403). Racial stacking is viewed as discriminatory because players are assigned certain positions based on racial stereotypes and not only actual ability (Anderson, 1993; Best, 1987; Chu & Segrave, 1981; Curtis & Loy, 1978a, 1978b; Eitzen & David, 1975; Eitzen & Tessendorf, 1978; Massengale & Farrington, 1977; Medoff, 1977; Sailes, 2010). Singer (2005) found that African American male football student athletes at Division I PWIs felt they were not afforded leadership and major decision-making opportunities in college or professional sports due to their race. The participants' experience with racial stacking negatively affected their perceptions of leadership opportunities available to them in sports. The underrepresentation of Blacks in sport leadership positions along with the concurrent prevalence of racial stacking reinforces the dominant race logic of White supremacy that has plagued both Blacks in sports and Blacks in the broader US society.

Discussion

Using a sociological imagination for the critical examination of Black athletes' experiences at PWIs provides insight into how these institutions can shift from simply operating as "modes of integration" merely reinforcing structural inequalities to "modes of historical change" that create true equality of opportunity for all individuals in the US (Mills, 1959, p. 47). History informs us that when societies (e.g. US) or organizations (e.g. NCAA), reach certain point of imbalance social movements or revolutions are inevitable. The aforementioned personal troubles and public issues accompanied by public distrust of the growing commercialization of major college sports should serve as notice to the NCAA that a revolution is mounting unless major structural reforms take place.

The NCAA's ideological stance operates under what Mills' (1959) described as a *Grand Theory* approach. The *Grand Theory* involves the establishment of social norms and social regularities within a social system to maintain social equilibrium. This social equilibrium is maintained in two ways, through socialization and social control. The NCAA's ideological stance is rooted in the principle of amateurism whereby student athletes participate in intercollegiate athletics primarily for intrinsic purposes as an extension of the educational experience. The key idea is that these student athletes are not being viewed as institutional employees and thus should not be compensated fully for their revenue generation. From the beginning of the recruiting process, Black athletes are groomed to view themselves as amateurs and thus view any behavior outside the confines of the NCAA bylaws as deviant. Social control is established through harsh punishments to violators (e.g. Reggie Bush (USC; football), Cameron Newton (Auburn; football), and Terrelle Pryor (Ohio State; football). The NCAA's use of a *Grand Theory* approach ensures the dominant power structure remains intact and those who are being exploited remained limited in their ability to alter the current structure (Mills, 1959).

The psychological benefit of the *Grand Theory* lies in the fact that its standards become the basis for adherence to the power structure as well as for opposition to it (Mills, 1959). Previous theorists have described "social norms as 'legitimations' (Max Weber), 'collective representation' (Emil Durkheim), 'dominant ideas' (Karl Marx), and 'public sentiments' (Herbert Spencer)" (Mills, 1959: p. 36). The core issue associated with these analyses is the possession and exertion of power. Although the *Grand Theory* suggests social equilibrium benefits all actors, often times the main benefactors of social equilibrium are the individuals in power. In the case of intercollegiate athletics, the NCAA bylaws serve as the social norms that retain social control over student athletes, but the individuals who benefit most from the multi-billion dollar college sport industry are the NCAA administrators, Bowl Championship Series (BCS) organizers, Conference Commissioners, Head Coaches, and the institutions and their athletic departments. The individuals who benefit the least from the system are the student athletes who fuel the system (Byers, 1995; Hawkins, 2010; Sellers, 2000; Smith, 2009; Zimbalist, 2001).

Moreover, liberalism is deeply rooted in the US political and social values (Mills, 1959). In regards to social sciences, liberal practicality has been applied in the examination of various social problems. Liberal practicality is the belief that a balance must be retained through the small individual reform efforts. For example, under liberal practicality, issues facing Blacks in the US such as poverty, mortality rates, health disparities, and academic achievement gap should be addressed separately. Inherent in the liberal practicality approach is the idea that social problems are scattered and thus must be addressed in a sequential fashion. The pluralist causation of these problems requires "piecemeal reform", but fails to take into account the interconnectedness of social problems that are created by social structures (Mills, 1959: p. 85). The sociological imagination provides an opportunity to show how social problems are interconnected to a socio-historical lineage and therefore must be addressed concurrently rather than separately. In other words, the personal troubles facing Black athletes at PWIs are not separate from the public issues facing Blacks in the broader US, thus both personal troubles and public issues must be addressed simultaneously since their inextricably linked (Mills, 1959).

Implications

A recommendation for addressing the personal trouble and public issue of racial discrimination/ social at PWIs is to implement effective strategies that fully integrate Black athletes into the student body. Many PWIs have diversity or multicultural offices that are designed to recruit racial/ethnic minority students and provide them with a support system that will enable them to have a positive college experiences and ultimately graduate. These programs should be integrated with the athletic departments to establish effective programs and services to assist this unique group of students. Another recommendation for integrating Black male student athletes into the general study body is to combine student athlete academic services with institutional student academic services for the student body. This integration would not require a total overhaul of successful student athlete academic support services, but merely strengthening the partnerships between the two so they do not operate in complete autonomy. The implementation of these recommendations could assist major FBS institutions in improving academic and social experiences of Black athletes.

A major reform measure that should be implemented immediately is the establishment and enhancement of partnerships between NCAA, member institutions, and the K-12 US public educational systems particularly those low resource schools to improve academic preparation prior to college enrollment (Edwards, 2000; Funk, 1991; Shropshire, 1997). Previous studies have revealed that a significant number of Black male student athletes particularly in the major revenue generating sports come from low-income communities and low resource schools which can impact their academic preparedness (AIR, 1988, 1989; Purdy et al., 1985; Sellers, 1992; Shulman & Bowen, 2001). These partnerships could address the issue of academic preparedness at earlier stages in a student athletes' life and thus enhance their chances of excelling academically in college (Edwards, 2000). In addition, these partnerships would send the message that these institutions are truly concerned with addressing the academic achievement gap and not simply interested in exploiting these Black athletes for their athletic abilities (Edwards, 2000; Hawkins, 2010; Smith, 2009).

The NCAA and its member institutions should also consider collaborating with other private and public organizations that promote Black academic achievement. For example, the NCAA could collaborate with organizations such as the Journal for Blacks in Higher Education (JBHE), the National Children's Defense Fund, the National Association for the Advancement of Colored People (NAACP), and the Science, Technology, Engineering, and Mathematics (STEM) Education Coalition among other similar organizations. These partnerships could focus on identifying and disseminating best practices for eliminating the current academic achievement gap as well as recognize schools that demonstrate significant improvement from year to year in eliminating the academic achievement gap among Black and White athletes. Similar to the annual TIDES reports, this alliance could create a national ranking of institutions that graduate Black male student athletes at high rates as well as institutions that show improvement from year to year and specifically highlight the programs they have implemented to accomplish this improvement. This partnership would optimize efforts directed at improving academic achievement and experiences of Black male student athletes at PWIs.

A recommendation to address the economic deprivation of Black athletes at PWIs is to eliminate the myth of amateurism principle as it is currently applied to FBS football and Division I men's basketball student athletes. Student athletes are already compensated in the form of scholarships; therefore, they should not be viewed as amateurs (Byers, 1995; Funk, 1991; Sack & Staurowsky, 1998; Zimbalist, 2001). This outdated label of amateurism denies student athletes of their fundamental right to fair compensation for their services and further supports the notion that the NCAA is serving as exploitive cartel of student athlete labor. One feasible option is to redistribute the profits generated through a commercial/education model through a revenue sharing plan that fairly compensates student athletes as well as place a higher emphasis on educational values (Acain, 1998). This revenue sharing plan is not an all-inclusive solution to the problem of economic exploitation in major intercollegiate athletics, but it represents a step in the direction of minimizing the exploitation of student athletes as well as avoiding any violation of current anti-trust lawsuits enacted by the Sherman Anti-Trust laws (Acain, 1998).

Recommendations for increasing leadership opportunities for Black males in intercollegiate athletics must also incorporate structural reform efforts. In 2003, the Black Coaches Association (BCA) funded the hiring report card project to serve as a watchdog on the hiring practices of NCAA Division I football programs (Keith, 2011). The Fritz Pollard Alliance (FPA) led by John Wooten advocated the hiring and promotion of minority candidates with both the NFL and NCAA. Increasing awareness of the hiring disparities is a key part of addressing the underrepresentation of Black leadership in intercollegiate athletics. The NCAA's Diversity and Inclusion Office published a Best Practices report outlining key recommendations for improving overall diversity among athletic departments. One list in the report outlines effective hiring practices such as implementing strategies that attract diverse candidates in the hiring process, provide job announcements to historically diverse colleges, and utilize grants or internships to hire racial/ ethnic minorities and women (NCAA, 2011b). College presidents, athletic directors, conference commissioners, coaches, faculty, and athletes must be committed to improving the problem in order for true change to take place (Brooks & Althouse, 2000). Noteworthy programs offered by this office include the football professional development programs, Fellows Leadership Development Programs, NCAA Postgraduate Internship Program, Ethnic Minority Enhancement Postgraduate Scholarship for Careers in Athletics, and Diversity Education (Diversity Training Workshops) (NCAA, 2011b).

Conclusions

This paper provides a socio-historical context for examining the relationship between the personal troubles of Black athletes at PWIs and the public issues facing Blacks throughout US history. Institutional policies and practices aimed at improving academic experiences and achievement of Black athletes at PWIs must be "sociologically grounded and historically relevant" (Mills, 1959: p. 143). Meaningful efforts, whether in theory or practice, must target the structural arrangements in the broader US society that perpetuate existing inequalities. Dr. Harry Edwards, renowned sports sociologist and social justice advocate, professed this inextricable connection: "Black athletes' academic problems are in large part rooted in and intertwined with Black youths' societal circumstances more generally there can be no effective resolution of the educational circumstances of Black athletes at any academic level except in coordination with commensurate efforts in society" (Edwards, 2000: p. 10).

The NCAA and its member institutions have an opportunity to take a leadership role in addressing significant personal troubles of Black male student athletes as well as public issues of Blacks in the broader US The implementation and constant improvement of these recommendations could enhance current services and programs as well as serve as example for other social institutions (Sage, 1998). This paper is a call to action for structural changes within the current structure of intercollegiate athletics. If institutions of higher education are the beacon of leadership and intellectual advancement, then these institutions must be willing to implement radical structural reform efforts that change the status quo of intercollegiate athletics. Only when the NCAA and its member institutions take bold steps will it live up to its mission to "govern competition in a fair, safe, equitable and sportsmanlike manner, and to integrate intercollegiate athletics into higher education so that the *educational experience of the student athlete is paramount*" (NCAA, 2011a: p. 1).

Acknowledgements

I would like to thank Dr. Billy Hawkins for his input and editorial assistance with this manuscript.

References

Acain, M. P. (1998). Revenue sharing: A simple cure for the exploitation of college athletes. *18 Loyola of Los Angeles Entertainment Law Review, 307*.

Adler, P. A., & Adler, P. (1991). *Backboards and blackboards: College athletics and role engulfment*. New York: Colombia University Press.

AIR (1988). Summary results from the 1987–1988 national study of intercollegiate athletics. *Studies in Intercollegiate Athletics*. Palo Alto, CA: Center for the Study of Athletics.

AIR (1989). The experiences of Black intercollegiate athletes at NCAA division I institutions. *Studies in Intercollegiate Athletics*. Palo Alto, CA: Center for the Studies of Athletics.

Amer, M. L. (2008). African American members of the United States congress: 1870–2008. *CRS Report for Congress*, 1–67. URL (last checked 17 February 2012) http://www.senate.gov/reference/resources/pdf/RL30378.pdf

Anderson, D. (1993). Cultural diversity on campus: A look at intercollegiate football coaches. *Journal of Sport and Social Issues, 17*, 61–66. doi:10.1177/019372359301700108

Anshel, M. H. (1990). Perceptions of Black intercollegiate football players: Implications for the sport psychology consultant. *Sport Psychologist, 4*, 235–248.

Azzarito, L., Burden, Jr., J., & Harrison, L. Jr., (2004). Perceptions of athletic superiority: A view from the other side. *Race, Ethnicity, and Education, 7*, 149–166. doi:10.1080/1361332042000234277

Barbalias, P. (2004). Black student-athletes: Improving their collegiate experience. URL (last checked on 17 February 2012). http://www.uvm.edu/~vtconn/v17/barbalias.html

Bell, D. A. (1992). *Faces at the Bottom of the Well: The permanence of racism*. New York: Basic Books.

Benson, K. (2000). Constructing academic inadequacy: African American athletes' stories of schooling. *The Journal of Higher Education, 71,* 223–246. doi:10.2307/2649249

Best, C. (1987). Experience and career length in professional football: The effect of positional segregation. *Sociology of Sport Journal, 4,* 410–420.

Branson, H. R. (1978). Black colleges of the North. In C. V. Willie, & R. R. Edmonds (Eds.), *Black Colleges in America*. New York: Teachers College Press.

Brooks, D., & Althouse, R. (2000). African American head coaches and administrators: Progress but...? In D. A. Brooks, & R. Althouse (Eds.), *Racism in College Athletics: The African American athlete's experience* (2nd ed., pp. 85–118). Morgantown, WV: Fitness Information Technology.

Browning, J., & Williams, J. (1978). History and goals of Black institutions of higher learning. In C. V. Willie, & R. R. Edmonds (Eds.), *Black Colleges in America*. New York: Teachers College Press.

Byers, W. (1995). *Unsportsmanlike Conduct: Exploiting college athletes*. Ann Arbor, MI: The University of Michigan Press.

Chu, D. B., & Segrave, J. O. (1981). Leadership and ethnic stratification in basketball. *Journal of Sport and Social Issues, 5,* 15–32. doi:10.1177/019372358100500102

Coakley, J. (2009). *Sports in Society: Issues and controversies* (10th ed.). New York, NY: McGraw-Hill.

Comeaux, E., & Harrison, C. K. (2007). Faculty and male student-athletes: Racial differences in the environmental predictors of academic achievement. *Race, Ethnicity, and Education, 10,* 199–214. doi:10.1080/13613320701330726

Comstock, A. P. (1912). Chicago housing conditions, VI: The problem of the negro. *American Journal of Sociology, 18,* 241. doi:10.1086/212075

Crouse, J., & Trusheim, D. (1988). *A Case Against the SAT*. Chicago, IL: University of Chicago Press.

Curtis, J. E., & Loy, J. W. (1978a). Positional segreation in professional baseball: Replication, trend data and critical observation. *International Review of Sport Sociology, 4,* 5–21. doi:10.1177/101269027801300401

Curtis, J. E., & Loy, J. W. (1978b). Race/ethnicity and relative centrality of playing positions in team sports. *Exercise and Sport Science Review, 6,* 285–313. doi:10.1249/00003677–197800060–00008

Dandaneau, S. P. (2000). *Taking it Big: Developing sociological consciousness in postmodern times*. Thousand Oaks, CA: Pine Forge Press.

Davis, T. (1999). Intercollegiate athletics in the next millenium: A framework for evaluating reform proposals. *Marquette Law Review, 9,* 253–271.

DeNavas-Walt, C., Proctor, B. D., & Smith, J. C. (2011). Income, poverty, and health insurance coverage in the United States: 2010. In U. S. C. Bureau (Ed.). Washington, DC: US Government Printing Office.

Denzin, N. K. (1990). Presidential address on the sociological imagination revisted. *The Sociological Quarterly, 31,* 1–22. doi:10.1111/j.1533–8525.1990.tb00314.x

Denzin, N. K. (2001). *Interpretive interactionism* (Vol. 16). Thousand Oaks, CA: Sage.

Denzin, N. K., & Lincoln, Y. S. (2005). *The Sage Handbook of Qualitative Research* (3rd ed.). Thousand Oaks, CA: Sage Publications.

Donnor, J. K. (2005). Towards an interest-convergence in the education of African-American football student-athletes in major college sports. *Race, Ethnicity, and Education, 8,* 48.

DuBois, W. E. (1996). *The Philadelphia Negro: A social study* (Reprint ed.). Philadelphia, PA: University of Pennsylvania Press.

Duderstadt, J. (2003). *Intercollegiate athletics and the American University: A university president's perspective.* Ann Arbor, MI: University of Michigan Press.

Edwards, H. (1973a). The Black athletes: 20th century gladiators for White America. *Psychology Today, 7,* 43–52.

Edwards, H. (1973b). *Sociology of Sport.* Homewood, IL: Dorsey Press.

Edwards, H. (1980). *The Struggle that Must Be: An autobiography.* New York, NY: Macmillan.

Edwards, H. (1984). The "Black dumb jock": An American sports tragedy. *The College Board Review, 131,* 8–13.

Edwards, H. (1985). Educating Black athletes. In D. Chu, J. U. Segrave, & B. J. Becker (Eds), *Sport and Higher Education* (pp. 373–384), Champaign, IL: Human Kinetics.

Edwards, H. (1994). *Playoffs and Payoffs: The African American athlete as an institutional resource.* Stanford, CA: Achieving Coaching Excellence.

Edwards, H. (2000). Crisis of Black athletes on the eve of the 21st century. *Society, 37,* 9–13. doi:10.1007/BF02686167

Eitzen, D. S., & David, C. S. (1975). The segregation of Blacks by playing positions in football: Accident or design? *Social Science Quarterly, 55,* 948–959.

Eitzen, D. S., & Tessendorf, I. (1978). Racial segregation by position in sports: The special case of basketball. *Review of Sport & Leisure, 3,* 109–128.

Ervin, L., Saunders, S. A., Gillis, H. L., & Hogrebe, M. C. (1985). Academic performance of student athletes in revenue generating sports. *Journal of College Student Personnel, 26,* 119–125.

ETS (2011). A strong start: Positioning young Black boys for educational success a statistical profile. In E. T. Service (Ed.), *ETS's Addressing Achievement Gaps Symposium* (pp. 1–5). Washington, DC: Educational Testing Service.

Ferris, E., Finster, M., & McDonald, D. (2004). Academic fit for student-athletes: An analysis of NCAA division I-A graduation rates. *Research in Higher Education, 45,* 555–575. doi:10.1023/B:RIHE.0000040263.39209.84

Fleming, J. (1984). *Blacks in College.* San Francisco: Jossey-Bass Publishers

Funk, G. D. (1991). *Major Violation: The unbalanced priorities in athletics and academics.* Champaign, IL: Leisure Press.

Gallien, L. B., & Peterson, M. S. (2005). *Instructing and Mentoring the African-American College Student: Strategies for success in higher education.* Upper Saddle River, NJ: Pearson Education, Inc.

Gaston-Gayles, J. L. (2005). The factor structure and reliability of the student athletes' motivation toward sports and academics questionnaire (SAMSAQ). *Journal of College Student Development, 46,* 317–327. doi:10.1353/csd.2005.0025

Gitlin, T. (2000). Afterword. *The Sociological Imagination: 40th anniversary edition* (pp. 229-242). New York: Oxford University Press.

Gutek, G. L. (1986). *Education in the United States: A historical perspective.* Englewood Cliffs, NJ: Prentice-Hall

Harrison, C. K. (2004). *"The Score": A hiring report card for NCAA Division IA and IAA football head coaching positions.* Orlando, FL: The Robeson Center and the Black Coaches Association (BCA).

Harrison, C. K., & Lawrence, S. M. (2004). College students' perceptions, myths, and stereotypes about African American athleticism: A qualitative investigation. *Sport, Education & Society, 9,* 33–52. doi:10.1080/1357332042000175809

Harrison, L. Jr. (2001). Understanding the influence of stereotypes: Implications for the African American in sport and physical activity. *Quest (00336297), 53,* 97–114. doi:10.1080/00336 297.2001.10491732

Hatt, B. (2007). Street smarts vs. book smarts: The figured world of smartness in the lives of marginalized, urban youth. *The Urban Review, 39,* 145–166. doi:10.1007/s11256-007-0047-9

Hawkins, B. (1999). Black student-athletes at predominantly White national collegiate athletic association (NCAA) division I Institutions and the pattern of oscillating migrant laborers. *The Western Journal of Black Studies, 23,* 1–9.

Hawkins, B. (2010). *The New Plantation: Black athletes, college sports, and predominantly White institutions.* New York: Palgrave-MacMillan.

Helms, J. E. (1994). The conceptualization of racial identity and other "racial" constructs. In E. J. Trickett, R. J. Watts, & D. Birman (Eds.), *Human Diversity: Perspectives on people in context* (pp. 285–311). San Francisco, CA: Jossey-Bass.

Henderson, F. T., & Kritsonis, W. A. (2007). Graduation rates at historically Black colleges and universities: A review of literature. *National Journal for Publishing and Mentoring Doctoral Student Research, 4,* 1–11.

Hikes, Z. (2005). Maximizing student success: A coupled approach to student retention In J. L. B. Gallien, & M. S. Peterson (Eds.), *Instructing and Mentoring the African American College Student: Strategies for success in higher education* (pp. 16–48). New York, NY: Pearson Education, Inc.

Hine, D. C., Hine, W. C., & Harrold, S. (2006). *The African-American Odyssey: Since 1965* (3rd ed., Vol. 2). Upper Saddle River, NJ: Pear-son Prentice Hall.

Hunt, T., Ivery, I., & Sailes, G. (2010). Talented genetics or genetically talented: The historical rationale for Black athletic success. In G. Sailes (Ed.), *Modern Sport and the African American Experience* (pp. 137-154). San Diego, CA: Cognella.

Jencks, C., & Phillips, M. (1998). *The Black-White Test Score Gap*. Washington, DC: Brookings Institution.

Jensen, A. R. (1969). How much can we boost I.Q. and scholastic achievement? *Harvard Educational Review, 33,* 1–123.

Johnson, D. Q. (1985). Educating misguided student-athletes: An application of contract theory. *Columbia Law Review, 85,* 96–129. doi:10.2307/1122405

Jones, R. (1998). Proving Blacks inferior: The sociology of knowledge. In J. A. Ladner (Ed.), *The death of White Sociology* (pp. 114–135). Baltimore, MD: Black Classic Press.

Keith, F. A. (2011). A change has finally come. URL (last checked on 29 March 2012). http://www.bcasports.org/index.php?option=com_content&view=article&id=74:february-10–2011&catid=12:press-releases

Lapchick, R. (1984). *Broken Promises: Racism in American sports*. New York: St. Martin's.

Lapchick, R. (1991). *Five Minutes to Midnight: Race and sport in the 1990s*. Lanham, MD: Madison Books.

Lapchick, R. (2006). Decisions from the top: Diversity among campus, conference leaders at Division IA institutions. URL (last checked 5 March 2012). http://tidesport.org/Grad%20Rates/2006_Demograhpic_release.pdf

Lapchick, R., Hoff, B., & Kaiser, C. (2011). The 2010 racial and gender report card: College sport. URL (last checked 12 February 2012). http://tidesport.org/RGRC/2010/2010_College_RGRC_FINAL.pdf

Lawrence, S. M. (2005). Short communication: African American athletes' experiences of race in sport. *International Review for the Sociology of Sport, 40,* 99–110. doi:10.1177/1012690205052171

Lincoln, Y. S., & Guba, E. G. (2000). Paradigmatic controversies, contradictions, and emerging confluences. In N. K. Denzin, & Y. S. Lincoln (Eds.), *The handbook of qualitative research* (2nd ed., pp. 1065–1122), Thousand Oaks, CA: Sage Publications.

Manning, J. E. (2011). Membership of the 112th Congress. A profile. *CRS Report for Congress: Prepared for Members and Committees of Congress* (Vol. 7–5700, pp. 1–11), URL (last checked 12 February 2012). http://www.senate.gov/reference/resources/pdf/R41647.pdf

Martin, B., Harrison, C. K., Stone, J., & Lawrence, S. M. (2010). Athletic voices and academic victories: African American male student—Athlete experiences in the Pac Ten. *Journal of Sport & Social Issues, 34,* 131–153. doi:10.1177/0193723510366541

Massengale, J. D., & Farrington, S. K. (1977). The influence of playing position centrality on the careers of college football coaches. *Review of Sport and Leisure, 2,* 107–115.

McBay, S. (1992). The condition of African American education: Changes and challenges. In J. Dewart (Ed.), *The State of Black America 1992* (pp. 141–156). New York, NY: National Urban League.

McDonald, M. G., & Birrell, S. (1998). *Reading Sport: Historical articulations of a method.* Las Vegas, NV: North American Society for the Sociology of Sport.

Medoff, M. (1977). Position segregation and professional baseball *International Review of Sport Sociology, 12,* 49–54.

Mills, C. W. (1959). *The Sociological Imagination.* New York: Oxford University Press

NCAA (2009). NCAA student-athlete ethnicity report 1999–2000–2007–2008. URL (last checked 29 March 2012). http://www.ncaapublications.com/productdownloads/SAEREP09.pdf

NCAA (2010). Trends in graduation success rates and federal graduation rates at NCAA division I institutions. URL (last checked on 29 March 2012). http://www.ncaa.org/wps/wcm/connect/f015f6004477d89f977cb749973c7da7/GSR+and+Fed+Trends+for+Web10_26_10+Final.pdf?MOD=AJPERES&CACHEID=f015f6004477d89f977cb749973c7da7

NCAA (2011a). About the NCAA. URL (last checked on 29 March 2012). http://www.ncaa.org/wps/wcm/connect/public/ncaa/about+the+ncaa

NCAA (2011b). NCAA best practices: Achieving excellence through diversity and inclusion. URL (last checked 29 March 2012). http://www.ncaa.org/wps/wcm/connect/c166120041b6686e9878b99cc9880460/Achieving+Excellence.pdf?MOD=AJPERES&CACHEID=c166120041b6686e9878b99cc9880460

NCAA (2011c). Trends in graduation success rates and federal graduation rates at NCAA division I institutions. URL (last checked 29 March 2012). http://www.ncaa.org/wps/wcm/connect/public/NCAA/PDFs/2011/Trends+in+Graduation-Success+Rates+and+Federal+Graduation+Rates+at+NCAA+Division+I+Institutions

NCAA (2012). Finances: Revenue. URL (last checked 29 March 2012). http://www.ncaa.org/wps/wcm/connect/public/NCAA/Finances/Revenue

NCES (2007). Digest of Education Statistics 2007 (NCES 2007–002). US Department of Education. URL (last checked on 17 February 2012). http://nces.ed.gov/pubs2007/2007039.pdf

NCES (2009). Status and trends in the education of racial and ethnic minorities. US Department of Education. URL (last checked on 17 February 2012). http://nces.ed.gov/pubs2010/2010015/tables/table_24_1.asp

Nettles, M. T., & Perna, L. W. (1997a). Higher and adult education. *The African American Education Data Book* (Vol. 1). Fairfax, VA: Frederick D. Patterson Research Institute of the College Fund/ UNCF.

Nettles, M. T., & Perna, L. W. (1997b). Preschool through high school. *The African American Education Data Book* (Vol. 2). Fairfax, VA: Frederick D. Patterson Research Institute of the College Fund/ UNCF.

Orfield, G. (2009). Reviving the goal of an integrated society: A 21st century challenge. Los Angeles, CA: The Regents of the University of California.

Palmer, R. T., & Gasman, M. (2008). It takes a village to raise a child: The role of social capital in promoting academic success for African American men at a Black college. *Journal of College Student Development, 49,* 52–70. doi:10.1353/csd.2008.0002

Pascarella, E. T., Bohr, L., Nora, A., & Terenzini, P. T. (1995). Intercollegiate athletic participation and freshman-year cognitive outcomes. *Journal of Higher Education, 66,* 369–387. doi:10.2307/2943793

Polite, F., & Hawkins, B. (2011). *Sport, Race, Activism, and Social Change: The impact of Dr. Harry Edwards' scholarship and service* San Diego, CA: Cognella.

Purdy, D. A., Eitzen, D. S., & Hufnagel, R. (1985). Are athletes also students? The educational attainment of college athletes. In D. Chu, J. O. Segrave, & B. J. Becker (Eds.), *Sport and Higher Education* (pp. 221–234). Champaign, IL: Human Kinetics

Rhoden, W. C. (1989). Many Black college student-athletes express feelings of isolation (Special Issue). URL (last checked on 5 February 2012). http://query.nytimes.com.gst/fullpage.html ?res=950DE1DB1431F935757C096F948260&sec=&spon=&pagewanted=1

Richardson, L. (1997). *Fields of Play: Constructing an academic life*. New Brunswick, NJ: Rutgers University Press.

Roebuck, J. B., & Murty, K. B. (1993). *Historically Black Colleges and Univerisities: Their place in Amerian higher education*. Westport, CT: Bergin and Garvey.

Sack, A., & Staurowsky, E. J. (1998). *College Athletes for Hire: The evolution and legacy of the NCAA's amateur myth*. Westport, CT: Praeger.

Sage, G. H. (1998). *Power and Ideology in American Sport* (2nd ed.). Champaign, IL: Human Kinetics

Sage, G. H. (2000). Introduction. In D. Brooks, & R. Althouse (Eds.), *Racism in College Athletics: The African American athlete's experience* (Vol. 2, pp. 2–12). Morgantown, WV: Fitness Information Technology.

Sailes, G. (1993). An investigation of campus stereotypes: The myth of black athletic superiority and the dumb jock stereotype. *Sociology of Sport Journal, 10,* 88–97.

Sailes, G. (2010). The African American athlete: Social myths and stereotypes. In G. Sailes (Ed.), *Modern Sport and the African American Athlete Experience* (pp. 55–68). San Diego, CA: Cognella.

Schwaneger, H. (1969). *The History of Higher Education in Deleware*. Ph.D. dissertation, Phila-delphia: University of Pennsylvania.

Sellers, R. M. (1992). Racial differences in the predictors for academic achievement of student-athletes in division I revenue producing sports. *Sociology of Sport Journal, 9,* 48–59.

Sellers, R. M. (2000). African American student-athletes: Opportunity or exploitation? In D. A. Brooks, R. (Ed.), *Racism in College Athletics: The African American athlete's experience* (2nd ed., pp. 133–154). Morgantown, WV: Fitness Information Technology, Inc.

Shapiro, T. M., Meschede, T., & Sullivan, L. (2010). The racial wealth gap increases fourfold. In I. O. A. A. S. Policy (Ed.), *Research and Policy Brief*. Waltham, MA: Brandeis University.

Shropshire, K. (1997). Colorblind propostions: Race, the SAT & the NCAA. *Stanford Law and Policy Review, 8,* 141–157.

Shulman, J., & Bowen, W. (2001). *The Game of Life: College sports and educational values*. Princeton, NJ: Princeton University Press.

Singer, J. N. (2005). Understanding racism through the eyes of African-American male student-athletes. *Race, Ethnicity, and Education, 8,* 365–386.

Singer, J. N. (2008). Benefits and detriments of African American male athletes' participation in a big-time college football program. *International Review for the Sociology of Sport, 43,* 399–408. doi:10.1080/13613320500323963

Smith, E. (2009). *Race, Sport and the American Dream* (2nd ed.). Durham, NC: Carolina Academic Press. doi:10.1177/1012690208099874

Spencer, N. E. (2010). Beyond the sociological imagination: Doing autoethnography to explore intersections of biography and history. In E. Smith (Ed.), *Sociology of sport and social theory*. Champaign, IL: Human Kinetics.

Steele, C. M., & Aronson, J. (1995). Stereotype threat and the intellecttual test perfor-mance of African Americans. *Journal of Personality and Social Psychology, 69,* 797–811. doi:10.1037/0022–3514.69.5.797

Stone, A. H. (1908). Is race friction between Whites and Blacks growing and inevitable? *American Journal of Sociology, 13,* 677. doi:10.1086/211624

US Bureau of the Census (1982). *Characteristics of the Population Below the Poverty Level: 1980.* Washington, DC: US Government Printing Office.

US Bureau of Census (2012). State and county quickfacts. *Population Estiamtes, American Com-munity Survey, Census of Population and Housing, State and County Housing Unit Estimates, County Business Patterns, Nonemployer Statistics, Economic Census, Survey of Business Owners, Building Permits, Consolidated Federal Funds Report.* URL (last checked on 17 February 2012). http://quickfacts.census.gov/qfd/states/00000.html

US Department of Commerce (1993). We the Americans: Blacks. In E. A. S. Administration (Ed.), Washington, DC: US Bureau of Statistics.

Van Evrie, J. H. (1870). *White Supremacy and Negro Subordination*. New York: Van Evrie, Hor-ton & Co.

Walther, E. S. (1994). *Some Readings on Historically Black Colleges and Universities.* Greensboro, NC: Management Information and Research.

Watson, J. C. (2006). Student-athletes and counseling: Factors influencing the decision to seek counseling services. *College Student Journal, 40,* 35–42.

Wiggins, D. K. (1991). Prized performers but frequently overlooked as students. *Research Quarterly for Exercise and Sport, 62,* 164–177.

Wiggins, D. K. (2000). Critical events affecting racism in athletics. In D. Brooks, & R. Althouse (Eds.), *Racism in College Athletics: The African American athlete's experience* (2nd ed., pp. 15–36). Morgantown, WV: Fitness Information Technology

Wiggins, D. K., & Miller, P. (2003). *The Unlevel Playing Field: A documentary history of the African-American experience in sport.* Urbana, IL: University of Illinois Press.

Willie, C. V., Grady, M. K., & Hope, R. O. (1991). *African-Americans and the Doctoral Experience: Implications for policy.* New York: Teachers College

Wilson, W. J. (1978). *The Declining Significance of Race: Blacks and changing American institutions.* Chicago, IL: University of Chicage Press.

Wilson, R. (1994). The participation of African Americans in Amerian higher education. In M. Justiz, R. Wilson, & L. Bjork (Eds.), *Minorities in Higher Education* (pp. 195-209). Phoenix: American Council on Education and the Orys Press.

Wilson, C. A. (1996). *Racism: From slavery to advanced capitalism.* Thousand Oaks, CA: Sage.

Wolff, A., & Keteyian, A. (1990). *Raw Recruits: The high stakes game colleges play to get their basketball stars—And what it costs to win.* New York, NY: Pocket Books.

Woods, R. (2011). *Social Issues in Sport.* Champaign, IL: Human Kinetics.

Wright-Edelman, M. (1988). Growing up in Black America. In J. H. Skolnick, & E. Currie (Eds.), *Crisis in American Institutions* (pp. 154). Glenview, IL: Scott, Foresman.

Zimbalist, A. (2001). *Unpaid Professionals.* Princeton, NJ: Princeton University Press.

Chapter 7

Power, Conflict, and Cultural Identity

17

Whatever Happened to the Black (American) Athlete?
The NBA's Cultural Renewal and Gentrification Program

Scott N. Brooks
Jermaine Cathcart
Edwin Elias
Michael A. McKail

The National Basketball Association (NBA) announced today that a record 101 international players from 37 countries and territories are on opening night rosters for the 2014-15 season. (NBA.com, 2014)

The number of international players in the league has more than doubled since 2000-01 (45 international players) and nearly quintupled since 1990-91 (21 international players). NBA games and programming are available in 215 countries and territories in 47 languages this season. (NBA.com, October 29, 2014)

IT'S EASY TO READ THE ANNOUNCEMENT ABOVE AS SIMPLE ACKNOWL-edgement of the end of black American men's total dominance in basketball. Following the epic *Sports Illustrated* cover story from 1997, "What Ever Happened to the White Athlete," the new cover story could be, "Whatever Happened to the Black American Basketball Player?" The original story focused on agency—why white kids (and boys especially) weren't playing basketball as much, weren't in certain positions on football teams, and the structure of opportunity. Blacks are considered the dominant racial group for athletics (but really only when speaking about basketball and football). But it didn't address the heart of the question: what was *done* to white athletes. And the same problem would undoubtedly surface in the new potential cover story. Asking how non-American players gained such a numerical foothold in an American sport and American professional leagues is the same as asking how blacks came to be the dominant athlete in a world where they had been largely excluded from competing with and against whites. Access and power happened to the white athlete and is now happening to the black American basketball player through interest convergence. Black athletes had been playing in parallel leagues before they were allowed to be a part of the post-WWII white sports world (Ashe 1988, Rhoden 2006). White colleges and universities, most of which were forced to open their admissions doors to blacks, began the collegiate arms race—the competition between colleges and universities for primarily black athletic muscle (Edwards 1984). The NBA, MLB, and NFL reintegrated professional sports and increased their competitiveness, and appealed to a black consumer base; sports became the beacon of racial and social progress. Colleges and universities and professional franchises and leagues granted access and changed the way they operated in order to increase their profits. The noticeable demographic change in the NBA now is the result of gentrification—a shift in business practices that has changed the league racially, globally, and culturally.

Black American males, as the preferred worker of American cash sports, have represented the best and worst of sports. The NBA bounced back from its nadir of the late 1970s by becoming a marketing stalwart under the leadership of Commissioner David Stern, who used Magic Johnson and Larry Bird in a cultural race war, before riding Nike and Air Jordan to astronomical growth and profits (Andrews 2001, 2006). The NBA rebuilt and achieved new heights of profitability in the late 1980s and 1990s by promoting certain, respectable black male athletes—who we call Cosby Jocks. With the curtain call of Michael Jordan's career, the NBA entered a transitional period that still has not fully reached equilibrium—the search for the next Michael Jordan continues. However, a new iconic figure of black athleticism took hold towards the end of Jordan's career—the era of the Thug Jock. Since the mid-1990s, the list of off-the-field crimes (sexual assault, rape, drug possession, weapon possession, even murder) has besieged the NBA (and NFL) with bad press, and the league has responded by becoming more insulated, tightening control over its workers, and focusing on protecting its brand reputation and marketability (Leonard 2012). Not coincidentally, the league's makeup of black American athletes has sharply decreased and the importation of players, including some of African descent, has grown at a rapid rate (Karen and Washington 2015). Former NBA commissioner Stern pushed the league into new frontiers, planting seeds throughout the world ("NBA Continues to Grow Internationally" 2012). The marketing of NBA stars and the game in other countries plus the influx of global talent has eased this process and the media distribution shows this—the NBA is now a global game.

Global Capitalism, Market Practices, and Race at Work

To study, describe, and explain the globalization of the NBA, one might consider scholarship in the area of labor markets and race and work. The supply of workers (and potential workers) can be affected by employers' actions, such as sanctioning or punishing workers that they don't want and encouraging new labor groups. Employers may decide, for several reasons, to seek alternative pools of labor. One reason may be to save on costs and reap greater profits, another may be that the current labor does not meet standards or a second group exceeds the standards of quality.[1] A third reason may be that a labor group has created trouble or hurt the company's image and reputation. Replacing a work group does not happen overnight, and is often done through a number of institutional practices for legitimacy: policies and rules are created that systematically lessen the probability of hiring or retaining particular groups of people; people in leadership positions use new criteria for evaluating prospective employees; the company may even initiate or participate in public media campaigns that villainize persons of a certain background; employers' new hiring and management practices are justified as part of a necessary movement to improve on the business that they do or the services that they provide; and, taken together, the collection of new practices sends the message to existing and aspiring employees that they need to "clean up their act" or they will be gone or never be hired. Ultimately, labor decisions are profit driven, and shifting completely or partially from one labor pool to another or creating a mixed, diverse labor force is less about social progress and much more about global capitalism and the maximization of profits.

Classic and contemporary scholarship highlights the American opportunity structure for groups of people based on the racial/ethnic hierarchy—race still matters. Studies have described the unequal opportunity structure (Drake and Cayton 1993 [1945]), theorized assimilation and mobility processes (Park 1964), and illuminated the informal processes that limit and block mobility (Collins 1997, Royster 2003, Pager 2007). Groups in elevated positions (whites and Asians) are advantaged and are best able to take advantage of high-status occupation opportunities when compared to Latinos and blacks. Opportunity structures can vary by industry and type of job. Professional sports jobs, and particularly those in basketball and football, are generally acknowledged as black jobs, with a few exceptions. However, niches can be fleeting and blacks have often experienced downsizing and replacement by other immigrant groups (DuBois 1901 [1899], Anderson 2011).

Gentrification and Urban Renewal

The NBA has implemented a cultural renewal program to address current problems. "Urban Renewal is the term used to describe the diversified efforts by localities, with the assistance of the Federal Government, for the elimination and prevention of slums and blight, whether residential or non-residential, and the removal of the factors that create slums and blighting conditions" (Colburn 1963). The urban renewal program originated with the United States Housing Act of 1937. It was a part of President Roosevelt's public works project, designed to improve housing

---

1 ESPN statistician Ryan Feldman (2015) has shown using both win shares and all-star selections that international players fare worse than American college players in the NBA.

conditions for low-income families while simultaneously pumping government dollars into the building industry and creating construction jobs (Colburn 1963). It underwent some revisions in 1949, 1954, and 1961, and ultimately came to have three main elements: "(1) slum prevention through neighborhood conservation and housing code enforcement; (2) rehabilitation of structures and neighborhoods; and (3) clearance and redevelopment of structures and neighborhoods" (Colburn 1963, 8). It is important to note that federal funds were made available to fund these local initiatives. The growth and timing of the last amended US Housing Acts in 1954 and 1961 coincided closely with deindustrialization, a decline in the central city economic core, and a growing national fear of the city and the high concentration of blacks (and other poor and working-class people of color) in cities. Put plainly, a public works project morphed into a program that has had disproportionately deleterious effects on poor and working-class inner city blacks in the United States. Black inner-city poor are a vulnerable population experiencing greater real and imagined concentrated poverty due to the decline of US manufacturing, leading to worsening employment opportunities for the inner-city low skilled and increasing social and economic isolation (Wilson 1987, Massey and Denton 1993).

Gentrification is a prong of urban renewal. It is the process of neighborhood transformation from poor to middle-class or affluent, and generally from black to white. Often this is made possible by the plummeting use value of land in urban areas, done deliberately by real estate owners and slum lords, while the exchange value speculatively skyrockets because of the promise of federal and local grants for redevelopment, low interest rates, and tax subsidies (Smith 1992). More than anything, the intentional dilapidation and blight is a cultural manipulation, playing into a fear of the city in support for revitalizing, rehabilitating, and recreating the city—to restore it to its previous stature or even improve upon what it once was. The end result is something new, contrived, and beyond physical structures; gentrification is a cultural phenomenon, highlighting how power controls and manages space (Zukin 1991).

Translating urban renewal and gentrification to the NBA requires thinking of each player in terms of use and exchange value (the current value of utility and the value if traded on the market as a commodity, respectively) relative to the value of other players in the league. The NBA leadership acts as a developer, creating and aiding neighborhoods (franchises), and pushing for the tearing down and building up of houses (players) that fit with the social, cultural, and economic transformation necessary to reap greater profits. The associated value with each part can be quantified, although value changes based on comparative perceptions and ideas of value, and what the market will bear—city image, good neighborhood, best, average or worst home in a particular neighborhood. Since the late 1990s and after the NBA's image and attendance reached lows, the NBA has engineered a cultural renewal program, ratcheting up punishment and getting rid of problem athletes, while opening opportunities to foreign athletes (gentrification). This process of gentrification has been a cultural cleansing towards gaining greater control of the league's public image, and transforming and/or rehabilitating the negative image—changing urban-ness' dilapidation and danger into hip, multicultural, and progressive. We will discuss how the NBA negotiated a racial and cultural transition during Commissioner David Stern's reign, focusing on changes in collective bargaining, player behavior and conduct policies, marketing, increasing the number of foreign athletes, and developing a successful global market strategy.

Expanding the Preferred Worker

It is easy to think that black males are simply the best athletes in the world from a Western perspective. American televised sports are dominated by football and basketball, with black males often the focus of attention, or at least in the greatest numbers. The myth is that blacks (females and males) dominate the cash sports (football and basketball for males, and basketball for females) because of genetic factors. However, science does not confirm this (Mukhopadhyay, Henzy, and Moses 2007, Goodman, Moses, and Jones 2012, Brooks 2009, Edwards 1973). Rather, environmental, class, gender, and even cultural factors weigh heavily on how we view athletics and competition, our motivation to participate, which sports we choose to compete in, and how we learn to participate and excel. One variable commonly left out of the picture is institutions. Institutions, such as colleges, universities, and sports franchises, recruit black athletes and rely upon them for revenue, enhancing their status and prestige, and winning. Beyond the myth of superior athleticism, class has also been important. Black athletes from working class and poor socioeconomic backgrounds have been highly sought after because it is believed that they participate with a particular attitude of toughness, fearlessness, and aggressiveness that makes them formidable (Brooks 2009). Moreover, being black (and working class or poor) comes with less social, cultural, and economic capital to resist institutional authority, exploitation, and poor treatment. Blacks have been historically, and remain today, cash sports' *preferred athletes*; they are the best athletes for the cheapest social and financial costs (Brooks and McKail 2008). This relationship is mutually beneficial but not equal. Sport capitalists have more power—they hire the athletes. They establish such a relationship for profitability, stability, and efficiency to insure that they are covered and that the athletes do their work as a priority, meeting their standards in terms of cost, quality, and dependability. The athlete feels some satisfaction in their preferred status and labor position—the black niche—as long as they have little competition.

However, the tide is changing. For various reasons, black athletes, males in particular, are costing more and their value to sport capitalists is steadily waning. Advanced technology has motored a sports revolution. Greater technology has extended the tentacles and reach of corporations, creating multinational corporations that can effectively bridge labor, production, and consumers across national and oceanic borders (LaFeber [1999] 2002). New global media has increased the audiences of sports, enabled cultural diffusion (in particular directions) from the core to periphery, and thus developed a taste for American culture, including sports.

While the 1980s and early 1990s marked the modern golden age of the NBA, the late 1990s and 2000s have been tumultuous, with great lows and very few highs, sparking fear in white owners.[2] The preferred worker has become a *troubled worker*, yet salaries and sponsorship have reached all-time highs. For the global sports elite, the non-US athlete labor pool, a product of new media and global sports capitalism, can act as a cheaper labor force, splitting the labor market, informally regulating the behavior of American black male athletes, and threatening their preferred status—American black males can be replaced by non-American blacks, Europeans and Asians. The NBA strengthened its position by hiring non-US athletes, adding to competition between labor pools, seeking new markets and consumers already engaged with American basketball and culture. The NBA's connections to global media outlets (some media corporations own part or whole sports franchises and others are sponsors) further empowers the NBA, as media plays the role of public relations agent, controlling the storylines, villainizing certain athletes, and rendering the global sports elite (owners) invisible, benign, and even victims at times.

The Troubled Worker and the Need for an NBA Renewal Program

The NBA changed in the late 1990s and early 2000s from the Cosby Jock[3] era to that of the troubled worker or Thug Jock, epitomized by Latrell Sprewell, Allen Iverson, Kobe Bryant, and Ron Artest. The effect was low NBA attendance. Some have compared this time and brand image to the 1970s NBA image held by its predominantly white fans; the league had simply become too black for many white fans to embrace (Powell 2004). A wave of incidents highlighted the NBA's state of basketball. First, Latrell Sprewell threatened to kill and then chocked his head coach P. J. Carlesimo during practice. The attack left visible marks on the coach's neck and NBA Commissioner David Stern responded by suspending Sprewell for the remainder of the season—sixty-eight games out of an eighty-two game season. Second, the arrest of Allen Iverson for a domestic dispute with his wife when, while carrying a gun, he barged into his cousin's apartment (Iverson was renting the apartment to his cousin) looking for his wife who, according to *The New York Times*, had been hiding from Iverson (Robbins 2002). The third major event that tarnished the NBA image, and perhaps the most controversial sports case since the O. J. Simpson trial, was the 2003 rape accusation against Kobe Bryant, at the time the most prominent NBA star since

---

2   Bruce Levinson (former owner of the Atlanta Hawks) was forced to sell his franchise after making remarks that the cheerleaders and fan base were too black and that was scaring off the wealthier white fan base.

3   We understand that Bill Cosby's image has declined greatly and justifiably as his numerous sexual assaults and rapes have been brought to light. Our use is in reference to the perception of Heathcliff Huxtable, how Bill Cosby was perceived in *The Cosby Show* in the 1980s. We use "Cosby Jock" to describe another construction of the black jock, which began after the NBA–ABA merger, carried by Julius Erving (Dr. J) and Earvin "Magic" Johnson. The NBA needed to restore its image, as it was losing the white middle class fan base and sponsors because it was predominantly black, there was fighting, and the players were characterized and drug addicts and thugs. Erving became one of the first players to receive a national endorsement deal, with Chapstick lip balm in 1981. In the first commercial, Erving changes his name from Dr. J to Dr. Chapstick and tells four children of different races and ethnicities about the products "emollients" and benefits. He is all at once black cool, black middle class, and a role model for kids. In a 1984 Coca-Cola commercial, Julius Erving and Bill Cosby are in the sitting room of a men's club with servers in tuxedos, discussing the taste of Coke. Here, both are presented as middle-class/upper-middle-class, articulate, college-educated (Erving and Cosby refer to each other as Doctor) black men.

Michael Jordan. The last major incident that cast a bad light on the NBA was the now-infamous "Malice at the Palace," where one Detroit Pistons player pushed an Indiana Pacers player, which escalated into an athletes–fans mauling. This event is frequently considered the tipping point for the rule changes in the NBA. It occurred on November 19, 2004, and involved (as the main actors) Ron Artest, Stephen Jackson, and Jermaine O'Neal from the Indiana Pacers, Ben Wallace from the Detroit Pistons, and various fans in the arena. The brawl with the fans started when a spectator, John Green, threw a cup of Diet Coke at Artest while he was lying on a scorer's table ("Fan Details Strides" 2009). Artest subsequently ran into the stands and began to fight the spectator who he believed had thrown the cup of soda at him. Chaos ensued, with fans stepping onto the court to fight with Jackson, Artest, and O'Neal. The players were suspended for a combined total of 146 games for the fight ("Suspensions Without Pay" 2004). Of even more importance, however, was the damage the fight did to the NBA brand. The league had once again slipped into being a league of thugs. To mitigate growing criticism, the NBA sought to implement stricter regulations on player conduct.

Taming the Troubled Worker:
The Cultural Renewal Program

The NBA felt it had to clean its image, and responded with cultural warfare. Immediate efforts to curb the social and cultural problems associated with the "urban" problem were sought and implemented via strategies to rebrand the image of NBA players. Several new rules were negotiated in the 2005 Collective Bargaining Agreement, most notably a new dress code, violations for taunting, and instituting a minimum age limit.

Dress Code

When viewing the NBA dress code, Allen Iverson wearing a do-rag, baggy shorts, and platinum chains immediately comes to mind. The NBA dress code utilizes coded racist language to ban attire typically associated with urban black youth culture and hip-hop culture (which the league routinely exploits in their videogame soundtracks and as hype music in their arenas), and is a deliberate attempt to control the behavior of black males (Leonard 2006, 2012). The "No T-shirts, Jerseys, or Sports Apparel" policy (unless team identified, approved by the team, and appropriate for the event, such as a basketball clinic) has to do with the throwback and retro jerseys frequently sported by black youth that were becoming increasingly popular in the NBA. This is in agreement with the obvious interest the NBA has in not disconcerting advertisers. The "No Headgear" rule states that "no headgear of any kind [can be worn] while a player is sitting on the bench or in the stands at a game, during media interviews, or during a team or league event or appearance (unless appropriate for the event or appearance, team-identified, and approved by the team)" ("Player Dress Code" 2005). The "No Shorts" policy is a response to the baggy shorts or capris worn by many black youth in inner cities. The "No Headgear (of any kind)" was principally introduced to stop do-rag usage. And the most glaring, race-based ban was the "no chains, pendants, or medallions worn over the player's clothes" rule ("Player Dress Code" 2005). There is a culture clash going on here and the league imposed white middle class norms of civility upon black male athletes. As Simons (2003, 12) points out,

> Dress is an important way to assert individuality and gain respect. In basketball changes in player hairstyles, shorts length, colors of uniforms and shoe styles have been an almost exclusively African American phenomenon, with mainstream White rule-makers unable to control it except by imposing a norm of neatness. ... The dominant White culture see these dress violations as calling attention to one self, and violating the White norm of uniformity and neatness. African Americans see them as expressive assertion of individuality.

This dress code should be rightly placed within a larger reactionary and conservative social context "that blames Black culture for the pollution and denigration of American life" (Leonard 2006).

Trash Talking and Taunting

> It was getting to the point where trash talking was causing fights because of the embarrassment players felt. People were reacting physically rather than verbally.
>
> – Rod Thorn, NBA vice president of basketball operations (cited in Phillips 1995)

The assumption and fear is that verbal aggression leads to physical aggression, which may ultimately cause the game to get out of control. This is largely based on stereotypical media-fueled images that connect young black males with hyperviolent, sexualized criminality (Simons 2003). Verbal jabbering is an acceptable and normal part of African American culture, on par with joking. Many black historians and literary critics consider this a long-standing oral tradition in black communities that has its cultural roots in Africa (Gates 1998). A problem with the trash talking/taunting rule is its highly subjective nature. The lack of specificity to these rules, combined with the overly stereotyped image of hyperviolent black males, leads to a situation where black males are much more likely to be penalized for behavior that is considered normal within their culture. Furthermore, rules in games are designed with the purpose of providing a set of regulations that prevent a player from gaining an unfair advantage (e.g., goal tending). Cultural bias and heavily subjective rules such as taunting and trash talking tend to have the opposite stated effect. It unnecessarily penalizes black athletes and gives an unfair advantage to others; all things being equal, teams with more black players are more likely to incur technical fouls for trash talking and taunting. In addition, general managers and coaches could consider drafting, hiring, playing fewer black players to avoid being penalized on the court and suffering bad media attention off the court. Some research has already shown that whiter teams are called less for fouls (Price and Wolfers 2010).

NBA Age Limit

> As a Black guy, you kind of think (race is) the reason why it's coming up. You don't hear about it in baseball or hockey. To say you have to be 20, 21 to get in the league, it's unconstitutional. If I can go to the U.S. Army and fight the war at 18, why can't you play basketball for 48 minutes and then go home?
>
> – Jermaine O'Neal (cited in Leonard 2006, 166)

> Well, they are physically mature enough to be part of the NBA, and they are great young players. But as you frame the issue, the question is whether a couple of years more of seasoning would increase their maturity, their skills, their collegiate programs and ultimately what it could do for sending messages to kids who are practicing their skills who should think about getting an education rather than coming right to [the] NBA.
>
> – David Stern, NBA commissioner (Stern 2001)

Age restrictions for players are not a universal in professional sports leagues; some have them, others don't, and age restrictions have changed over time. Certain leagues, both in America and abroad, consider it an investment to train young athletes and develop their skill in the best facilities in the world.[4] Stern, in the above transcript with Wolf Blitzer, claims altruistic motives are at the heart of the age limit. But in reality, the restriction is simply a power move. The NBA age limit, also known as the one-and-done rule, has been called a stop-gap or intersection where the NBA and NCAA have more control over the labor pool and can add an additional layer of obstacles and "conditioning" before the black athletes become professionals (Aldridge 2012).

In essence, the NBA decided to take action against risky high school players who might cripple franchises and fan interest. Risk is assessed by the league and the franchise rather than the athlete who gets paid, regardless of how much trouble they might create for themselves. Tom Ziller (2011) conducted a study that looked at the draft results from the years preceding and the years following the implementation of the NBA age limit. The main conclusion Ziller drew was that general managers made approximately the same number of top-ten draft mistakes as they did before the age limit restriction.[5] The reality is not that high school draft picks bust more often than college picks, but rather, there is simply more attention on high school picks.

---

4 The US soccer federation has just begun this type of developmental program. Kids serious about playing soccer will attend ten-month programs in soccer "development academies." See *The New York Times* article by Sam Borden for more on this (Borden 2012).

5 Ziller (2011) explains: In the four years before the age minimum was put into place, teams saw decent success in the top 10 in the draft. A rough sorting reveals 21 top-10 picks in the four years (2002-05) as successes, nine as disappointments and 10

Black NBA players have been impacted by the one-and-done rule, as shown by Jermaine O'Neal's feelings expressed above. It is common knowledge that many NBA players come from some of the most disadvantaged and impoverished backgrounds. Stern has touted the merits of sending a message for kids to stay in school and not chase hoop dreams, but what difference does one year make? And what about the role that the NBA and colleges have played in the creation of the hoop dream? Would hoop dreams exist without the pie-in-the-sky multimillion dollar contracts, sneaker deals, and scholarships to colleges in the power conferences? For student athletes, with the right resources, right connections, and right culture, college can open the doors. However, for many black student athletes it is a momentary shine of their talents and a return to low social status (Brooks and Kim 2007). Thus, the rule serves to keep impoverished, black, low-income athletes in another year of poverty while latently serving the interests of the exploitative, profit-seeking, big-time college sports organization (Zimbalist 2001). As Tennessee Congressman Steve Cohen notes, "My concern is that the players who must abide by this rule are harmed by the league's pursuit of these business interests." He continued: "Age discrimination prevents players from supporting their families. ... I am concerned that the careers of young men who possess all the skills necessary to succeed in the NBA ... may be sacrificed in favor of the bottom lines of the teams on which they hope to play" (Cohen cited in NBC sports 2009).

Social scientist David Leonard (2006) views the implementation of the age limit, dress code and the various other rule changes levied at black NBA athletes as "not just a response to the brawl but a method of surveillance and an instrument of control aimed at the uninhibited 'invasion' of hip-hop, a threatening and potentially unprofitable inscription of Black masculinity" (Leonard 2006, 160). What Leonard recognizes is the change in black male athletes' status from preferred (and unchallenged) worker to troubled worker.

The NBA's Gentrification Process

> Ultimately, gentrification—a process that seems to reassert a purely *local* identity —represents downtown's social transformation in terms of an *international* market culture. (Zukin 1991, 187)

Sharon Zukin explains the limitation of considering gentrification only in terms of housing and neighborhood demographic change—the level of change that is deemed gentrification doesn't happen through individual decisions or one block or neighborhood changing. Instead, gentrification is a series of events preceded by power plays between local officials, developers, and communities, making the once dangerous city a safe space with better, urban culture and a plush lifestyle. The new urbanity increasingly appeals to cosmopolitanism, as a space that can accommodate international culture and tastes, as well as international elites and white-collar workers. The

---

as busts.

NBA's gentrification hasn't totally lost the racial feel—like baseball, many of the non-American players are racially brown or black, visibly having some African ancestry.[6]. In this way, the NBA is still dominated by blacks and thus, symbolically, still played by the dominant athletic group; but it has also gained new numbers of non-black and traditionally Western Europeans.

The NBA paid little attention to non-American basketball players before 1984. However, the revitalized NBA, led by Magic Johnson, Larry Bird, and Michael Jordan, became a global cultural phenomenon. With this came the potential for new labor pools and an expanded consumer base. Businesses consider new labor pools when looking to increase profit and a cheaper and/or more efficient labor source able to produce the same or an acceptable level of quality. In the case of the NBA, non-American or imported workers have provided a high level of quality, which has improved dramatically over time, and opened the gates for new and larger consumer groups and markets. The change in labor has been slow and bumpy—between 1971 and 1983 a total of six international players were selected in the NBA draft, but none signed or played until 1984, when Hakeem Olajuwon signed with the Houston Rockets. It is now in full swing. (See Figure 17.1 to see how the draft has been used to bring in international players from 1993 to 2015.)

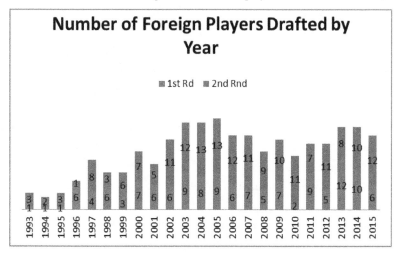

The annual Nike Hoop Summit, which started in 1995, showcases the world's upcoming basketball talent in one game. This game, USA versus The World, features the USA Basketball Men's Junior National Select Team, composed of the top high school boy senior players, playing against a World Select Team, top players 19-years-old or younger from around the world. An overwhelming number of these World players have gone on to become NBA players, including Dirk Nowitzki, Tony Parker, Luis Scola, Andrea Bargnani, Wang Zhi, and Enes Kanter ("USA Men's Nike Hoop Summit"). The NBA followed Nike's lead. In 2001, the NBA began its Basketball Without Borders Camp, a cross-continent program between FIBA and the NBA (NBA.com).

---

6   The previous two number one overall picks in the NBA draft were non-American black players: Anthony Bennet and Andrew Wiggins from Canada.

Furthermore, this past year, the NBA replaced its traditional Frosh/Soph Rising Stars Challenge (where the best rookies play the best sophomores) with a USA versus The World Frosh/Soph game ("USA vs. World" 2015). Although the goal of this program is to promote and educate people on the NBA, it also breeds competitiveness.[7]

Historically, the most successful international players have been college players, and more recently, high school imports, who've learned the game in the United States and are fairly acculturated and known before becoming professionals. Hakeem Olajuwon's career reflects the best NBA import success story. Although Hakeem was born and raised in Nigeria, he received his formal basketball training in the United States during his tenure at the University of Houston. This not only raised Hakeem's basketball performance, by putting him in the position to compete against Americans and the best competition at the time, but it also served as an easier and longer transition than someone who would make their first trip to America and have to jump right into being a professional, while also adjusting to culture shock. Hakeem competed against professionals like Hall of Famer Moses Malone during the summer, who was playing for the Houston Rockets at the time, before being the first selection of the 1984 draft and playing eighteen seasons as a professional.[8]

Since the late 1980s, imported players have fit a different profile: they are younger, often have no US college experience, yet know American culture, come from Eastern Europe, France, England, or South America, and are highly skilled. Canada is the exceptional exception: elite Canadians are typically going to powerhouse high school boarding schools and/or top colleges, and the country has the most non-American first-round draft picks, and thirteen total players on 2014–2015 NBA rosters (Cooper 2014). Basketball has been played all over the world and several countries (Russia, Greece, Turkey, Spain, Italy, and Brazil) and international professional clubs (Žalgiris Kaunas, Maccabi Tel-Aviv, Real Madrid, and Olimpia Milano) have been recognized for some time. But the competitive level picked up with the increase in television coverage via new technology; a visible and growing number of international players in US colleges and universities and in the NBA; American global cultural diffusion; and the dominance of the 1992 US Olympic Team (the "Dream Team") on the world stage (LaFeber [1999] 2002). Over the past ten years, there have been 147 international players selected who had no previous US experience, including 11 in the 2011 draft (Figure 17.1). Many of these players have come as young men, rather than being seasoned and proven veterans in Europe or Asia. Because American culture is global, they know much more about the United States than the United States knows about them—the good and the bad—and a majority are able English speakers. Thus, transitioning is less risky. Imported players are not simply giants or "freaks" from African (or Nigerian or Sudanese) or Eastern European countries anymore; now they are all shapes and sizes, coming from all over the world. Scouting has grown and expanded to a global scale. Still, some trends in national origins have begun to

---

7   Basketball Without Borders is now on every major continent in the world and holds a camp where the hundred best players in a given region are invited to attend, given instruction by US coaches, and set to compete against each other.
8   Olajuwon won two NBA championships, earned league MVP, Defensive Player of the Year and Finals MVP all in the same season (the first and only person to ever accomplish this) and was inducted into Basketball's Hall of Fame in 2008.

take shape. Former Soviet bloc countries (Serbia-Montenegro, Russian, Lithuania, Yugoslavia, Slovenia, Croatia) and France, Spain, Puerto Rico, Argentina, Australia, and England lead the way. These contemporary imports sometimes come from basketball or elite athletic pedigrees, like Boris Diaw. Diaw's mother is considered one of France's best-ever basketball players, and his father is a former Senegalese high jump champion. Another example is Joakim Noah, who is son of French tennis legend Yannick Noah. Their skills are being developed early in national athletic training programs, and professional clubs are increasing their competitiveness, knowledge of the game, and quality as professionals. In addition, imported players are now given credit for changing the game, as some skills and moves are considered non-American, such as the "euro step," and players are typified as "euro big men," rather than simply finesse or power, which are traditional American ideal types for bigger, taller players.

American dominance is no longer a foregone conclusion. In 2002 and 2006 the US team lost in the FIBA world championships (capturing sixth and third place, respectively) and earned the bronze medal in the 2004 Olympics. The US team returned to capture the gold in 2008, but only narrowly defeated Spain in a much-anticipated final game that featured nineteen NBA players (or former NBA players), with all of the US players and seven of the Spanish players being in the NBA. In all, forty-two current and former NBA players played for their national teams, with ten out of the twelve competing teams having at least one NBA player (NBA.com). The US team had the most active or current (at that time) NBA players, all twelve, while Spain and Argentina were tied for second most with four each; Spain also had three former players and Argentina had one former player.

Globalization and Global Capitalism of the NBA

> It shows that basketball is getting bigger all over the world. Basketball used to be a smaller sport, but now everybody plays it. The NBA has fans all over the world. It's becoming a global game.
>
> – Dirk Notwitzki, German import who plays for the Dallas Mavericks, reflecting on the number of NBA players in the Olympics representing different nations

The American sports machine has had multiple innovations. Sports moved from local to regional activities, rivalries were established, and opposing fans traveled to support their team in hostile away games (Hoch 1973). There was big money to be made in this, rather than simply relying on the small, local, partisan crowd. Bigger arenas and stadiums were built to house the "war" and increasingly the rivalry extended beyond the teams and people directly related; regional loyalty suggested allegiances whether or not a person attended or had any formal attachment to the university or organization that owned/sponsored the athletic team. Loyalty developed into tradition. Radio and newspaper coverage of sporting events were central to informing the legions of fans regarding their team's everyday activities, reporting scores, expectations, progress and problems, and acting as sources of hype. Television was tremendous in making every game a home game for fans; the world was made smaller, as one could watch games that had or were happening in other parts of the country. Cable television has expanded coverage exponentially, while at the same time offering customized service, such that a person has a lot of power to decide what they want to see, and personal television recording has given consumers control over when they see their games. Most recently, online programming has bridged multiple media options—newsprint, game coverage, news analysts and commentators, personal interest accounts and documentaries, and consumer involvement (via blogging, Twitter, et cetera). In short, sports today are media based (Brandt 2011).

Perhaps no sport has been better at realizing and taking advantage of the media revolution than the NBA. The NBA makes a significant share of its basketball-related income from broadcast rights, national and local; it has global television network partners, and recently started its own television network, NBA TV. The NBA negotiates from a favorable position because of basketball's popularity. The NBA's earnings from broadcast rights have exploded since Magic Johnson and Larry Bird's first professional season (1979–1980), when the USA network paid $1.5 million for three years (see Table 1). For the 2011–2012 season, the NBA was paid $930 million in national broadcast rights from ESPN/ABC and TNT, $485 million and $445 million, respectively (Sporting News 2011). The new TV deal the NBA signed with ESPN and Turner amounts to $24 billion over nine years. That is approximately $2.6 billion per year ("NBA Extends Television Deals" 2014).

TABLE 1. NBA CABLE TELEVISION CONTRACTS

Season	Station	Contract amount
1979–80 to 1981–82	USA	$1.5 million/3 years
1982–83 to 1983–84	USA/ESPN	$11 million/2 years
1984–85 to 1985–86	TBS	$20 million/2 years
1986–87 to 1987–88	TBS	$25 million/2 years
1988–89 to 1989–90	TBS/TNT	$50 million/2 years
1990–91 to 1993–94	TNT	$275 million/4 years
1994–95 to 1997–98	TNT/TBS	$397 million/4 years
1998–99 to 2001–02	TNT/TBS	$840 million/4 years
2002–03 to 2007–08	TNT	$2.2 billion/6 years
2003–	TNT/TBS	$930 million/4 years
2002–03 to 2007–08	TNT	$2.2 billion/6 years
2007–	TNT/TBS	$930 million/4 years
2002–03 to 2007–08	TNT	$2.2 billion/6 years

Each team shares national television broadcast rights (this contract is worth $31 million per team), and each team can make individual (non-shared) local television deals, with some teams earning more from local deals than from their share of the league's national deal.[9] "Between 1985 and 1990, the broadcast of NBA games overseas doubled to 70 countries" (Falcous and Maguire 2005). These broadcasts generated $5 million for the NBA. By 2002 the NBA was broadcasting games in a staggering 212 countries, earning $35 million dollars. NBA TV, which started in 1999, has been operated by Cox Communications, Cablevision, and Time Warner Cable since 2003. This multimillion-dollar arrangement allows NBA TV to reach forty-five million–plus American homes and be seen in forty countries via global partners. It also has an innovative offering, an online subscription to a worldwide audience. NBA TV carries NBA regular season games and some first-round playoff games, WNBA games, Euroleague and Maccabi Tel Aviv (Israel) team games, and a host of international games, all broadcast in high definition. In "April 2005, the channel televised the Chinese Basketball Association finals for the first time."[10]

The NBA could not be a global sport without cultural diffusion. Manipulating non-American media markets so that games could be covered internationally was aided by Nike's global saturation and the technology that could project images and report on events simultaneously or with very little time delay. Michael Jordan, as a business model, represents Nike's brilliance in brand marketing and strategy. Jordan has been much more than a basketball player; he represents a cultural icon that sells a cool, black, urban image; shoes and apparel; and American dominance. Through Jordan's worldwide acceptance, Nike began (and continues) taking its athlete icons overseas as cultural ambassadors to host youth tournaments. Nike shoes and apparel sales have leaped since the late 1980s when Jordan's iconic figure was constructed, and the company has even infiltrated traditionally closed markets like China. Jordan was the initial brand icon, but Tiger Woods, Lebron James, and Kobe Bryant have pushed Nike even deeper into the global sphere, epitomized by Kobe becoming one of China's most popular athletes (Medina 2012). Kobe began visiting China to promote his Nike shoes and has since "filmed a commercial touting Smart Car [in] China ... appeared in a Sprite commercial and music video featuring Asian pop singer **Jay Chou, ... [and]** even had his own reality show" (Medina 2012). In four of the past five seasons, Bryant's jersey was the most in demand. In addition, twenty percent of NBA merchandise was sold overseas for a profit of $430 million (Eisenberg 2003).

Conclusion: How Race Explains Global Sport

Beyond winners and losers, the NBA's racial and ethnic/international demographics tells us about labor and race relations in America, and also illuminates sports labor and race relations globally. While players of African descent, regardless of where they're from, are considered black, there is baggage that comes with being black and American. Imported black players are considered ath-

---

9   The Los Angeles Lakers signed a 20-year deal with Time Warner in 2011. The amount is undisclosed but is known to be in excess of $30 million per year, and less than $150 million (*Los Angeles Times*, February 14, 2011, "Time Warner Cable, Lakers Strike 20-year TV Deal"). The most recent deal shows the Lakers making $200 million a year for both TWCsportsnet and TWC deportes (http://www.forbes.com/sites/christinasettimi/2014/01/22/the-nbas-richest-local-television-deals/).
10   "Chinese Basketball Association Coverage Expands to U.S." NBA.com, April 13, 2005.

letic, but being of European ethnicity or nationality gives them some positive borrowed identity in comparison to black players from African countries. Many of the black players from Europe come from recognizable biracial backgrounds. White European players, on the other hand, are chameleons. They can be honorary black, since they play in a predominantly black league, and are not white American. Yet, they are white and can pass, with the loss of their accent, for white American or as part of the global white elite, since being European comes with a greater sense of authenticity with regard to whiteness; it is higher culture, less diluted, and more worldly. In this way, white European success in the NBA gives hope that whiteness really is best when focused and trained right—they are overachievers like white Americans, successful basketball players who are able to play with blacks at this time because of their pure European blood and intelligence. White racial unity is apparent in some white players' abilities to claim non-American ancestry, blood, and nationality. Some have played for Germany, France, or other countries, with little to no eyebrow raising (e.g., Grand Rapids, Michigan, native Chris Kaman played for Germany in the 2008 Olympics).

The combined actions by the NBA, its corporate partners, and other actors (such as the NCAA) exemplify the institutional power of whites and how blacks' position as workers is maintained. Whether the different actors are consciously engaged in marginalizing black athletes or not is unimportant; the effects have directly and indirectly significant effects. Black American players feel threatened by the increasing numbers of others, and sometimes voice their displeasure publicly in ethnocentric and derogative terms, blinded by competition, rather than focusing on the people and institutions in power.[11] Edna Bonacich's classic theory of the split-labor market is instructive. Owners profit from group competition and "divide and conquer" worker interests to advance their own agendas. They split the labor market and manipulate workers to accept lower wages and to compete with other groups via racial/ethnic antagonism (Bonacich 1972). A split labor market is effectively created through the NBA's direct importation of talent, as well as the efforts of universities that recruit players from abroad, and sports corporations like Nike that push beyond American borders to grow new markets and promote international talent in events like their annual summit. The NBA's globalization has brought new consumer markets and corporate partners, extended its reach and visibility, and tapped into potential new labor pools. This also adds to the number of stakeholders, as more interests are served and hurt by NBA activities, including a lockout. David Carter, executive director of the Sports Business Institute at the University of Southern California's Marshall School of Business, expressed the new interests of convergence and how this strengthens the NBA. "The big winners are anyone involved in marketing and financing in the NBA—the advertisers, the sponsors, they've got continuity now. A lot of people are focusing on what this means right away, but you have to look at it as 10 years that marketing

---

11   In the NBA, black American athletes have focused their angst on "white" players, including imports Steve Nash and Dirk Nowitzki. But in baseball, comments by Gary Sheffield in 2007 and Tori Hunter in 2010 have been made about black Latinos being "impostors" (not really black), but preferred over black Americans because they talk back less and will play for less money.

partners and TV partners know they have this" (quoted in Clark 2011). With the average career of an NBA player lasting 4.71 years, the NBA's strength lies in its stability, corporate power, and persistence—it will outlast its workers, continue to become a global enterprise, and act in ways to maintain leverage over its workers through social regulation (rules), revenue sharing, salary caps, and the threat of imported workers, while simultaneously partnering with media that villainizes workers and renders the owners invisible. As DuBois highlighted more than a hundred years ago, structure and power, both in the hands of whites, overwhelmingly determines black employment and life chances. What is seen in the case of basketball exists in all sports where blacks have been allowed to participate, and where they play in significant numbers.

The case of international football (soccer), in terms of recruiting and hiring black talent, reflects the similar patterns found in American sports. The inclusion of blacks (mostly non-American) has been checkered, and discrimination remains in overt and covert forms. Black pioneer of English football Jack Leslie played professionally in the 1920s, although he was not allowed to play for England (Morley 2012). Moreover, blacks were playing in noticeable numbers by the 1970s. The British Premier League is looking into adopting the NFL's Rooney Rule, which guarantees that at least one minority candidate is interviewed when a coaching position is open. And the continuing history of the racial abuse experienced by black players is peaking (Franklin 2012, Morley 2012). In response, FIFA, international football's global governing body, has made anti-racism one of its goals, due to the embarrassing displays of racism by the significant number of fans from white supremacist groups in Europe. This issue has become dangerous, particularly with the growing number of players of African descent (European, North American, South American, and African). Although football is much more global than any other sport, blacks are only now gaining a solid foothold across nations and in most of the premier leagues around the world. This is not random; the decision to have a black player or not is becoming the standard for measuring whether an owner is serious about competing or not at the national or continental level (Foer 2004).

In a 1963 interview with social psychologist Kenneth Clark, James Baldwin discussed urban renewal as a mechanism for displacing and alienating blacks. Baldwin quoted a 16-year-old teen from an earlier television event:

> He said, "I got no country. I got no flag." Now he's only 16 years old, and I couldn't say, "you do." I don't have any evidence to prove that he does. They were tearing down his house because San Francisco is engaging ... most cities are engaged in ... something called urban renewal, which means moving Negroes out. It means the federal government is an accomplice to this fact - negro removal, that is what it means. (Standley and Pratt 1989, 42)

Returning to the first question: whatever happened to the black athlete? The labor gentrification of the NBA was a rehabilitation, or remove and renovate, or rebuild program, whereby the player pool was opened wide for non-American players. NBA leadership returned to old manners of exclusion: putting up barriers to entry, such as an age limit, which was in place prior to 1950 when blacks weren't drafted by NBA teams. Wilt Chamberlain couldn't enter the NBA right away because he had to wait for his college class to graduate (Ashe 1988). Media played a significant role in the image and myth making, and in covering the renewal of the NBA as the NBA became a "global" league. A time may be coming, like it has in baseball, where some black American players will look around and realize that they're becoming extinct and feel as though they've been squeezed out by the gentrification process, but by then it'll be far too late.

References

Aldridge, David. 2012. "Altruism far down on the list of motives for NBA's age limit." *NBA.com*, April 9. http://www.nba.com/2012/news/features/david_aldridge/04/09/morning-tip-nba-draft-age-limit-debate/.

Andrews, David. 1999. "Whither the NBA, whither America?" *Peace Review* 11 (4): 505–16.

Andrews, David, ed. 2001. *Michael Jordan Inc.: Corporate Sport, Media Culture, and Late Modern America.* Albany, NY: SUNY Press.

Andrews, David. 2006. *Sport-Commerce-Culture: Essays on Sport in Late Capitalist America.* New York: Peter Lang.

Ashe Jr., Arthur R. 1988. *A Hard Road to Glory: The African American Athlete in Basketball.* New York: Amistad Books.

Associated Press. 2009. "NBA defends minimum age rule to Congress." *NBC Sports.* http://nbc-sports.msnbc.com/id/32012358/ns/sports-nba/

Bonacich, Edna. 1972. "A theory of ethnic antagonism: The split labor market." *American Sociological Review* 37 (October): 547–59.

Borden, Sam. 2012. "High school players forced to choose in soccer's new way." *The New York Times.* http://www.nytimes.com/2007/05/02/sports/basketball/02refs.html?pagewanted=all.

Brooks, Scott N. 2009. *Black Men Can't Shoot.* Chicago: University of Chicago Press.

Brooks, Scott, and Linda Kim. 2007. "The dilemmas and contradictions of 'getting paid.'" In *Racism in College Athletics: The African American Experience* (2nd ed), edited by Dana Brooks and Ronald Althouse. Morgantown, WV: Edition Fitness Information Books.

Brooks, Scott N., and Michael McKail. 2008. "The preferred work: A structural explanation for black male dominance in basketball." *Critical Sociology* 34 (3): 369–87.

"Bryant distracted, scared amid sex assault case." 2003. *SI.com*, December 26. http://sportsillustrated.cnn.com/2003/basketball/nba/12/26/kobe.interview.ap/index.html?cnn-yes.

Colburn, Fern M. 1963. *The Neighborhood and Urban Renewal.* New York: National Federation of Settlements and Neighborhood Centers.

Collective Bargaining Agreement. 2005. National Basketball Players Association. http://www.nbpa.org/cba/2005.

Collins, Sharon M. 1997. *Black Corporate Executives: The making and breaking of a Black middle class.* Philadelphia: Temple University Press.

Desens, Carl. 1994. "The NBA's Fast Break Overseas." *Business Week Online*, December 4. http://www.businessweek.com/archives/1994/b340279.arc.htm.

Drake, St. Clair, and Horace R. Cayton. 1993 [1945]. *Black Metropolis: A study of Negro life in a Northern city.* Chicago: University of Chicago Press.

DuBois, W. E. B. 1999 [1899]. *A Philadelphia Negro.* Philadelphia: University of Pennsylvania Press.

Edwards, Harry. 1984. "The Collegiate athletic arms race: Origins and implications of the 'rule 48' controversy." *Journal of Sport & Social Issues* March (8): 4–22.

Eisenberg, Daniel. 2003. "The NBA's global game plan." *Time* 17: 59.

Falcous, Mark, and Joseph Maguire. 2006. "Imagining America: The NBA and local-global mediascapes." *International Review for the Sociology of Sport* 41 (1): 59–78.

Falcous, Mark, and Joseph Maguire. 2005. "Globetrotters and local Heroes? Labor migration, basketball, and local identities." *Sociology of Sport Journal* 22 (2): 137–57.

"Fan details strides made since brawl." 2009. *ESPN*, November 19. http://sports.espn.go.com/nba/news/story?id=4670842.

Feldman, Ryan. 2015. "NBA Draft: The Numbers on International Players." *ESPN*, June 23. http://espn.go.com/blog/statsinfo/post/_/id/106856/nba-draft-the-numbers-on-international-lottery-picks.

Foer, Franklin. 2004. *How Soccer Explains the World: An unlikely story of globalization.* New York: Harper.

Franklin, Joshua. 2012. "Blowing the whistle on racism in English soccer." *The Boston Globe*, February 13. http://www.boston.com/bostonglobe/editorial_opinion/blogs/the_angle/2012/02/blowing_the_whi.html.

Gates, Henry Louis. 1998. *The Signifying Monkey: A theory of African American literary criticism.* New York: Oxford University Press.

Goodman, Alan, Yolanda T. Moses, and Joseph Jones. 2012. *Race, Are We So Different?* Hoboken, NJ: Wiley-Blackwell.

Gumbel, Bryant. 2011. *Real Sports with Bryant Gumble* [television broadcast]. HBO, October 18.

Hill-Collins, Patricia. 2004. *Black Sexual Politics.* New York: Routledge.

Hoch, Paul. 1973. *Rip Off the Big Game.* New York: Double Day.

Howard-Cooper, Scott. 2014. "A New Basketball Generation Comes of Age in Canada." *NBA.com,* November 1. http://www.nba.com/2014/news/features/scott_howard_cooper/11/01/international-influence-canada/.

LaFeber, Walter. [1999] 2002. *Michael Jordan and the New Global Capitalism.* New York: Norton.

Lapchick, Richard. 2002. *Smashing Barriers*. New York: Madison.

Leonard, David. 2004. "The Next MJ or the Next OJ? Kobe Bryant, Race, and the Absurdity of Colorblind Rhetoric." *Journal of Sport and Social Issues* 28 (3): 284–313.

Leonard, David. 2006. "The real color of money: Controlling Black bodies in the NBA." *Journal of Sport and Social Issues* 30 (2): 158–79.

Leonard, David. 2012. *After Artest: The NBA and the assault on Blackness*. Albany, NY: State University of New York Press.

"Leon Smith Checks Out of Hospital, Looks to Future." 2000. *CNNSI.com*, January 7. http://sportsillustrated.cnn.com/basketball/nba/news/2000/01/07/smith_update_ap/.

Massey, Douglas S., and Nancy A. Denton. 1993. *American Apartheid: Segregation and the Making of the Underclass*. Boston: Harvard University Press.

Medina, Mark. 2012. "Kobe Bryant's Presence Remains Strong in China." *Los Angeles Times* (Lakers blog), February 19. http://lakersblog.latimes.com/lakersblog/2012/02/kobe-bryant.html.

Morley, Gary. 2012. "Racism in Football, 'It's Not Black and White.'" *CNN*, February 23. http://edition.cnn.com/2012/02/23/sport/football/football-racism-england/index.html.

Mukhopadhyay, Carole, Rosemary Henze, and Yolanda T. Moses. 2007. *How Real Is Race? A Sourcebook on Race, Culture and Biology*. New York: Rowman and Littlefield.

"NBA continues to grow internationally." 2012. *NBA.com*, October 26. http://www.nba.com/2012/news/10/26/nba-international-growth.ap/.

"NBA Extends Television Deals." 2014. *ESPN*, October 7. http://espn.go.com/nba/story/_/id/11652297/nba-extends-television-deals-espn-tnt.

"NBA Minimum Salary." 2005. *InsideHoops*, August 10. http://www.insidehoops.com/minimum-nba-salary.shtml.

Pager, Devah. 2007. *Marked: Race, Crime, and Finding Work in an Era of Mass Incarceration*. Chicago: University of Chicago Press.

Park, Robert E. 1964. *Race and Culture. Essays in the Sociology of Contemporary Man*. New York: Free Press.

Phillip, Mary-Christine. 1995. "Cultural difference or foul mouth." *Black Issues in Higher Education* 20 (April): 20–24.

"Player Dress Code." 2005. *NBA.com*, October 20. http://www.nba.com/news/player_dress_code_051017.html.

Powell, Shaun. 2008. *Soled Out: How Blacks Are Winning and Losing in Sports*. Champaign, IL: Human Kinetics.

Price, Joseph, and Wolfers, Justin. 2010. "Racial discrimination among NBA referees." *The Quarterly Journal of Economics* 125 (4): 1859–87.

"Record 101 international players on opening day rosters." 2014. *NBA.com*, October 28. http://www.nba.com/2014/news/10/28/international-players-on-opening-day-rosters-2014-15/.

Rhoden, William C. *40 Million Dollar Slaves*. New York: Three Rivers Press.

Robbins, Liz. 2002. "BASKETBALL; Iverson faces felony charges in trespassing and gun case." *New York Times*, July 12. http://www.nytimes.com/2002/07/12/sports/basketball-iverson-faces-felony-charges-in-trespassing-and-gun-case.html?pagewanted=all&src=pm.

Royster, Deidre. 2003. *Race and the Invisible Hand: How White networks exclude Black men from blue-collar jobs.* Berkeley: University of California Press.

Simons, Herbert. 2003. "Race and penalized sports behavior." *International Review for the Sociology of Sport* 38 (1).

Smith, Neil. 1992. "New city, new frontier: The lower East side as wild, wild West." In *Variation on a Theme Park: The new American city and the end of public space*, edited by Michael Sorkin, 61–93. New York: Hill and Wang.

"Spanish Basketball." 2010. *Eurobasket*. www.eurobasket.com/esp.intro.asp

Standley, Fred L., and Louis H. Pratt, eds. 1989. *Conversations with James Baldwin.* Jackson: University of Mississippi Press.

Stern, David. 2001. "All stars too soon: The NBA Age Dilemma." *CNN.com* [transcript of televised interview], February 11. http://transcripts.cnn.com/TRANSCRIPTS/0102/11/se.01.html.

"Suspensions without pay, won't be staggered." 2004. *ESPN*, November 22. http://sports.espn.go.com/nba/news/story?id=1928540.

"Taunting." 2001 *NBA.com*, October 23. http://www.nba.com/analysis/rules_p.html?nav=ArticleList.

"USA Men's Nike Hoop Summit alumni NBA draft choices, 1995-2011." *USAbasketball.com*. http://www.usabasketball.com/mens/hoopsummit/hsum_nbadraft.html.

"USA vs. World in New BBVA rising stars challenge format." 2015. *NBA.com*, January 21. http://www.nba.com/2015/news/as.rising.stars/01/21/new-format-for-rising-stars-challenge/.

Van Riper, Tom. 2012. "NBA TV on a Roll." *Forbes*.

Wilson, William Julius. 1987. *The Truly Disadvantaged: The inner city, the underclass, and public policy.* Chicago: University of Chicago Press.

Ziller, Tom. 2011. "Age minimum hasn't limited NBA draft busts, and extending it to 20 won't help." *SBNation*, May 30. http://www.sbnation.com/nba-draft/2011/5/30/2197120/nba-draft-busts-age-minimum.

Zimbalist, Andrew. 1999. *Unpaid Professionals: Commercialism and conflict in big time college sports.* Princeton, NJ: Princeton University Press.

Zukin, Sharon. 1991. *Landscapes of Power: From detroit to disney world.* Berkeley: University of California Press.

18

African American Racial Identity and Sport

Louis Harrison, Jr.
C. Keith Harrison
Leonard N. Moore

THE TOPIC OF RACE IS OFTEN IGNORED, GLOSSED OVER, OR DILUTED with other concepts such as multicultural issues or diversity. We know that racial opinions, feelings, and beliefs operate in both subtle and powerful ways even when there is no explicit intention. Unfortunately, racial discourse is curiously absent or under-discussed in the academic arena (Apple, 1999). In the academic domain where the quest for knowledge is at the center of our mission, the discourse on race is conspicuously absent. This topic is long overdue for frank, constructive, and productive discussion (Carter & Goodwin, 1994).

The study of race as a biological or genetic variable, especially with regard to sport, has a historically inauspicious and questionable reputation (Wiggins, 1997). Genetically speaking, the boundary lines drawn between races have been profoundly blurred. In this country there are some classified as African American that have more features common to Europeans than Africans. The study of the genetic and biological basis for race has been deemed fruitless and is composed of 'lose and leaky' categories that defy logic and are inherently inconsistent (Dole, 1995). According to LaVeist (1996), race is a social rather than biological factor that reveals a common socio-political history. Being African American has more to do with shared experiences than shared genetic material. Recent works by Hoberman (1997) and Entine (2000) tend to reinforce biological determinism and cloud the empirical realities of how racism manipulates patterns of identity, sport, and social distinction.

Even though many recognize the complexity and meaning of assigning individuals to racial categories, it is still the most widely used method of classification. Hewstone et al. (1991) attest to the prevalence of race as a prominent organizing principal in memory categorization. Our inclination to categorize people in terms of race is influenced by our social surroundings, culture, customs, beliefs, and political associations, which in turn guide our conceptions of ourselves as well as others (Haslam et al., 1999). Racial ideology has been entrenched in hundreds of years of history and has a firm hold on the social and psychological composition of the United States. Racial classification may apply either externally, internally, or both, but once established, it is extremely resistant to change (Harris, 1997).

Being African American presupposes a myriad of connotations in the minds of both African Americans and non-African Americans alike. Consider all the adjectives that come to mind when this racial designation is considered. Whenever engaging in this psychological exercise with others, the terms athlete or sport often surface. While these general terms are employed, most acknowledge that a specific and narrow range of sports are alluded to which tend to have an over-representation of African American participants (e.g. basketball, football, track & field). The implication is that, in most cases, being African American denotes an identification, either directly or indirectly, with specific sport activities. Consequently, in many cases development of African American racial identity may be tied to the development of an identification with particular sports.

The objective of this paper is to examine the Cross model of African American racial identity development and examine parallels and theoretical implications in the development of sport competency and participation patterns. Knowledge in this realm may cultivate a better understanding of the sport and physical activity performance and participation patterns in the African American population.

African American Racial Identity Development

Every person goes through a process of defining themselves in terms of personal and social importance and meaning attached to being a part of a particular racial group. The social construction of these groups tends to change over time, but in the United States there are important and significantly different experiences of people that vary by racial categorization (Tatum, 1997). The development of identity is a socialization process shaped by experiences with one's family, community, school, group and social affiliations. It undergoes trials and tests to serve to make the owner feel focused and stable by making life predictable (Cross, 1995). While change in the environment is tolerated and sometimes welcomed, a change in our identity can be disturbing and difficult.

Cross (1995) outlines the metamorphic process whereby African Americans 'become Black'. This developmental process in which African Americans develop a manner of thinking about and evaluating themselves in terms of being 'Black' is called Nigrescence (Cross, 1995; Helms, 1985). Cross depicts Nigrescence as a resocializing experience that steers one's preexisting racial identity from Eurocentric to Afrocentric. This comprehensive model of African American racial identity development provides a rational and logical structure which can be applied to the development of preferences for sport and physical activity participation to support the understanding of the relationship of racial identity development and sport. Additionally, Cross et al. (1991) cite the broad applicability of this model by alluding to the fact that several authors in different parts of the country were developing parallel models independently indicating that African American racial identity development was essentially the same across several regions of the United States. In fact, this model has even been applied with slight modifications to the people of South Africa (Hocoy, 1999).

Cross' (1995) revision of his original racial identity model includes refinements that better coincide with today's social forces. The original four-stage process was modified through review of research findings on racial identity development. It is important to note that Nigrescence is not a process that follows normal physical growth and development. It is a mechanism by which African Americans who are assimilated, deculturalized and in many cases miseducated develop into more Afrocentric people. The following are brief summaries of Cross' revised Nigrescence model with inclusion of examples that depict sport and physical activity as part of the Nigrescence process.

Stage 1: Pre-encounter

The African American in the pre-encounter stage exhibits a racial attitude that ranges from race neutral to anti-Black. These individuals may not deny being physically of African American decent, but consider it to be insignificant in their life or in some cases, a negative trait. In this stage some see race as a problem or stigma. In extreme cases, some may espouse potent anti-Black attitudes and internalize negative stereotypes and attitudes that approach those of white racists. Those in this stage will rarely exhibit any pride in their race and tend to blame African Americans for their own racial problems. They are often miseducated and see no value in 'Black studies'. They often exaggerate and romanticize the talents and capacities of Whites while showing skepticism and apprehension about the abilities of African Americans in the same position. Their preferred sport and physical activity, if there be any, would likely focus on traditionally European American activities as they strive to shun any identification with African Americans. In the pre-encounter stage the individual would probably not embrace traditionally African American activities such as basketball. In this stage the individual is socialized to favor a Eurocentric cultural perspective. This participation in activities that encourages greater contact with European Americans tend to be preferred. This stage may be extended for some African American males who enjoy social success because of athletic talent. Our culture embraces African American athletes; thus young African Americans gifted with athletic ability may be shielded for some time from the experiences that potentially trigger the encounter stage.

Stage 2: Encounter

This stage is usually identified by a series of incidents, episodes, or circumstances that erode or transform the individual's present outlook or world view. The individual must though personalize the encounter information in a way that changes the way the person sees the world and him/herself. The encounter nudges the individual outside his or her comfort zone and may cause them to be perplexed, apprehensive, or even depressed. Examples of encounter episodes are surprisingly common. In the Autobiography of Malcolm X, Haley (1964) notes the response of an European American teacher. When Malcolm told the teacher he aspired to be a lawyer, the teacher responded 'A lawyer—that's no realistic goal for a nigger' (p. 36). Even though he was an A student and president of his class, this teacher framed Malcolm's potential within the perceived confines of his race. This encounter obviously had a huge impact on Malcolm X. Even though blatant examples of racist attitudes may not be as common today, there are still many encounter-producing occurrences. Many African American athletes enjoy a large degree of social acceptance in predominantly European American settings. Often the cultural acceptance of the African American athlete is severely strained if the African American athlete begins to date a European American female. Because of the often unspoken taboo against interracial dating, particularly in the South, there is a fertile setting for encounter episodes. Furthermore, encounters with law enforcement officers who are unaware of the African American athlete's status is common (Slansky, 1997) and also provides encounter opportunities.

In this stage the person may seek additional information and validation for their newly developing identity. This state may be accompanied by emotion, guilt, and anger that is generalized toward Whites. In this stage sport and physical activity choices may not be significantly effected. Even though significant changes are taking place in the individual's identity, there may be little outward manifestation.

Stage 3: Immersion-Emersion

The immersion-emersion stage of Nigrescence is characterized by destruction of the previous identity while simultaneously constructing the new Afrocentric identity. There is a commitment to replace the old world view with a new one, but the new self is not clearly defined. Therefore, symbols and attitudes thought to represent the new self attract individuals in this stage. Symbols such styles of dress, hairstyles, involvement in particular organizations and political groups typify those in this stage. Individuals in immersion-emersion stage adopt a dichotomized world view where everything is simply Black or White. African American youth at this stage may also begin to segregate themselves by race. This self-segregation is not just an attempt to be 'Black'. It comes about through disengagement from European Americans who 'don't get it' and engagement with other African Americans who can more readily validate and identify with what the person is feeling (Tatum, 1997). This self-segregation is a form of support group that the African American individual cannot find elsewhere. They want to be with peers who know how to be 'Black'.

Participation in sports or physical activities that identify the individuals 'Blackness' are likely sought out in an effort to completely immerse themselves in 'Blackness'. Physical activities that identified as 'White' may be shunned even if the individual shows potential for outstanding performance in the sport or activity.

After immersing themselves into an almost totally Afrocentric attitude and posture, the individual emerges from this oversimplified ideological perspective to a more reflective and profound understanding of African American issues. The individual understands and views the immersion as a period of transformation and moves on to a deeper understanding of Nigrescence.

Stage 4: Internalization

Internalization represents a sense of contentment with the self that calms the internal struggle of the previous stages. The militant and radical attitudes are transformed into thoughtful examination of oppression and racism. The individual is saturated with sincere connection to and love and acceptance of African American communities. Sports and physical activities are then viewed as a mode of exercise or recreation rather than a source of identity. Participation in a traditionally European American sport or activity may no longer elicit dissonance in the individual. Internalization accompanies a soothing of internal psychological stress and the re-construction of one's basic personality along with the intermeshing of one's Blackness with other role identities (e.g. spiritual, occupational).

Stage 5: Internalization-Commitment

The Nigrescence voyage ends for some with curtailment of activities or discontinuation of active involvement exclusively in African American activities. Some on this voyage begin to dedicate a substantial degree of time and effort forging this new world view into tangible efforts to further the cause of Blackness. Nigrescence theory suggests that this commitment to sincere involvement in activities that further causes that are of interest to the African American community is the only partition between the previous stage and this one. This commitment may include activities or actions that are not considered Afrocentric. For example, the individual may commit to remaining physically fit via any mode that is attractive and available rather than being overly concerned with the Afrocentricity of the mode. This can be observed in the increasing numbers of African Americans becoming involved in activities once considered 'White sports'.

The activation and consummation of the Nigrescence experience is not the same for all African Americans. In some highly unlikely situations the individual may never develop past the pre-encounter stage while others progress through all stages before reaching adulthood. Thomas and Speight (1999) indicate that African American parents' racial identity attitudes were related to racial socialization attitudes. That is, parents with pre-encounter, encounter, and immersion attitudes did not have strong racial socialization attitudes and thus tended not to have strong socializing effects on their children. African American parents with internalization attitudes had strong racial socialization attitudes and were more likely to socialize their children to have a positive racial identity. These African American parents overwhelmingly felt that racial socialization was important and necessary to prepare children for the reality of racism. Plummer (1995) indicates that African American adolescents from nurturing environments display primarily internalization attitudes. Plummer reiterates that African American adolescents in her study were prepared by their parents with the skills necessary to function in a predominately European American environment. Plummer also cautions that because their views of society are so narrow and devoid of life experiences, their internalization attitudes may be premature and idealized rather than based on experience and thoughtful analysis. It is doubtful that today's African American adolescent begins Nigrescence development at the pre-encounter stage.

The Role of Stereotypes in Identity Development

Sport and physical activity attitudes and choices may be closely linked to racial identity attitudes. Viewing a sport or physical activity as identity appropriate may strongly influence participation, practice and persistence in the sport or activity of choice. African American youth with immersion attitudes may consider basketball, football, and track and field as appropriate for participation while excluding participation in other activities deemed inappropriate. These attitudes may develop skills, interests, and competencies in a narrow range of activities to the exclusion of most others.

Stereotypes are defined as beliefs about the personal characteristics of a group. These beliefs are often overgeneralized and erroneous, but resistant to change (Meyer, 1993). Nevertheless, stereotypes significantly influence the way we view other groups as well as our own behavior. Stereotypes function to organize and simplify information, preserve important social values, maintain group beliefs, justify collective actions and sustain positive group distinctiveness (Oakes et al., 1994). Stereotyping or social categorization that operates in the self-concept precipitates self-stereotyping which changes individuals into psychological group members (Oakes et al., 1994).

The process of self-stereotyping and producing psychological groups are meshed in the development of social identity. Social identity deals with the inclination to maintain an optimistic view of the self through identifying with or establishing favorable comparisons between one's own group and other groups (Crocker & Luhtanen, 1990). This social identity derives from the knowledge of group membership and development of collective self-esteem. This is evident in the self-segregation of young African Americans, particularly in immersion stage. In African American culture, the overwhelming success of African American athletes in particular sports would conceivably prompt the development of elevated collective self-esteem and perpetuate positive self-stereotypes in the realm of sport (Harrison, 2001). Biernat el al. (1996) suggest that the process of self-stereotyping is selective. They argue that those operating within the stereotyped group have immersed themselves in the group identity and display protective behavior with regard to their collective self-esteem. This again is clearly evident in the self-segregating behavior of many

African American youth in sport settings. Goodstein and Ponterotto (1997) indicate that racial identity and self-esteem are significantly correlated for African Americans, but not for European Americans. In a society where being African American evokes so many negative stereotypes, it is easy to fathom why there would be fervent identification with a positive stereotype. The superior African American athlete stereotype has a unique history (Wiggins, 1997) that is pervasive among the general population. Stone et al. (1997) gave evidence of the ubiquitous perception of African American sport superiority in the general population. Given the same information and listening to a radio broadcast of a basketball game, the participants rated perceived African American athletes as having more athletic ability while perceived European American athletes were rated as having more basketball intelligence and hustle. There is also empirical evidence that suggests that the presence and salience of racial stereotypes can actually influence intellectual (Steele, 1997; Steele & Aronson, 1995) and athletic performance (Stone et al., 1999). In light of the fact that stereotypes and self-stereotypes can form the basis of group identity, or in this case African American racial identity, it is tenable to say that developing skills in a particular sport may be intrinsic in the development of African American racial identity.

Racial Identity in Adolescence

Awareness of racial differences is apparent in children as young as preschoolers (Ramsey, 1987). According to Ramsey, children, regardless of race, use race to categorize people more often than any other trait. Spencer and Markstrom-Adams (1990) indicate that in studies of preschool and elementary school-aged children there is an inclination towards a pro-European American bias in racial preference, attitudes, and identification. This indicates the realization of the preferences and privilege that accompany being European American. However, one's identity becomes crucial in adolescence. Adolescence is a time when one fervently seeks an identity. For African American children it is a time when the individuals define themselves as African American as part of the developmental process (Plummer, 1995). During this time the adolescent confirms preferences and beliefs consistent with his/her group affiliations. The adolescent begins to ask 'who am I ethnically and/or racially?' Race becomes salient to the adolescent mainly because his/her race becomes salient to the rest of the world (Tatum, 1997, p. 53). Those once perceived as 'cute' children grow up and are often seen as threatening adolescents. This greatly increases the opportunity for encounter episodes.

African American adolescents tend to be more committed to a racial identity than European Americans (Spencer & Markstrom-Adams, 1990). The meaning and significance of being African American becomes salient to the African Adolescent in many areas of life. For an African American adolescent it is virtually impossible to be unaware of the implications one's racial designation imposes on one's life. Hatcher and Troyna (1993) contend that racism is a profound factor in the educational experiences of African American and European American children. Because of the abundance of negative stereotypes imposed on African Americans, the influence of perceived positive racial stereotypes may have a refreshing influence on the development of the adolescent's racial identity. It may provide a comfortable place to 'immerse' one's self during identity development. As stated earlier, self-stereotyping has a self-protective facet that embraces positive traits and rejects the negative. Of the few positive stereotypes of African Americans, sport performance is probably the most salient. Thus other than entertainment, African American adolescents have few positive images on which to anchor their racial identity.

Goodstein and Ponterotto (1997) indicate that unlike European Americans, for African Americans, an elevated degree of racial identity indicates increased self-esteem. In a society in which both blatant and subliminal messages communicate negative images of African Americans, African American adolescents can find positive images in few domains. One of the few areas where African Americans are depicted positively is sport. African American athletes are highly visible and occupy a lofty status in the eyes of American society, while in the mainstream of American society African Americans are rendered virtually invisible. In an attempt to cope with the alienation and frustration some African American athletes channel their creative energies into the creation of distinctive and demonstrative sport skills, styles of demeanor, language, gestures, gait patterns, and the like (Majors, 1990). When these behaviors are observed by African American adolescents who are engaged in a search for identity, and those observed are rewarded and admired for their actions, the behaviors are easily incorporated in the individual's identity and become a convenient place for immersion. Many of these young people are heavily exposed to the prevalent stereotypes about African Americans particularly in the realm of sport. In an effort to form a positive racial identity it is plausible to think they would adhere to and identify with what they perceive as positive stereotypical views of African Americans of which one of the most prominent is the African American athlete. It is easy to understand why African American adolescents, many of whom may be in immersion stage, would adopt the hairstyles, demeanor, and sport choices of those they perceive to be African American role models.

During adolescence young people are exposed to ideas and values outside of those taught and established in the family. They move from a strong family influenced setting to a peer dominated domain. Parents and other significant authority figures gradually lose their persuasive power while the need for peer approval escalates (Payne & Isaacs, 1999, pp. 51–52). For males, especially African American males, involvement in sport and athletic ability are powerful determinants of social acceptability and group membership. According to Payne and Isaacs, sport and physical activity involvement not only determine group membership, but sport skills are molded and pressure is exerted to improve skills in the accepted activities to gain respect and approval. All this occurs at a time when young people are growing rapidly in size and strength, the requisite parameters for exceptional sport performance. These young people, particularly those in immersion stage, are not only developing an identity with their peer group, they are identifying with and immersing themselves in the sports and physical activities they are participating in.

For most youth this means identifying with and participating in activities that are popular with the peer group whose identification is likely with high status models. For African American youth this means participation in sports in which they see other successful African Americans participate (e.g. basketball, football, track & field). Harrison et al. (1999) demonstrated that African American adolescents physical activity choices were significantly different from and less eclectic than those of European American adolescents. These students identified overwhelmingly with the stereotypical African American activities such as basketball, football, and track. Additionally, when compared to others, African American males appear to be more positively affected by sport models. Further, the results of the study also showed that African Americans expected or aspired to participate at higher levels (e.g. collegiate, professional) than European American students. According to this study these choices were rooted in the development of the adolescent's self-schema. It is likely that these schemata, because they coincide with racial identity development, intensely influence sport and physical activity choices throughout life.

Interaction of Racial and Athletic Identity

In the evolving study of African American racial identity one must consider the stableness of such a construct. Of what import is African American racial identity if it is malleable based on situational factors? Shelton and Sellars (2000) address this issue and conclude that African American racial identity has both situational and stable properties. These authors also ascertain that under conditions where race is an important factor, African American racial identity moves to the forefront.

But what happens when sport is considered an important part of one's identity? What happens when an African American develops a strong affinity and identity in the realm of sport? While some believe that it is racial identity that stimulates the development of athletic identity, what happens when the athletic identity moves to the forefront? Brewer et al. (1993) identify athletic identity as the degree to which an individual identifies with the athletic role. Brown et al. (1997) investigated the role of both racial and athletic identity among college athletes, and concluded that while racial identity and athletic identity were positively correlated in European American athletes, these constructs were negatively correlated in African American athletes. The authors suggest that while competing in intercollegiate athletics African American athletes are shielded from racism and discrimination, which allows their athletic identities to come to the forefront. Jackson et al. (1997) also found some support for the increasing importance of athletic identity and the decreasing importance of racial identity among African American athletes. In this emerging vein of research, much more work needs to be done involving valid and reliable measures of both racial and athletic identity before we really understand the interaction of these constructs.

Racial Identity: Crossing Economic Class Lines

There are those that suggest that the differences observed in sport and physical activity participation patterns and performance can be attributed to differences in socio-economic status (SES) (Wilson, 1978). It has been postulated that people of lower income have fewer options and opportunities for securing high status and lucrative employment. Professional sports provide one of the few ways this can be accomplished. Furthermore, it is speculated that sports like basketball are popular among poorer people because of the ease of accessibility to facilities. According to these hypotheses, African Americans are over-represented in particular sports because they are disproportionately represented in lower SES. While these theories appear logical, they also distort, dilute, oversimplify, and underestimate the meaning and impact of developing an African American identity in the realm of sport.

Several researchers and theorists give evidence that the significance of being African American and the development of African American racial identity cross SES lines (Pettigrew, 1980; Willie, 1989). In most cases African Americans feel they have more in common and more shared experiences with other African Americans than with European Americans of the same income level. African Americans share many common negative experiences that majority individuals rarely experience. These experiences leave enduring impressions on their minds and become entwined in and influence the development of the individual's racial identity. Experiences such as being detained by authorities on a DWB (driving while Black) occur frequently (Slansky, 1997) and are not confined to African Americans of low SES. In fact, African Americans of higher SES report high incidences of being stopped or arrested by police officers while shopping in upscale neighborhoods or driving expensive cars (Jet, 1993). African American motorists stopped on DWBs often experience harsher treatment and are detained longer than majority motorists. These negative experiences which evoke strong emotional responses are shared among many African Americans. As stated earlier, these kinds of incidents may provide the stimulus for movement into the encounter stage or send the African American youth deeper into immersion.

Durant and Sparrow (1997) found that regardless of their social class, African Americans in their study perceived that their opportunities were limited because of their race. Furthermore, it was revealed that African Americans in this study were more race conscious than class conscious. In fact middle class African Americans were even more race conscious than lower class African Americans. This indicates that regardless of social class, African Americans feel that race is still a profoundly important component in determining the opportunities and limitations on their lives. This seems to indicate that Nigresence is apparently a stronger factor than social class. What is blatantly obvious to African American youth is the over-representation of successful African American athletes in spite of the apparent limitations in other spheres.

This often unspoken consciousness helps explain why many African American youth, regardless of SES, place a tremendous emphasis on and identity with athletic achievement. It is one of the few venues in American life where the possibilities of success appear limitless. Although many

African American youths have scores of potential role models in their schools, churches, homes, or communities, they understand that no matter how much schooling or education they acquire, they will still confront frequent episodes of racism in mainstream America. These episodes appear with less frequency in sport participation.

African American Masculinity, Popular Culture and Sport: Effects of Nigresence

Harrison et al. (1999) findings indicate African American adolescents' physical activity choices were significantly different from and less eclectic than those of European American adolescents. What is implicit in these findings is the possible transference of this athletic and racial schematic identity into broader societal occupational structures. In other words, if identities are narrow and monolithic for African American youth (particularly males) inside the vacuum of sport, then how might these same perceptions reflect their outside sport or occupational choices? How does it impact the Nigresence process, or how is it impacted by the Nigresence process?

There is some evidence that limited media exposure of African American youth manipulates choices of identity for African American males. Johnson et al. (1995) found that when compared to a control group, subjects in a rap video exposure condition were more likely to say that they wanted to be like the materialistic young man and were less confident that another young man, who chose to engage in academic pursuits, would achieve his educational goals. Clearly, a link exists between sport and entertainment as the attainable images of success to African American youth. The findings of this study also indicate that exposure to violent rap music videos has an effect on the attitudes and perceptions of young African American males. While not specifically tested in their study, it is logical to hypothesize that the bombardment of African American youth with images of African American athletes in a few sports can alter, confound, and shape the racial identity development of these young minds, especially when entering or going through immersion stage. The perceptions of the African American youth in this study indicate a negative effect regarding educational goals. African American adolescents in immersion stage may view academic attainment as 'acting White' (Ogbu, 1990) and instead channel their energies into sport and entertainment endeavors. This relates to African American youth focusing on particular sports as a means of achieving success. The antithesis to this question is to consider whether African American youth, particularly males, have negative perceptions of occupational aspirations outside sport. How do these perceptions influence or impact the individual in later identity development stages? Scholar Cornel West (1993), in his essay, articulates that African American males have different forms of expression in terms of navigating oppression, racism, and patriarchal power structures. Thus, many African American males channel their efforts towards sports and entertainment because this is the one vessel and space that offers them stylistic options. Others suggest the context of expression, African American masculinity, and space are critical when examining

African American men, either empirically or exploratory (Majors, 1990; Spraggins, 1999; White & Cones, 1999). The challenge in the twenty-first century is not to exclude African American male confidence and expression by channeling them away form sport. The real challenge is to discover how to socialize this ethnic gender to invest in education with the same enthusiasm, work ethic and creative/artistic expression that they do on the playing fields and gyms (Harrison el at, 2000). Perhaps a better understanding of the Nigresence process will aid in meeting the challenge. Another challenge is to persuade European Americans to embrace and support African American racial development identity with the same level of acceptance given to athletic competency. Much more investigation is necessary to understand the perceptions of young African American male youth and how the image of African American professional athletes and entertainers accessing the mainstream economic structures without the status quo (suit and tie versus hip hop) attire and behaviors correlate, influence, and affect their daily investment in rigorous learning and scholarship for the delayed gratification of occupational and vocational success.

The emergence of the hip-hop athlete in the mid-1990s has further elevated the status of the African American athlete in American culture, and African American youth have taken notice. African American youngsters in crucial spates of racial identity development observe today's superstar athletes, such as Allen Iverson, and profess a desire to emulate him. This is not surprising when one considers that Iverson's athletic ability has enabled him to play by his own rules, a rarity for an African American man in America. For instance, Iverson pays homage to the hip-hop African American culture by openly sporting braids and tattoos. He openly defies European American authority by coming to practices and games late (sometimes missing practice). He routinely travels with a roughish-looking entourage, and recently released a profanity-laden rap CD. This behavior would be unacceptable in nearly any other work environment. Nonetheless, because he is a gifted athlete he makes in excess of $10 million dollars a year in salary and endorsements. What is the effect on young African Americans struggling with identity?

Many African American youth see themselves as the next potential Allen Iverson largely because there were very few perceived external obstacles placed in his path to stardom. They learn at an early age that America views an educated African American as threatening, while this same community will embrace, support, and encourage them in their athletic pursuits. Unless these perceived barriers are removed athletics will continue to occupy a central place in the African American community simply because it is one of the few places where an African American man can be a man.

Conclusions

Nigresence theory appears to provide a credible framework for the discussion of African American racial identity and its relationship to sport. Cross' model of African American racial identity development appears to provide additional evidence to corroborate many of the sociological theories that attempt to explain the over-representation of African Americans in particular sports and physical activities. The Cross model provides a stable theoretical framework on which future research maybe anchored. More research is needed to shed light on the relationship of African American racial identity development and development of other identities in other domains such as athletic identity. Deeper understanding of these phenomena may help to stifle the oppressive funneling of the limitless dreams of African American youth into an extremely limited pool of athletic opportunities.

Understanding the development of African American racial identity and characteristics of its various stages can also be an invaluable tool for the teachers and other professionals working in diverse environments with African American youth. Because the world is becoming more diverse it is becoming more and more imperative that those in leadership positions understand all of the people they serve. This would indicate that all those who prepare teachers, coaches and others who will occupy leadership positions have a better understanding of racial identity development. Often racial problems stem from a lack of understanding and communication. Understanding racial identity development may provide the stimulation necessary to avert these problems.

References

Apple, M.W. (1999) The absent presence of race in educational reform, *Race, Ethnicity and Education*, 2, pp. 9–16.

Biernat, M., Vescio, T.K. & Green, M.L. (1996) Selective self-stereotyping, *Journal of Personality and Social Psychology*, 71, pp. 1194–1209.

Brewer, B.W., Raalte, J.L.V. & Linder, D. (1993) Athletic identity: Hercules' muscles or achilles heel?, *International Journal of Sport Psychology*, 24, pp. 237–254.

Brown, T.N., Manuel, W.J., Jackson, J.S., Keiper, S. & Sellers, R.M. (1997) There's 'no race' on the playing field: examining perceptions of racial discrimination among White American and African American intercollegiate student-Athletes, paper presented at the annual meeting of the American Psychological Association, Chicago, IL.

Carter, R.T. & Goodwin, A.L. (1994) Racial identity and education, in: Darling-Hammond (Ed.) *Review of Research in Education* (Washington, DC, American Educational Research Association).

Crocker, J. & Luhtanen, R. (1990) Collective self-esteem and ingroup bias, *Journal of Personality and Social Psychology*, 58, pp. 60–67.

Cross, W.E. (1995) The psychology of Nigrescence: revising the Cross model, in: J.G. Ponterotto, J.M. Casas, L.A. Suzuki & C.M. Alexander (Eds) *Handbook of Multicultural Counseling* (Thousand Oaks, CA, Sage).

Cross, W.E., Parham, T.A. & Helms, J.E. (1991) The stages of Black identity development: Nigrescence models, in: R.E. Jones (Ed.) *Black Psychology* (New York, Harper & Row).

Dole, A.A. (1995) Why not drop race as a term? *American Psychologist*, 54, p. 40.

Durant, T.J. Jr. & Sparrow, K.H. (1997) Race and class consciousness among lower- and middle-class Blacks, *Journal of Black Studies*, 27, pp. 334–351.

Entine, J. (2000) *Taboo: Why black athletes dominate sports, and why we are afraid to talk about it* (New York, Public Affairs).

Goodstein, R. & Ponterotto, J.G. (1997) Racial and ethnic identity: their relationship and their contribution to self-esteem, *Journal of Black Psychology*, 23, pp. 275–292.

Haley, A. & X.M. (1964) *Vie Autobiography of Malcom X* (New York, Balantine Books).

Harris, O. (1997) Stereotypes, stacking and superspades, paper presented at the American Psychological Association Meeting in Chicago, IL.

Harrison, C.K., Holmes, S., Moore, D. & Manning, T. (2000) The effects of media ads on intercollegiate student-athletes: exposure to athletic and professional occupational imagery, paper presented a the North American Society for the Sociology of Sport Annual Meeting, Colorado Springs, CO.

Harrison, L. Jr. (2001) Understanding the influence of stereotypes: implications for the African American in sport and physical activity, *Quest*, 53, pp. 97–114.

Harrison, L. Jr., Lee, A. & Belcher, D. (1999) Self-schemata for specific sports and physical activities: the influence of race and gender, *Journal of Sport and Social Issues*, 23, pp. 287–307.

Haslam, S.A., Oakes, P.J., Reynolds, K.J. & Turner, J.C. (1999) Social identity and the emergence of stereotype consensus, *Personality and Social Psychology Bulletin*, 25, pp. 809–818.

Hatcher, R. & Troyna, B. (1993) Racialization and children, in: C. McCarthy & W. Crichlow (Eds) *Race Identity and Representation in Education* (New York, Routledge).

Helms, J.E. (1985) An overview of Black racial identity theory, in: J.E. HELMS (Ed.) *Black and While Racial Identity: Theory, research, and practice* (New York, Greenwood).

Hewstone, M., Hantzi, A. & Johnston, L. (1991) Social categorization and person memory: the pervasiveness of race as an organizing principle, *European Journal of Social Psychology*, 21, pp. 517–528.

Hoberman, J. (1997) *Darwin's Athletes: How sport has damaged Black America and preserved the myth of race* (New York, Houghton Mufflin).

Hocoy, D. (1999) The validity of cross's model of Black racial identity development in the South African context, *Journal of Black Psychology*, 25, pp. 131–152.

Jackson, J., Keiper, S., Brown, K.T., Brown, T.N. & Manuel, W.J. (1997) Athletic identity, racial attitudes, & aggression in first year Black and White intercollegiate athletes, unpublished paper, NCAA Work Group, University of Michigan.

Jet (1993) *National study reports white cops' beatings of blacks reveal dirty secrets of racism, May*, pp. 14–18.

Johnson, J.D., Jackson, L.A. & Gatto, L. (1995) Violent attitudes and deferred academic aspirations: deleterious effects of exposure to rap music, *Basic and Applied Social Psychology*, 16, pp. 27–41.

LaVeist, T.A. (1996) Why we should continue to study race ... but do a better job: an essay on race, racism and health, *Ethnicity and Disease*, 6, pp. 21–29.

Majors, R. (1990) Cool pose: Black masculinity and sports, in: M.A. Messner & D.F. Sabo (Eds) *Sport, Men, and the Gender Order: Critical feminist perspectives* (Champaign, IL, Human Kinetics).

Meyer, D.G. (1993) *Social Psychology* (New York, McGraw-Hill)

Oakes, P.J., Haslam, S.A. & Turner, J.C. (1994) *Stereotyping and Social Reality* (Cambridge, Blackwell).

Ogbu, J.U. (1990) Minority education in comparative perspective, *Journal of Negro Education*, 59, pp. 45–55.

Payne, G. & Isaacs, L. (1995) *Human Motor Development: A lifespan approach* (3rd ed.) (Mountain View, CA, Mayfield).

Pettigrew, T. (1980) The changing—not declining—significance of race, *Contemporary Sociology*, 9, pp. 19–21.

Plummer, D.L. (1995) Patterns of racial identity development of African American adolescent males and females, *Journal of Black Psychology*, 21, pp. 168–180.

Ramsey, P.G. (1987) Young children's thinking about ethnic differences, in: J.S. Phinney & M.J. Rotheram (Eds) *Children's Ethnic Socialization* (Newbury Park, Sage).

Shelton, N.J. & Sellers, R.M. (2000) Situational stability and variability in African American racial identity, *Journal of Black Psychology*, 26, pp. 27–49.

Slansky, D.A. (1997) *Traffic Stops, Minority Motorists, and the Future of the Fourth Amendment, Supreme Court Review, Annual,* pp. 273–329.

Spencer, M.B. & Markstrom-Adams, C. (1990) *Identity Processes Among Racial and Ethnic Minority Children in America, Child Development*, 61, pp. 290–310.

Spraggins, J.D. (1999) African american masculinity: power and expression, *Journal of African American Men*, 4, pp. 45–72.

Steele, C.M. (1997) A threat in the air: how stereotypes shape intellectual identity and performance, *American Psychologist*, 52, pp. 613–629.

Steele, C.M. & Aronson, J. (1995) Stereotype threat and the intellectual test performance of African Americans, *Journal of Personality and Social Psychology*, 69, pp. 797–811.

Stone, J., Perry, Z.W. & Darley, J.M. (1997) 'White men can't jump': evidence for the perceptual confirmation of racial stereotypes following a basketball game, *Basic and Applied Social Psychology*, 19, pp. 291–306.

Stone, J., Lynch, C.I., Sjomeling, M. & Darley, J.M. (1999) Stereotype threat effects on black and white athletic performance, *Journal of Personality and Social Psychology*, 77, pp. 1213–1227.

Tatum, B. (1997) *Why Are All the Black Kids Sitting Together in the Cafeteria? And Other Conversations about Race* (New York, Basic Books).

Thomas, A.J. & Speight, S.L. (1999) Racial identity and racial socialization attitudes of African American parents, *Journal of Black Psychology*, 25, pp. 152–170.

WEST, C. (1993) *Race Matters* (Boston, Beacon Press).

White, J. & Cones, J. (1999) *Black Men Emerging* (New York, Routledge).

Wiggins, D.K. (1997) 'Great speed but little, stamina': the historical debate over black athletic superiority, in: S.W. Pope (Ed.) *The New American Sport History: Recent approaches and perspectives* (Urbana, IL, University of Illinois Press).

Willie, C. (1989) *Caste and Class Controversy on Race and Poverty* (Dix Hills, NY, General Hall).

Wilson, W.J. (1978) *The Declining Significance of Race* (Chicago, University of Chicago Press).

19

Keepin' in the Fields
The NFL and Black Slavery

Kevin Thomas
F. Erik Brooks

Background

SLAVERY IN THE UNITED STATES WAS TIME OF SHEER BRUTALITY FOR African people, later known as African Americans. African people were taken from their native continent of Africa, sold to European conquerors, and shipped across the Atlantic Ocean to a strange, cruel world. Many people did not survive this atrocious journey; those who survived were subject to harsh, dehumanizing, and anguishing treatment from slave owners greedy to provide capital for a growing country. The process of becoming a slave started with a period of "seasoning." Seasoning is the process of mentally breaking down a person to make them fit for servitude. This process took about two to three months and people were not sent to plantations unless overseers were reassured they were mentally able to endure such demanding circumstances.

The myth of African or black physical superiority can be traced back to the days of the European conquest of Africa. Europeans thought that the tremendous builds of the men they encountered upon landing on the continent, coupled with the tremendous monuments that were erected there, revealed their physical superiority to Europeans, making them prime subjects for hard labor. Furthermore, African people did not die as easily from European diseases when they made contact with Europeans. The expectations placed on slaves were extraordinary, in an effort to generate capital for a growing country.

During slavery, the masters entertained themselves by having the slaves violently compete against one another in blood sports such as wrestling, often fighting until someone died. The slave masters would take their best fighting slave and have him compete against other slaves to test his dominance. Competitors for the right price could even buy these slaves. The slave would be rewarded with alcohol, special clothes, and more leisure time to himself, as long as he was winning fights. However, if the slave began to lose more fights than he won, he could be sold to another plantation or even killed. The gruesome horror around this entertainment still rears its head in modern sports like boxing, mixed martial arts, and football.

Review of Literature

Sailes's 1993 work, "An Investigation of Campus Stereotypes: The Myth of Black Athletic Superiority and the Dumb Jock Stereotype," addresses the stereotypes of college athletes on college campuses and universities. He challenges the "dumb jock" stereotype that college athletes are given because they play sports at the university level.

Sailes's 1991 article, "The Myth of Black Sports Supremacy," explores the myth of black players being superior in sports to white players. He asserts that while there are some physical differences and mental aptitudes that allow for better results from black players, that does not inherently translate into black athletes being more able to perform in sports than whites.

In "Zulu Masculinities, Warrior Culture and Stick Fighting: Reassessing Male Violence and Virtue in South Africa," Carton and Morrell (2012) explore African understanding of masculinities through the culture of Zulu stick fighting.

In "Examining Productive Conceptions of Masculinities: Lessons Learned from Academically Driven African American Male Student-Athletes," Martin and Harris (2006) use interviews to understand the behaviors and socialized conceptions of manhood for student athletes with regard to academics.

Jansinski's 2007 article, "Constituting Antebellum African American Identity: Resistance, Violence, and Masculinity in Henry Highland Garnet's (1843) 'Address to the Slaves,'" explores the claims of Henry Highland Garnet about slaves resisting the harsh treatment of their masters.

Moore (2010), "Fine Specimens of Manhood: The Black Boxer's Body and the Avenue to Equality, Racial Advancement, and Manhood in the Nineteenth Century," explores the sport of boxing, which was used a means for black men to regain a sense of masculinity in the eyes of white America.

Rhoden (2006), *Forty Million Dollar Slaves: The Rise and Redemption of the Black Athlete*, tracks the history of African American males in sports and how African Americans are marketed to professional teams for monetary purposes.

Wolff (1995), "'Masculinity' in Uncle Tom's Cabin," explores masculinity in the book *Uncle Tom's Cabin*, giving insights into life for enslaved African men.

Harper (2004), "The Measure of a Man: of Conceptualizations Masculinity among High- Achieving African American Male College Students," explores masculinity for African Americans who excel academically in college.

Wilson, Kirtland, Ainsworth, and Addy (2006), in "Socioeconomic Status and the Perception of Access and Safety for Physical Activity," explore the correlation between socioeconomic status and the perceptions of access to physical safety with regard to sports.

Theoretical Perspective

The critical lens this paper will use in order to determine results will be critical race theory (CRT). According to Daniel Solorzano, Miguel Ceja and Tara Yosso (2000), "the basic CRT model consists of five elements focusing on: (a) the centrality of race and racism and their intersectionality with other forms of subordination, (b) the challenge to dominant ideology, (c) the commitment to social justice, (d) the centrality of experiential knowledge, and (e) the trans disciplinary perspective" (Solorzano, 1997, 1998; Solorzano & Delgado Bernal, in press; Solorzano & Yosso, 2000). This paper will first seek to present information about the National Football League (NFL) as it relates to African American men from a gender, race, and class perspective. The relativity of gender is essential to comprehend because it offers a glimpse of the value of African American men to a capitalistic system. Second, it offers a perspective on the physical aspects widely attributed to men and how they used to market the product that is the NFL. Third, it gives perspective on the intellectual stereotypes attributed to African American football players in relation to their usefulness to the NFL and society in general. Race will be denoted throughout the entire paper because it helps to focus the perspective of observers to a specific demographic when seeking to understand the differences in stereotype to the dominant society. Last, class will be briefly visited, because it give a more holistic view of the player's economic status prior to playing in the NFL.

Methodology

The scientific method I used to obtain data for this research is similar to the scientific method. My overarching question is, "Is NFL the like a slave plantation?" I would posit that it is, because the people who own the teams make enormous amounts of money at the expense of the players, who sacrifice their bodies with each game. After my research question was solidified, I began to conduct interviews with three professors within the sport management/kinesiology departments. I interviewed noted scholar Dr. Gary Sailes, from the University of Indiana, Bloomington. Next, I interviewed Dr. Alegerian Hart from Western Illinois University. Lastly, I interviewed Dr. Billy Hawkins, from the University of Georgia. I interviewed professors, who are all about the same age, in hopes that they could provide a prospective for this project that included a historical component, a cultural component (all identify as African American), and some of the substantial information they had acquired over the years. I transcribed my interviews for coding purposes. I looked for common themes that occurred in all the interviews to make comparisons and conduct an analysis. After my analysis I came to a conclusion with regard to my research project.

Analysis

My analysis will include a chart comparing the common themes found in the interviews with the professors (Table 1). A common theme in the interviews was the type of athlete that draws the attention of the NFL. How does the NFL go about acquiring the person for a team? What is the process for determining the value of a prospect? Then, after the player is drafted, what is done with regards to their compensation? What sorts of council does the NFL provide the players to manage their money well? Next, what is done to prepare these players for the tremendous "beating" they will undergo every week for sixteen straight weeks? Does the NFL care about the physical toll these players go through? Then, what liberties are the players allowed to vocalize things that are important to them on and off the field? Finally, are there any similarities between a slave plantation and the NFL one can see with a critical lens?

TABLE 1. COMMON THEMES IN INTERVIEWS ABOUT THE EXPERIENCES OF BLACK NFL PLAYERS

	Physical traits	Pre-draft	Draft	Physicality of NFL	Space for players concerns
Sailes	Big, strong, fast, eye-catching athleticism	Tested based on sports science; people are interviewed who can attest to their character	Players selected based on need; general manager and head coaches play major roles	Players expected to be able to perform; not to be exploited because they are paid well	Mainly organized through Player's Association; political contro-versy is not good for sponsors
Hart	Great motor, big on intangibles	Players tested extensively for skills; value is determined based on arbitrary scales; interviews take place with people who can vouch for character	Owners stay behind the scenes; gen-eral manager and head coaches are front and center; players selected based on need	Players are expected to perform; physical toll is known, but is not a deterrent for system; money isn't guaranteed	Organized through Player's Association; not a lot of political outspokenness; consciousness of the system by players is most seen in contractual structuring sessions
Hawkins	Talented athletically, posses good social skills	N/A	N/A	Players are expected to perform; aware-ness of concussions is more prevalent	Players are not qualified to make an political statements

The aforementioned chart breaks down the similarities in statements given by the interviewees about the nature of the NFL with regard to African American players. All the professors said that the NFL looks for extreme, athletically gifted players. The players usually exhibit a significant type of stamina to keep pushing to victory no matter the odds; they exhibit a level of tremendous speed; and they grow stronger as time moves forward. Dr. Hawkins notes the players can have a certain level of charisma and flair for being naturally entertaining to general audiences. The professors also made mention of "stacking" by NFL teams when it comes to certain positions. There were no definite statements made as to whether this practice was done on purpose, but they said the numbers overwhelmingly show more players of color in skilled positions like corner back, wide receiver, running back, and the like; however, recently there has been an increase in the number of black quarterbacks in the NFL. A report by TideSports.org asserts the following regarding stacking:

Most observers agree that the issue of stacking in the NFL is no longer a concern of significance. In the 2013 NFL season, African Americans held 17.1 percent of the quarterback positions, decreasing by 2.9 percentage points from 2012. The quarterback has been football's central "thinking" position. Historically, the positions of running back, wide receiver, cornerback, and safety have had disproportionately high percentages of African Americans. The latter positions rely a great deal on speed and reactive ability. The quarterback position was the primary concern since it was so central to the game and now that African Americans have broken down that barrier, concern about stacking has been greatly diminished.

However, Dr. Hart suggests that there are subtleties used to distinguish black quarterbacks from the white quarterbacks. The example he gave was the nicknames given to black quarterbacks versus addressing white quarterbacks more frequently by their government listed name. RG3 (Robert Griffin III) versus Tom Brady is listed in the example. However, he does not say this is inherently negative or a slight to black quarterbacks, but it can used a way to still distinguish black quarterbacks from white quarterbacks, mainly in terms of playing styles.

Next, the professors noted that the players are expected to hone their craft intensely while maintaining their eligibility in college. Furthermore, if they are drafted they are expected to work hard in the off-season in order to increase the likelihood they will be productive during the season. Next, the professors note the efforts of the NFL to help the players adequately manage their money, through the rookie camps given at the beginning of the off-season. These camps include former players sharing their experiences with their money and how the rookies can do better than they did at the time. Also, there are financial advisors present to give the players advice on how to keep and invest their money. Next, the professors addressed the roles of team executives in scouting the players to make sure they are worth investing their money in, from a character standpoint. These background checks can include a lot of people, but the player's parents may not always be contacted, for various reasons. Next, Dr. Hawkins and Dr. Hart addressed the brutality of the sport and the tremendous risk the players take to make an NFL team, and what they do to earn money that is not guaranteed contractually.

The professors also mentioned the limited capacity the players have to voice their concerns off the field, but they all believe the Player's Association does an adequate job of making sure the players are treated well at the bank. The lack of player input about issues off the field is the fear of losing money from sponsors or being "blackballed" from the league. Dr. Sailes notes that the players mainly speak out about injustices off the field after they have retired from the sport.

Conclusions

With regard to my original question that lead to the development of this project, I would have to say my results supported the validity of the statement that "the NFL is like a slave plantation." I will admit that there are elements within the NFL system that are reminiscent of slavery. For example, highly recommending that players train hard during the off-season to prepare for the regular season can be demanding a lot from the players. It limits time with their families and also suggests that players don't have as much control over their lives in the NFL as they could. Furthermore, the "blood sport" mentality, similar to that of a gladiator, can be seen as barbaric. Dr. Hart makes the remark that, according to sports science, every time two linemen (offense and defense) square off at the line of scrimmage it is the equivalent of being in a car wreck. This type of trauma can lead to concussions, spine injuries, and even death. The players do wear equipment to help ease the impact, but it is still risky in nature. Moreover, the fact that contracts are not guaranteed, while the players face tremendous risk every week, is astounding. It would appear that the NFL is more insistent on getting players to earn money for the sport than providing security for the duration of the player's lives. The racial environment is present on the field; however, according to Dr. Hart, is not well represented in terms of executive positions for players after they retire from the sport.

On one hand the physical aspects of the NFL can be demanding, but on the other, the financial compensation plus the national exposure can be great for players. The players receive several hundred thousand to millions of dollars every week for sixteen weeks, but then the money stops until the next season. In theory this should provide adequate income levels for players to maintain an acceptable standard of living within our society. However, sometimes the money is misappropriated by players who are young and come from impoverished backgrounds, as noted by Dr. Sailes. The majority of players come from disenfranchised backgrounds and they are too easy with their money. Over twelve percent of NFL players file for bankruptcy after they finish their careers. However, some players do a good job of keeping their money to invest in their future. The money compensation eases some of the pain endured in the traumatic experiences players suffer every week while playing. Some people feel that the business side of the NFL overshadows the individuals, making it hard to put an end to any exploitation within the league. In my opinion, there needs to be a more concerted effort to see the players as people owners employ, rather than good or bad investments owners make to win games and increase their revenue.

References

Carton, Benedict, and Robert Morrell. 2012. "Zulu masculinities, warrior culture and stick fghting: Reassessing male violence and virtue in South Africa." *Journal of Southern African Studies* 31–53.

Harper, Shaun. .2004. "The measure of a man: Conceptualizations of masculinity among high-achieving African American male college students." *Berkeley Journal of Sociology* 48: 89–107.

Jasinski, James. 2007. "Constituting antebellum African American identity: Resistance, violence, and masculinity in Henry Highland garnet's (1843) 'Address to the Slaves.'" *Quarterly Journal of Speech*: 27–57.

Lapchick, Richard. 2014. "The 2014 racial and gender report card: National Football League." *Tide Sports*, September 10.

Lussana, Sergio. 2010. "To see who was best on the plantation: Enslaved fighting contests and masculinity in the antebellum plantation South." *Journal of Southern History* 76 (4): 901–22.

Martin, Brandon, and Frank Harris. 2006. "Examining productive conceptions of masculini-ties: Lessons learned from academically driven African American male student-athletes." *The Journal of Men's Studies*: 359–78.

Moore, L. 2010. "Fine specimens of manhood: The Black boxer's body and the avenue to equal-ity, racial advancement, and manhood in the nineteenth century." *MELUS: Multi-Ethnic Literature of the United States* (): 59–84.

Rhoden, William C. 2006. *$40 Million Slaves: The rise, fall, and redemption of the Black athlete.* New York: Crown.

Sailes, G. A. 1991. "The myth of Black sports supremacy." *Journal of Black Studies*: 480–87.

Solorzano, Daniel, Miguel Ceja, and Tara Yosso. 2000. "Critical race theory, racial microaggres-sions, and campus racial climate: The experiences of African American college students." *The Journal of Negro Education* 69 (1/2): 60–73.

"United States Census Bureau." USA QuickFacts from the US Census Bureau.

Wolff, Cynthia Griffin. 1995. "'Masculinity' in *Uncle Tom's Cabin*." *American Quarterly*: 595.

CPSIA information can be obtained
at www.ICGtesting.com
Printed in the USA
FSHW020034230121
77915FS